CHRIS BRYANT'S CCNP

ROUTE 300-101 STUDY GUIDE

CHRIS BRYANT'S CCNP

ROUTE 300-101 STUDY GUIDE

CHRIS BRYANT

Chris Bryant, CCIE #12933
"The Computer Certification Bulldog"

ISBN: 1517583942
ISBN-13: 9781517583941

Contents

A VERY Brief Introduction Before We Get Started...

Thank you for making The Bryant Advantage part of your CCNP success story! I know you have a lot of training options out there, from books to videos and everything in between, and all of us here at TBA are very appreciative of your purchase.

During your studies, check out my YouTube channel! I'm starting an all-new CCNP ROUTE Playlist in April 2016, and with over 300 free videos there already, I know there's something there you'll enjoy.

https://www.youtube.com/user/ccie12933

My all-new website launches in April 2016, and there will be plenty of CCNA and CCNP written tutorials, flash cards, practice exams, and videos there to help you succeed in the exam room and in real life. See you there!

http://www.bryantadvantage.com

You'll find additional free resources via these links:

Facebook: http://bit.ly/bulldogfacebook

Google+: http://bit.ly/bulldoggoogle

LinkedIn: http://bit.ly/bulldoglinkedin

Thanks again for your purchase, and now, *let's get started!*

Chris Bryant

"The Computer Certification Bulldog"

Chapter 1: REVIEWING THE FUNDAMENTALS

Before we tackle EIGRP, OSPF, and BGP, let's take a few minutes for a review of some important networking fundamentals! (Besides, you never know when this stuff just might pop up on your Route exam!)

A Dollop of TCP and UDP

Both TCP and UDP run at the Transport layer of the OSI model, and they both perform something called "multiplexing"—that's about it for the similarities! Let's review the major differences between TCP and UDP.

TCP guarantees segment delivery, it performs error detection, and it performs windowing. TCP is *connection oriented*, meaning a two-way communication between the endpoints takes place before data is actually exchanged.

UDP performs best-effort delivery, which is good but not guaranteed. It has no error-detection mechanism, since it lacks the Sequence and ACK numbers needed to perform error detection. UDP offers no windowing, and it's *connectionless*. There is no "pregame communication" between the endpoints—the data exchange just starts!

Even if you're a little rusty on the concept of windowing, you have to admit that TCP sounds a lot better than UDP. I'll take a guarantee of delivery over best-effort delivery any day of the week. That alone sounds like a great reason to use TCP for everything and UDP for nothing!

As a future CCNP, you know darn well that isn't the case. Traffic doesn't get any more delay sensitive than voice and video traffic, and both of those use UDP. Why? Think about that while we take a look at this curious little TCP process.

TCP and the Three-Way Handshake

You've shaken hands many times in life, but have you ever had a three-way handshake? Is a three-way handshake even *possible*?

Such a handshake is difficult for humans, but it's easy for TCP. Before TCP will allow data-segment transmission, the involved devices must agree on basic parameters, including the Initial Sequence Number (ISN). These parameters are agreed upon during the three-way handshake, which all starts with the initiator sending a TCP segment with the synchronization bit set. The primary value synched here is the TCP Sequence Number.

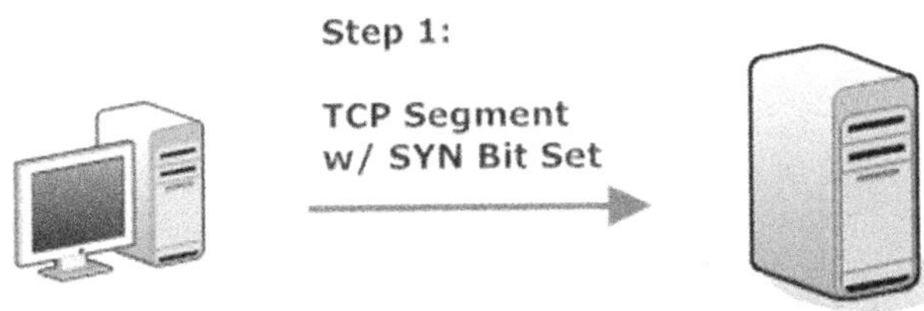

The recipient responds with a TCP segment of its own, this one with the ACKnowledgment (see what I did there?) bit set in addition to the SYN bit.

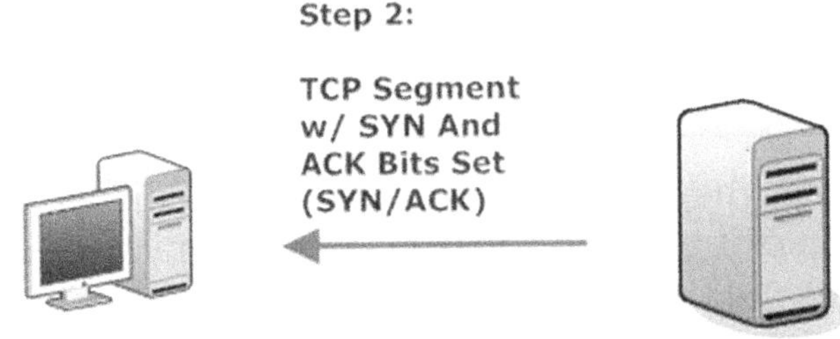

Part of that SYN/ACK is the server acknowledging receipt of the original SYN, so it makes sense for the server receiving the SYN/ACK to ACK it in turn. That's the final shake of our three-way handshake!

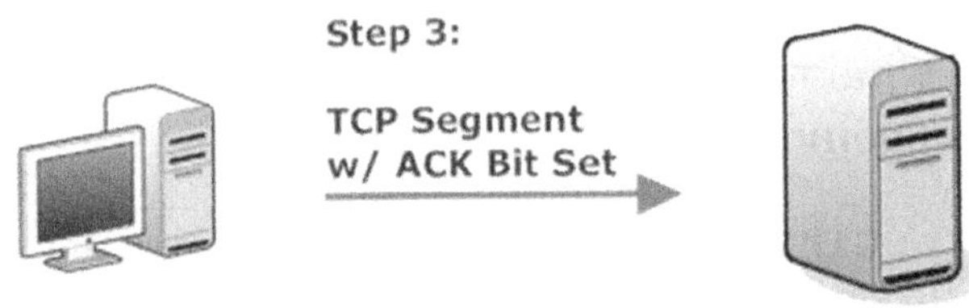

And now, an exclusive illustration of the UDP three-way handshake:

That's it! UDP doesn't have a three-way handshake, which does sound like yet another strike against the use of UDP.

Flow Control and Windowing

The initial *size of the window*, one of the values negotiated during the three-way handshake, determines how many bytes of data the recipient is willing to take in before it must send an ACK.

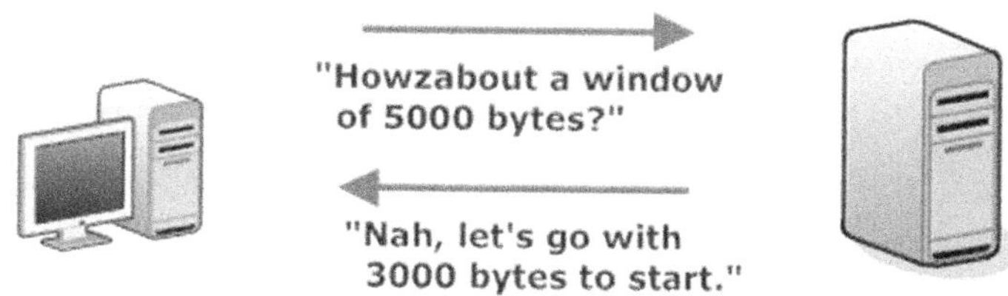

This window is dynamic in size. As the recipient realizes it can handle that initial window size comfortably, the recipient will indicate to the sender that the window size can be expanded. This dynamic behavior gives this feature the name *TCP sliding window.*

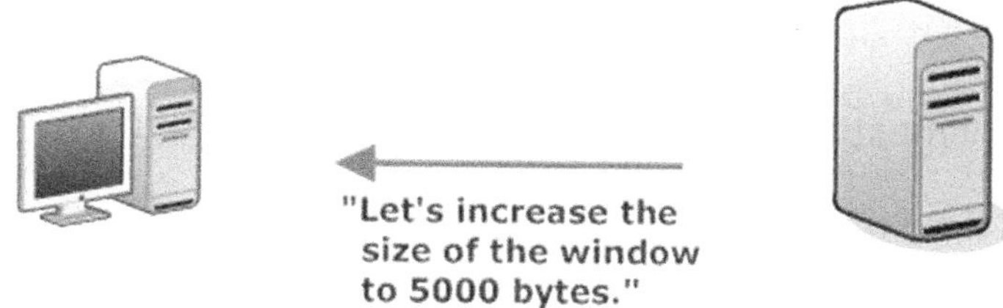

As the recipient begins to be a tad overwhelmed by the amount of incoming data, it can tell the recipient to slow that flow down by shrinking the size of the window.

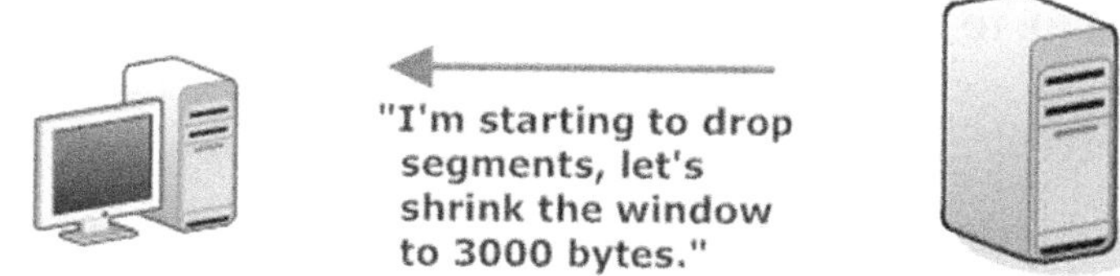

This flow control allows segment transmission to stay close to the maximum input rate of the recipient while allowing the recipient to put the brakes on when needed. *Yeah, science!*

A related feature is the *TCP window scale* option, which allows us to go *way* beyond the TCP receive window maximum of 65,535 bytes. This feature should be used with care and only in certain situations, since some firewalls and routers can't run it properly. The situations where TCP window scale can be used are far beyond the scope of the CCNP Route exam, but I do highly recommend the following Wikipedia page for outside reading:

https://en.wikipedia.org/wiki/TCP_window_scale_option

To enable TCP window scale on a Cisco router, use *ip tcp window-size*. The numeric value involved is bytes, which this particular IOS version assumes you know!

```
R1(config)#ip tcp ?
  async-mobility      Configure async-mobility
  chunk-size          TCP chunk size
  ecn                 Enable Explicit Congestion Notification
  intercept           Enable TCP intercepting
  mss                 TCP initial maximum segment size
  path-mtu-discovery  Enable path-MTU discovery on new TCP connections
  queuemax            Maximum queue of outgoing TCP packets
  selective-ack       Enable TCP selective-ACK
  synwait-time        Set time to wait on new TCP connections
  timestamp           Enable TCP timestamp option
  window-size         TCP window size

R1(config)#ip tcp
% Incomplete command.

R1(config)#ip tcp window-size ?
  <0-1073741823>  Window size
```

Naturally, this feature must be enabled on both hosts involved in the TCP session.

Back to flow control for a moment…

UDP has no form of flow control. You'd think that would always be a strike against UDP, but TCP having flow control and UDP not having it can actually work against TCP when congestion occurs. Let's say you have UDP and TCP flows going across your network, and congestion is detected. How will each protocol react?

TCP will use flow control to throttle back on transmission.

UDP will do no such thing.

In effect, TCP is surrendering bandwidth that UDP immediately takes for itself. That's kind of rude on UDP's part, but that's what happens. Whether you call this TCP starvation or UDP dominance, it's not a good situation. You can avoid this starvation and dominance by using traffic classes to indicate which traffic should be dropped when congestion occurs and which traffic should not be dropped in that situation.

Mixing UDP and TCP traffic without using traffic classes or some form of QoS isn't a good idea. You end up with lower throughput for your TCP traffic while still running into latency issues, since UDP is taking for itself any bandwidth that TCP gives up.

TCP's flow control feature can also lead to *global synchronization.* If you have many hosts with active TCP sessions and the recipient is overloaded, flow control kicks in, and the hosts will throttle back on transmission. Problem is, they all slow down at the same time, and as congestion eases, flow control indicates to the hosts that they should pick up the transmission pace, and they all end up doing that at the same time.

These peaks and valleys mean the bandwidth is either underutilized or saturated—there's no in between with global synchronization. *Weighted Random Early Detection* (WRED) is a handy tool in the fight against global synchronization.

So why do we keep UDP around, anyway? For a hint, let's compare the TCP and UDP headers.

TCP:

<table>
<tr><td colspan="3">Source Port</td><td>Destination Port</td></tr>
<tr><td colspan="4">Sequence Number</td></tr>
<tr><td colspan="4">Acknowledgement Number</td></tr>
<tr><td>Data Offset</td><td>Res.</td><td>Flags</td><td>Window</td></tr>
<tr><td colspan="3">Checksum</td><td>Urgent</td></tr>
<tr><td colspan="4">Options and Padding</td></tr>
<tr><td colspan="4">Data</td></tr>
</table>

UDP:

<table>
<tr><td>Source Port</td><td>Destination Port</td></tr>
<tr><td>Length</td><td>Checksum</td></tr>
<tr><td colspan="2">Data</td></tr>
</table>

The difference in size gives us a hint to UDP's advantage over TCP—*less overhead.* TCP offers many more features than UDP, and as always, network features come at a cost. With

TCP, that cost comes in the form of additional overhead. With the amount of delay-sensitive voice and video traffic on today's networks, that's overhead we really can't afford. That's why UDP is used for voice and video traffic!

Let's continue the case of UDP vs. TCP with a similarity between the two.

When 10.1.1.11 sends packets to 10.1.1.100, it's all sunshine and lollipops if there's only one type of traffic being transmitted, but what if there are multiple types? The host could be simultaneously sending a TFTP file transfer, e-mail via SMTP, and website data via HTTP.

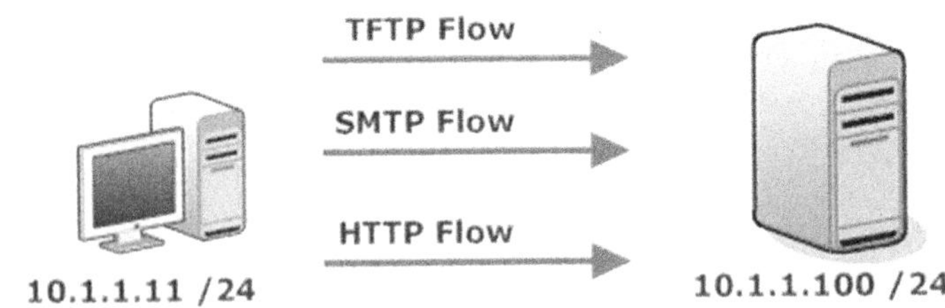

The server needs a way to keep incoming flows separate so it can send each type of data to the appropriate application. That's where well-known port numbers come in, including these three you bumped into during your CCNA studies!

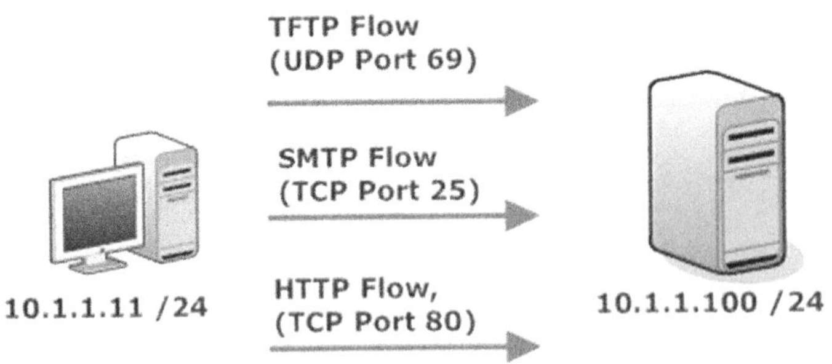

These well-known port numbers allow the recipient to know how to handle the incoming traffic flows; when a host receives data marked with UDP port 69, it knows that traffic needs to go to the TFTP application, and so on. These port numbers also allow the host to mix the data types during transmission rather than sending all the TFTP data first, then the SMTP data, and then HTTP data. This mixing of data streams is called *multiplexing* and is supported by both UDP and TCP.

Some Additional TCP Features

We know TCP sequence and ACK numbers can be used to detect lost segments, but that process isn't always as efficient as we'd like. While lost segments are detected and retransmitted, we do end up with some segments being retransmitted when it's not necessary. *TCP Selective Acknowledgements* make the overall process much more efficient, since the client can indicate exactly which segments it did receive.

Without selective ACKs, the recipient could only ACK segment 1, without adding that 3 and 4 got through.

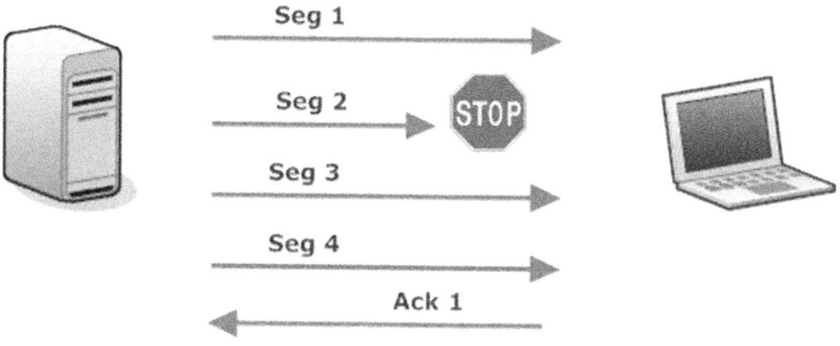

The sender then resends segments 2, 3, *and* 4.

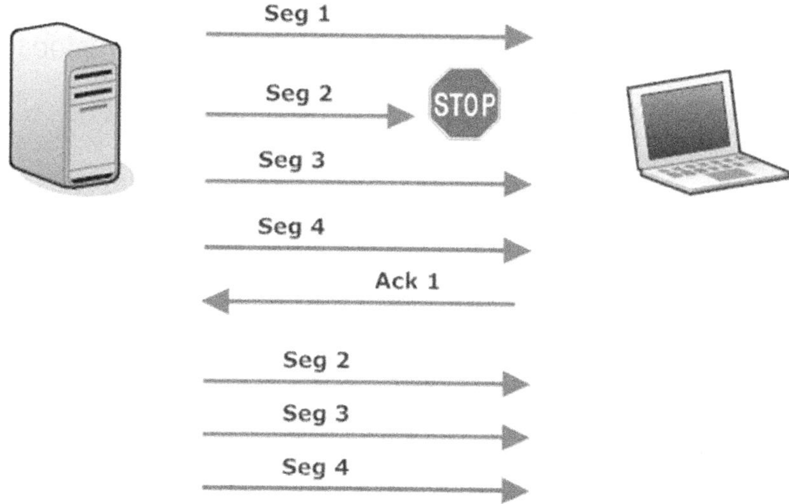

We're appreciative of the resend, but still, we hate to see segments re-sent that actually got through the first time. TCP Selective Acknowledgements give the recipient the ability to indicate which segments were received in addition to the segments being acknowledged. Here, the recipient ACKs Segment 1 while also letting the sender know Segments 3 and 4 were received.

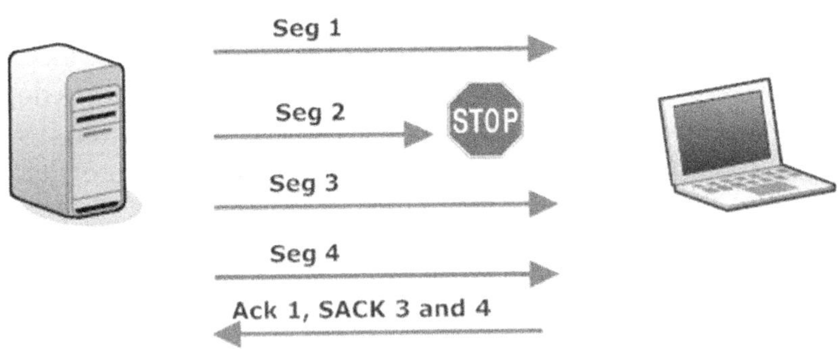

The sender now knows that it only needs to resend Segment 2, and that's just what it does.

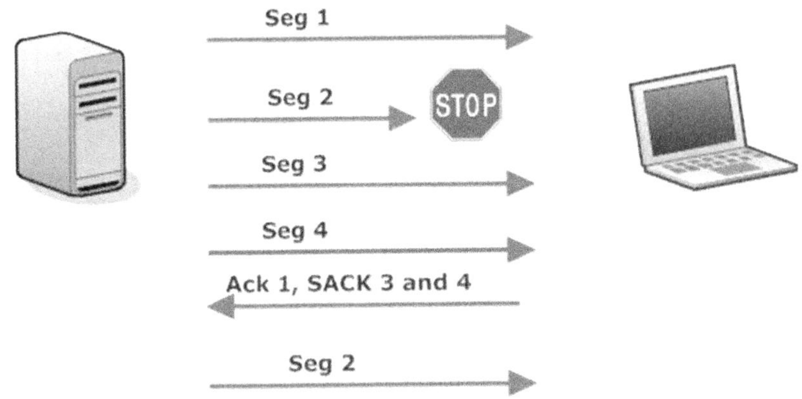

To enable this feature on a Cisco router, run *ip tcp selective-ack* in global config mode.

```
R1(config)#ip tcp ?
  async-mobility       Configure async-mobility
  chunk-size           TCP chunk size
  ecn                  Enable Explicit Congestion Notification
  intercept            Enable TCP intercepting
  mss                  TCP initial maximum segment size
  path-mtu-discovery   Enable path-MTU discovery on new TCP connections
  queuemax             Maximum queue of outgoing TCP packets
  selective-ack        Enable TCP selective-ACK
  synwait-time         Set time to wait on new TCP connections
  timestamp            Enable TCP timestamp option
  window-size          TCP window size

R1(config)#ip tcp selective-ack ?
  <cr>
```

A quick word about those TCP timestamps while we're here, courtesy of ForensicsWiki.org:

"TCP timestamps are used to provide protection against wrapped sequence numbers. It is possible to calculate system uptime (and boot time) by analyzing TCP timestamps. These calculated uptimes (and boot times) can help in detecting hidden network-enabled operation systems, linking spoofed IP and MAC addresses together...etc."

Sounds great, but as with the next feature we'll discuss, there are concerns with security vulnerabilities. Do serious research on your particular network devices before using this feature. On Cisco routers, enable with *ip tcp timestamp*. Note: TCP Header Compression does not work when TCP timestamps are enabled.

The TCP Keepalive Feature

I get asked a lot about this one in my CCNA course. It shows up in the *service* IOS Help readout, and new students see it and wonder if it's necessary to run this service to make TCP services run. (They usually ask this after I hit them with all the L2 keepalives we run into.)

```
R1(config)#service ?
  alignment              Control alignment correction and logging
  compress-config        Compress the nvram configuration file
  config                 TFTP load config files
  dhcp                   Enable DHCP server and relay agent
  disable-ip-fast-frag   Disable IP particle-based fast fragmentation
  exec-callback          Enable exec callback
  exec-wait              Delay EXEC startup on noisy lines
  finger                 Allow responses to finger requests
  hide-telnet-addresses  Hide destination addresses in telnet command
  linenumber             enable line number banner for each exec
  nagle                  Enable Nagle's congestion control algorithm
  old-slip-prompts       Allow old scripts to operate with slip/ppp
  pad                    Enable PAD commands
  password-encryption    Encrypt system passwords
  prompt                 Enable mode specific prompt
  pt-vty-logging         Log significant VTY-Async events
  sequence-numbers       Stamp logger messages with a sequence number
  slave-log              Enable log capability of slave IPs
  tcp-keepalives-in      Generate keepalives on idle incoming network
                         connections
  tcp-keepalives-out     Generate keepalives on idle outgoing network
                         connections
  tcp-small-servers      Enable small TCP servers (e.g., ECHO)
  telnet-zeroidle        Set TCP window 0 when connection is idle
  timestamps             Timestamp debug/log messages
  txacc-accounting       Enable transmit credit accounting
  udp-small-servers      Enable small UDP servers (e.g., ECHO)
```

The two commands are simple and self-explanatory, but the reasons to use them are really few and far between. These services are disabled by default and not necessary for normal TCP operation. A search on "Cisco tcp keepalive" brings up a document on how to use this feature to prevent hung Telnet sessions. It's outside the scope of the ROUTE exam, but worth a quick read:

http://www.cisco.com/c/en/us/support/docs/dial-access/asynchronous-connections/14957-tcpkeepalive.html

Many admins consider these keepalives to be security risks. Personally, I've played with them both in lab environments but haven't used them in the field. It's good to know they're available, but unless you have some specific need for them, I'd leave them off.

TCP Explicit Congestion Notification

The name is really the recipe with this feature! Enabling TCP ECN allows a router to notify hosts at the endpoints of a communication that there's congestion afoot, providing support for traffic that is particularly delay sensitive (voice and video!).

To enable TCP ECN, run *ip tcp ecn* in global config mode. There are no options with this command.

```
R1(config)#ip tcp ?
  async-mobility      Configure async-mobility
  chunk-size          TCP chunk size
  ecn                 Enable Explicit Congestion Notification
  intercept           Enable TCP intercepting
  mss                 TCP initial maximum segment size
  path-mtu-discovery  Enable path-MTU discovery on new TCP connections
  queuemax            Maximum queue of outgoing TCP packets
  selective-ack       Enable TCP selective-ACK
  synwait-time        Set time to wait on new TCP connections
  timestamp           Enable TCP timestamp option
  window-size         TCP window size

R1(config)#ip tcp ecn ?
  <cr>

R1(config)#ip tcp ecn
```

PPP—oE and Otherwise

We'll do a quick and important review of PPP with this link:

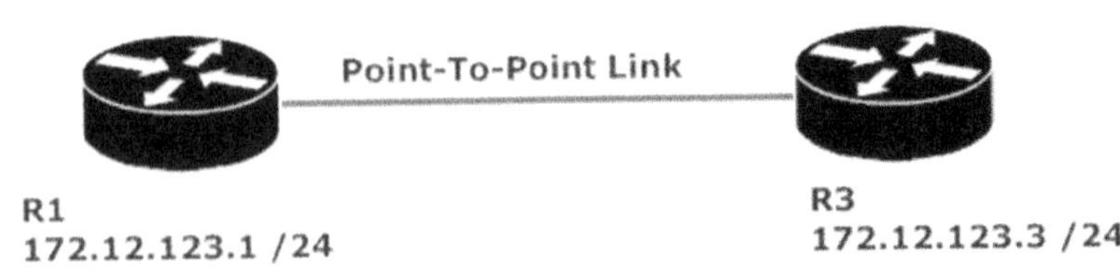

The default Cisco router Serial interface encapsulation is HDLC...

```
R1#show int serial 1/0
Serial1/0 is up, line protocol is up
  Hardware is CD2430 in sync mode
  Internet address is 172.12.123.1/24
  MTU 1500 bytes, BW 128 Kbit, DLY 20000 usec,
    reliability 255/255, txload 1/255, rxload 1/255
  Encapsulation HDLC, loopback not set
```

...which we'll change via the *encapsulation* command.

```
R1(config)#int serial 1/0
R1(config-if)#encap ?
  alc             Airline Line Control (ALC)
  atm-dxi         ATM-DXI encapsulation
  bstun           Block Serial tunneling (BSTUN)
  frame-relay     Frame Relay networks
  hdlc            Serial HDLC synchronous
  lapb            LAPB (X.25 Level 2)
  ppp             Point-to-Point protocol
  sdlc            SDLC
  sdlc-primary    SDLC (primary)
  sdlc-secondary  SDLC (secondary)
  smds            Switched Megabit Data Service (SMDS)
  stun            Serial tunneling (STUN)
  uts             Unisys TS
  x25             X.25

R1(config)#int serial 1/0
R1(config-if)#encap ppp

R3(config)#int serial 1
R3(config-if)#encap ppp

R1#show int serial 1/0
Serial1/0 is up, line protocol is up
  Hardware is CD2430 in sync mode
  Internet address is 172.12.123.1/24
  MTU 1500 bytes, BW 128 Kbit, DLY 20000 usec,
    reliability 255/255, txload 1/255, rxload 1/255
  Encapsulation PPP, LCP Open
```

Why the switch from HDLC to PPP? PPP offers quite a few features that HDLC does not, including authentication options and vital error-detection and error-recovery features. Let's have a look at those authentication options in action right now!

The Challenge Authentication Protocol (CHAP) is much more aggressive than the Password Authentication Protocol (PAP). If R1 is running PAP here, the router that needs to be authenticated (R3) must actively present the password to R1. R1 is not going to start the process.

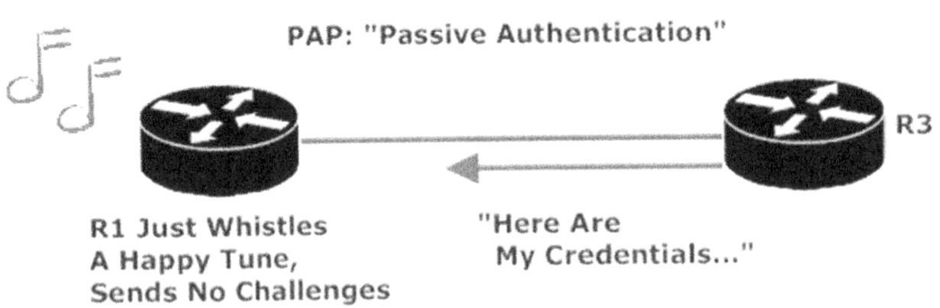

With CHAP, R1 will actively challenge R3 to prove its identity.

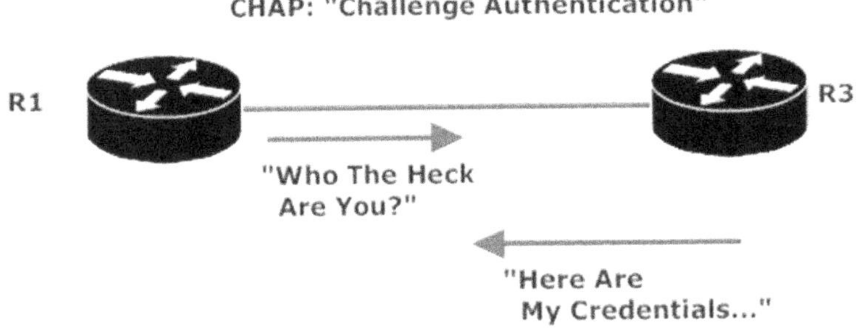

We'll start our CHAP config by creating a username/password database. Two of them, actually! R3 will have a one-line database containing R1's name and password (CCNP), and R1 will have a one-line database containing R3's name and password (also CCNP).

```
R1(config)#username R3 password CCNP

R3(config)#username R1 password CCNP
```

CHAP is applied to the interface with *ppp authentication chap*. To see the authentication in action, we'll run *debug ppp authentication* on R3 before finishing the config.

```
R1(config)#int serial 1/0
R1(config-if)#ppp authen chap

R3(config)#int serial 1
R3(config-if)#ppp authen chap

2d01h: Se1 CHAP: O CHALLENGE id 33 len 23 from "R3"
2d01h: Se1 CHAP: I CHALLENGE id 50 len 23 from "R1"
2d01h: Se1 CHAP: O RESPONSE id 50 len 23 from "R3"
2d01h: Se1 CHAP: I RESPONSE id 33 len 23 from "R1"
```

```
2d01h: Se1 CHAP: O SUCCESS id 33 len 4
2d01h: Se1 CHAP: I SUCCESS id 50 len 4
```

That's just what we wanted to see! A challenge from each router, a response from each, and success for each authentication! Note the "O" and "I" letting us know whether the message is outbound or inbound.

Here's the result of *debug ppp authentication* after CHAP was removed and PAP was used instead. The authentication went fine, but there are no challenges.

```
2d01h: Se1 PAP: I AUTH-REQ id 1 len 12 from "R1"
2d01h: Se1 PAP: O AUTH-REQ id 1 len 12 from "R3"
2d01h: Se1 PAP: Authenticating peer R1
2d01h: Se1 PAP: O AUTH-ACK id 1 len 5
2d01h: Se1 PAP: I AUTH-ACK id 1 len 5
```

That's all well and good, but the real reason we don't care for PAP is that PAP sends both the username and password out in clear text! In today's world, that's just unacceptable. You're likely to see PAP only on your Cisco certification exams. There's just no room for it in today's real-world networks.

In this example, I used PPP over a point-to-point serial link, but that's hardly the only type of link that can use PPP. It's still used over dial-up access links, which brings up two age-old questions:

- Under what circumstances will the dial-up link be dialed?
- How long will the line stay up?

With dial-up links, we don't want just any old traffic to bring up the line, or we could get a pretty big dial-up phone bill at the end of the month! With dial-up links, we define certain types of traffic that can bring up the line. This interesting traffic was defined with ACLs. Define the amount of time the link can stay up in the absence of interesting traffic, and you're all set. (A relatively new feature, *dialer persistent*, allows a dial-up link to be brought up without interesting traffic.)

PPP over Ethernet (PPPoE) is a combination of PPP and Ethernet that's used primarily by ISPs. PPP is actually encapsulated inside Ethernet, allowing transmission over any Ethernet-friendly interface.

From Cisco's website: "PPPoE clients are typically personal computers connected to an ISP over a remote broadband connection, such as DSL or cable service. ISPs deploy PPPoE because it supports high-speed broadband access using their existing remote access infrastructure and because **it is easier for customers to use.**" (Bolding is mine. We'll take customer ease of use any time we can get it!)

The first part of a successful PPPoE session is the *Active Discovery* phase. What's being actively discovered, you ask? This phase is where the PPPoE client is looking for a PPPoE server. Once that happens, we're off to the PPP *Session* phase, where PPP authentication and negotiation take place. (Better go with CHAP authentication!) When that phase is complete, our L2 encap is now in place, and data can be sent over the link.

A Review of the Routing Process

No routing protocols were harmed in the making of these walkthroughs, especially since none are in use.

When 192.168.1.1 wants to send packets to 10.1.1.5, the sending host knows darn well that the intended recipient is on a different subnet. That's where the default gateway comes in. The IP address on the router's Fast 0/0 interface can serve as the default gateway for hosts on the 192.168.1.0 /24 subnet. When a transmitting host sends packets to the default gateway, it's basically saying, "I have no idea where this destination subnet is, so I'll send the packets to the DG and let that device handle it."

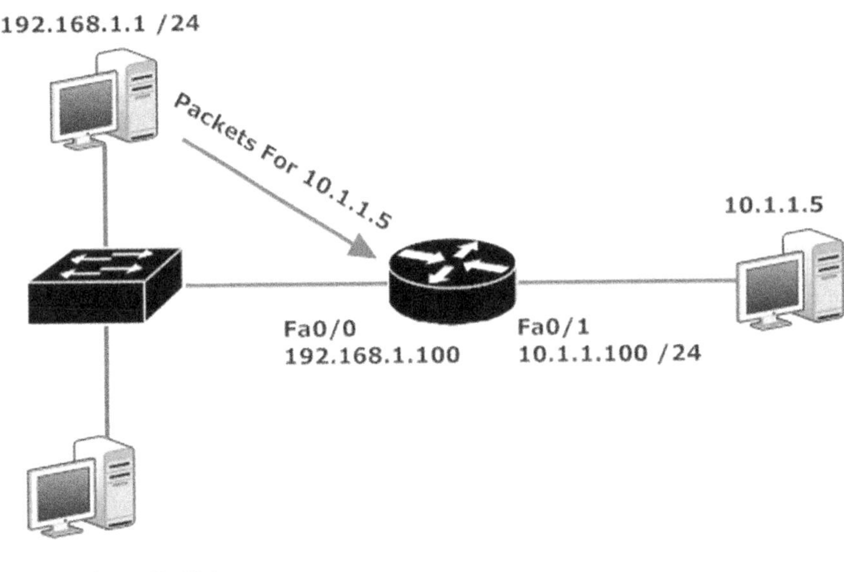

When a router receives a packet, there are three possibilities regarding the packet's destination.

- A directly connected network
- A nondirectly connected network the router *has* an entry for in its IP routing table
- A nondirectly connected network the router has *no* entry for in its IP routing table

Let's have a look at each possibility!

The Directly Connected Network

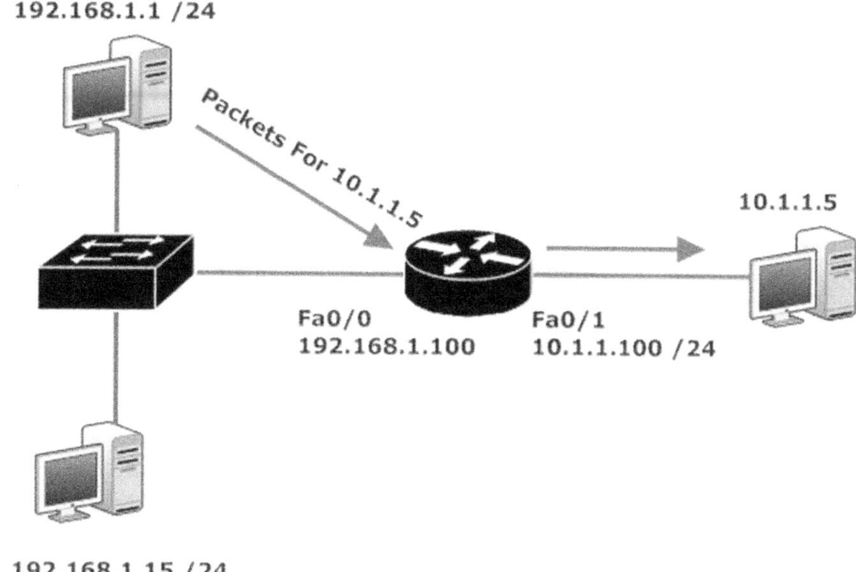

The router looks in its IP routing table, sees the 10.1.1.0 /24 network is directly connected to its Fa0/1 interface, and sends the packets out its Fa0/1 interface. Nothing to it! Let's add a router to our network and make the decision just a little more difficult.

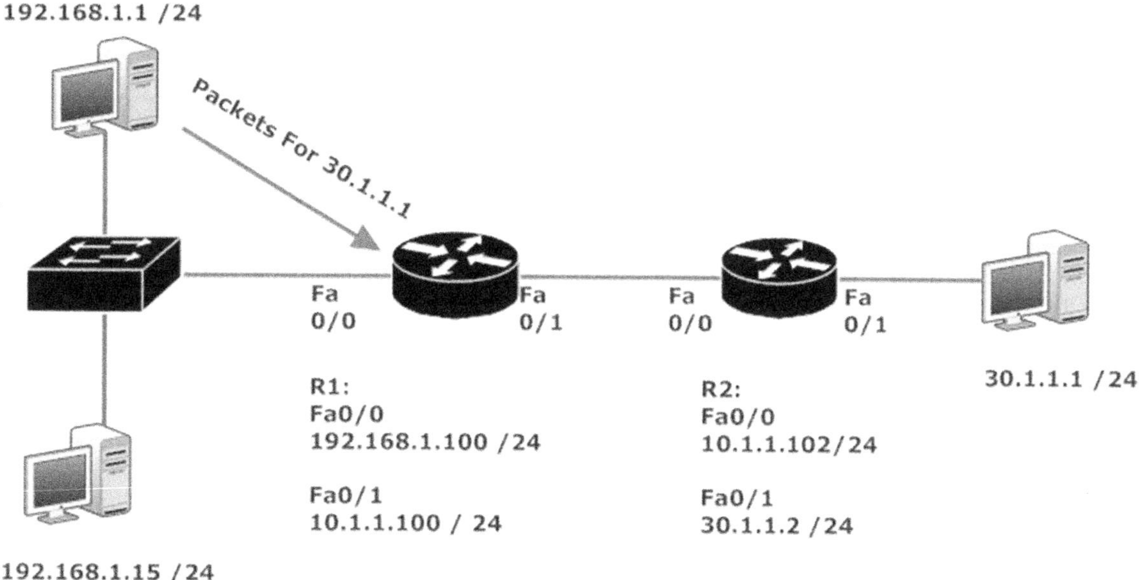

The problem here? R1 knows only of the directly connected networks 192.168.1.0 /24 and 10.1.1.0 /24, so a routing table lookup for 30.1.1.1 will fail. Unless we put a static route on R1 or get a dynamic routing protocol up and running, we're Sure out of Luck (SOOL). This static route would get the job done:

```
R1(config)#ip route 30.1.1.0 255.255.255.0 10.1.1.102
```

We'd need another static route to allow 30.1.1.1 to send packets back to 192.168.1.1, since R2 has no route for 192.168.1.0 /24.

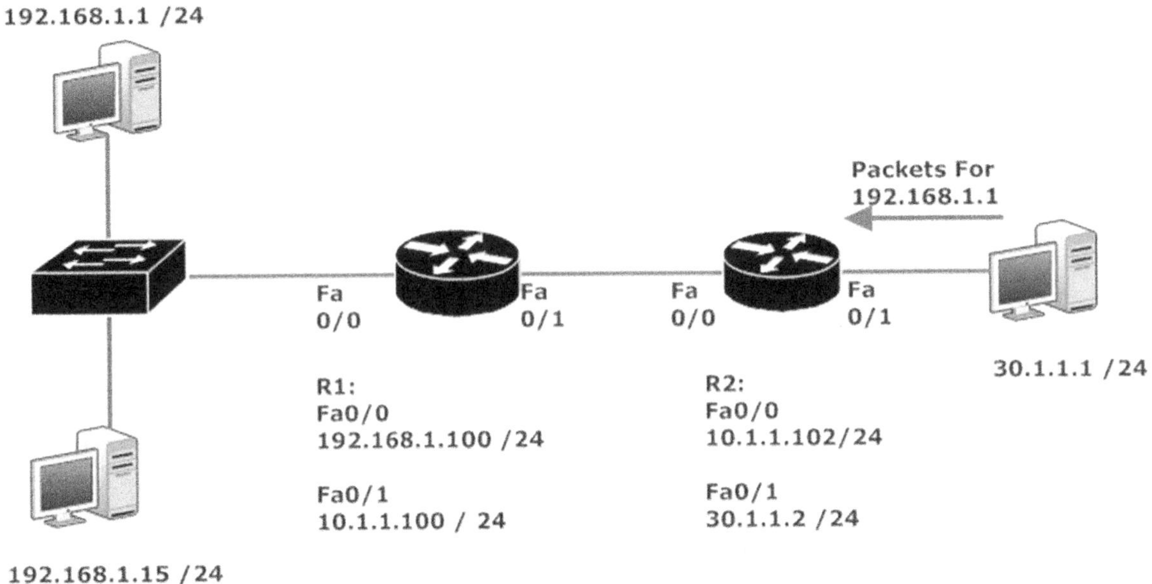

Watch that kind of thing when you're working with an environment free of dynamic routing protocols. Point A may be able to get packets to Point B, but that doesn't automagically mean Point B can get the packets back to Point A without an additional static route!

A Brief and Thorough Review of Unicasts, Broadcasts, and Multicasts

Unicasts are intended for a single host, broadcasts are intended for all hosts, and multicasts are intended for members of a multicast group. End of review, and on to EIGRP!

Chapter 2: EIGRP FUNDAMENTALS

Raise your hand if you thought you learned almost everything there is to know about EIGRP during your CCNA studies!

If you raised your hand, don't feel bad. I thought the same thing after earning my CCNA. There's a lot more to EIGRP than what we both learned during our NA studies. Before we explore new EIGRP territory, let's spend some serious time going over EIGRP fundamentals.

EIGRP is the enhanced version of the Interior Gateway Routing Protocol (IGRP). IGRP is no longer supported by Cisco and isn't on the exams. EIGRP is known as a hybrid protocol, since it officially has characteristics of link state and distance vector protocols. As you'll see, EIGRP acts much more like an LS protocol than a DV protocol. The main DV behavior shown by EIGRP is the initial exchange of full routing tables between EIGRP neighbors.

New EIGRP neighbors initially exchange full routing tables.

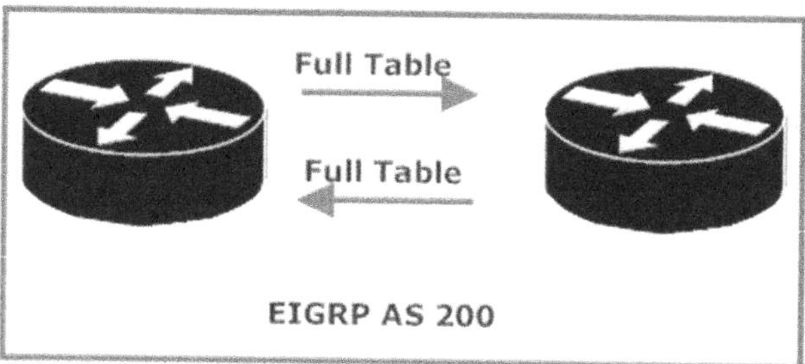

After that initial exchange of full tables, an EIGRP router will send an update only when there's a change in the network. That update will reflect only those changes and will not consist of a full routing table.

RP brings several major benefits to our network:

- Rapid convergence when a change in the network is detected, since backup routes ("feasible successors") are calculated before they're actually needed due to the loss of a primary route ("successors")
- Multiprotocol support, including IP, IPX, and Appletalk
- Support for VLSM and CIDR

Those benefits can't benefit us until adjacencies form between our EIGRP-speaking routers. Actually, nothing can happen between our EIGRP routers until adjacencies form, so let's spend some time with the packet that makes these happen.

EIGRP uses hello packets (multicast to 224.0.0.10) to establish and maintain neighbor relationships. The Reliable Transport Protocol (RTP) is used to handle the transport of messages between EIGRP-enabled routers.

EIGRP uses autonomous systems (AS) to identify routers that belong to the same logical group. EIGRP speakers that are in separate ASs cannot become neighbors.

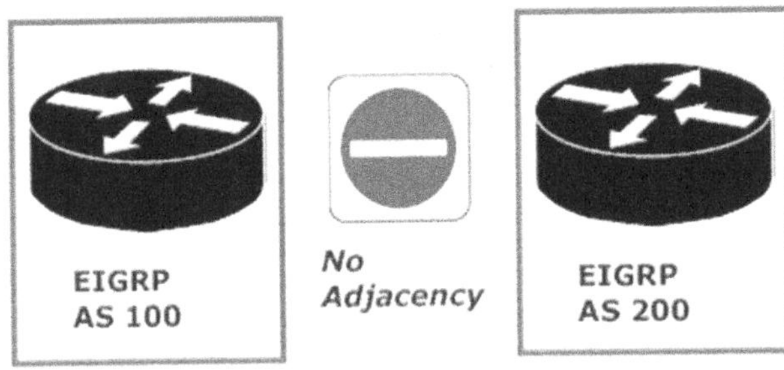

Once the adjacency is formed, it's kept alive by a steady flow of hello packets from the neighbor. If those Hellos stop coming, the adjacency is eventually dropped.

The Successor and Feasible Successor

EIGRP keeps three important tables. The route table stores the best route to each remote network the router knows of. The topology table keeps all known valid, loop-free routes to those same networks. Finally, the neighbor table keeps exactly what you'd think it would keep—information on the router's EIGRP neighbors.

The route and topology tables play a vital role in EIGRP's rapid recovery from a lost route. Here, R1 has two paths to R4. EIGRP has determined the path through R2 is the best. That route will be placed into both the route *and* topology tables. The route through R3 is valid and has been determined by EIGRP to be free of routing loops, so that route (a feasible successor) is placed into the topology table.

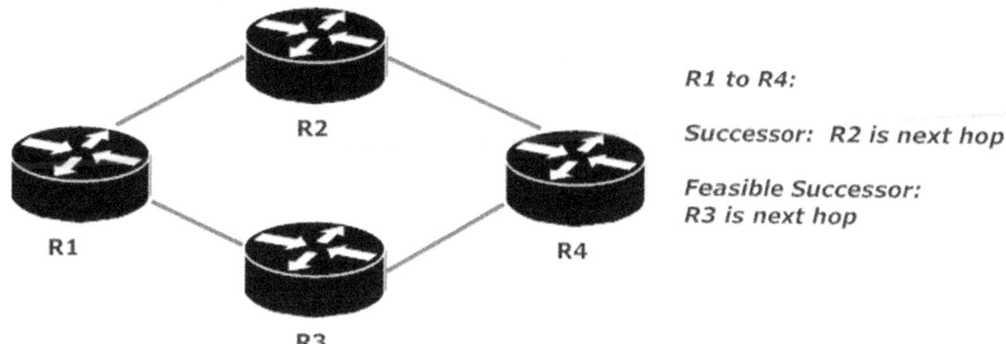

Should the primary route (the successor) be lost, EIGRP doesn't need to calculate a new route. EIGRP would then name the route through R3 as the successor, and routing goes on.

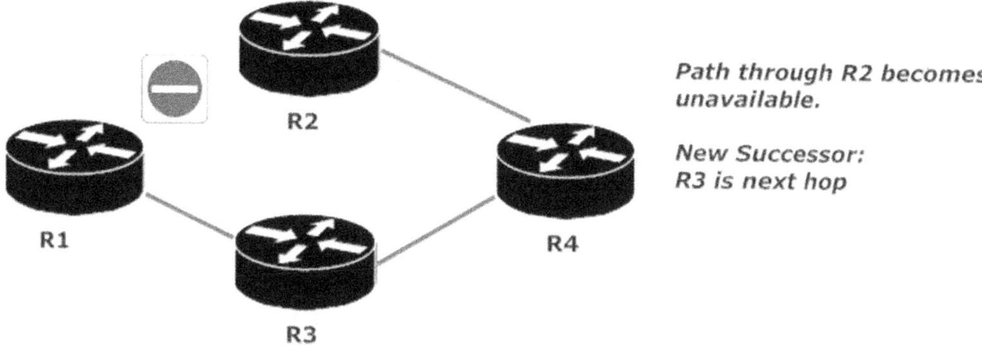

We'll see the successor and feasible successor in action on live Cisco routers throughout our EIGRP labs. Let's start our first lab right now by configuring and verifying EIGRP adjacencies on the following network.

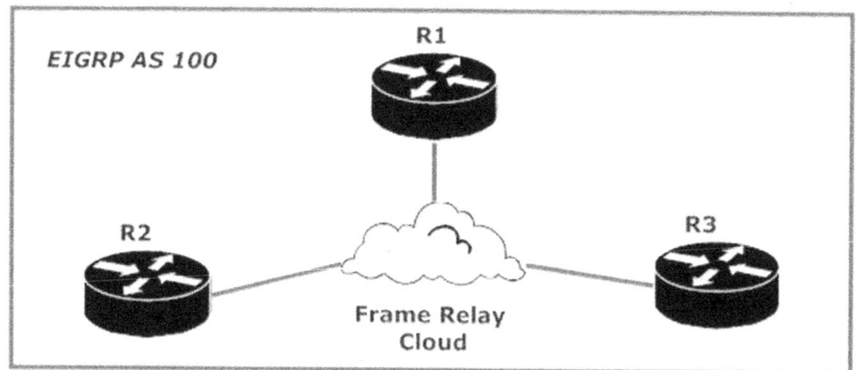

Each router's Serial 0/1/0 interface is connected to the frame relay network, and we're using the 172.12.123.0 /24 subnet for IP addressing. The router numbers are used for the fourth octet of the address—R1's Serial 0/1/0 interface is 172.12.123.1, and so forth.

We'll use the *network* command to enable EIGRP. The command *network 172.12.123.0 0.0.0.255* enables EIGRP on any interface in the 172.12.123.0 /24 subnet. The use of wildcard masks is optional, but you'll see them in 99 percent of real-world EIGRP deployments. Watch that detail on your CCNP ROUTE and TSHOOT exams. EIGRP and OSPF both use wildcard masks, but they're required only in OSPF. The network 172.12.123.0 command is legal in EIGRP, as verified by IOS Help on R1.

```
R1(config)#router eigrp 100
R1(config-router)#no auto-summary
R1(config-router)#network 172.12.123.0 ?
  A.B.C.D EIGRP wild card bits
  <cr>

R1(config-router)#network 172.12.123.0 0.0.0.255

R2(config)#router eigrp 100
R2(config-router)#no auto-summary
R2(config-router)#network 172.12.123.0 0.0.0.255

R3(config)#router eigrp 100
R3(config-router)#no auto
R3(config-router)#network 172.12.123.0 0.0.0.255
```

I disabled something called "auto-summary" on all three routers before I even put in the network command. More on this later, but for now note that EIGRP has autosummarization on by default on many Cisco routers and switches. Autosummarization is off by default in almost all router IOS versions starting with 15.

Just a few seconds after enabling EIGRP on all three routers, this console message appeared on R1:

```
May  6 10:42:02: %DUAL-5-NBRCHANGE: EIGRP-IPv4 100: Neighbor 172.12.123.2 (Seria
l0/1/0) is up: new adjacency
May  6 10:42:02: %DUAL-5-NBRCHANGE: EIGRP-IPv4 100: Neighbor 172.12.123.3 (Seria
l0/1/0) is up: new adjacency
```

EIGRP hello packets have discovered two potential neighbors, and all must have been well, because those potential neighbors quickly became *actual* neighbors! We'll verify with *show ip eigrp neighbors.*

```
R1#show ip eigrp neighbor
EIGRP-IPv4 Neighbors for AS(100)
H     Address        Interface    Hold Uptime    SRTT     RTO    Q     Seq
                                  (sec)          (ms)            Cnt   Num
1     172.12.123.3   Se0/1/0      165  00:02:05  1577     5000   0     3
0     172.12.123.2   Se0/1/0      161  00:02:05  1968     5000   0     3
```

From left to right, the key values are the IP addresses of the EIGRP AS 100 neighbors, the local interface upon which they were discovered, and the uptime of the adjacency.

We have EIGRP adjacencies, but do we have any EIGRP routes? Let's check via *show ip route eigrp*. (The code tables have been removed from the following command outputs.)

```
R1#show ip route eigrp

R1#
```

When a show command drops you right back at the enable prompt, that means there's nothing to show you! We have no EIGRP routes because an address from the 172.12.123.0 /24 subnet is on a directly connected interface on each router.

```
R1#show ip route connected

      172.12.0.0/16 is variably subnetted, 2 subnets, 2 masks
C        172.12.123.0/24 is directly connected, Serial0/1/0
L        172.12.123.1/32 is directly connected, Serial0/1/0
```

Let's get some EIGRP routes into our lab by adding a loopback to each router. We'll use the router number for each octet in the address along with a /24 mask.

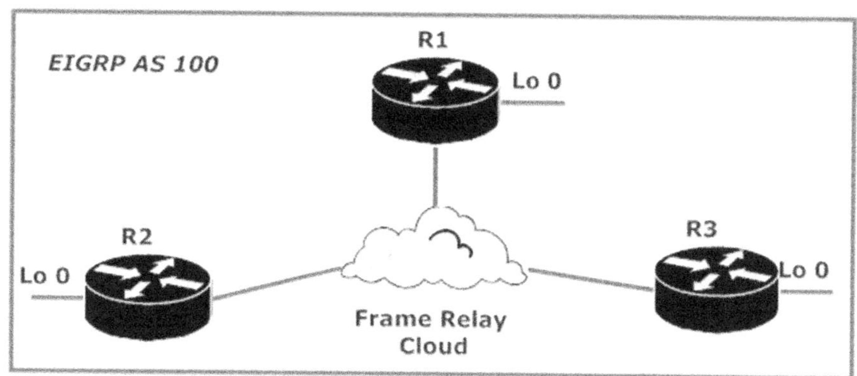


```
R1(config)#router eigrp 100
R1(config-router)#network 1.1.1.0 0.0.0.255

R2(config)#router eigrp 100
R2(config-router)#network 2.2.2.0 0.0.0.255

R3(config)#router eigrp 100
R3(config-router)#network 3.3.3.0 0.0.0.255
```

Let's have a look at each router's EIGRP route table.

```
R1#show ip route eigrp
      2.0.0.0/24 is subnetted, 1 subnets
D        2.2.2.0 [90/2297856] via 172.12.123.2, 01:07:00, Serial0/1/0
      3.0.0.0/24 is subnetted, 1 subnets
D        3.3.3.0 [90/2297856] via 172.12.123.3, 01:06:46, Serial0/1/0
```

```
R2#show ip route eigrp
      1.0.0.0/24 is subnetted, 1 subnets
D        1.1.1.0 [90/2297856] via 172.12.123.1, 01:07:19, Serial0/1/0
```

```
R3#show ip route eigrp
      1.0.0.0/24 is subnetted, 1 subnets
D        1.1.1.0 [90/2297856] via 172.12.123.1, 01:07:24, Serial0/1/0
```

Curious! R1 is showing the EIGRP routes we'd expect, but neither spoke router can see the loopback network on the other spoke router. That's due to *split horizon*, an important routing loop prevention behavior that can on occasion play havoc with your routing tables.

There is no direct connection between R2 and R3. Any traffic sent by one of those routers to the other must pass through the hub router (R1), and that's where split horizon comes in. The rule of split horizon dictates that a router cannot advertise a route back out the same interface upon which it was originally learned. R1 is learning about R3's loopback network via an EIGRP update received on Serial 0/1/0, so R1 can't advertise that same network via that same interface. Therefore, R2 can't learn about that network.

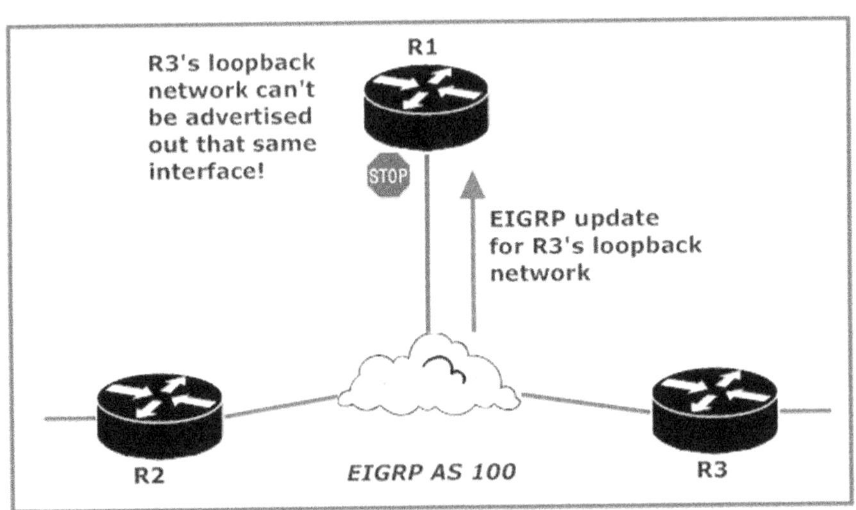

R1 is learning about R2's loopback network via an update received on Serial 0/1/0 as well, so R1 can't advertise that network via that same interface. R3 is left out in the cold!

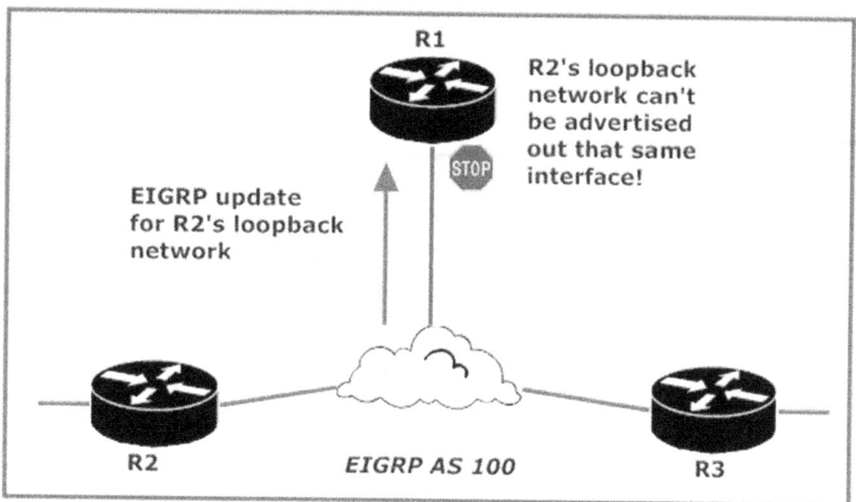

Split horizon can be disabled, and in a lab environment, doing so doesn't worry me (mostly). In a production network, I'd be very careful about doing so. While you may get the result you want, you might get other results that you don't want!

Note that SH is disabled at the interface level and that the AS must be specified.

```
R1(config)#int serial 0/1/0
R1(config-if)#no ip split-horizon ?
     Eigrp  Enhanced Interior Gateway Routing Protocol (EIGRP)
     <cr>

R1(config-if)#no ip split-horizon eigrp ?
     <1-65535>   AS number

R1(config-if)#no ip split-horizon eigrp 100
```

A few seconds later, I received these console messages:

```
May  6 12:20:13: %DUAL-5-NBRCHANGE: EIGRP-IPv4 100: Neighbor 172.12.123.3 (Seria
l0/1/0) is resync: split horizon changed
May  6 12:20:13: %DUAL-5-NBRCHANGE: EIGRP-IPv4 100: Neighbor 172.12.123.2 (Seria
l0/1/0) is resync: split horizon changed
```

In the past, disabling or enabling split horizon resulted in the temporary loss of EIGRP adjacencies. The messages here mention the neighbor being "resynched" instead of lost. The uptime from *show ip eigrp neighbor* verifies the adjacencies didn't come all the way down. Had the adjacencies been lost, the uptime would show just a few seconds rather than over one hundred minutes.

```
R1#show ip eigrp neighbor
EIGRP-IPv4 Neighbors for AS(100)
H     Address        Interface    Hold Uptime     SRTT    RTO    Q     Seq
                                  (sec)           (ms)           Cnt   Num
1     172.12.123.3   Se0/1/0      140  01:41:02   165     990    0     16
0     172.12.123.2   Se0/1/0      164  01:41:02   184     1104   0     16
```

Disabling SH on the hub router's Serial interface has the desired result, as R2 and R3 now see each other's loopbacks. I've also pinged every interface from every router with 100 percent success (ping results not shown), so we're good to go!

```
R2#show ip route eigrp
      1.0.0.0/24 is subnetted, 1 subnets
D        1.1.1.0 [90/2297856] via 172.12.123.1, 01:29:46, Serial0/1/0
      3.0.0.0/24 is subnetted, 1 subnets
D        3.3.3.0 [90/2809856] via 172.12.123.1, 00:04:34, Serial0/1/0

R3#show ip route eigrp
      1.0.0.0/24 is subnetted, 1 subnets
D        1.1.1.0 [90/2297856] via 172.12.123.1, 01:29:51, Serial0/1/0
      2.0.0.0/24 is subnetted, 1 subnets
D        2.2.2.0 [90/2809856] via 172.12.123.1, 00:04:39, Serial0/1/0
```

We're now going to add the 172.12.23.0 /27 network to our lab. Addresses from that subnet will be used on the new Ethernet segment connecting R2 and R3.

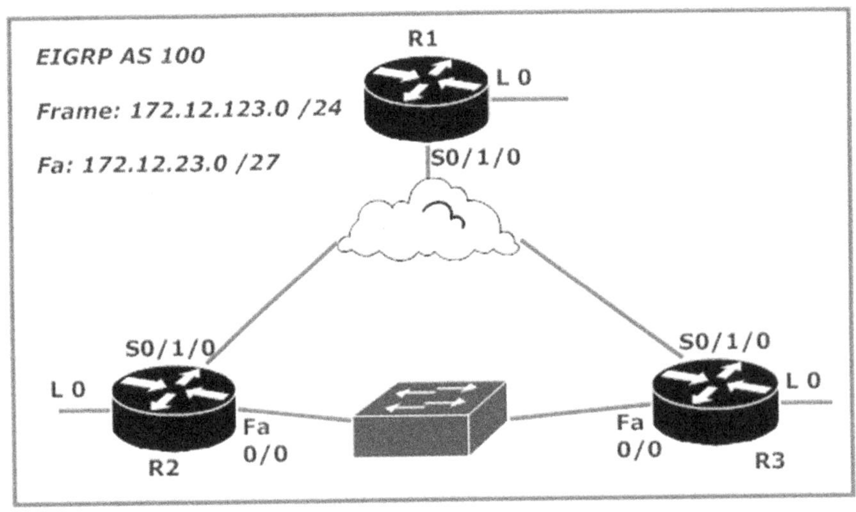


```
R2(config)#router eigrp 100
R2(config-router)#network 172.12.23.0 0.0.0.31

R3(config)#router eigrp 100
R3(config-router)#network 172.12.23.0 0.0.0.31
```

```
May 5 12:43:16: %DUAL-5-NBRCHANGE: EIGRP-IPv4 100: Neighbor 172.12.23.2
(FastEthernet0/0) is up: new adjacency
```

Looks good! Let's verify and proceed.

```
R3#show ip eigrp neighbor
EIGRP-IPv4 Neighbors for AS(100)
H   Address        Interface   Hold Uptime   SRTT   RTO   Q    Seq
                               (sec)         (ms)         Cnt  Num
1   172.12.23.2    Fa0/0       13  00:00:44  1      200   0    21
0   172.12.123.1   Se0/1/0     168 02:01:50  40     240   0    23

R2#show ip eigrp neighbor
EIGRP-IPv4 Neighbors for AS(100)
H   Address        Interface   Hold Uptime   SRTT   RTO   Q    Seq
                               (sec)         (ms)         Cnt  Num
1   172.12.23.3    Fa0/0       11  00:00:49  3      200   0    22
0   172.12.123.1   Se0/1/0     162 02:01:55  41     246   0    22
```

Interestingly enough, we now have two entries for the 172.12.23.0 /27 network in R1's EIGRP route table.

```
R1#show ip route eigrp
      2.0.0.0/24 is subnetted, 1 subnets
D        2.2.2.0 [90/2297856] via 172.12.123.2, 00:06:03, Serial0/1/0
      3.0.0.0/24 is subnetted, 1 subnets
D        3.3.3.0 [90/2297856] via 172.12.123.3, 00:06:03, Serial0/1/0
      172.12.0.0/16 is variably subnetted, 3 subnets, 3 masks
D        172.12.23.0/27 [90/2172416] via 172.12.123.3, 00:06:03, Serial0/1/0
                        [90/2172416] via 172.12.123.2, 00:06:03, Serial0/1/0
```

This is equal-cost load balancing, a default behavior of EIGRP. Since the metric for these two paths to 172.12.23.0 /27 is exactly the same (2172416), both paths are put into the EIGRP route table, and the load to that network is balanced over the two paths.

All routes in the EIGRP route table are successors, but what of those feasible successors I made such a big deal about earlier? You'll find feasible successors and successors in the EIGRP topology table.

```
R1#show ip eigrp topology
EIGRP-IPv4 Topology Table for AS(100)/ID(172.12.123.1)
Codes: P - Passive, A - Active, U - Update, Q - Query, R - Reply,
       r - reply Status, s - sia Status

P 172.12.123.0/24, 1 successors, FD is 2169856
        via Connected, Serial0/1/0
```

```
P 172.12.23.0/27, 2 successors, FD is 2172416
        via 172.12.123.2 (2172416/28160), Serial0/1/0
        via 172.12.123.3 (2172416/28160), Serial0/1/0
P 2.2.2.0/24, 1 successors, FD is 2297856
        via 172.12.123.2 (2297856/128256), Serial0/1/0
        via 172.12.123.3 (2300416/156160), Serial0/1/0
P 3.3.3.0/24, 1 successors, FD is 2297856
        via 172.12.123.3 (2297856/128256), Serial0/1/0
        via 172.12.123.2 (2300416/156160), Serial0/1/0
P 1.1.1.0/24, 1 successors, FD is 128256
        via Connected, Loopback0
```

Two successors do indeed exist for 172.12.23.0/27, and both are in the EIGRP route table. There are also two routes for 2.2.2.0 /24 and 3.3.3.0 /24 in this table, but only one for each in the EIGRP route table. R1 has two valid, loop-free routes to 2.2.2.0 /24 in the topology table, but the metrics are unequal. As a result, the path with the lowest metric (2297856) is named the successor and is placed into the EIGRP route table. The other path is a feasible successor and will become the successor if the current successor leaves the table.

```
P 2.2.2.0/24, 1 successors, FD is 2297856
        via 172.12.123.2 (2297856/128256), Serial0/1/0
        via 172.12.123.3 (2300416/156160), Serial0/1/0
```

Let's test that! R1 is currently using 172.12.123.2 as the next-hop IP address for traffic heading for 2.2.2.0 /24. I'll disable EIGRP on R2 for the 172.12.123.0 /24 network, and then check all three of R1's EIGRP tables.

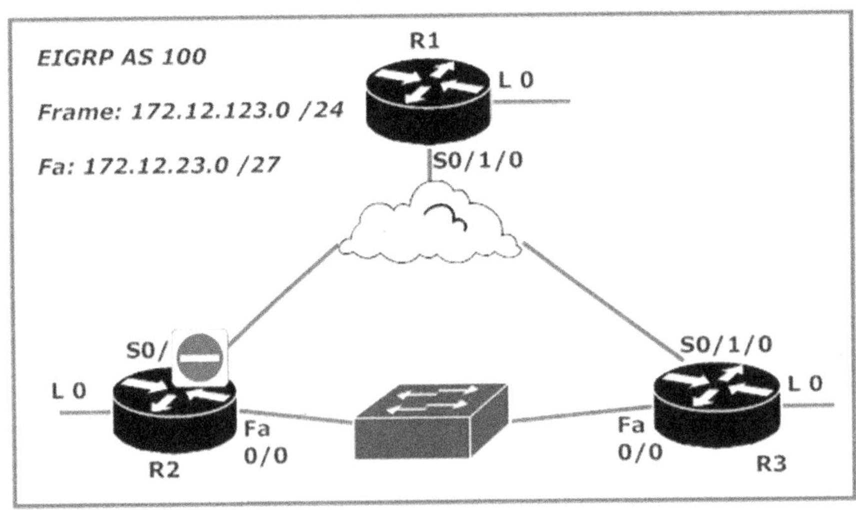


```
May 6 14:47:31: %DUAL-5-NBRCHANGE: EIGRP-IPv4 100: Neighbor 172.12.123.2 (Serial0/1/0)
is down: holding time expired

R1#show ip eigrp neighbor
EIGRP-IPv4 Neighbors for AS(100)
```

```
H     Address        Interface   Hold Uptime     SRTT    RTO    Q     Seq
                                 (sec)           (ms)           Cnt   Num
1     172.12.123.3   Se0/1/0     173  04:07:40   80      480    0     23
```

```
R1#show ip route eigrp
      2.0.0.0/24 is subnetted, 1 subnets
D        2.2.2.0 [90/2300416] via 172.12.123.3, 00:00:10, Serial0/1/0
      3.0.0.0/24 is subnetted, 1 subnets
D        3.3.3.0 [90/2297856] via 172.12.123.3, 00:00:25, Serial0/1/0
      172.12.0.0/16 is variably subnetted, 3 subnets, 3 masks
D        172.12.23.0/27 [90/2172416] via 172.12.123.3, 00:00:10, Serial0/1/0

R1#show ip eigrp topology
EIGRP-IPv4 Topology Table for AS(100)/ID(172.12.123.1)
Codes: P - Passive, A - Active, U - Update, Q - Query, R - Reply,
       r - reply Status, s - sia Status

P 172.12.123.0/24, 1 successors, FD is 2169856
         via Connected, Serial0/1/0
P 172.12.23.0/27, 1 successors, FD is 2172416
         via 172.12.123.3 (2172416/28160), Serial0/1/0
P 2.2.2.0/24, 1 successors, FD is 2297856
         via 172.12.123.3 (2300416/156160), Serial0/1/0
P 3.3.3.0/24, 1 successors, FD is 2297856
         via 172.12.123.3 (2297856/128256), Serial0/1/0
P 1.1.1.0/24, 1 successors, FD is 128256
         via Connected, Loopback0
```

The route that was the feasible successor is now the successor, and R1 can still ping R2's loopback.

```
R1#ping 2.2.2.2

Type escape sequence to abort.
Sending 5, 100-byte ICMP Echos to 2.2.2.2, timeout is 2 seconds:
!!!!!
Success rate is 100 percent (5/5), round-trip min/avg/max = 64/64/68 ms
```

I'll now reenable EIGRP on R2's Serial interface.

```
R2(config-if)#router eigrp 100
R2(config-router)#network 172.12.123.0 0.0.0.255
May 6 14:56:02: %DUAL-5-NBRCHANGE: EIGRP-IPv4 100: Neighbor 172.12.123.1 (Serial0/1/0)
is up: new adjacency
```

Let's revisit R1's topology table.

```
R1#show ip eigrp top
EIGRP-IPv4 Topology Table for AS(100)/ID(172.12.123.1)
Codes: P - Passive, A - Active, U - Update, Q - Query, R - Reply,
       r - reply Status, s - sia Status

P 172.12.123.0/24, 1 successors, FD is 2169856
           via Connected, Serial0/1/0
P 172.12.23.0/27, 2 successors, FD is 2172416
           via 172.12.123.2 (2172416/28160), Serial0/1/0
           via 172.12.123.3 (2172416/28160), Serial0/1/0
P 2.2.2.0/24, 1 successors, FD is 2297856
           via 172.12.123.2 (2297856/128256), Serial0/1/0
           via 172.12.123.3 (2300416/156160), Serial0/1/0
P 3.3.3.0/24, 1 successors, FD is 2297856
           via 172.12.123.3 (2297856/128256), Serial0/1/0
           via 172.12.123.2 (2300416/156160), Serial0/1/0
P 1.1.1.0/24, 1 successors, FD is 128256
           via Connected, Loopback0
```

The metrics for 2.2.2.0 /24 and 3.3.3.0 /24 are soooo close! They're so close that we really should load balance over all available paths, even though the metrics aren't quite equal. EIGRP runs equal-cost load balancing by default, but *un*equal-cost balancing requires a little configuration. *Very* little configuration, as it turns out!

The variance Command

One magic word enables unequal-cost load balancing in EIGRP. Typing the word is the easy part—it's the number that follows the word that you gotta watch! The *variance* command is simply a multiplier and has a default value of 1. The router will multiply the Feasible Distance by this value. Any feasible successor with a metric less than that new value will be entered into the routing table.

In print, I admit that sounds a little confusing—perhaps even a tad askew. Thankfully, the reality of this command is simple. Consider the two paths from R1 to R2's loopback in the topology table.

```
P 2.2.2.0/24, 1 successors, FD is 2297856
           via 172.12.123.2 (2297856/128256), Serial0/1/0
           via 172.12.123.3 (2300416/156160), Serial0/1/0
```

The successor has a metric of 2297856. By setting the EIGRP variance to 2 on R1, any route with a metric of less than 4595712 (2 times 2297856) will be entered into the EIGRP routing table and will participate in unequal-cost load sharing. The only feasible successor to that route has a metric of 2300416, so it certainly qualifies! Let's run *variance 2* on R1.

```
R1(config)#router eigrp 100
R1(config-router)#variance ?
  <1-128> Metric variance multiplier

R1(config-router)#variance 2
```

R1's EIGRP routing table now shows both the successor and feasible successor for 2.2.2.0 /24, and unequal-cost load balancing is in effect!

```
R1#show ip route eigrp
      2.0.0.0/24 is subnetted, 1 subnets
D        2.2.2.0   [90/2300416] via 172.12.123.3, 00:00:56, Serial0/1/0
                   [90/2297856] via 172.12.123.2, 00:00:56, Serial0/1/0
      3.0.0.0/24 is subnetted, 1 subnets
D        3.3.3.0   [90/2297856] via 172.12.123.3, 00:00:56, Serial0/1/0
                   [90/2300416] via 172.12.123.2, 00:00:56, Serial0/1/0
```

The feasible successor and successor are also showing up for R3's loopback network. This illustrates a very important point regarding *variance*—it's an all-or-nothing command. When you change variance, you're changing it for your router's entire EIGRP configuration.

With unequal-cost load balancing in effect, the load each link carries is proportional to the metric. If one path's metric is twice as good as another, that path will carry roughly twice as much data.

The *show ip protocols* command verifies the variance setting and brings you a lot of other important routing information!

```
R1#show ip protocols
*** IP Routing is NSF aware ***

Routing Protocol is "eigrp 100"
  Outgoing update filter list for all interfaces is not set
  Incoming update filter list for all interfaces is not set
  Default networks flagged in outgoing updates
  Default networks accepted from incoming updates
  Redistributing: eigrp 100
  EIGRP-IPv4 Protocol for AS(100)
    Metric weight K1=1, K2=0, K3=1, K4=0, K5=0
    NSF-aware route hold timer is 240
    Router-ID: 172.12.123.1
    Topology : 0 (base)
      Active Timer: 3 min
      Distance: internal 90 external 170
      Maximum path: 4
      Maximum hopcount 100
      Maximum metric variance 2
```

```
Automatic Summarization: disabled
Maximum path: 4
Routing for Networks:
1.1.1.0/24
  Gateway          Distance        Last Update
  172.12.123.0/24
Routing Information Sources:
   Gateway          Distance        Last Update
   172.12.123.3           90        00:05:05
   172.12.123.2           90        00:05:05
   Distance: internal 90 external 170
```

Note the maximum path value of 4. This value defines how many equal-cost paths can be used for the same destination. You can change the value from the default of 4 with the maximum-paths command, but if you set it to 1, you're disabling load balancing!

```
R1(config)#router eigrp 100
R1(config-router)#maximum-paths ?
  <1-32> Number of paths
```

Let's go back to *variance*. You might have looked at that lab and thought, "Hey, I don't need to do any math. I'll just enter *variance 255*, and I'll get all the load balancing I want!"

You'll also get load balancing you *don't* want. Let's say we have three valid paths to the same network. Path 1 has a metric of 5000, Path 2 a metric of 7000, and Path 3 a metric of 55000. That gives us two links close in speed and a third path that's waaaay slower than the others. Do you really want to load balance over that third path? Probably not. It's a good backup link, but not one I want to use in load balancing. *Do the math!*

DUAL Queries and "Passive" Routes

It's fine if a router has a successor for a given route without having a feasible successor—as long as the successor route is available.

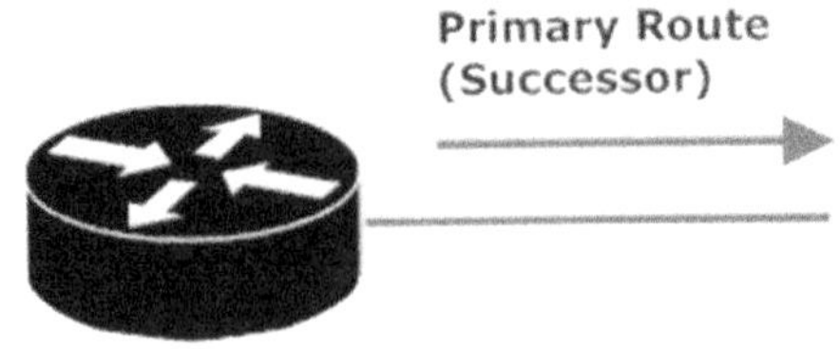

In an earlier lab, we saw a feasible successor step in for a successor that was suddenly unavailable. We love that quick cutover, but what if there's no feasible successor to cut over to?

EIGRP uses DUAL to calculate route metrics *and* to query neighboring routers in the situation described here. DUAL will first mark the route in question as active, and at first glance that sounds like a good thing. The term "active" refers to the fact that EIGRP is actively calculating the route, *not* that the route is active and can carry data. An EIGRP active route is actually unavailable to carry data!

With the route marked active, DUAL will now send queries out to the router's EIGRP neighbors. This query is basically just one neighbor asking another, "Hey, do you know how to get to this network? I just lost my route to it."

If the first queried router doesn't have such a route, that router then asks *its* neighbors.

This process continues until a queried router replies with the desired route, or the routers being queried run out of other routers to ask!

Routes come out of active state so quickly that it's hard to spot one, and that's the way we like it. Routes that are no longer being calculated by DUAL and are therefore ready to be used to route data are in passive mode, and this is one time where passive is better than active!

```
R1#show ip eigrp topology
EIGRP-IPv4 Topology Table for AS(100)/ID(172.12.123.1)
Codes: P - Passive, A - Active, U - Update, Q - Query, R - Reply,
       r - reply Status, s - sia Status

P 172.12.123.0/24, 1 successors, FD is 2169856
           via Connected, Serial0/1/0
P 172.12.23.0/27, 2 successors, FD is 2172416
           via 172.12.123.2 (2172416/28160), Serial0/1/0
           via 172.12.123.3 (2172416/28160), Serial0/1/0
P 2.2.2.0/24, 2 successors, FD is 2297856
           via 172.12.123.2 (2297856/128256), Serial0/1/0
           via 172.12.123.3 (2300416/156160), Serial0/1/0
P 3.3.3.0/24, 2 successors, FD is 2297856
           via 172.12.123.3 (2297856/128256), Serial0/1/0
           via 172.12.123.2 (2300416/156160), Serial0/1/0
P 1.1.1.0/24, 1 successors, FD is 128256
           via Connected, Loopback0
```

With these EIGRP fundamentals down cold, let's hit some EIGRP *non*fundamentals.

Chapter 3: ADVANCED EIGRP

Before we dive into more EIGRP configs, let's take a more detailed look at the packets that make everything happen! EIGRP uses the *Reliable Transport Protocol* (RTP) to handle the guaranteed and reliable delivery of EIGRP packets. "Guaranteed and reliable" sounds a lot like TCP, but the two are quite different in how they operate. Not *all* EIGRP packets will be sent reliably.

Hello packets handle neighbor discovery and serve as keepalives for established adjacencies. They're multicast to 224.0.0.10.

Acknowledgement packets are simply hello packets that carry no data. Neither ACKs nor hellos use RTP and are therefore considered unreliable.

Update packets are sent to new neighbors, allowing that neighbor to build accurate routing and topology tables. They're also sent upon a change in the network. Update packets are generally multicast packets, but this is networking, so you know there's an exception. More on that in just a few minutes!

Query packets are sent when a router loses a successor and has no feasible successor.

Reply packets are sent in response to query packets. It's a happy response, because reply packets indicate a new route to the destination in question has been found! Reply packets use RTP and are considered reliable, as are update and query packets.

To see how many of these packets have passed through, run *show ip eigrp traffic.*

```
R1#show ip eigrp traffic
EIGRP-IPv4 Traffic Statistics for AS(100)
  Hellos sent/received: 4412/5447
  Updates sent/received: 44/38
  Queries sent/received: 2/5
  Replies sent/received: 5/2
  Acks sent/received: 39/45
```

When the query, update, and reply packets remain the same, the network is stable. If you see them constantly incrementing, you likely have a flapping link in your network. The query and reply values increment only when a successor is lost.

The Initial EIGRP Route Exchange

Let's take a detailed look at the forming of an EIGRP adjacency and the route exchange that follows. The festivities begin when EIGRP is enabled on an interface. EIGRP hello packets are then multicast (to 224.0.0.10, natch!) via that interface in an attempt to find potential neighbors.

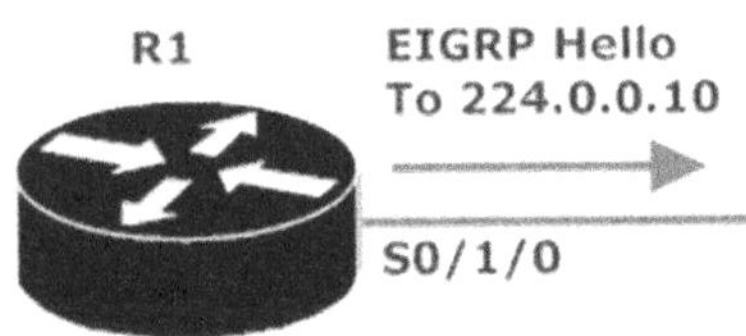

R2 receives the hello, and if certain values are agreed upon by the two routers involved, R2 will respond with an update packet. That packet contains all the EIGRP-learned routes R2 knows of. Update packets are usually multicast, but in this case the update is a unicast.

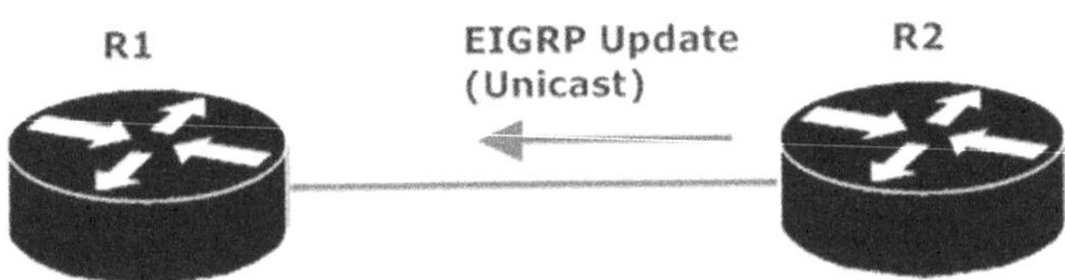

R1 now sends an EIGRP ACK back to R2, letting R2 know the routes were received. R1 will also send an update packet of its own, unicast to R2, containing all the EIGRP routes R1 knows of. R2 will respond with an EIGRP ACK of its own, and the initial route exchange is complete. This is the only time EIGRP routers exchange full routing tables. After this, only network changes are advertised.

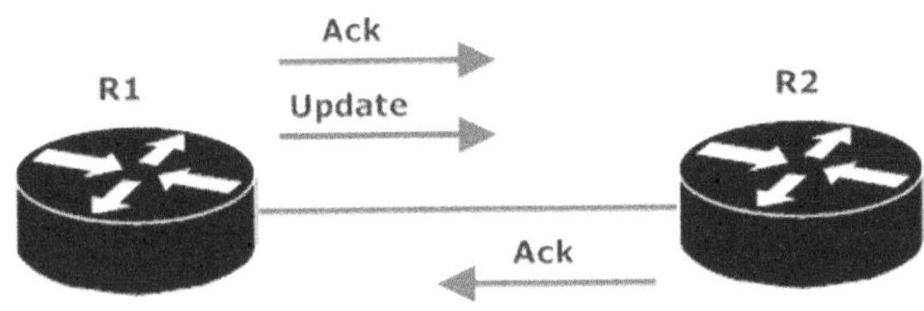

Other EIGRP Adjacency Issues (and Nonissues)

The EIGRP hold time has the same function as OSPF dead time. They each define the amount of time in which a hello must be received in order to retain the neighbor relationship. The default EIGRP hold time is three times the hello time (more on that soon). Unlike OSPF, the hello and hold timers in EIGRP do not have to agree between potential neighbors in order for them to become neighbors. We'll prove that in the next lab, using R2 and R3 in their own little autonomous system.

Before we get started, it would be nice to know what the current timer settings are! They're slightly hidden in EIGRP but revealed with *show ip eigrp interface detail.*

```
R3#show ip eigrp interfaces detail fast0/0
EIGRP-IPv4 Interfaces for AS(100)
                         Xmit Queue    Mean   Pacing Time   Multicast    Pending
Interface      Peers     Un/Reliable   SRTT   Un/Reliable   Flow Timer   Routes
Fa0/0            1          0/0        1218       0/1          6092         0
  Hello-interval is 5, Hold-time is 15
  Split-horizon is enabled
  Next xmit serial <none>
  Un/reliable mcasts: 0/17 Un/reliable ucasts: 34/12
  Mcast exceptions: 0 CR packets: 0 ACKs suppressed: 0
  Retransmissions sent: 0 Out-of-sequence rcvd: 2
  Topology-ids on interface - 0
  Authentication mode is not set
```

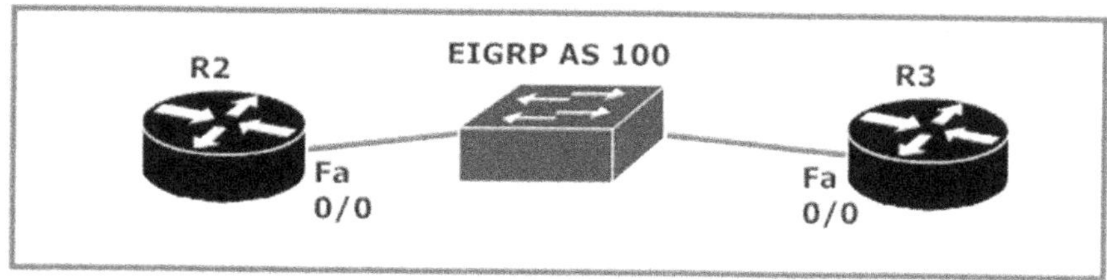

Let's verify adjacencies and then screw around with the config a bit!

```
R2#show ip eigrp neighbor
EIGRP-IPv4 Neighbors for AS(100)
H    Address       Interface   Hold Uptime      SRTT     RTO    Q     Seq
                               (sec)            (ms)            Cnt   Num
1    172.12.23.3   Fa0/0       11 06:58:47      4        200    0     36

R3#show ip eigrp neighbor
EIGRP-IPv4 Neighbors for AS(100)
H    Address       Interface   Hold Uptime      SRTT     RTO    Q     Seq
                               (sec)            (ms)            Cnt   Num
1    172.12.23.2   Fa0/0       10 07:00:32      5        200    0     47
```

Let's change the hello interval to 7 seconds on R3 and see what happens.

```
R3(config)#int fast 0/0
R3(config-if)#ip hello ?
  Eigrp   Enhanced Interior Gateway Routing Protocol (EIGRP)

R3(config-if)#ip hello eigrp ?
  <1-65535>   AS number

R3(config-if)#ip hello eigrp 100 ?
  <1-65535>   Seconds between hello transmissions

R3(config-if)#ip hello eigrp 100 7

R3#show ip eigrp neighbor
EIGRP-IPv4 Neighbors for AS(100)
H     Address        Interface     Hold Uptime       SRTT     RTO     Q     Seq
                                                     (sec     (ms)    Cnt   Num
0     172.12.23.2    Fa0/0         11 00:09:04       1218     5000    0     62
```

Nothing happened! The uptime wasn't reset, and no console messages were received, so the adjacency is still intact. That means we can set the hello timer to anything we like, and the adjacency will still be there, right?

Welllllll...

```
R3(config)#int fast 0/0
R3(config-if)#ip hello eigrp 100 30
```

I just set the hello timer to thirty seconds, and nothing happened right away. No messages about the adjacency being lost. No nothin', I tell you! *Until...*

```
May 5 20:01:31: %DUAL-5-NBRCHANGE: EIGRP-IPv4 100: Neighbor 172.12.23.2
(FastEthernet0/0) is down: Interface PEER-TERMINATION received

May 5 20:01:35: %DUAL-5-NBRCHANGE: EIGRP-IPv4 100: Neighbor 172.12.23.2
(FastEthernet0/0) is up: new adjacency

May 5 20:01:50: %DUAL-5-NBRCHANGE: EIGRP-IPv4 100: Neighbor 172.12.23.2
(FastEthernet0/0) is down: Interface PEER-TERMINATION received

May 5 20:01:55: %DUAL-5-NBRCHANGE: EIGRP-IPv4 100: Neighbor 172.12.23.2
(FastEthernet0/0) is up: new adjacency
```

This isn't your garden-variety adjacency loss. This is a *flapping adjacency*—up one second and down just a few seconds later. This is what happens when the EIGRP hello timer on one router is set to a larger value than the EIGRP hold timer on the neighbors! R3 is sending a hello packet every thirty seconds. Problem is, R2 is expecting one every fifteen seconds.

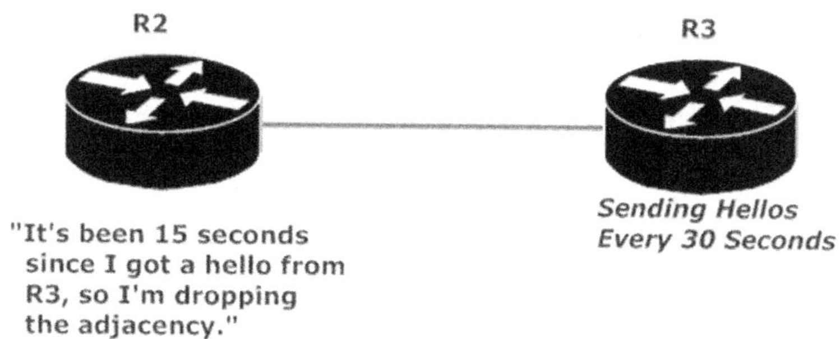

When that timer on R2 hits zero, the adjacency is dropped. When the hello does arrive at R2, the adjacency forms again. That'll keep happening until the timer issue is resolved. Moral of the story: don't set the hello timer higher than the hold timer!

EIGRP hello packets are sent every five seconds on high-speed links, which includes Ethernet segments (and higher variations of Ethernet), Frame Relay multipoint circuits running at over T1 speed, and point-to-point Serial links. Hello packets go out every sixty seconds over slower links, including Frame Relay multipoint circuits running at less than T1 speed. The EIGRP hold time is always three times the hello time.

show ip eigrp neighbors

Let's take a closer look at this vital command. The last four values are used only in more advanced EIGRP troubleshooting, and you can only use them if you know what they are!

```
R3#show ip eigrp neighbor
EIGRP-IPv4 Neighbors for AS(100)
H    Address       Interface    Hold Uptime      SRTT    RTO    Q    Seq
                                (sec)            (ms)           Cnt  Num
0    172.12.23.2   Fa0/0        11 00:21:46      2       200    0    74
```

From left to right:

The top line indicates the IP version in use and the EIGRP AS.

H—The order in which the neighbors were discovered.

Address—The IP address of the neighbor.

Interface—The interface upon which the router is receiving hellos from that address.

Hold—The EIGRP hold time we're now so familiar with!

Uptime—The length of time the adjacency has been in place.

SRTT—Smooth Round-Trip Time. The number of milliseconds it takes for an EIGRP packet to be sent to that neighbor and for an ACK to come back from that neighbor.

RTO—Retransmission Time Out. The length of time until a packet will be retransmitted to this neighbor.

Q Cnt—Queue Count. The number of EIGRP packets waiting to be sent.

Seq Num—Sequence Number. The number on the last update, reply, or query packet that was received from this neighbor.

While we're examining numbers, let's take a detailed look at a couple of distances.

The Feasible and Advertised Distances

We've been working with the topology table for a while now, and you've certainly taken notice of the two numbers in parentheses following each next-hop IP address. We'll use the first EIGRP lab for this discussion. All defaults are back in place.

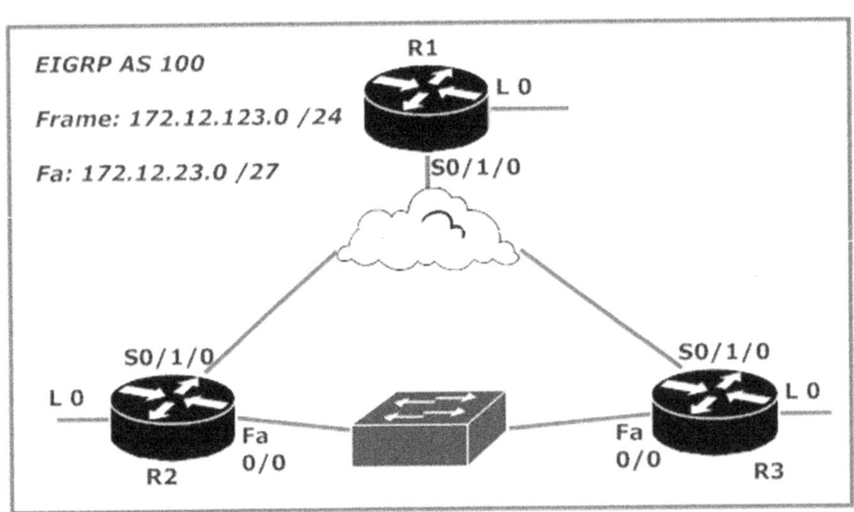

Here are the EIGRP topology table entries for 172.12.23.0 /27 on R1:

```
P 172.12.23.0/27, 2 successors, FD is 2172416
            via 172.12.123.2 (2172416/28160), Serial0/1/0
            via 172.12.123.3 (2172416/28160), Serial0/1/0
```

The first number, 2172416, is the route's *feasible distance*. This is the full metric of the route to the destination network. A route's feasible distance also appears in the route table, right next to the administrative distance of that same route.

The second number, 28160, is the route's *advertised distance.* Nothing complicated here. It's just the metric from the next-hop router to the destination network. The AD is visible only in the EIGRP topology table.

Note: The advertised distance is also known as the reported distance (RD). I'm going to use "advertised distance" throughout this section. There's a possibility your ROUTE exam may use either or both terms for this value.

For the path to be considered loop-free, the advertised distance must be less than the feasible distance. This routing loop prevention mechanism ensures the next-hop router is closer to the destination than the local router.

These distances are also used by EIGRP to determine feasible successors. Let's walk through this important process using R1's topology entries for 3.3.3.0 /24.

```
P 3.3.3.0/24, 1 successors, FD is 2297856
            via 172.12.123.3 (2297856/128256), Serial0/1/0
            via 172.12.123.2 (2300416/156160), Serial0/1/0
```

The table is kind enough to tell us the successor's FD is 2297856, which matches that of the route using 172.12.123.3 as the next-hop address. What of the other route? It can't be a successor, since its FD is higher than the FD of the successor. Can the other route possibly be a feasible successor? It can, because its *advertised* distance of 156160 is lower than the *feasible* distance of the successor. That's the *feasibility condition*, and since the condition has been met, the second route is a feasible successor.

Let's get some practice in with the feasibility condition using some slightly smaller numbers. We'll assume a successor route and three possible feasible successors.

Successor: FD 5, AD 4

Possible FS 1: FD 9, AD 7

Possible FS 2: FD 8, AD 6

Possible FS 3: FD 6, AD 4

Whether the AD is one digit, eight digits, or more, the feasibility condition works the same. If the AD of a potential FS is less than the FD of the successor, the potential FS is indeed a feasible successor. Only the third route meets that condition, so that's our only feasible successor.

Using that same principle, we need to determine the successor and feasible successor(s) for the path from R1 to R3 in the following network:

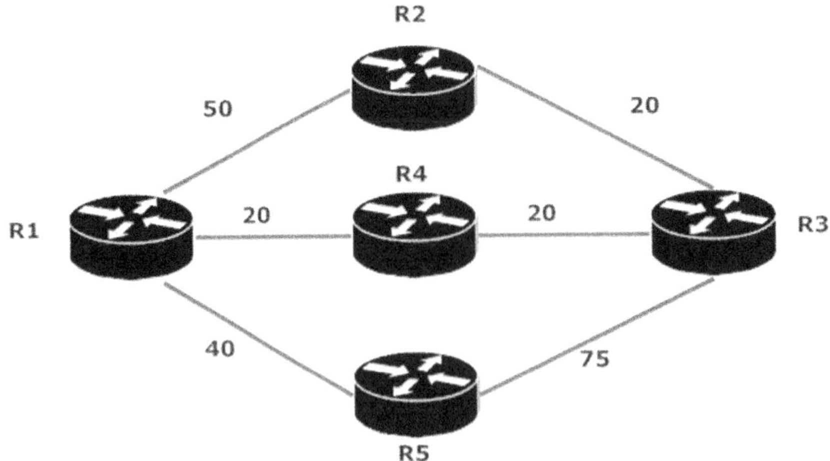

Before we even begin with the feasibility condition, we have to know the AD and FD for each path! The advertised distance is the next-hop router's metric to the destination, and the feasible distance is the local router's metric to that same destination. From R1's point of view, the FD and AD of each path are as follows:

R1—R4—R3: FD 40, AD 20

R1—R2—R3: FD 70, AD 20

R1—R5—R3: FD 115, AD 75

The route with the best metric is the successor, and that's the R1-R4-R3 path. Can either or both of the other two routes become a feasible successor? Only if the AD of the candidate route is less than the FD of the successor (in this case, 40). The R1-R2-R3 path's AD is less than 20, so that route is a feasible successor. The R1-R5-R3 path's AD is larger than 40, so that route is not a feasible successor.

R1—R4—R3: FD 40, AD 20 (successor)

R1—R2—R3: FD 70, AD 20 (feasible successor)

R1—R5—R3: FD 115, AD 75 (neither)

The Feasibility Condition and Variance

A route that doesn't meet the feasibility condition cannot be used in unequal-cost load balancing. In the previous example, the R1-R5-R3 path couldn't be used for load balancing.

It's a great idea to write out the FD and AD of all routes in your network before deciding on the variance value and to determine whether all of the desired paths can actually be used in unequal-cost load balancing...as in the following illustration:

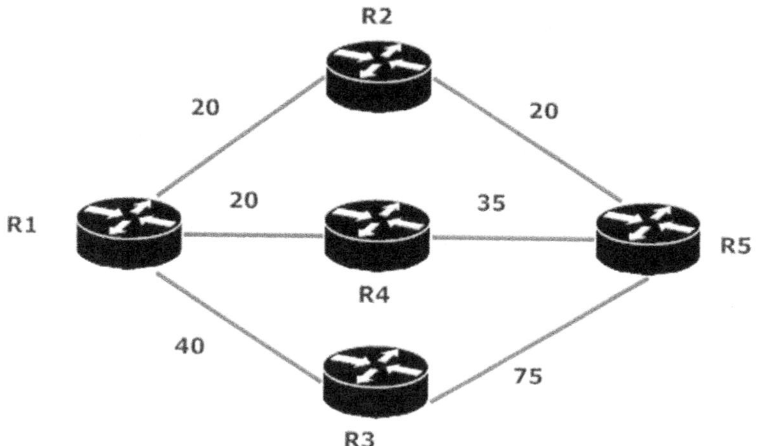

Using *variance* to configure unequal-cost load balancing for traffic going from R1 to R5 seems simple enough. We just need to get the path metrics and go from there. The individual path metrics are 40, 55, and 115, so using *variance 3* would allow all three paths to be placed into our routing table. All set, right?

Not quite. Our math is fine; it's the feasibility condition that's going to bite us in the arse. Let's have a look at the FD and AD for each path. Which path will be the successor? Which path will be a feasible successor, if any?

R1—R2—R5: FD 40, AD 20

R1—R4—R5: FD 55, AD 35

R1—R3—R5: FD 115, AD 75

The R1-R2-R5 path is the successor. R1-R4-R5 meets the feasibility condition, since its AD of 35 is less than the FD of the successor (40). The R1-R3-R5 path does not meet this condition, since its AD of 75 is larger than the successor's FD. You could actually set the variance to 2 in this situation, which would allow unequal-cost load sharing over the single feasible successor. (For exam and real-world purposes, make it your best practice to set the variance as low as possible while still getting the load balancing you want.) No matter the variance, the third path cannot participate in load balancing.

The Triple Threat: EIGRP Administrative Distances

With OSPF, you have one basic administrative distance: 110.

Regular OSPF route? AD is 110. OSPF route learned by redistribution? AD is 110. OSPF E1 route? AD is 110. OSPF E2 route? AD is 110.

This is one area where OSPF and EIGRP differ greatly. We actually have three different EIGRP administrative distances:

Internal routes, introduced to EIGRP with the *network* command, have an AD of 90 and a routing table code of "D." ("E" was already in use by EGP, the External Gateway Protocol.)

External routes, introduced to EIGRP via route redistribution, have an AD of 170 and a routing table code of "D EX."

Summary routes, the result of manual route summarization, have an AD of 5. That is, if you know where to look. And you will. Soon.

According to theory, then, a network could have an AD of 90 or an AD of 170, depending on how it's advertised. Let's test that theory with this network! An EIGRP adjacency already exists between these two routers, but the loopback interface on R1 (1.1.1.1 /24) has not yet been introduced to EIGRP AS 100.

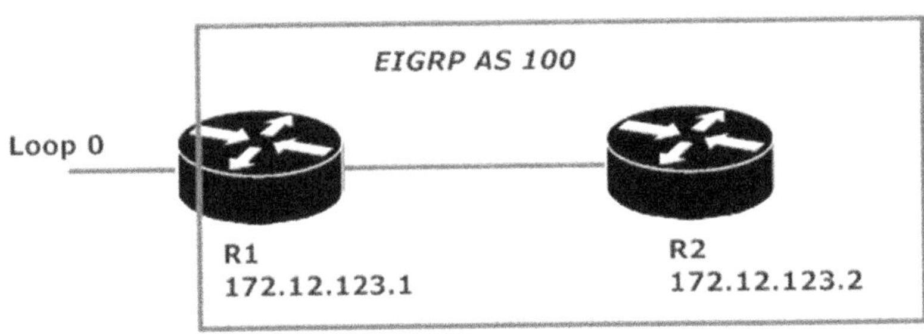

I'll use *network* to advertise R1's loopback to R2, making this an internal route. R2's EIGRP route table shows the route with a code of "D" and an admin distance of 90, just what we expect to see with an EIGRP internal route.

```
R1(config)#router eigrp 100
R1(config-router)#network 1.1.1.0 0.0.0.255

R2#show ip route eigrp
      1.0.0.0/24  is subnetted, 1 subnets
D        1.1.1.0  [90/2297856] via 172.12.123.1, 00:00:06, Serial0/1/0
```

If route redistribution is used instead of *network*, the result is an EIGRP external route. I'll remove the *network* command and then use *redistribute connected* to introduce all connected segments to the EIGRP AS. (*Much* more on redistribution later in the course!)

```
R1(config)#router eigrp 100
R1(config-router)#no network 1.1.1.0 0.0.0.255
R1(config-router)#redistribute connected
```

The same route still appears on R2 but as an external route with an AD of 170 and a routing table code of "D EX."

```
R2#show ip route eigrp
      1.0.0.0/24  is subnetted, 1 subnets
D EX     1.1.1.0  [170/2297856] via 172.12.123.1, 00:01:49, Serial0/1/0
```

You can change the AD of external or internal routes on the local route with the *distance eigrp* command. You have to specify both internal and external AD even if you're changing it for only one of those route types. You will lose adjacencies as a result of this command, but if nothing else has been changed, they'll come right back up.

```
R2(config)#router eigrp 100
R2(config-router)#distance ?
  <1-255>  Set route administrative distance
  Eigrp    Set distance for internal and external routes

R2(config-router)#distance eigrp ?
  <1-255>  Distance for internal routes

R2(config-router)#distance eigrp 90 ?
  <1-255>  Distance for external routes

R2(config-router)#distance eigrp 90 100 ?
  <cr>

R2(config-router)#distance eigrp 90 100

  %DUAL-5-NBRCHANGE: EIGRP-IPv4 100: Neighbor 172.12.123.1 (Serial0/1/0) is down:
route configuration changed
  %DUAL-5-NBRCHANGE: EIGRP-IPv4 100: Neighbor 172.12.123.1 (Serial0/1/0) is up: new
adjacency

R2#show ip route eigrp
      1.0.0.0/24  is subnetted, 1 subnets
D EX     1.1.1.0  [100/2297856] via 172.12.123.1, 00:00:07, Serial0/1/0
      3.0.0.0/24  is subnetted, 1 subnets
D         3.3.3.0  [90/156160] via 172.12.23.3, 00:00:34, FastEthernet0/0
```

We'll see the third EIGRP AD in action in the next section, which just happens to start right now!

EIGRP Route Summarization: Automatic and Manual

EIGRP has a pesky little default behavior. *Autosummarization* occurs when routes are advertised across classful network boundaries. That doesn't sound all that bad, but when you have *discontiguous networks*, it can cause real trouble. Discontiguous networks are subnets of the same major network number that are separated by another network number. In the following lab, we have subnets of 20.0.0.0 separated by a different major network number, 172.12.0.0.

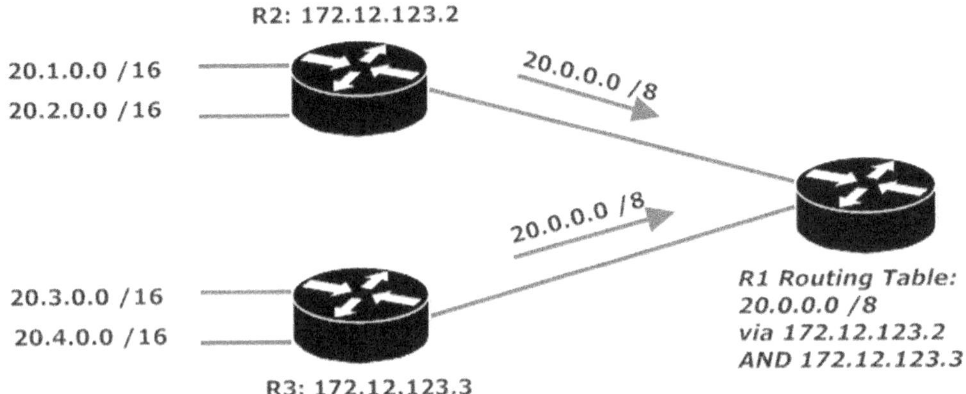

With EIGRP's default autosummarization left on, R1 will receive two advertisements for the 20.0.0.0 /8 network—one from R2 and one from R3. Combined with equal-cost load sharing (also on by default!), there's an excellent chance that half of the packets sent by R1 that are destined for any subnet of 20.0.0.0 will end up going the wrong way.

Let's test that theory! The adjacency between R1 and the spoke routers R2 and R3 is already in place. Watch what happens when I start to add R2's 20.0.0.0 subnets to EIGRP.

```
R2(config)#router eigrp 100
R2(config-router)#network 20.1.0.0 0.0.255.255
May  7  10:27:19:  %DUAL-5-NBRCHANGE:  EIGRP-IPv4  100:  Neighbor  172.12.123.1
(Serial0/1/0) is resync: summary up, remove components
R2(config-router)#network 20.2.0.0 0.0.255.255
```

The adjacency resynched, and the message mentions "summary up." Sounds like something got summarized! Let's check R1's routing table.

```
R1#show ip route eigrp
D     20.0.0.0/8   [90/2172416] via 172.12.123.2, 00:00:30, Serial0/1/0
```

R1 is receiving a summarized route from R2 due to autosummarization. Let's see what happens when we add R3's 20.0.0.0 subnets to our EIGRP deployment.

```
R3(config)#router eigrp 100
R3(config-router)#network 20.3.0.0 0.0.255.255
May  6  10:31:27:  %DUAL-5-NBRCHANGE:  EIGRP-IPv4  100:  Neighbor  172.12.123.1
(Serial0/1/0) is resync: summary up, remove components
R3(config-router)#network 20.4.0.0 0.0.255.255
```

R1's resulting routing table:

```
ILLUSTRATION need the routing table, I can get this done tonight and check that
20.1.0.0 ping result.
```

The problem comes in when R1 tries to ping any of the four individual addresses from the 20.0.0.0 subnets on R2 and R3. We end up with a real mess:

```
R1#ping 20.1.1.1
U.U.U
Success rate is 0 percent (0/5)

R1#ping 20.2.1.1
U.U.U
Success rate is 0 percent (0/5)

R1#ping 20.3.1.1
U.U.U
Success rate is 0 percent (0/5)

R1#ping 20.4.1.1
U.U.U
Success rate is 0 percent (0/5)
```

We know autosummarization is causing the problem, so turning it off should help. Question is, just *where* do we need to turn it off? Where *exactly* is the problem? In the real world, we'd likely just turn autosummarization off on all our EIGRP-speaking routers. Exam questions and job interview questions aren't always "real world," though. If I asked you to disable autosummarization only where it needed to be disabled in order to solve this problem, where would you do so?

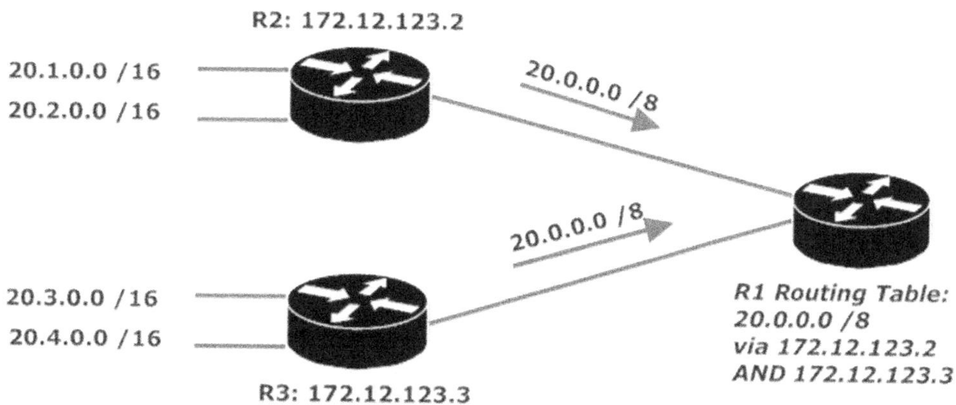

It's intuitive to think that disabling autosummarization on the hub router will solve the problem, but that won't get the job done. The routes are already summarized by the time they reach R1, and they can't be "unautosummarized." The summarization is taking place on the spoke routers, and it's there that autosummarization must be disabled. After doing so, we'll revisit R1's routing table.

```
R2(config)#router eigrp 100
R2(config-router)#no auto

R3(config)#router eigrp 100
R3(config-router)#no auto
```

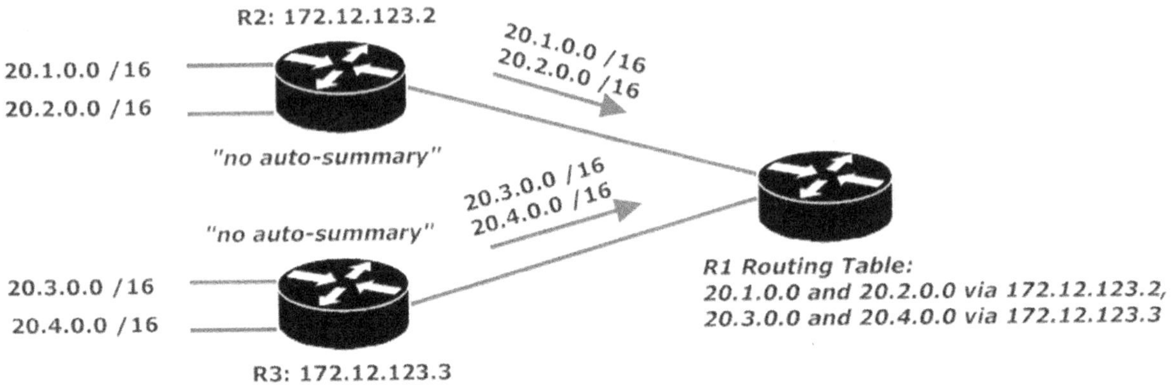

R2: 172.12.123.2
20.1.0.0 /16
20.2.0.0 /16
20.1.0.0 /16
20.2.0.0 /16
"no auto-summary"
20.3.0.0 /16
20.4.0.0 /16
"no auto-summary"
20.3.0.0 /16
20.4.0.0 /16
R3: 172.12.123.3
R1 Routing Table:
20.1.0.0 and 20.2.0.0 via 172.12.123.2,
20.3.0.0 and 20.4.0.0 via 172.12.123.3

```
R1#show ip route eigrp
     20.0.0.0/16  is subnetted, 4 subnets
D       20.1.0.0  [90/2172416] via 172.12.123.2, 00:15:16, Serial0/1/0
D       20.2.0.0  [90/2172416] via 172.12.123.2, 00:09:07, Serial0/1/0
D       20.3.0.0  [90/2172416] via 172.12.123.3, 00:15:08, Serial0/1/0
D       20.4.0.0  [90/2172416] via 172.12.123.3, 00:08:04, Serial0/1/0
```

Ta-da! R1 now has the proper routing information and can ping all four remote addresses.

```
R1#ping 20.1.1.1
!!!!!
Success rate is 100 percent (5/5), round-trip min/avg/max = 64/65/68 ms

R1#ping 20.2.1.1
!!!!!
Success rate is 100 percent (5/5), round-trip min/avg/max = 64/65/68 ms

R1#ping 20.3.1.1
!!!!!
Success rate is 100 percent (5/5), round-trip min/avg/max = 64/65/68 ms

R1#ping 20.4.1.1
!!!!!
Success rate is 100 percent (5/5), round-trip min/avg/max = 64/65/68 ms
```

Manual Summarization

Autosummarization is a pain, but manual summarization is a great thing when used at the proper points in your network. Here are just a few reasons why:

- The routing tables are smaller, making the entire routing process faster.
- Since the tables are smaller, the load on the CPU from the routing process is lessened.
- Routing updates themselves are smaller.
- The more-specific network numbers are hidden, which gives a small boost to our overall network security plan.
- The impact of flapping links on the rest of the network is lessened.
- The overall number of EIGRP queries can be lessened.

The key to success with route summarization is you, the network admin, deciding where route summarization should take place. Not the router, not the protocol. You.

In this lab, R1 has seven subnets it's advertising to EIGRP neighbor R2.

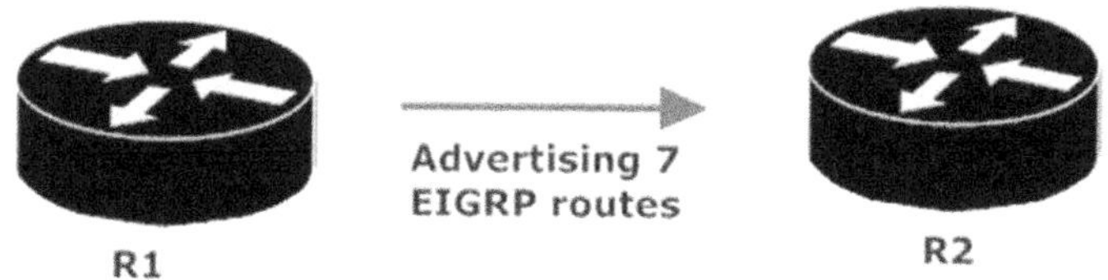

R2 sees all seven routes.

```
R2#show ip route eigrp
     100.0.0.0/16  is subnetted, 7 subnets
D       100.1.0.0  [90/2297856] via 172.12.123.1, 00:00:31, Serial0/1/0
D       100.2.0.0  [90/2297856] via 172.12.123.1, 00:00:31, Serial0/1/0
D       100.3.0.0  [90/2297856] via 172.12.123.1, 00:00:31, Serial0/1/0
D       100.4.0.0  [90/2297856] via 172.12.123.1, 00:00:31, Serial0/1/0
D       100.5.0.0  [90/2297856] via 172.12.123.1, 00:00:31, Serial0/1/0
D       100.6.0.0  [90/2297856] via 172.12.123.1, 00:00:31, Serial0/1/0
D       100.7.0.0  [90/2297856] via 172.12.123.1, 00:00:31, Serial0/1/0
```

Nothing wrong with that table, but we'd like to keep our routing tables as complete and concise as possible. Manual route summarization can knock those seven routes down to *one line*! All we need to do is break each route down into binary strings.

100.1.0.0 **01100100 00000**001 00000000 00000000
100.2.0.0 **01100100 00000**010 (every route ends in 16 zeroes)

100.3.0.0 **01100100 00000**011
100.4.0.0 **01100100 00000**100
100.5.0.0 **01100100 00000**101
100.6.0.0 **01100100 00000**110
100.7.0.0 **01100100 00000**111

That's actually the hardest part of summarizing routes!

The next step is to work from left to right and identify the common bits. The decimal value of the common bits yields the summary route, and the number of common bits yields the summary mask. The value of the common bits (in bold) is 100.0.0.0. We have 13 common bits, expressed in /13 in prefix notation and 255.248.0.0 in dotted decimal (11111111 11111000 00000000 00000000 in binary). There's your summary route and mask! Apply it to the advertising interface, and you're all set!

```
R1(config)#int serial 0/1/0
R1(config-if)#ip summary-address ?
  eigrp  Enhanced Interior Gateway Routing Protocol (EIGRP)
  rip    Routing Information Protocol (RIP)

R1(config-if)#ip summary-address eigrp ?
  <1-65535>  AS number

R1(config-if)#ip summary-address eigrp 100 ?
  A.B.C.D  IP address

R1(config-if)#ip summary-address eigrp 100 100.0.0.0 ?
  A.B.C.D  IP network mask

R1(config-if)#ip summary-address eigrp 100 100.0.0.0 255.248.0.0

  May  7  13:49:02:  %DUAL-5-NBRCHANGE:  EIGRP-IPv4  100:  Neighbor  172.12.123.3
(Serial0/1/0) is resync: summary configured
  May  7  13:49:02:  %DUAL-5-NBRCHANGE:  EIGRP-IPv4  100:  Neighbor  172.12.123.2
(Serial0/1/0) is resync: summary configured
```

The routing table on R2 reflect the summary route only. R1 is no longer advertising the more-specific routes on Serial 0/1/0.

```
R2#show ip route eigrp
      100.0.0.0/13  is subnetted, 1 subnets
D        100.0.0.0  [90/2297856] via 172.12.123.1, 00:00:43, Serial0/1/0
```

There's also a new EIGRP route in an unexpected place—R1.

```
R1#show ip route eigrp
D     100.0.0.0/13 is a summary, 00:02:42, Null0
```

On the summarizing router, the summary route is seen as a route to "Null0." Basically, this is a route to the trash can. If a packet comes in that doesn't match one of the seven more-specific routes that have been summarized, that packet will be dropped. This EIGRP default behavior helps to prevent routing loops.

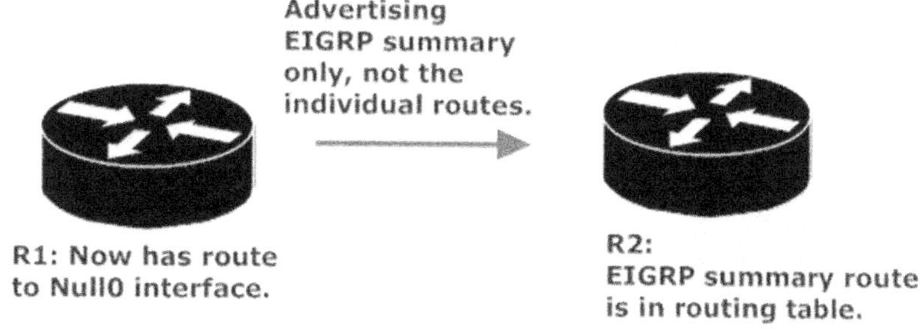

You likely noticed R2 has an AD of 90 assigned to that summary route.

```
D       100.0.0.0   [90/2297856] via 172.12.123.1, 00:05:40, Serial0/1/0
```

That's the value we expect it to have, since the summary will have an AD of 5 only on the summarizing router. However, the summary route on R1 doesn't show *any* AD.

```
R1#show ip route eigrp
D    100.0.0.0/13   is a summary, 00:02:42, Null0
```

Hmm. Let's try another variation of *show ip route.*

```
R1#show ip route 100.0.0.0 ?
  A.B.C.D          Network mask
  longer-prefixes  Show route matching the specified Network/Mask pair only
  |                Output modifiers
  <cr>
```

Let's try the *mask* option.

```
R1#show ip route 100.0.0.0 255.248.0.0
Routing entry for 100.0.0.0/13
  Known via "eigrp 100", distance 5, metric 128256, type internal
  Redistributing via eigrp 100
  Routing Descriptor Blocks:
  * directly connected, via Null0
      Route metric is 128256, traffic share count is 1
      Total delay is 5000 microseconds, minimum bandwidth is 10000000 Kbit
      Reliability 255/255, minimum MTU 9676 bytes
      Loading 1/255, Hops 0
```

Ta-da!

EIGRP Stub Routing

Stub routing is a fantastic method of limiting the size of some routing tables in your EIGRP network while at the same time limiting the scope of DUAL queries. EIGRP doesn't have the stub area options that OSPF has, but EIGRP does allow a router to be configured as a stub. This is often done with a hub-and-spoke configuration like the one we've used in this course.

Whether you're looking at this from R2 or R3's point of view, the next-hop IP address for all packets sent will be 172.12.123.1. There's no other option. There could be 75 networks connected to R1 and/or R3, and packets sent by R2 to any of those networks will always have that same next-hop IP address. There's no reason for R2 to have a huge routing table if the next-hop address is the same for every route.

Some EIGRP stub routing notes:

When an EIGRP-speaking router loses a successor and no feasible successor is known, *that router will not query stub routers.* This limits the overall scope of query packets.

By default, EIGRP stub routers advertise information about two route types back to the hub—directly connected networks and summary routes. That's it!

Only one router in a given adjacency can be a stub. Two routers configured as stubs cannot form an adjacency.

Use *eigrp stub* to configure an EIGRP router as a stub. To change the default route advertisement mentioned previously, use that same command followed by the route types you want the stub to advertise to the hub. (We'll save *leak-map* for future studies.)

```
R2(config)#router eigrp 100
R2(config-router)#eigrp stub ?
  connected      Do advertise connected routes
  leak-map       Allow dynamic prefixes based on the leak-map
  receive-only   Set receive only neighbor
```

```
redistributed Do advertise redistributed routes
static        Do advertise static routes
summary       Do advertise summary routes
```

Generally, the defaults are fine. Don't get too clever with the options, especially *receive-only*. Let me show you what I mean with this network:

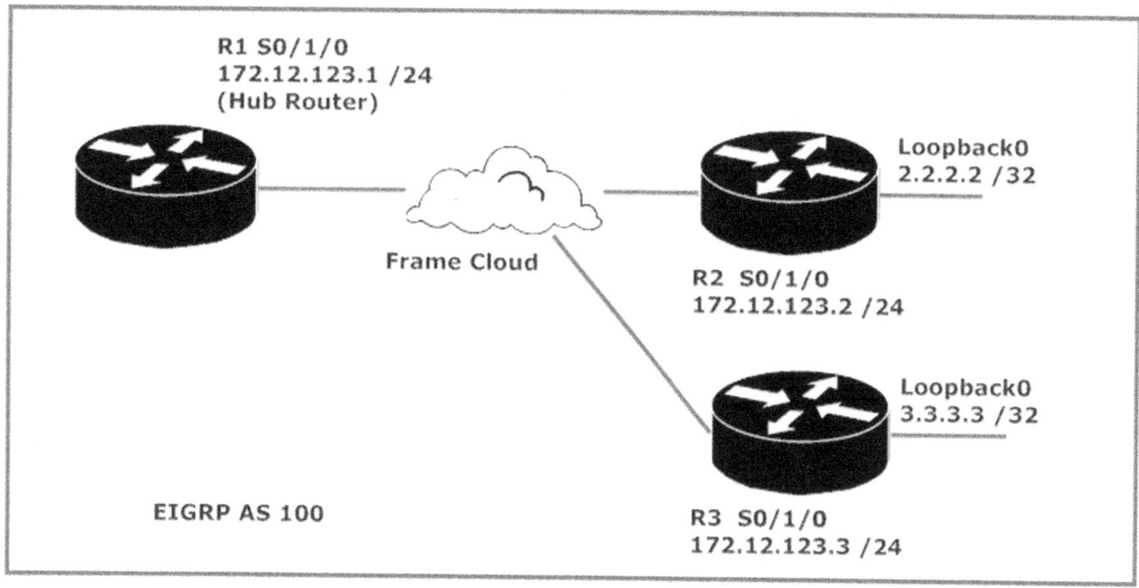

R2 and R3 are perfect stub-routing candidates—the next hop for any traffic they send will be 172.12.123.1—so let's make it so with *eigrp stub.*

```
R2(config)#router eigrp 100
R2(config-router)#eigrp stub
*May 15 13:43:16.903: %DUAL-5-NBRCHANGE: EIGRP-IPv4 100: Neighbor 172.12.123.1
(Serial0/1/0) is down: peer info changed
*May 15 13:43:51.967: %DUAL-5-NBRCHANGE: EIGRP-IPv4 100: Neighbor 172.12.123.1
(Serial0/1/0) is up: new adjacency
```

Hey, did you know making an EIGRP router a stub makes it drop all existing adjacencies? If you didn't, now you do! We did get this one back in about thirty-five seconds. Let's take care of R3:

```
R3(config)#router eigrp 100
R3(config-router)#eigrp stub
*May 15 13:30:55.723: %DUAL-5-NBRCHANGE: EIGRP-IPv4 100: Neighbor 172.12.123.1
(Serial0/1/0) is down: peer info changed
*May 15 13:31:36.791: %DUAL-5-NBRCHANGE: EIGRP-IPv4 100: Neighbor 172.12.123.1
(Serial0/1/0) is up: new adjacency
```

By the way, the EIGRP stub defaults appear in the config:

```
router eigrp 100
 network 3.3.3.0 0.0.0.255
 network 172.12.123.0 0.0.0.255
 eigrp stub connected summary
```

R1 still sees the loopbacks advertised by R2 and R3:

```
R1#show ip route eigrp
      2.0.0.0/24  is subnetted, 1 subnets
D        2.2.2.0  [90/2297856] via 172.12.123.2, 00:03:43, Serial0/1/0
      3.0.0.0/24  is subnetted, 1 subnets
D        3.3.3.0  [90/2297856] via 172.12.123.3, 00:02:46, Serial0/1/0
```

If we get a little too stubbish and make R3 a receive-only stub...

```
R3(config)#router eigrp 100
R3(config-router)#eigrp stub ?
  connected       Do advertise connected routes
  leak-map        Allow dynamic prefixes based on the leak-map
  receive-only    Set receive only neighbor
  redistributed   Do advertise redistributed routes
  static          Do advertise static routes
  summary         Do advertise summary routes
  <cr>

R3(config-router)#eigrp stub receive-only
 *May 15 13:37:25.699: %DUAL-5-NBRCHANGE: EIGRP-IPv4 100: Neighbor 172.12.123.1
(Serial0/1/0) is down: peer info changed
 *May 15 13:38:18.571: %DUAL-5-NBRCHANGE: EIGRP-IPv4 100: Neighbor 172.12.123.1
(Serial0/1/0) is up: new adjacency
```

...R1 loses the route to R3's loopback.

```
R1#show ip route eigrp
      2.0.0.0/24  is subnetted, 1 subnets
D        2.2.2.0  [90/2297856] via 172.12.123.2, 00:08:06, Serial0/1/0
```

Moral of the story: if you're missing subnets after configuring EIGRP stub routers, watch the options.

Now...*what time is it?*

It's Time to Get Passive

One fine day, you might find yourself needing to advertise a network via EIGRP while not sending EIGRP-related traffic via the interface that's part of that network.

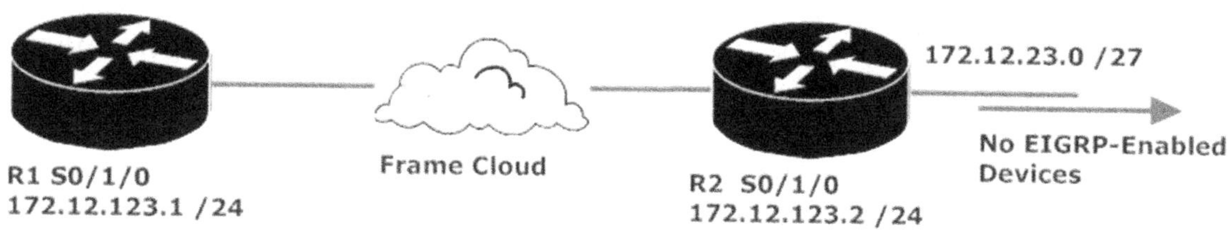

R2 wants to advertise the 172.12.23.0 /27 network via EIGRP to R1. In doing so, EIGRP hellos will go out the 172.12.23.2 interface every five seconds, verified by *debug eigrp packet*. Hellos are being sent and received on serial0/1/0 but only sent on fast0/0.

```
*May 14 13:30:01.522: EIGRP: Received HELLO on Serial0/1/0 nbr 172.12.123.1
*May 14 13:30:01.550: EIGRP: Sending HELLO on Serial0/1/0
*May 14 13:30:04.182: EIGRP: Sending HELLO on FastEthernet0/0
*May 14 13:30:08.466: EIGRP: Sending HELLO on FastEthernet0/0
*May 14 13:30:13.026: EIGRP: Sending HELLO on FastEthernet0/0
*May 14 13:30:17.442: EIGRP: Sending HELLO on FastEthernet0/0

R2#u all
All possible debugging has been turned off
```

The *passive-interface* command allows us to advertise a network via EIGRP while suppressing the transmission of EIGRP control traffic by interfaces on that same network. (That's fancy talk for, "Hellos don't go out of interfaces they don't need to go out.")

```
R2(config)#router eigrp 100
R2(config-router)#passive-interface fast0/0
```

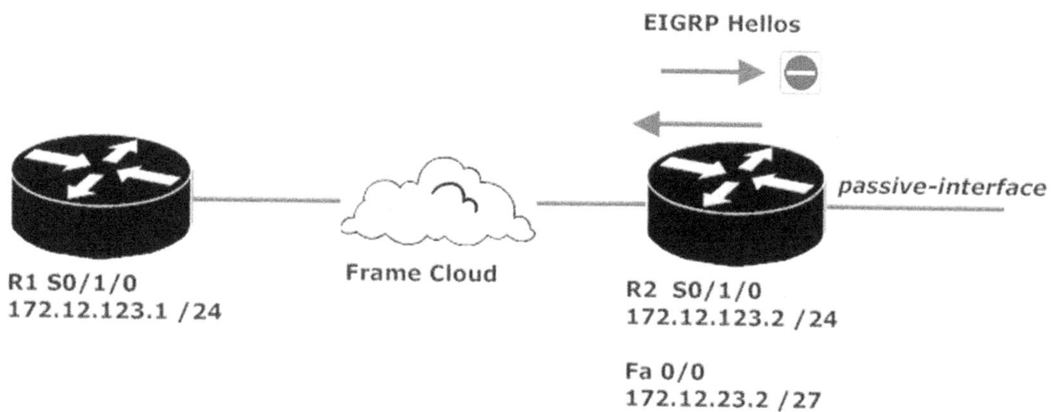

R1 still sees the 172.12.23.0 /27 network in its routing table…

```
R1#show ip route eigrp

     172.12.0.0/16   is variably subnetted, 3 subnets, 3 masks
D 172.12.23.0/27    [90/2172416] via 172.12.123.2, 00:05:21, Serial0/1/0
```

…but R2 is no longer sending hellos out 172.12.23.2. *debug eigrp packet* shows only hellos going out and being received on Serial1/0/1.

```
*May 14 13:32:42.330: EIGRP: Received HELLO on Serial0/1/0 nbr 172.12.123.1
*May 14 13:32:48.450: EIGRP: Sending HELLO on Serial0/1/0
*May 14 13:33:36.158: EIGRP: Received HELLO on Serial0/1/0 nbr 172.12.123.1
*May 14 13:33:48.450: EIGRP: Sending HELLO on Serial0/1/0
```

You could also use *passive-interface* to prevent adjacencies with downstream routers. If you wanted to prevent such an adjacency between R2 and R3 in the following scenario, *passive-interface* does the job nicely.

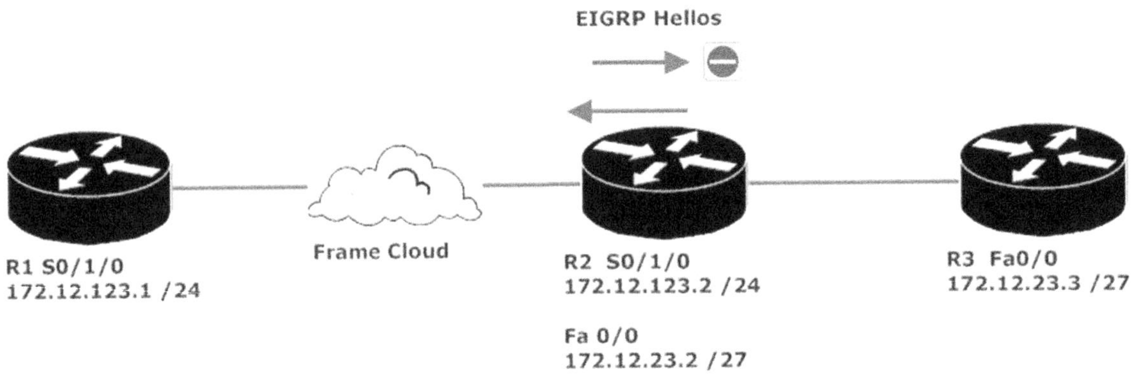

One more *passive-interface* option before we move on! You can make all of your router interfaces passive with *passive-interface default.* If you then realize you need an interface or two to be nonpassive, use *no passive-interface* followed by that particular interface name. In the following config, after making all interfaces on the router passive, the router informed me I lost an adjacency as a result! I quickly used *no passive-interface serial 0/1/0* to make that interface nonpassive, and the adjacency quickly came back.

```
R2(config)#router eigrp 100
R2(config-router)#passive-int default
*May 14 13:58:18.622: %DUAL-5-NBRCHANGE: EIGRP-IPv4 100: Neighbor 172.12.123.1
(Serial0/1/0) is down: interface passive

R2(config-router)#no passive-int serial 0/1/0
*May 14 13:58:25.662: %DUAL-5-NBRCHANGE: EIGRP-IPv4 100: Neighbor 172.12.123.1
(Serial0/1/0) is up: new adjacency
```

Those Special K-Values

Potential EIGRP neighbors must agree on the k-weight settings, viewable in *show ip protocols.*

```
R2#show ip protocols
Routing Protocol is "eigrp 100"
  Outgoing update filter list for all interfaces is not set
  Incoming update filter list for all interfaces is not set
  Default networks flagged in outgoing updates
  Default networks accepted from incoming updates
  Redistributing: eigrp 100
  EIGRP-IPv4 Protocol for AS(100)
    Metric weight K1=1, K2=0, K3=1, K4=0, K5=0
```

EIGRP uses the metric weights to determine how much importance to give a particular value when calculating route metrics. The k-values, in order, are as follows:

K1: bandwidth
K2: load
K3: delay
K4: reliability
K5: MTU

By default, EIGRP takes bandwidth and delay into consideration when calculating route metrics while ignoring the other values. To be even more blunt with you than usual, you're more likely to run into a k-value mismatch in an exam or lab environment than in a real-world network. Most of the time, real-world networks use the default k-values.

You can change the k-values with the *metric weights* command. Just for fun, let's do just that!

```
R2(config)#router eigrp 100
R2(config-router)#metric weights ?
  <0-8> Type (Only TOS 0 supported)

R2(config-router)#metric weights 0 ?
  <0-255> K1

R2(config-router)#metric weights 0 1 ?
  <0-255> K2

R2(config-router)#metric weights 0 2 ?
  <0-255> K2

R2(config-router)#metric weights 0 2 0 ?
  <0-255> K3
```

```
R2(config-router)#metric weights 0 2 0 1?
<0-255>

R2(config-router)#metric weights 0 2 0 1 ?
  <0-255> K4

R2(config-router)#metric weights 0 2 0 1 0 ?
  <0-255> K5

R2(config-router)#metric weights 0 2 0 1 0 0
```

There are only five k-values, but the *metric weights* command requires six values. The first is the Type of Service value for EIGRP packets. We're given a range of 0–8, but the router will only accept zero! After that, just enter the k-weights you want. This config would have EIGRP consider bandwidth twice as strongly as it would delay, and the other values would continue to be ignored.

About one microsecond after changing those values, this message popped up:

```
  *May 14 14:12:17.286: %DUAL-5-NBRCHANGE: EIGRP-IPv4 100: Neighbor 172.12.123.1
(Serial0/1/0) is down: metric changed
```

I quickly negated the metric weights command to revert to the defaults, and the adjacency pops right back up!

```
R2(config-router)#no metric weights 0 2 0 1 0 0

  *May 14 14:12:32.082: %DUAL-5-NBRCHANGE: EIGRP-IPv4 100: Neighbor 172.12.123.1
(Serial0/1/0) is up: new adjacency
```

Know this command for your exam, but in the real world, leave those k-values alone!

Tweaking the Bandwidth Value to Match Your Network Design

Here are some (very) general guidelines when it comes to designing networks that will be running EIGRP:

- Invest the time necessary to set up a solid IP address allocation scheme before deploying your addresses. Measure twice, configure once!
- Maximize your opportunities for manual route summarization.
- Avoid discontiguous networks when possible, and keep EIGRP's autosummarization behavior in mind when you can't avoid them.

Your hub routers in any hub-and-spoke network will have the largest workload of all, so be sure those routers have the CPU and memory resources they need.

There are extra details to attend to when allocating bandwidth over an NBMA network. The typical Serial interface will have multiple Virtual Circuits (VCs), and the calculation for the *bandwidth* command varies according to the type of interface used on the hub and the CIR assigned to each circuit.

Some good questions to answer before you start configuring:

- What *is* the current CIR?
- What are the current bandwidth values of our interfaces?
- Does the client have any special requests or policies that need to be taken into consideration? Bandwidth maximums or minimums, stub routing, and the like?

We'll now take a look at several different scenarios and how they affect the bandwidth setting.

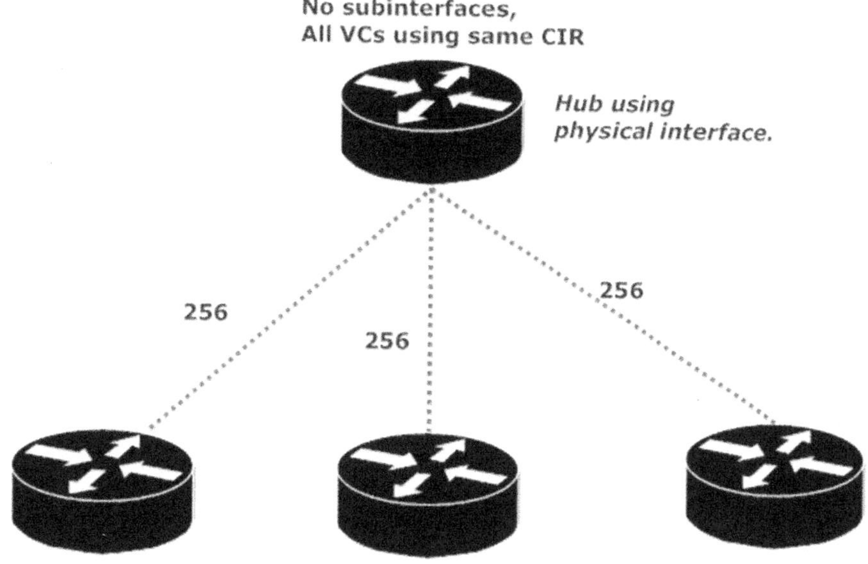

With no subinterfaces in use and the CIR the same for every VC, just add the CIRs, and you have your bandwidth value. This ensures none of the circuits are overloaded, which could happen if we left bandwidth at the default of 1544.

```
R1(config)#int serial 0/1/0
R1(config-if)#bandwidth ?
  <1-10000000>    Bandwidth in kilobits
  inherit         Specify that bandwidth is inherited
  receive         Specify receive-side bandwidth

R1(config-if)#bandwidth 768
```

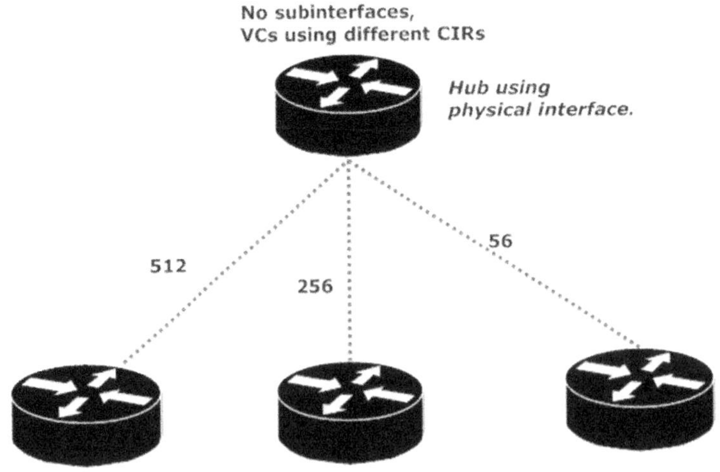

In this situation, Cisco has stated you can take the lowest CIR value and multiply it by the number of VCs to obtain the optimal bandwidth setting. It's not the recommended solution, but it is a valid one. This solution would give us *bandwidth 168* on the hub router's serial interface.

```
R1(config)#int serial 0/1/0
R1(config-if)#bandwidth 168
```

A better solution is creating point-to-point interfaces and assigning an individual bandwidth value to each CIR.

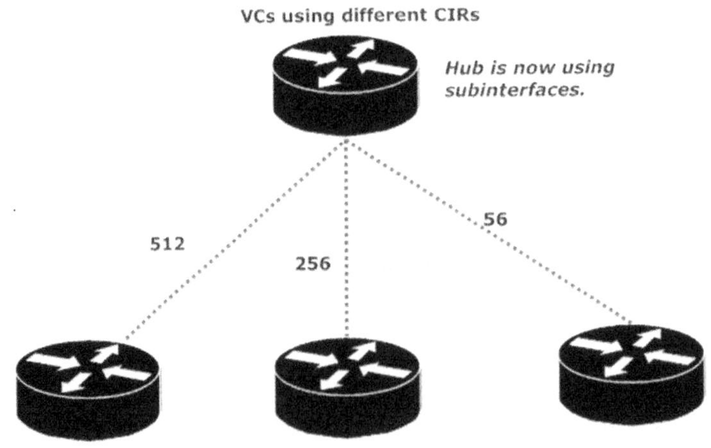


```
R1(config)#int serial 0/1/0.1 point-to-point
R1(config-subif)#ip address 20.1.1.1 255.255.255.0
R1(config-subif)#bandwidth 512

R1(config)#int serial 0/1/0.2 point-to-point
R1(config-subif)#ip address 20.2.1.1 255.255.255.0
R1(config-subif)#bandwidth 256
```

```
R1(config)#int serial 0/1/0.3 point
R1(config-subif)#ip address 20.3.1.1 255.255.255.0
R1(config-subif)#bandwidth 56
```

Speaking of subinterfaces, what if we had a single multipoint subinterface instead of three point-to-pointers?

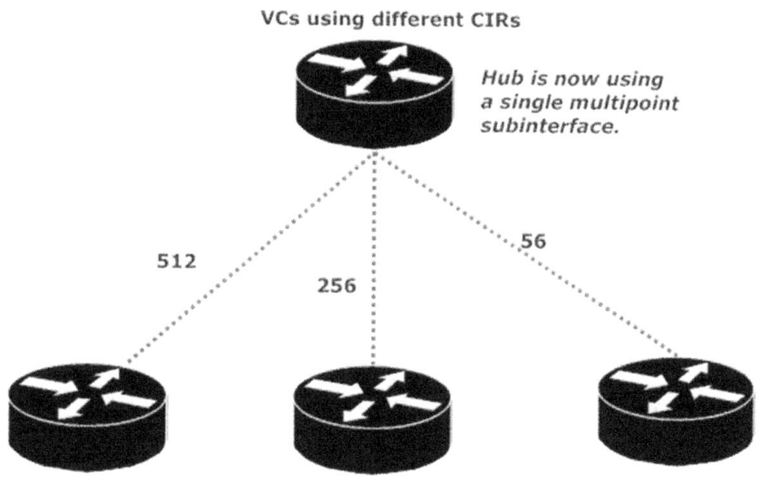

Just add the CIR values to get the correct bandwidth value for the subinterface.

```
R1(config)#int serial 0/1/0.123 multipoint
R1(config-subif)#bandwidth 824
```

Let's shift our focus to EIGRP's default bandwidth usage, which is 50 percent of the interface's bandwidth as set by the bandwidth command. To change this default, use *ip bandwidth-percent eigrp*. IOS Help reminds us we have to specify the AS.

```
R1(config)#int serial 0/1/0.123 multipoint
R1(config-subif)#bandwidth 824
R1(config-subif)#ip bandwidth-percent eigrp ?
  <1-65535> AS number

R1(config-subif)#ip bandwidth-percent eigrp 100 ?
  <1-999999> Maximum bandwidth percentage that EIGRP may use

R1(config-subif)#ip bandwidth-percent eigrp 100 300
```

Hmm. According to IOS Help, I can set the interface to allow EIGRP to use 999999 percent of the available bandwidth. That's great! I can automagically create bandwidth just by using the supermagical command!

No no no no no no no no. That's not how this works. That's not how *any* of this works. We know better. It does seem odd that I could set that max bandwidth percentage to

300 percent and not get an error. How in the world am I able to do that? An IOS bug, perhaps?

Nope! The actual physical speed of the interface can exceed the logical setting. We could take an interface with a 512 kbps capacity and configure it with *bandwidth 56*. If we then wanted the line to allow EIGRP to use 168 kbps of the available bandwidth, we'd set the bandwidth-percent value to 300. That allocates 300 percent of 56 kbps to EIGRP, which is 168 kbps.

Sounds goofy, but it's legal, as we proved above. Just watch your syntax. The first number is the EIGRP AS, and the second number is the bandwidth percentage.

Propagating a Default Route in EIGRP

There's nothing quite as simple as OSPF's *default information-originate* command, but there's nothing complex here, either. We can either inject a static route into EIGRP via route redistribution, or we can indicate a default network with *ip default-network.*

For the first option, we'll create a default route on R1 and use its Fast0/0 interface as the exit interface. We'll then redistribute that route into the EIGRP AS.

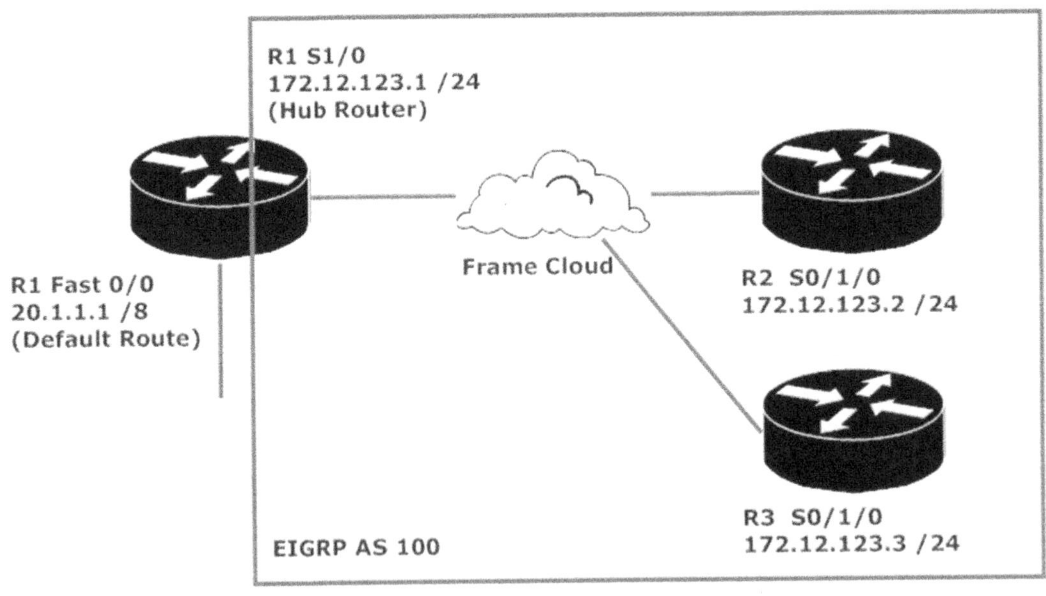


```
R1(config)#ip route 0.0.0.0 0.0.0.0 fast 0/0
R1(config)#router eigrp 100
R1(config-router)#redistribute static ?
  Metric      Metric for redistributed routes
  route-map   Route map reference
  <cr>
```

```
R1(config-router)#redistribute static metric ?
  <1-4294967295> Bandwidth metric in Kbits per second

R1(config-router)#redistribute static metric 1544 ?
  <0-4294967295> EIGRP delay metric, in 10 microsecond units

R1(config-router)#redistribute static metric 1544 ?
  <0-4294967295> EIGRP delay metric, in 10 microsecond units

R1(config-router)#redistribute static metric 1544 10 ?
  <0-255> EIGRP reliability metric where 255 is 100% reliable

R1(config-router)#redistribute static metric 1544 10 255 ?
  <1-255> EIGRP Effective bandwidth metric (Loading) where 255 is 100% loaded

R1(config-router)#redistribute static metric 1544 10 255 1 ?
  <1-65535> EIGRP MTU of the path

R1(config-router)#redistribute static metric 1544 10 255 1 1500
```

Much more on route redistribution in a later section of the course. For now, you need to know that EIGRP requires a metric to be configured for a redistributed route, and this is one of the two ways to do it. The result on the downstream routers is a default route that's also an external EIGRP route, and it's one that allows both spokes to ping 20.1.1.1.

```
R2#show ip route eigrp
(code table removed for clarity)
Gateway of last resort is 172.12.123.1 to network 0.0.0.0
D*EX 0.0.0.0/0 [170/2172416] via 172.12.123.1, 00:00:16, Serial0/1/0


R2#ping 20.1.1.1
Type escape sequence to abort.
Sending 5, 100-byte ICMP Echos to 20.1.1.1, timeout is 2 seconds:
!!!!!
Success rate is 100 percent (5/5), round-trip min/avg/max = 64/65/68 ms


R3#show ip route eigrp
(code table removed for clarity)
Gateway of last resort is 172.12.123.1 to network 0.0.0.0
D*EX 0.0.0.0/0 [170/2172416] via 172.12.123.1, 00:01:28, Serial0/1/0


R3#ping 20.1.1.1
Type escape sequence to abort.
Sending 5, 100-byte ICMP Echos to 20.1.1.1, timeout is 2 seconds:
```

```
!!!!!
Success rate is 100 percent (5/5), round-trip min/avg/max = 64/64/68 ms
```

First, I'll show you how the *ip default-network* command *should* work, and that's what you should go with on your exam. It works a little odd in IOS 15, and while the CCNP Route exam is not IOS specific, you should be aware of the quirkiness of this command with that particular IOS.

You can advertise a nonzero network number as the default route with *ip default-network*, but you have to watch out for a little something. Actually, it's a *big* something.

The router that originates this advertisement MUST have that network number in its IP routing table.

Why am I making such a big deal out of this? With OSPF, we have the option of advertising a default route even when the router didn't have a default route in its routing table ("*default-information originate always*"). We have no such option with EIGRP.

Let's remove the previous lab's default static route and *redistribute* command.

```
R1(config)#router eigrp 100
R1(config-router)#no redistribute static metric 1544 10 255 1 1500
```

To configure the classful network 20.0.0.0 /8 as the default route for the EIGRP AS, first use the *network* command to introduce it.

```
R1(config)#router eigrp 100
R1(config-router)#network 20.0.0.0 0.255.255.255
```

R2 will see the route, but it's not marked as a candidate default route.

```
R2#show ip route
Gateway of last resort is not set

D     20.0.0.0/8 [90/2172416] via 172.12.123.1, 00:00:20, Serial0/1/0
```

We'll make that route a candidate default route on R1 with *ip default-network* and then revisit R2's routing table.

```
R1(config)#ip default-network 20.0.0.0

R2#show ip route eigrp

Gateway of last resort is 172.12.123.1 to network 20.0.0.0

D*    20.0.0.0/8 [90/2172416] via 172.12.123.1, 00:00:31, Serial0/1/0
```

The route is now shown on R2 as a candidate default, and the next-hop IP address to that network is shown as the gateway of last resort.

That's the *theory* of *ip default-network*, and that's what you should go with on your exam. A lot of people are bumping into an issue with this command in IOS 15. I ran the exact same config on routers all running IOS 15, and here's the end result on R2—the route is marked as a candidate default, but the gateway of last resort is not set.

```
R2#show ip route eigrp
Gateway of last resort is not set

D*    20.0.0.0/8 [90/2172416] via 172.12.123.1, 00:03:06, Serial0/1/0
```

There's been quite a bit of online chatter on this output, and I want you to know that if it happens to you, you're not going crazy. Again, if you bump into any questions on this command during your exam, go with the theory and the operation of the command on previous IOS versions.

Time for an EIGRP breather. Let's switch gears and tackle OSPF.

Chapter 4:

OSPF FUNDAMENTALS

The distance vector protocol RIP is gone from the CCNP exams, but I'm going to bring it back for a moment for comparison's sake.

The routing updates sent by RIP are sent at regularly scheduled intervals, even when there have been no changes in the network. That makes for unnecessary work on the part of the sender and the receiver.

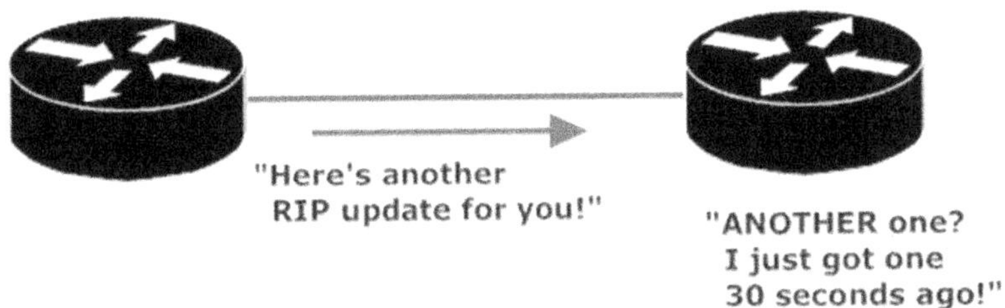

On the other hand, link state routers that have formed adjacencies exchange Link State Updates (LSUs), which contain Link State Advertisements (LSAs). These LSAs are placed into a link state database, such as the one shown here with *show ip ospf database*. Once the OSPF network has reached a state of convergence, the routers will have synchronized link state databases.

```
R1#show ip ospf database

            OSPF Router with ID (1.1.1.1) (Process ID 1)

                Router Link States (Area 0)

Link ID         ADV Router      Age         Seq#        Checksum    Link count
1.1.1.1         1.1.1.1         1790        0x80000004  0x00D5A8    1
```

```
2.2.2.2         2.2.2.2         1794    0x80000004    0x0097DD    1
3.3.3.3         3.3.3.3         1646    0x80000003    0x005B12    1

                Net Link States (Area 0)

Link ID         ADV Router      Age     Seq#          Checksum
172.12.123.1    1.1.1.1         1645    0x80000002    0x0027BC
```

The Dijkstra algorithm (also known as the Shortest Path First algorithm, or simply SPF) is run against the contents of the database to create the OSPF routing table, shown here with *show ip route ospf.*

```
R1#show ip route ospf
      2.0.0.0/8 is variably subnetted, 2 subnets, 2 masks
O IA     2.2.2.2/32 [110/65] via 172.12.123.2, 00:00:13, Serial0/1/0
      3.0.0.0/8 is variably subnetted, 2 subnets, 2 masks
O IA     3.3.3.3/32 [110/65] via 172.12.123.3, 00:00:02, Serial0/1/0
```

LSA Sequence Numbers

To ensure that OSPF routers have the most recent information possible in their databases, the LSAs are assigned sequence numbers. When an OSPF-enabled router receives an LSA, that router checks its OSPF database for any preexisting entries for that link.

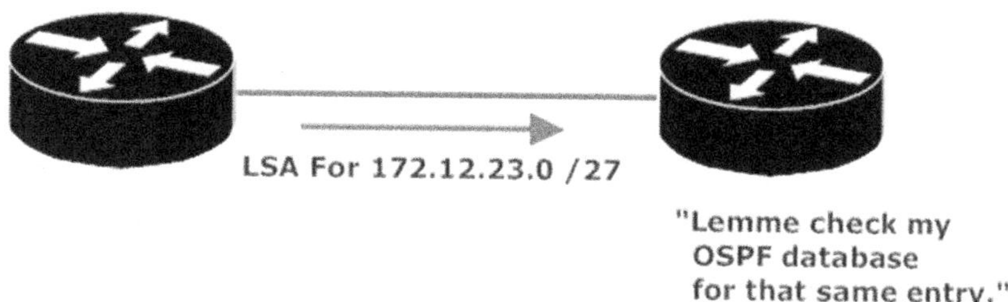

If there isn't an entry for that link, the receiving router will make one in its database and will then flood that LSA out every OSPF-enabled interface except the interface the LSA came in on. (Sounds familiar!)

If there is an entry for the link, the sequence numbers come into play:

- *Sequence number is the same*: LSA is ignored, no additional action taken.
- *Sequence number is lower*: The router ignores the update and transmits an LSU containing an LSA back to the original sender. Basically, the router with the most recent information is telling the original sender, "Hey, you sent me old information. Here's the latest information on that link."

- *Sequence number is higher*: The router adds the LSA to its database and sends an LSAcknowledgment back to the original sender. The router floods the LSA and updates its own routing table by running the SPF algorithm against the now-updated database.

Once the initial exchange of LSAs takes place, there will not be another exchange unless there's a change in the network topology. An OSPF-speaking router will also send out a summary LSA every thirty minutes.

Before the LSA exchange begins, OSPF-speaking routers must become neighbors by forming an adjacency. Routers must agree on the area number, the hello and dead timer settings, and whether the area is a stub area. If link authentication is configured, it must be configured on both sides of the adjacency. The OSPF process number itself is locally significant only and does not have to be agreed upon for an adjacency to form. (We'll see all of these values along with the following *show* commands in action during our labs.)

Verify OSPF adjacencies with *show ip ospf neighbor* and *show ip ospf interface*. Only *show ip ospf neighbor* shows you the status of database loading (FULL, 2WAY, etc.). *show ip ospf interface* gives you the local router's OSPF RID, its role on that segment (DR, BDR, DROther), the RID of the DR and BDR for that segment, how many adjacencies the local router has formed on that segment, and much more. It's an excellent starting point for OSPF troubleshooting.

```
R1#show ip ospf neighbor

Neighbor ID     Pri   State           Dead Time   Address         Interface
2.2.2.2           0   FULL/DROTHER    00:01:55    172.12.123.2    Serial0/1/0
3.3.3.3           0   FULL/DROTHER    00:01:55    172.12.123.3    Serial0/1/0

R1#show ip ospf int serial 0/1/0
Serial0/1/0 is up, line protocol is up
  Internet Address 172.12.123.1/24, Area 0
  Process ID 1, Router ID 1.1.1.1, Network Type NON_BROADCAST, Cost: 64
  Topology-MTID    Cost    Disabled    Shutdown    Topology Name
        0           64        no          no           Base
  Transmit Delay is 1 sec, State DR, Priority 1
  Designated Router (ID) 1.1.1.1, Interface address 172.12.123.1
  No backup designated router on this network
  Timer intervals configured, Hello 30, Dead 120, Wait 120, Retransmit 5
oob-resync timeout 120
Hello due in 00:00:23
  Supports Link-local Signaling (LLS)
  Cisco NSF helper support enabled
  IETF NSF helper support enabled
  Index 1/1, flood queue length 0
  Next 0x0(0)/0x0(0)
  Last flood scan length is 1, maximum is 1
  Last flood scan time is 0 msec, maximum is 4 msec
  Neighbor Count is 2, Adjacent neighbor count is 2
```

```
    Adjacent with neighbor 2.2.2.2
    Adjacent with neighbor 3.3.3.3
  Suppress hello for 0 neighbor(s)
```

The Role of the DR and BDR

A major drawback of distance vector protocols is their slow convergence. Convergence refers to the network state where every router has a similar and accurate view of the network, particularly after a topology change such as a down route. The slow convergence of distance vector protocols such as RIP can lead to suboptimal routing and routing loops.

Link state protocols converge almost immediately upon a change in the network. OSPF uses designated routers and backup designated routers to make network convergence a fast and orderly process. When a router on an OSPF segment with a DR and BDR detects a change in the network, the detecting router will not notify *all* of its neighbors. The detecting router will send a multicast to 224.0.0.6, the *All Designated Routers* address, where both the DR and BDR will hear it.

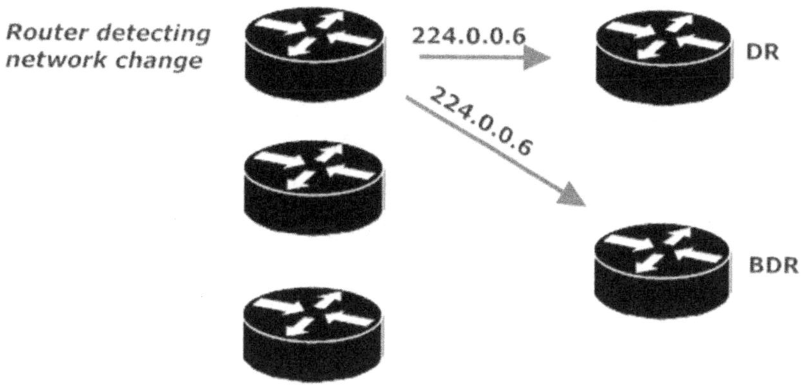

The DR then sends a multicast to 224.0.0.5, the *All OSPF Routers address,* where every OSPF-speaking router on that segment will hear it. The BDR updates its OSPF database in order to stay ready to step into the DR role if needed, but only the DR sends this multicast.

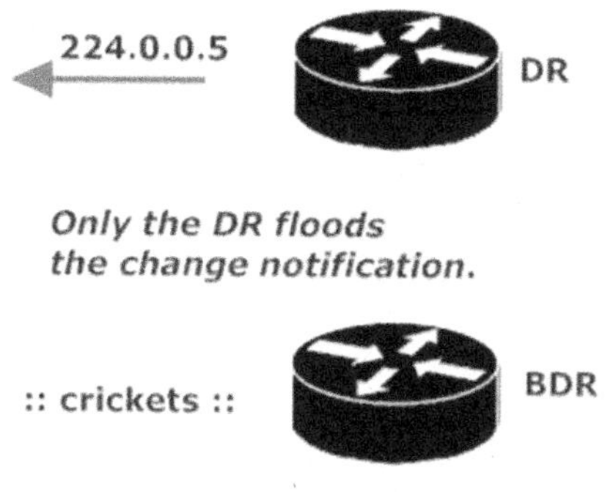

The DROthers, routers on that segment that are neither the DR nor the BDR, then send an LSAcknowledgment (LSA) back to the DR to indicate receipt of that update.

Four Routers Enter, One Router Leaves

Let's take a close look at the rules and regulations regarding the DR and BDR elections on an OSPF broadcast segment. One router will become the DR, another the BDR, and the other two DROthers.

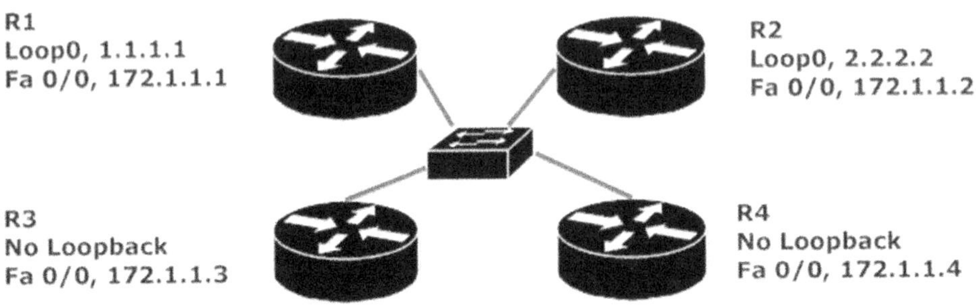

Here's an overview of the DR/BDR election process:

- All router interfaces on the segment with an OSPF interface priority of one or greater are eligible to participate in the election. The priority default is one. Setting the interface priority to zero will disqualify that router from participating in the election.
- The router with the highest interface priority is elected DR.
- If there's a tie, the OSPF Router ID (RID) is the tiebreaker. The router with the highest RID wins.
- This process is repeated to elect a new BDR. A single router cannot be the DR and BDR for the same segment.

With the RID playing such an important role in these elections, we need to know exactly how the router arrives at the RID. The RID of any given router will be the highest IP address assigned to a loopback interface on that router, regardless of whether that loopback is actually OSPF-enabled. A loopback interface whose address is serving as the OSPF RID is not automatically advertised by OSPF.

What if there *is* no loopback, you ask? In that case, the OSPF RID will be the highest IP address assigned to a physical interface. Again, that interface need not be OSPF-enabled in order for its IP address to serve as the RID.

Both rules can be overridden with the *router-id* command, which allows you to set the OSPF RID manually. The router must be reloaded or the OSPF processes cleared before the command will take effect.

We'll see those RID rules in operation soon. Right now, let's go back to our four-router network. What would the RID of each router be? Which router would be the DR? Which would be the BDR?

R1
Loop0, 1.1.1.1
Fa 0/0, 172.1.1.1

R2
Loop0, 2.2.2.2
Fa 0/0, 172.1.1.2

R3
No Loopback
Fa 0/0, 172.1.1.3

R4
No Loopback
Fa 0/0, 172.1.1.4

The RIDs:

Router 1: 1.1.1.1

Router 2: 2.2.2.2

Router 3: 172.1.1.3

Router 4: 172.1.1.4

R4 is the DR, R3 the BDR, and the other two routers would be DROthers.

Summing up, there are three ways to manipulate the DR and BDR selection:

- Changing the OSPF interface priority with *ip ospf priority*
- Setting the OSPF RID manually with *router-id*
- Setting the OSPF RID to an appropriate value with a loopback interface's IP address

The DR Is Dead! Long Live The DR!

What exactly happens when a DR goes offline? What happens when it comes back? Let's find out by taking the DR offline in this three-router network. We'll get all the DR/BDR information we need with *show ip ospf neighbor* on R1.

```
R1#show ip ospf neighbor

Neighbor ID     Pri   State           Dead Time   Address         Interface
2.2.2.2          50   FULL/BDR        00:00:37    10.1.1.2        FastEthernet0/0
3.3.3.3          10   FULL/DROTHER    00:00:38    10.1.1.3        FastEthernet0/0
```

R1 is the DR, R2 the BDR, and R3 the sole DROther.

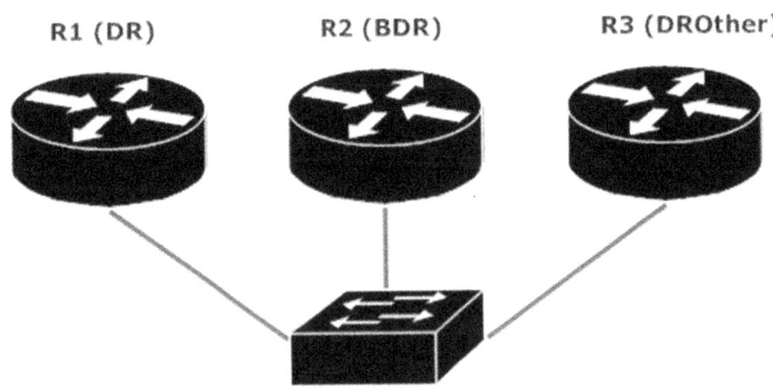

I'll run *show ip ospf neighbor* on R2 after reloading R1 and waiting for the adjacency to time out.

```
R1#reload

  R2#
*May 22 19:28:56: %OSPF-5-ADJCHG: Process 1, Nbr 9.9.9.9 on FastEthernet0/0 from
FULL to DOWN, Neighbor Down: Dead timer expired

R2#show ip ospf neighbor

Neighbor ID     Pri   State           Dead Time   Address         Interface
3.3.3.3          10   FULL/BDR        00:00:38    10.1.1.3        FastEthernet0/0
```

R3 is now the BDR, leaving only R2 for the DR role, as verified by the truncated output of *show ip ospf int fast 0/0.*

```
R2#show ip ospf int fast 0/0
FastEthernet0/0 is up, line protocol is up
Internet Address 10.1.1.2/24, Area 0
Process ID 1, Router ID 2.2.2.2, Network Type BROADCAST, Cost: 1
  Topology-MTID    Cost    Disabled    Shutdown    Topology Name
        0           1         no          no          Base
Transmit Delay is 1 sec, State DR, Priority 50
Designated Router (ID) 2.2.2.2, Interface address 10.1.1.2
Backup Designated router (ID) 3.3.3.3, Interface address 10.1.1.3
```

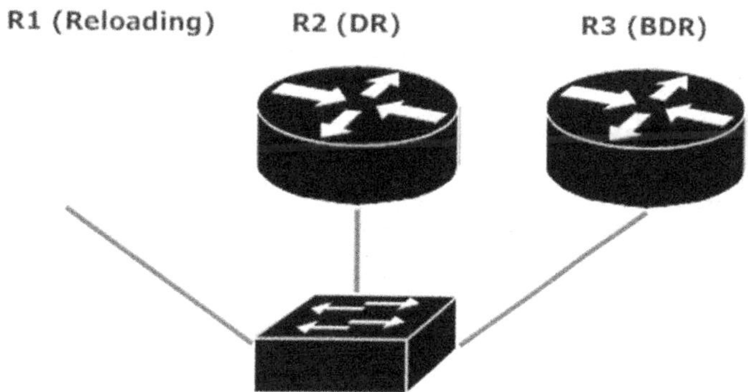

Once R1 comes back, the adjacencies reform—but what of the DR role? Will R1 take it back, or will R2 retain the championship? Let's find out...

```
OSPF-5-ADJCHG: Process 1, Nbr 3.3.3.3 on FastEthernet0/0 from
  LOADING to FULL, Loading Done

OSPF-5-ADJCHG: Process 1, Nbr 2.2.2.2 on FastEthernet0/0 from
  LOADING to FULL, Loading Done

R1#show ip ospf neigh

Neighbor ID     Pri   State           Dead Time   Address         Interface
2.2.2.2          50   FULL/DR         00:00:38    10.1.1.2        FastEthernet0/0
3.3.3.3          10   FULL/BDR        00:00:36    10.1.1.3        FastEthernet0/0
```

R1 is back online but is now the DROther of this segment. R2 and R3 retain their respective roles of DR and BDR.

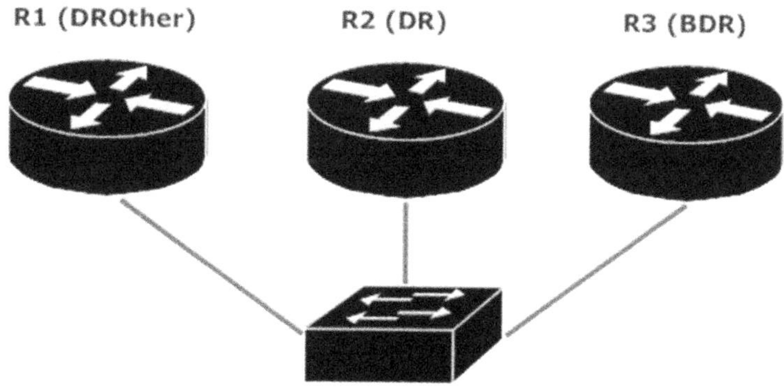

You'd have to do some more bouncing to get the role of DR back on R1!

The OSPF Network Types

We're now going to build an OSPF network from scratch, one segment at a time, starting with a broadcast segment between R1 and R5. We'll put this 10.1.1.0 /24 subnet into Area 0.

Each router has a single loopback that uses the router number for each octet.

Loopback interfaces will be advertised all at once later in this lab.

All previous OSPF-related commands have been removed from every router.

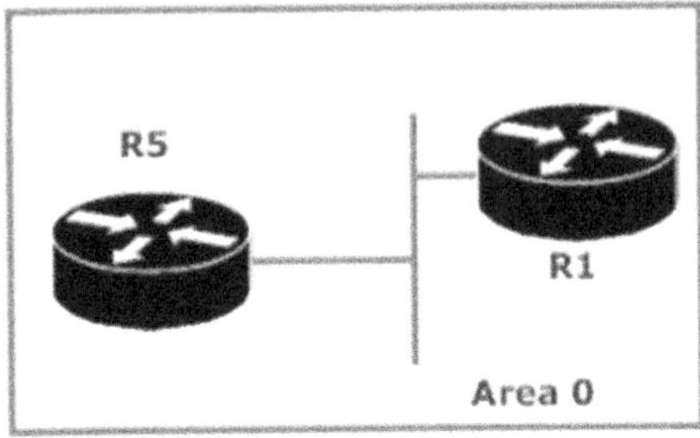

An OSPF config on a broadcast network will not so surprisingly default to an OSPF Broadcast network. Let's get the config up and running on R1 and R5 and then do some verifyin'.

```
R5(config)#router ospf 1
R5(config-router)#network 10.1.1.0 0.0.0.255 area 0

R1(config)#router ospf 1
R1(config-router)#network 10.1.1.0 0.0.0.255 area 0

R1#show ip ospf neigh

Neighbor ID     Pri   State           Dead Time   Address         Interface
5.5.5.5           1   FULL/DR         00:00:38    10.1.1.5        FastEthernet0/0


R5#show ip ospf neighbor

Neighbor ID     Pri   State           Dead Time   Address         Interface
1.1.1.1           1   FULL/BDR        00:00:33    10.1.1.1        GigabitEthernet0/0
```

We have a full adjacency, R5 is the DR due to its higher RID, and R1 is the BDR. *show ip ospf interface* also verifies the adjacency. This command gives you a lot of info, and you'll find the neighbor information at the bottom of the output.

```
R5#show ip ospf int
GigabitEthernet0/0 is up, line protocol is up
```

```
  Internet Address 10.1.1.5/24, Area 0
  Process ID 1, Router ID 5.5.5.5, Network Type BROADCAST, Cost: 1
  Topology-MTID    Cost    Disabled    Shutdown     Topology Name
        0           1         no          no            Base
  Transmit Delay is 1 sec, State DR, Priority 1
  Designated Router (ID) 5.5.5.5, Interface address 10.1.1.5
  Backup Designated router (ID) 1.1.1.1, Interface address 10.1.1.1
  Timer intervals configured, Hello 10, Dead 40, Wait 40, Retransmit 5
    oob-resync timeout 40
    Hello due in 00:00:02
  Supports Link-local Signaling (LLS)
  Cisco NSF helper support enabled
  IETF NSF helper support enabled
  Index 1/1, flood queue length 0
  Next 0x0(0)/0x0(0)
  Last flood scan length is 2, maximum is 2
  Last flood scan time is 0 msec, maximum is 0 msec
  Neighbor Count is 1, Adjacent neighbor count is 1
    Adjacent with neighbor 1.1.1.1        (Backup Designated Router)
  Suppress hello for 0 neighbor(s)

R1#show ip ospf int
FastEthernet0/0 is up, line protocol is up
  Internet Address 10.1.1.1/24, Area 0
  Process ID 1, Router ID 1.1.1.1, Network Type BROADCAST, Cost: 1
  Topology-MTID    Cost    Disabled    Shutdown     Topology Name
        0           1         no          no            Base
  Transmit Delay is 1 sec, State BDR, Priority 1
  Designated Router (ID) 5.5.5.5, Interface address 10.1.1.5
  Backup Designated router (ID) 1.1.1.1, Interface address 10.1.1.1
  Timer intervals configured, Hello 10, Dead 40, Wait 40, Retransmit 5
    oob-resync timeout 40
    Hello due in 00:00:06
  Supports Link-local Signaling (LLS)
  Cisco NSF helper support enabled
  IETF NSF helper support enabled
  Index 1/1, flood queue length 0
  Next 0x0(0)/0x0(0)
  Last flood scan length is 1, maximum is 1
  Last flood scan time is 0 msec, maximum is 0 msec
  Neighbor Count is 1, Adjacent neighbor count is 1
    Adjacent with neighbor 5.5.5.5        (Designated Router)
  Suppress hello for 0 neighbor(s)
```

There's no requirement as to which router needs to be the DR on an OSPF Broadcast network, but that's not true of our next OSPF network type!

The OSPF NBMA Network

We'll now add an Non-Broadcast Multi-Access network to our budding OSPF network. The new segment will use 172.12.123.0 /24 as its subnet. R1 has a frame relay PVC to both R2 and R3. There is no spoke-to-spoke PVC, so all spoke-to-spoke traffic must go through the hub. Just to make things difficult for myself, the interface numbers are a bit different for each router:

R1: Serial 1/0

R2: Serial 0/1/0

R3: Serial 0

The difference in interface numbering doesn't impact the lab in any way.

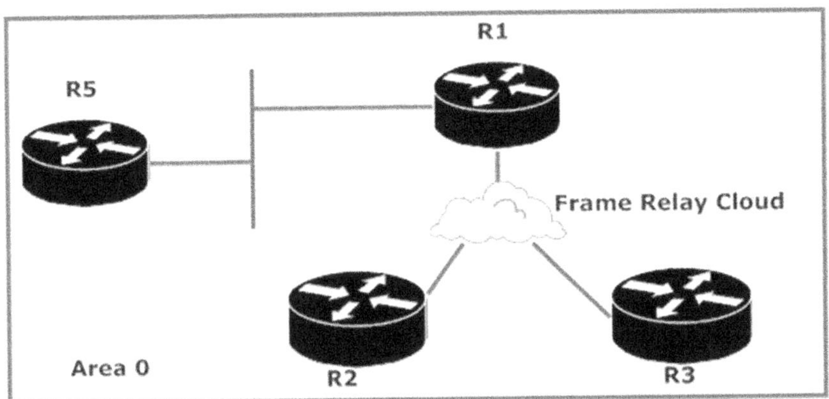

R1 must be made the DR on this segment, and there should be no BDR. It's vital for both the DR and BDR to be able to get a multicast to all other routers on the segment. With a hub-and-spoke topology, a spoke router cannot get a multicast to the other spoke. All spoke-to-spoke traffic goes through the hub router, and routers do not forward broadcasts or multicasts.

Helpful lab hint: be sure you have the *broadcast* option enabled on your frame map statements, or your multicasts ain't goin' anywhere!

```
R1#show frame map
Serial1/0 (up): ip 172.12.123.2 dlci 122(0x7A,0x1CA0), static,
              broadcast,
              CISCO, status defined, active
Serial1/0 (up): ip 172.12.123.3 dlci 123(0x7B,0x1CB0), static,
              broadcast,
              CISCO, status defined, active
```

We'll prevent R2 and R3 from participating in the DR/BDR election for that segment with the *ip ospf priority* command. Changing that value from the default of one down to zero disqualifies the interface from taking part in the election.

```
R2(config)#int serial 0/1/0
R2(config-if)#ip ospf pri ?
  <0-255>   Priority

R2(config-if)#ip ospf pri 0

R3(config)#int serial 0
R3(config-if)#ip ospf pri 0
```

We'll leave the priority alone on R1, but there is a statement that needs to be made on that router—twice! The hub router in this particular network type needs a *neighbor* statement for each spoke. Don't put *neighbor* statements *on* the spokes, though. It doesn't really hurt anything if you do, but for exam purposes, it's good to know they're only required on the hub.

```
R1(config)#router ospf 1
R1(config-router)#neighbor 172.12.123.2
R1(config-router)#neighbor 172.12.123.3
```

Finally, it's time to configure the *network* command on each router! This segment will be a part of Area 0 as well.

```
R1(config)#router ospf 1
R1(config-router)#network 172.12.123.0 0.0.0.255 area 0

R2(config)#router ospf 1
R2(config-router)#network 172.12.123.0 0.0.0.255 area 0

R3(config)#router ospf 1
R3(config-router)#network 172.12.123.0 0.0.0.255 area 0
```

Let's take a look at things from R1's point of view.

```
R1#show ip ospf neighbor

Neighbor ID     Pri   State          Dead Time   Address        Interface
2.2.2.2           0   FULL/DROTHER   00:01:57    172.12.123.2   Serial1/0
3.3.3.3           0   FULL/DROTHER   00:01:57    172.12.123.3   Serial1/0
5.5.5.5           1   FULL/DR        00:00:37    10.1.1.5       FastEthernet0/0
```

Both R2 and R3 are seen by R1 as DROthers, which is exactly the way we want it. We'll verify above and beyond with *show ip ospf int serial 0/1/0.*

```
R1#show ip ospf int serial 1/0
Serial1/0 is up, line protocol is up
  Internet Address 172.12.123.1/24, Area 0
  Process ID 1, Router ID 1.1.1.1, Network Type NON_BROADCAST, Cost: 781
  Transmit Delay is 1 sec, State DR, Priority 1
  Designated Router (ID) 1.1.1.1, Interface address 172.12.123.1
  No backup designated router on this network
  Timer intervals configured, Hello 30, Dead 120, Wait 120, Retransmit 5
oob-resync timeout 120
Hello due in 00:00:08
  Supports Link-local Signaling (LLS)
  Index 3/3, flood queue length 0
  Next 0x0(0)/0x0(0)
  Last flood scan length is 1, maximum is 1
  Last flood scan time is 0 msec, maximum is 4 msec
  Neighbor Count is 2, Adjacent neighbor count is 2
    Adjacent with neighbor 2.2.2.2
    Adjacent with neighbor 3.3.3.3
  Suppress hello for 0 neighbor(s)
```

Larger networks may have multiple hub routers, and we love that redundancy! In this case, one hub router would need to serve as the DR with the other serving as the BDR.

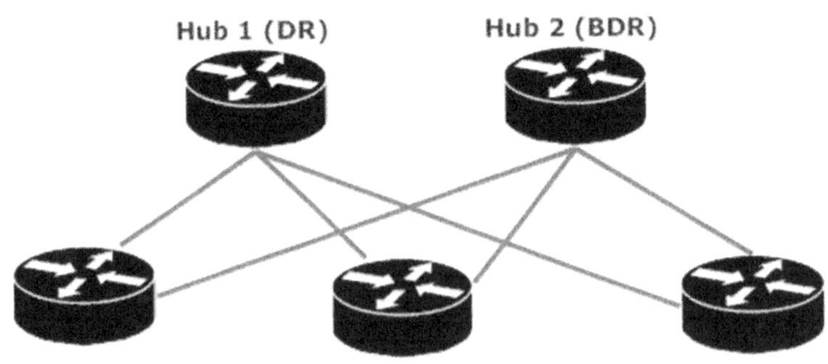

Off to our next network type!

The OSPF Point-to-Point and Point-to-Multipoint Networks

We'll add a direct connection between R1 and R3 and put this one into Area 13. The network number is 172.12.13.0 /27. R1 is using its Serial 1/1 interface and R3 its Serial 1 interface.

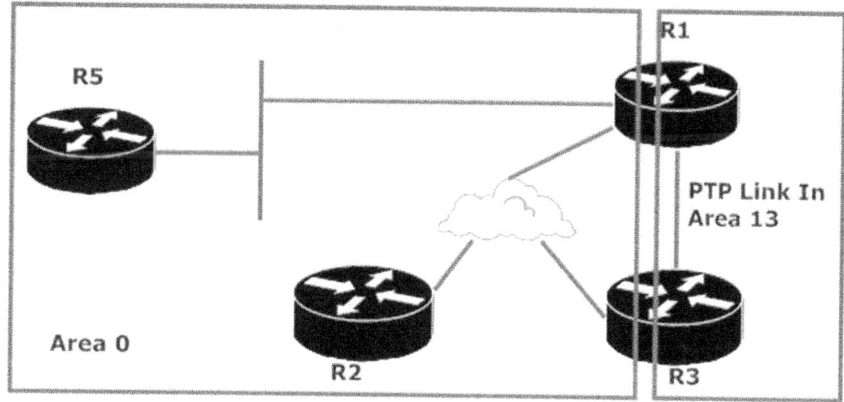

All nonbackbone areas—that is to say, all nonzero areas—must contain a router that has a physical or logical interface in Area 0. Both routers in Area 13 meet that criteria, so the config is legal.

show ip ospf interface tells us this OSPF segment defaulted to the point-to-point network type. This output also shows the default hello and dead timers for this network type, which are quite different from the NBMA timers. There's also a little something this command *doesn't* show us right now.

```
R1#show ip ospf int serial 1/1
Serial1/1 is up, line protocol is up
  Internet Address 172.12.13.1/27, Area 13
  Process ID 1, Router ID 1.1.1.1, Network Type POINT_TO_POINT, Cost: 781
  Transmit Delay is 1 sec, State POINT_TO_POINT,
  Timer intervals configured, Hello 10, Dead 40, Wait 40, Retransmit 5
    oob-resync timeout 40
    Hello due in 00:00:05
  Supports Link-local Signaling (LLS)
  Index 1/4, flood queue length 0
  Next 0x0(0)/0x0(0)
  Last flood scan length is 1, maximum is 1
  Last flood scan time is 0 msec, maximum is 0 msec
  Neighbor Count is 1, Adjacent neighbor count is 1
    Adjacent with neighbor 3.3.3.3
  Suppress hello for 0 neighbor(s)
```

Did you note the lack of a DR and BDR? Let's run *show ip ospf neighbor.*

```
R1#show ip ospf neighbor

Neighbor ID     Pri   State           Dead Time   Address         Interface
2.2.2.2           0   FULL/DROTHER    00:01:33    172.12.123.2    Serial1/0
3.3.3.3           0   FULL/DROTHER    00:01:44    172.12.123.3    Serial1/0
5.5.5.5           1   FULL/DR         00:00:32    10.1.1.5        FastEthernet0/0
3.3.3.3           0   FULL/ -         00:00:30    172.12.13.3     Serial1/1
```

We have a full adjacency to R3 via the point-to-point connection, which is great. What we don't have is a DR or BDR. Instead, there's a dash. Is something wrong here? If so, what?

Nothing wrong here! That dash is there because we don't *have* a DR or BDR on a point-to-point OSPF network. There's no need for one.

Why not, you ask? Well, one of the main purposes of a DR election is to decide which router will handle flooding of network changes to the other routers on the segment. The thing is, with a point-to-point segment, there's no need to flood such news. Once one router tells the other, every router on the segment knows about the change, since a point-to-point network can only contain two routers—one at each endpoint!

```
R3#show ip ospf neighbor

Neighbor ID     Pri   State           Dead Time   Address         Interface
1.1.1.1           1   FULL/DR         00:01:41    172.12.123.1    Serial0
1.1.1.1           1   FULL/ -         00:00:35    172.12.13.1     Serial1
```

You'd see the same dash on a *point-to-multipoint OSPF network*, which OSPF considers to be a collection of point-to-point links.

Let's add another broadcast segment to our network!

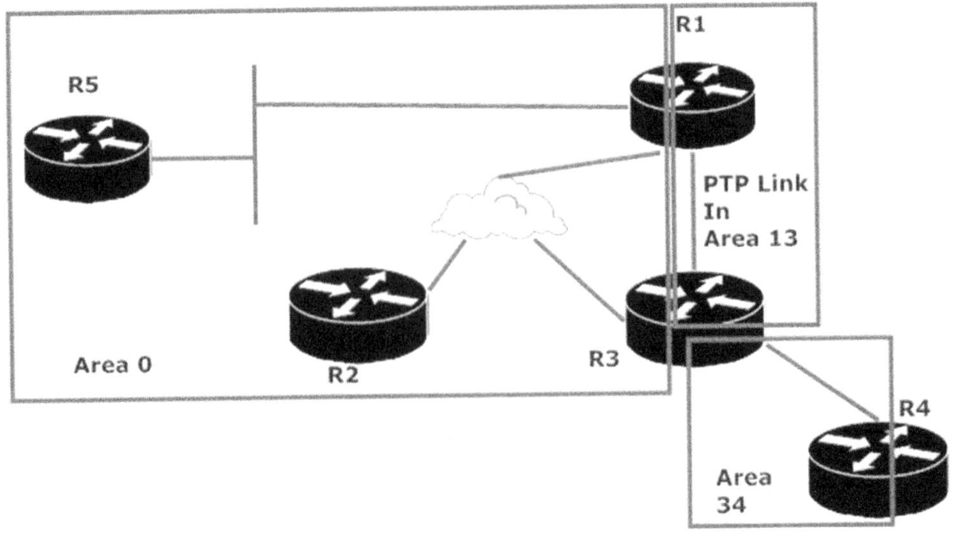

R3's Ethernet interface and R4's FastEthernet interface are on the 172.12.34.0 /24 network, and we'll add them to our OSPF network in Area 34.

```
R4(config)#router ospf 1
R4(config-router)#network 172.12.34.0 0.0.0.255 area 34

R3(config)#router ospf 1
R3(config-router)#network 172.12.34.0 0.0.0.255 area 34

R3#show ip ospf neighbor

Neighbor ID     Pri   State           Dead Time   Address         Interface
1.1.1.1           1   FULL/DR         00:01:59    172.12.123.1    Serial0
1.1.1.1           1   FULL/ -         00:00:35    172.12.13.1     Serial1
4.4.4.4           1   FULL/DR         00:00:33    172.12.34.4     Ethernet0

R4#show ip ospf neighbor

Neighbor ID     Pri   State           Dead Time   Address         Interface
3.3.3.3           1   FULL/BDR        00:00:30    172.12.34.3     FastEthernet0/0
```

Success! With our adjacencies and areas in place, let's add the loopback on each router to its own individual area—R1's loopback in Area 1, R2's loopback in Area 2, and so forth. We'll work our way from the top of the network down to the "bottom," where R4 resides.

Let's have a look at things from R5's point of view.

```
R5#show ip route ospf

      1.0.0.0/32  is subnetted, 1 subnets
O IA     1.1.1.1  [110/2] via 10.1.1.1, 00:02:55, GigabitEthernet0/0
      2.0.0.0/32  is subnetted, 1 subnets
O IA     2.2.2.2  [110/783] via 10.1.1.1, 00:02:31, GigabitEthernet0/0
      3.0.0.0/32  is subnetted, 1 subnets
O IA     3.3.3.3  [110/783] via 10.1.1.1, 00:02:26, GigabitEthernet0/0
      172.12.0.0/16 is variably subnetted, 3 subnets, 2 masks
O IA  172.12.13.0/27 [110/782] via 10.1.1.1, 00:03:23, GigabitEthernet0/0
O IA  172.12.34.0/24 [110/792] via 10.1.1.1, 00:03:24, GigabitEthernet0/0
O     172.12.123.0/24 [110/782] via 10.1.1.1, 00:03:24, GigabitEthernet0/0
```

From top to bottom, R5 sees all three loopback networks, the link connecting R1 and R3 (172.12.13.0 /27), the broadcast segment connecting R3 and R4 (172.12.34.0 /24), and the NBMA network (172.12.123.0 /24), so we're all set!

Wait a minute. Three loopback networks? What happened to R4's loopback? Odd. Let's check R1's OSPF route table:

```
R1#show ip route ospf
        2.0.0.0/32  is subnetted, 1 subnets
O IA      2.2.2.2   [110/782] via 172.12.123.2, 00:06:20, Serial1/0
        3.0.0.0/32  is subnetted, 1 subnets
O IA      3.3.3.3   [110/782] via 172.12.123.3, 00:06:20, Serial1/0
        5.0.0.0/32  is subnetted, 1 subnets
O IA      5.5.5.5   [110/2] via 10.1.1.5, 00:06:20, FastEthernet0/0
        172.12.0.0/16 is variably subnetted, 3 subnets, 2 masks
O IA      172.12.34.0/24 [110/791] via 172.12.123.3, 00:06:20, Serial1/0
```

Since the frame network and point-to-point link are connected to R1, we don't see them here in the OSPF route table, but we expected that. We still don't see R4's loopback. What about R2 and R3?

```
R2#show ip route ospf

        1.0.0.0/32  is subnetted, 1 subnets
O IA      1.1.1.1   [110/65] via 172.12.123.1, 00:08:00, Serial0/1/0
        3.0.0.0/32  is subnetted, 1 subnets
O IA      3.3.3.3   [110/65] via 172.12.123.3, 00:07:40, Serial0/1/0
        5.0.0.0/32  is subnetted, 1 subnets
O IA      5.5.5.5   [110/66] via 172.12.123.1, 00:08:00, Serial0/1/0
        10.0.0.0/24 is subnetted, 1 subnets
O         10.1.1.0  [110/65] via 172.12.123.1, 00:08:00, Serial0/1/0
        172.12.0.0/16    is variably subnetted, 4 subnets, 3 masks
O IA    172.12.13.0/27   [110/128] via 172.12.123.3, 00:08:00, Serial0/1/0
O IA    172.12.34.0/24   [110/74] via 172.12.123.3, 00:08:00, Serial0/1/0
```

```
R3#show ip route ospf
        1.0.0.0/32  is subnetted, 1 subnets
O IA      1.1.1.1   [110/65] via 172.12.123.1, 00:07:49, Serial0
        2.0.0.0/32  is subnetted, 1 subnets
O IA      2.2.2.2   [110/65] via 172.12.123.2, 00:07:49, Serial0
        5.0.0.0/32  is subnetted, 1 subnets
O IA      5.5.5.5   [110/66] via 172.12.123.1, 00:07:50, Serial0
        10.0.0.0/24 is subnetted, 1 subnets,
O         10.1.1.0  [110/65] via 172.12.123.1, 00:07:50, Serial0
```

Not even R4's OSPF neighbor, R3, has the route to R4's loopback in its routing table. The problem here is actually in the design of the network, since the design violates a very important OSPF rule. Let's have a look at our OSPF deployment with the new areas added.

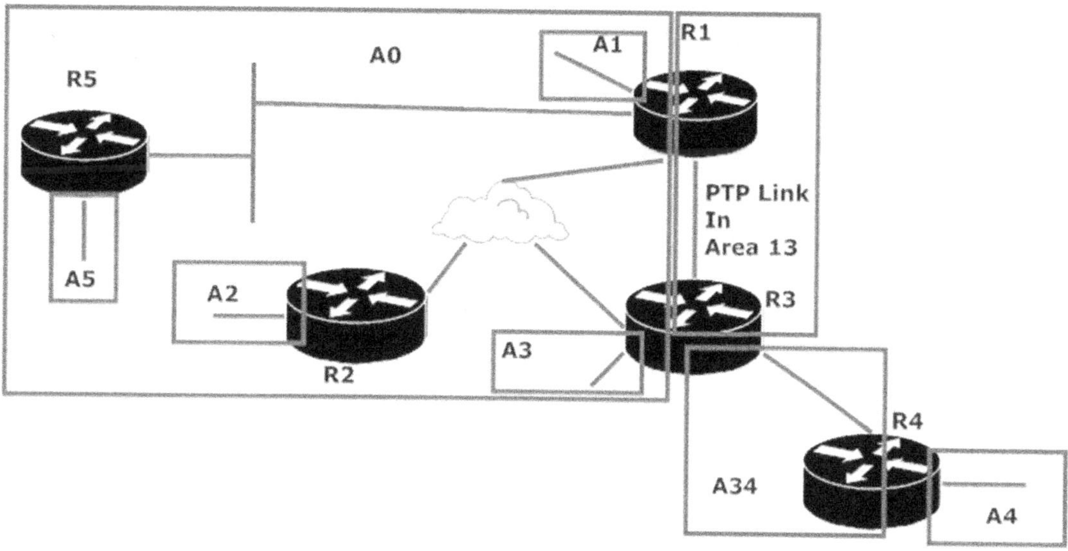

The number one rule of OSPF design is that every area must contain an interface on a router that has a physical or logical interface in Area 0 (A0). Four of our newest areas have no problem with that rule, but Area 4 does. Router 4 does not have a physical interface in Area 0, and for our routers to have full routing tables, we have to fix that. This rule allows a physical or logical connection to Area 0, and since we've seen plenty of physical interfaces put into Area 0, we'll now create a logical interface that gets the job done.

The OSPF Virtual Link

The area through which the virtual link is built, the transit area, cannot be a stub area of any kind. We're going to spend more time with stub areas later in this part of the course, and for right now it's enough to know that our transit area (Area 34) is not a stub.

Building a virtual link is actually pretty easy. You just have to know to ignore the message you'll get halfway through!

```
R3(config)#router ospf 1
R3(config-router)#area 34 ?
  authentication  Enable authentication
  default-cost    Set the summary default-cost of a NSSA/stub area
  nssa            Specify a NSSA area
  range           Summarize routes matching address/mask (border routers only)
  stub            Specify a stub area
  virtual-link    Define a virtual link and its parameters

R3(config-router)#area 34 virtual-link ?
  A.B.C.D ID (IP addr) associated with virtual link neighbor

R3(config-router)#area 34 virtual-link 4.4.4.4
```

```
R3(config)#router ospf 1
R3(config-router)#area 34 ?
  authentication  Enable authentication
  default-cost    Set the summary default-cost of a NSSA/stub area
  nssa            Specify a NSSA area
  range           Summarize routes matching address/mask (border routers only)
  stub            Specify a stub area
  virtual-link    Define a virtual link and its parameters

R3(config-router)#area 34 virtual-link ?
  A.B.C.D ID (IP addr) associated with virtual link neighbor


R3(config-router)#area 34 virtual-link 4.4.4.4

R4(config)#router ospf 1
R4(config-router)#area 34 virtual-lin
May 25 13:33:19.195: %OSPF-4-ERRRCV: Received invalid packet: mismatch area ID,
from backbone area must be virtual-link but not found from 172.12.34.3, FastEthe
rnet0/0
R4(config-router)#area 34 virtual-link 3.3.3.3
```

Unless you type really fast (or cut and paste), you're going to get at least one of these messages after you configure one side of the virtual link. The words "received invalid packet" tend to make anyone a bit panicky, but all this message means is that you haven't finished the virtual link. Once you do, the message will go away, and you'll see this one in its place:

```
May 25 13:33:29.243: %OSPF-5-ADJCHG: Process 1, Nbr 3.3.3.3 on OSPF_VL0 from
LOADING to FULL, Loading Done
```

Verify your new virtual link with *show ip ospf neighbor* and *show ip ospf virtual-link.* Note the interface type used by the new adjacency and that our virtual link is seen by OSPF as a point-to-point network.

```
R4#show ip ospf neighbor

Neighbor ID     Pri   State           Dead Time   Address         Interface
3.3.3.3           0   FULL/  -        -           172.12.34.3     OSPF_VL0
3.3.3.3           1   FULL/BDR        00:00:31    172.12.34.3     FastEthernet0/0


R4#show ip ospf virtual-link
Virtual Link OSPF_VL0 to router 3.3.3.3 is up
Run as demand circuit
DoNotAge LSA allowed.
Transit area 34, via interface FastEthernet0/0
```

```
Topology-MTID    Cost    Disabled    Shutdown    Topology Name
      0            1        no          no           Base
Transmit Delay is 1 sec, State POINT_TO_POINT,
Timer intervals configured, Hello 10, Dead 40, Wait 40, Retransmit 5
  Hello due in 00:00:05
  Adjacency State FULL (Hello suppressed)
  Index 1/2, retransmission queue length 0, number of retransmission 1
  First 0x0(0)/0x0(0) Next 0x0(0)/0x0(0)
  Last retransmission scan length is 1, maximum is 1
  Last retransmission scan time is 0 msec, maximum is 0 msec
```

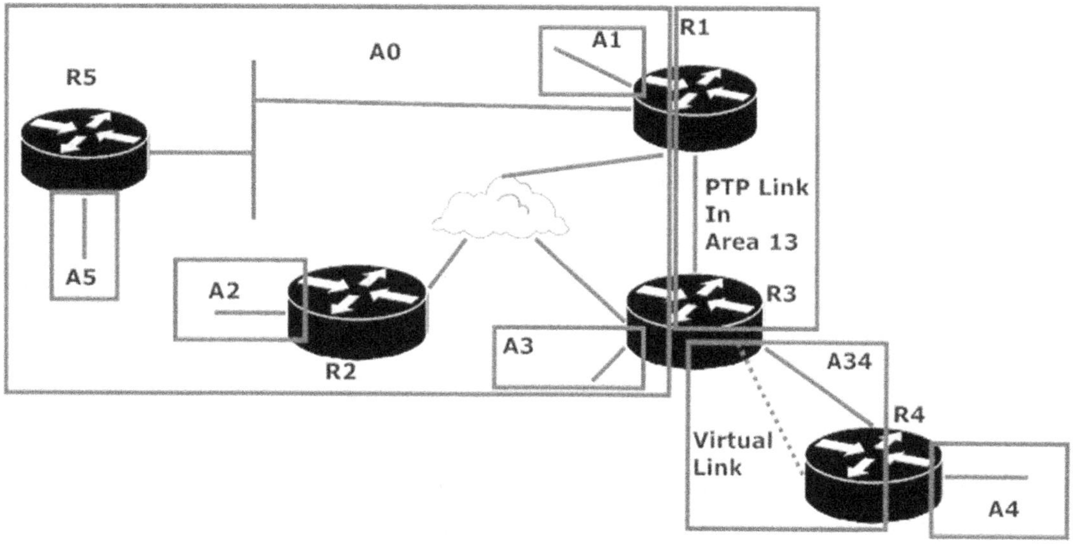

With our virtual link in place, does R5 have connectivity to R4's loopback?

```
R5#show ip route ospf

Gateway of last resort is not set

      1.0.0.0/32  is subnetted, 1 subnets
O IA     1.1.1.1  [110/2] via 10.1.1.1, 00:35:23, GigabitEthernet0/0
      2.0.0.0/32  is subnetted, 1 subnets
O IA     2.2.2.2  [110/783] via 10.1.1.1, 00:34:59, GigabitEthernet0/0
      3.0.0.0/32  is subnetted, 1 subnets
O IA     3.3.3.3  [110/783] via 10.1.1.1, 00:34:54, GigabitEthernet0/0
      4.0.0.0/32  is subnetted, 1 subnets
O IA     4.4.4.4  [110/793] via 10.1.1.1, 00:08:13, GigabitEthernet0/0
      172.12.0.0/16 is variably subnetted, 3 subnets, 2 masks
O IA  172.12.13.0/27 [110/782] via 10.1.1.1, 00:35:52, GigabitEthernet0/0
O IA  172.12.34.0/24 [110/792] via 10.1.1.1, 00:35:52, GigabitEthernet0/0
O     172.12.123.0/24 [110/782] via 10.1.1.1, 00:35:52, GigabitEthernet0/0
```

```
R5#ping 4.4.4.4
!!!!!
Success rate is 100 percent (5/5), round-trip min/avg/max = 64/76/120 ms
```

Yes and yes! Had that route not shown up, I would have checked the following three values, since they're responsible for 99 percent of virtual link problems:

- Using the wrong RID value in the virtual-link command
- Trying to use a stub area as the transit area
- Failure to configure authentication on the virtual link when authentication is in use in Area 0 (More on authentication later, I promise!)

Why the %)$%(Don't We Just Use One Big Area 0?*

After you see or hear about the importance of Area 0 for the zillionth time, you just might start thinking, "Why not just put everything into Area 0? That way you have no design issues, virtual links, or worries!"

We use areas because that allows us to create a hierarchy in our OSPF deployment. That sounds great, and Cisco loves the word "hierarchical"—but what the heck does it mean? Here's the latest and greatest definition from Google:

"adj: classified according to various criteria into successive levels or layers"

Using OSPF areas allows us to build a layered network. That does help to reduce the wear and tear on router resources such as memory and CPU. Thanks to this layered approach, you'll run into situations where a router doesn't need a huge routing table in order to reach the destinations it needs to reach. Why have a full routing table when a lesser number of routes will do?

Logically dividing an OSPF network into areas helps to limit LSU and LSA traffic, since notifications of changes in a multi-area OSPF network can be limited to the area in which the change took place. This limiting of LSAs in turn helps to limit the overall number of routing table recalculations.

Summing it up, using OSPF areas brings us more efficient routing thanks to complete and concise routing tables, fewer overall SPF recalculations, and less LSA/LSA traffic.

Speaking of SPF recalculations, you can see how many times that's happened with *show ip ospf.* If you continually see this number rising, you likely have an unstable segment in that OSPF area. Check out the full output of this command, especially the bolded information.

```
R5#show ip ospf
  Routing Process "ospf 1" with ID 5.5.5.5
  Start time: 2d00h, Time elapsed: 03:43:11.936
  Supports only single TOS(TOS0) routes
  Supports opaque LSA
```

```
Supports Link-local Signaling (LLS)
Supports area transit capability
Event-log enabled, Maximum number of events: 1000, Mode: cyclic
It is an area border router
Router is not originating router-LSAs with maximum metric
Initial SPF schedule delay 5000 msecs
Minimum hold time between two consecutive SPFs 10000 msecs
Maximum wait time between two consecutive SPFs 10000 msecs
Incremental-SPF disabled
Minimum LSA interval 5 secs
Minimum LSA arrival 1000 msecs
LSA group pacing timer 240 secs
Interface flood pacing timer 33 msecs
Retransmission pacing timer 66 msecs
Number of external LSA 0. Checksum Sum 0x000000
Number of opaque AS LSA 0. Checksum Sum 0x000000
Number of DCbitless external and opaque AS LSA 0
Number of DoNotAge external and opaque AS LSA 0
Number of areas in this router is 2. 2 normal 0 stub 0 nssa
Number of areas transit capable is 0
External flood list length 0
IETF NSF helper support enabled
Cisco NSF helper support enabled
Reference bandwidth unit is 100 mbps
  Area BACKBONE(0)
      Number of interfaces in this area is 1
      Area has no authentication
      SPF algorithm last executed 00:23:46.568 ago
      SPF algorithm executed 31 times
      Area ranges are
      Number of LSA 16. Checksum Sum 0x07326D
      Number of opaque link LSA 0. Checksum Sum 0x000000
      Number of DCbitless LSA 0
      Number of indication LSA 0
      Number of DoNotAge LSA 3
      Flood list length 0
  Area 5
      Number of interfaces in this area is 1 (1 loopback)
      Area has no authentication
      SPF algorithm last executed 00:51:14.332 ago
      SPF algorithm executed 2 times
      Area ranges are
      Number of LSA 9. Checksum Sum 0x0415A5
      Number of opaque link LSA 0. Checksum Sum 0x000000
      Number of DCbitless LSA 0
      Number of indication LSA 0
```

```
Number of DoNotAge LSA 0
Flood list length 0
```

Cisco offers these OSPF design guidelines to help you decide when it's time to add areas to your deployment:

- No router should be in more than three areas.
- No area should contain more than 50 routers.
- No router should have more than 60 neighbors.
- A router can be a DR or a BDR for more than one network segment, but monitor the workload on that switch carefully. Watch for an overtaxed CPU.
- Do not run more than one OSPF process on an Area Border Router (ABR).

More on multi-area OSPF in the next section. (Yeah, there's more!) Right now, let's revisit an old friend and important OSPF value.

OSPF Path Cost Determination

In our OSPF routing table, there are two great values in that itty-bitty set of brackets.

```
R5#show ip route ospf
      1.0.0.0/32  is subnetted, 1 subnets
O IA     1.1.1.1  [110/2] via 10.1.1.1, 01:00:08, GigabitEthernet0/0
      2.0.0.0/32  is subnetted, 1 subnets
O IA     2.2.2.2  [110/783] via 10.1.1.1, 00:59:44, GigabitEthernet0/0
      3.0.0.0/32  is subnetted, 1 subnets
O IA     3.3.3.3  [110/783] via 10.1.1.1, 00:59:39, GigabitEthernet0/0
      4.0.0.0/32  is subnetted, 1 subnets
O IA     4.4.4.4  [110/793] via 10.1.1.1, 00:32:58, GigabitEthernet0/0
      172.12.0.0/16 is variably subnetted, 3 subnets, 2 masks
O IA  172.12.13.0/27 [110/782] via 10.1.1.1, 01:00:37, GigabitEthernet0/0
O IA  172.12.34.0/24 [110/792] via 10.1.1.1, 01:00:37, GigabitEthernet0/0
O     172.12.123.0/24 [110/782] via 10.1.1.1, 01:00:37, GigabitEthernet0/0
```

The first value is 110, the default admin distance of OSPF. The second is the *cost* of the path, the metric used by OSPF. OSPF assigns a cost to every OSPF-enabled interface, and that cost is based on the port's speed. The default formula OSPF uses to calculate the interface cost is (*reference bandwidth / interface bandwidth*), which is easy to work with as long as you know the default reference bandwidth is 100 Mbps. If you have an Ethernet interface, you know it's running at 10 Mbps, so 100 divided by 10 equals an OSPF cost of 10. I just happen to have an Ethernet interface running OSPF on R3...

```
R3#show ip ospf int e0
Ethernet0 is up, line protocol is up
  Internet Address 172.12.34.3/24, Area 34
  Process ID 1, Router ID 3.3.3.3, Network Type BROADCAST, Cost: 10
```

...and there it is!

See if you can spot the possible issue in this list of default OSPF interface costs:

56k = 1785

64k = 1562

T1 line = 64

Ethernet = 10

Fast Ethernet = 1 (100 / 100)

Gig Ethernet = 1 (100 / 1000)

When the formula for determining OSPF interface cost was developed, there were no Fast Ethernet or Gig Ethernet interfaces, much less 10-Gig Ethernet! The formula works well until you get to Gig Ethernet. If you have both Fast and Gig Ethernet interfaces in your OSPF network, you don't want those interfaces to have the same cost when one is *much* faster than the other!

You can change the "reference bandwidth" part of the formula with the *auto-cost reference-bandwidth* command. (That's right—two hyphens!) You can just type *auto ref* if you like, but please be familiar with the full command. I'll change the default of 100 to 1000 on R3 and then view R3 to see the results.

```
R3(config)#router ospf 1
R3(config-router)#auto-cost ?
  reference-bandwidth Use reference bandwidth method to assign OSPF cost
  <cr>

R3(config-router)#auto-cost reference-bandwidth 1000
% OSPF: Reference bandwidth is changed.
    Please ensure reference bandwidth is consistent across all routers.

R3#show ip ospf int e0
Ethernet0 is up, line protocol is up
  Internet Address 172.12.34.3/24, Area 34
  Process ID 1, Router ID 3.3.3.3, Network Type BROADCAST, Cost: 100
```

The effect is immediate, and there's no need to clear OSPF processes to have this command take effect. You must pay attention to the warning we received after entering the command. If you change this value on one router in your OSPF domain, you should change it on all routers. Failure to do so could easily lead to suboptimal routing. You don't want Fast Ethernet interfaces to have an OSPF cost of 10 on some routers and 1 on others.

Should you need to change a particular interface's OSPF cost without affecting this calculation, use the interface-level *ip ospf cost* command. Using this command overrules or overrides (take your choice) the cost calculated with the reference bandwidth.

```
R3(config)#int e0
R3(config-if)#ip ospf cost 10

R3#show ip ospf int e0
Ethernet0 is up, line protocol is up
  Internet Address 172.12.34.3/24, Area 34
  Process ID 1, Router ID 3.3.3.3, Network Type BROADCAST, Cost: 10
```

We'll tweak bandwidth in the following lab to give OSPF a more accurate view of our network. Every segment is in Area 0.

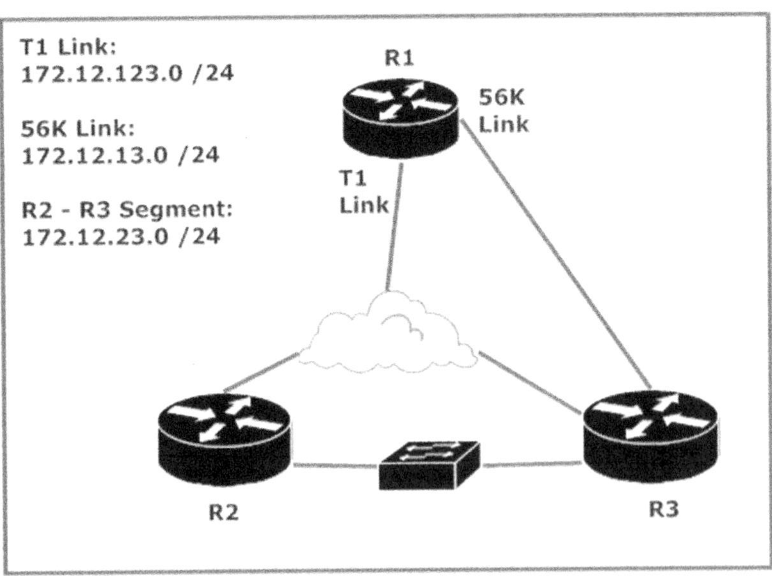

According to R1's OSPF route table, there's some serious load balancing going on. OSPF will load balance over four paths by default, and we're already up to three.

```
R1#show ip route ospf
     172.12.0.0/24 is subnetted, 3 subnets
O       172.12.23.0  [110/65] via 172.12.123.3, 00:09:22, Serial1/0
                     [110/65] via 172.12.123.2, 00:09:22, Serial1/0
                     [110/65] via 172.12.13.3, 00:09:22, Serial1/1
```

We don't mind the load balancing over the paths using a T1 link, but that 56k link is best used as a backup. *show int serial 1/1* reveals the current bandwidth setting.

```
R1#show int serial 1/1
Serial1/1 is up, line protocol is up
  Hardware is CD2430 in sync mode
  Internet address is 172.12.13.1/24
  MTU 1500 bytes, BW 1544 Kbit, DLY 20000 usec,
```

Let's let OSPF know this is only a 56k link and then verify the changes.

```
R1(config)#int serial 1/1
R1(config-if)#bandwidth 56

R1#show int serial 1/1
Serial1/1 is up, line protocol is up
  Hardware is CD2430 in sync mode
  Internet address is 172.12.13.1/24
  MTU 1500 bytes, BW 56 Kbit, DLY 20000 usec,
     reliability 255/255, txload 1/255, rxload 1/255

R1#show ip route ospf
     172.12.0.0/24 is subnetted, 3 subnets
O       172.12.23.0  [110/65] via 172.12.123.3, 00:00:07, Serial1/0
                     [110/65] via 172.12.123.2, 00:00:07, Serial1/0
```

Done and done! OSPF is now load balancing over the two faster paths. Should those two paths become unavailable, perhaps by an interface mysteriously going down…

```
R1(config)#int serial 1/0
R1(config-if)#shut (or not so mysteriously)

May 25 15:09:36.386: %OSPF-5-ADJCHG: Process 1, Nbr 172.12.123.2 on Serial1/0 fr
om 2WAY to DOWN, Neighbor Down: Interface down or detached
May 25 15:09:36.386: %OSPF-5-ADJCHG: Process 1, Nbr 172.12.123.3 on Serial1/0 fr
om 2WAY to DOWN, Neighbor Down: Interface down or detached
May 25 15:09:37.203: %SYS-5-CONFIG_I: Configured from console by console
May 25 15:09:38.385: %LINK-5-CHANGED: Interface Serial1/0, changed state to admi
nistratively down
May 25 15:09:39.387: %LINEPROTO-5-UPDOWN: Line protocol on Interface Serial1/0,
changed state to down
```

…the slower path reenters the OSPF route table.

```
R1#show ip route ospf
     172.12.0.0/24 is subnetted, 2 subnets
O       172.12.23.0  [110/1786] via 172.12.13.3, 00:00:00, Serial1/1
```

The big issue with the *bandwidth* command is that it's not OSPF specific. That bandwidth value is used by other routing protocols as well as IOS features. Watch your router's active features, and make sure they're still doing what you want them to do after changing this value.

The OSPF Adjacency States

It's hard to see every adjacency state during the actual forming of the adjacency! Here's a review of those states along with a description of what's going on during each state.

Down: No hellos received from that neighbor. Nothing much going on yet!

Attempt: Unicast hello packets are being sent to the neighbor. You'll only see this stage on the hub router in an NBMA network:

```
R1#show ip ospf neighbor

Neighbor ID     Pri   State             Dead Time   Address         Interface
N/A               0   ATTEMPT/DROTHER   00:01:55    172.12.123.2    Serial1/0
N/A               0   ATTEMPT/DROTHER   00:01:55    172.12.123.3    Serial1/0
```

Init: Hey, we're getting somewhere! The first hello packet has been received from the neighbor.

2-Way: When you're here, you're almost gold. At this point, each router has received a hello packet containing its own RID, indicating bidirectional communication. When a router receives a hello packet containing its own RID, it's not just talking to itself; that's the remote router's way of saying, "I received that hello packet you sent me earlier."

Exstart: Following the DR/BDR election, the exchange of link state database information can begin! The router with the highest RID will begin the exchange and increment the initial sequence number, which is determined during this stage.

Exchange: Database Descriptor (DBD) packets are exchanged. As you'd expect, these packets contain a description of the link state database.

Loading: Routers now send Link State Request (LSR) packets to the almost-neighbor.

Full: Router databases are synched, and the adjacency has been formed.

We know to use *show ip ospf neighbor* to verify our adjacencies; keep *show ip ospf interface* in mind. The first command gives you fundamental information about the adjacency, while the second gives you more detail about the neighbors.

```
R1#show ip ospf neighbor

Neighbor ID     Pri   State           Dead Time   Address         Interface
172.12.123.2      0   FULL/DROTHER    00:01:44    172.12.123.2    Serial1/0
172.12.123.3      0   FULL/DROTHER    00:01:33    172.12.123.    Serial1/0
```

```
R1#show ip ospf int serial 1/0
Serial1/0 is up, line protocol is up
  Internet Address 172.12.123.1/24, Area 0
  Process ID 1, Router ID 172.12.123.1, Network Type NON_BROADCAST, Cost: 64
  Transmit Delay is 1 sec, State DR, Priority 1
  Designated Router (ID) 172.12.123.1, Interface address 172.12.123.1
  No backup designated router on this network
  Timer intervals configured, Hello 30, Dead 120, Wait 120, Retransmit 5
    oob-resync timeout 120
    Hello due in 00:00:03
  Supports Link-local Signaling (LLS)
  Index 1/1, flood queue length 0
  Next 0x0(0)/0x0(0)
  Last flood scan length is 1, maximum is 2
  Last flood scan time is 0 msec, maximum is 0 msec
  Neighbor Count is 2, Adjacent neighbor count is 2
    Adjacent with neighbor 172.12.123.2
    Adjacent with neighbor 172.12.123.3
    Suppress hello for 0 neighbor(s)
```

Adjacencies, OSPF, and Multiple Routers

It's important to know when to troubleshoot and just as important to know when *not* to troubleshoot. Here's such a situation:

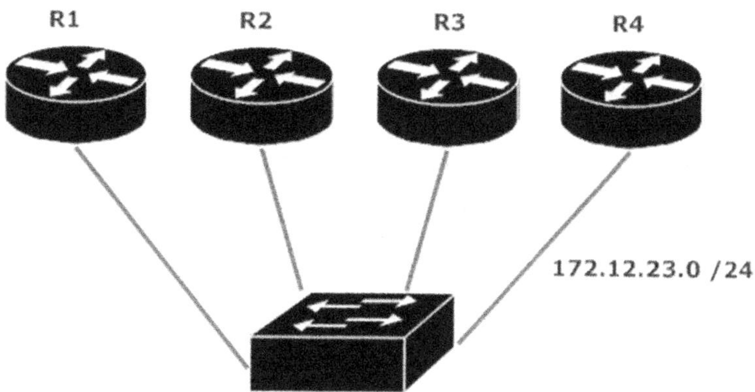

Let's have a look at our neighbor tables, shall we?

```
R4#show ip ospf neighbor

Neighbor ID     Pri   State          Dead Time   Address        Interface
172.12.23.1       1   FULL/DROTHER   00:00:39    172.12.23.1    FastEthernet0/0
172.12.23.2       1   FULL/DROTHER   00:00:35    172.12.23.2    FastEthernet0/0
172.12.23.3       1   FULL/BDR       00:00:37    172.12.23.3    FastEthernet0/0
```

```
R3#show ip ospf neighbor

Neighbor ID     Pri   State           Dead Time   Address         Interface
172.12.23.1       1   FULL/DROTHER    00:00:33    172.12.23.1     Ethernet0
172.12.23.2       1   FULL/DROTHER    00:00:39    172.12.23.2     Ethernet0
172.12.23.4       1   FULL/DR         00:00:33    172.12.23.4     Ethernet0

R2#show ip ospf neighbor

Neighbor ID     Pri   State           Dead Time   Address         Interface
172.12.23.1       1   2WAY/DROTHER    00:00:38    172.12.23.1     FastEthernet0/0
172.12.23.3       1   FULL/BDR        00:00:33    172.12.23.3     FastEthernet0/0
172.12.23.4       1   FULL/DR         00:00:37    172.12.23.4     FastEthernet0/0

R1#show ip ospf neighbor

Neighbor ID     Pri   State           Dead Time   Address         Interface
172.12.23.2       1   2WAY/DROTHER    00:00:36    172.12.23.2     FastEthernet0/0
172.12.23.3       1   FULL/BDR        00:00:38    172.12.23.3     FastEthernet0/0
172.12.23.4       1   FULL/DR         00:00:31    172.12.23.4     FastEthernet0/0
```

What do those 2-way adjacencies have in common?

The only adjacency that's in 2-way is the one between R1 and R2, the two DROthers. This is by design. The adjacency between the DROthers is never going to finish. We could come back tomorrow, and they'd still be in 2-way! This is actually a default behavior of OSPF that helps to cut down on the number of LSAs transmitted on a broadcast segment that contains more than two OSPF speakers.

The only routers that will have a full adjacency to all other routers on the segment are the DR and BDR. Each DROther will have a full adjacency with both the DR and BDR, but the DROthers on a broadcast segment will never have a full adjacency. Since the router detecting a network change tells both the DR and BDR, and it's then up to the DR to tell everyone, there's no reason for the DROthers to have a full adjacency.

Now that we have the many fundamentals of OSPF down cold, let's tackle multi-area OSPF and throw in a little route summarization for good measure!

Chapter 5:

ADVANCED OSPF

We know from previous labs that Area 0 is the backbone area of our OSPF network and that every nonbackbone area must contain a router that has a physical or logical (virtual link!) connection to Area 0. Traffic going from one nonbackbone area to another must cross Area 0.

For these reasons, Area 0 is generally found at the center of an OSPF network, and the following network will be no exception! We'll begin by placing the serial interfaces of R1, R2, and R3 into the 172.12.123.0 /24 network. This is our Area 0. As with any hub-and-spoke OSPF network, the spokes will be disqualified from participating in the DR/BDR election via the *ip ospf priority* command, and the hub will be configured with *neighbor* statements.

R1:

```
router ospf 1
  log-adjacency-changes
  network 172.12.123.0 0.0.0.255 area 0
  neighbor 172.12.123.2
  neighbor 172.12.123.3
```

R2:

```
interface Serial0/1/0
  ip address 172.12.123.2 255.255.255.0
  encapsulation frame-relay
  ip ospf priority 0
  frame-relay map ip 172.12.123.3 221 broadcast
  frame-relay map ip 172.12.123.1 221 broadcast
  no frame-relay inverse-arp
!
router ospf 1
  network 172.12.123.0 0.0.0.255 area 0
```

R3:

```
interface Serial0/1/0
  ip address 172.12.123.3 255.255.255.0
  encapsulation frame-relay
  ip ospf priority 0
  frame-relay map ip 172.12.123.2 321 broadcast
  frame-relay map ip 172.12.123.1 321 broadcast
  no frame-relay inverse-arp
!
router ospf 1
network 172.12.123.0 0.0.0.255 area 0

R1#show ip ospf neighbor

Neighbor ID     Pri   State           Dead Time   Address         Interface
172.12.123.2      0   FULL/DROTHER    00:01:42    172.12.123.2    Serial1/0
172.12.123.3      0   FULL/DROTHER    00:01:45    172.12.123.3    Serial1/0
```

R1 sees both R2 and R3 as DROthers, just as we want, and we're off to the races!

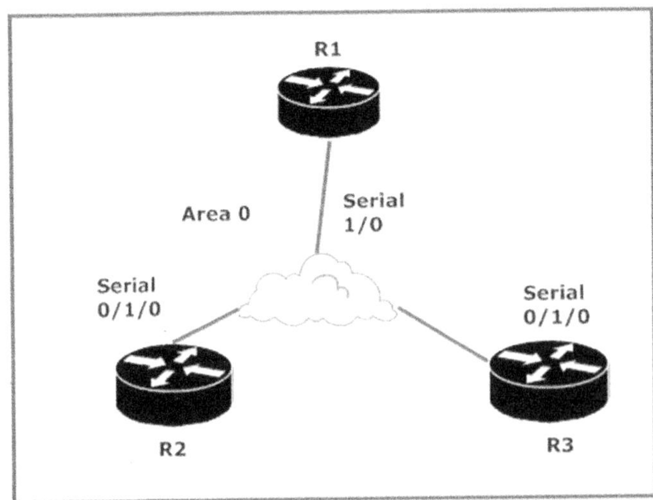

I've created a loopback on each router, using the router number for each octet along with a /32 mask. We'll introduce those to OSPF by placing them into a nonbackbone area, using the router number as the area number.

```
R1(config)#router ospf 1
R1(config-router)#network 1.1.1.1 0.0.0.0 area 1

R2(config)#router ospf 1
R2(config-router)#network 2.2.2.2 0.0.0.0 area 2

R3(config)#router ospf 1
R3(config-router)#network 3.3.3.3 0.0.0.0 area 3
```

Let's check the OSPF routing table on each router.

```
R1#show ip route ospf
       2.0.0.0/32  is subnetted, 1 subnets
O IA      2.2.2.2  [110/782] via 172.12.123.2, 00:02:24, Serial1/0
       3.0.0.0/32  is subnetted, 1 subnets
O IA      3.3.3.3  [110/782] via 172.12.123.3, 00:02:19, Serial1/0

R1#show ip route ospf
       2.0.0.0/32  is subnetted, 1 subnets
O IA      2.2.2.2  [110/782] via 172.12.123.2, 00:02:24, Serial1/0
       3.0.0.0/32  is subnetted, 1 subnets
O IA      3.3.3.3  [110/782] via 172.12.123.3, 00:02:19, Serial1/0

R2#show ip route ospf
O IA      1.1.1.1  [110/65] via 172.12.123.1, 00:02:32, Serial0/1/0
       3.0.0.0/32  is subnetted, 1 subnets
O IA      3.3.3.3  [110/65] via 172.12.123.3, 00:02:11, Serial0/1/0

R3#show ip route ospf
       1.0.0.0/32  is subnetted, 1 subnets
O IA      1.1.1.1  [110/65] via 172.12.123.1, 00:02:35, Serial0/1/0
       2.0.0.0/32  is subnetted, 1 subnets
O IA      2.2.2.2  [110/65] via 172.12.123.2, 00:02:35, Serial0/1/0
```

Each router has an OSPF route to the loopback networks on the other router. These routes are all marked "O IA." The "O" naturally refers to "OSPF." The "IA" refers to an *inter-area route*, a route to a destination located in an OSPF area that is not a part of the local router. Each router is our network is now an Area Border Router, since each borders Area 0 and a nonbackbone router.

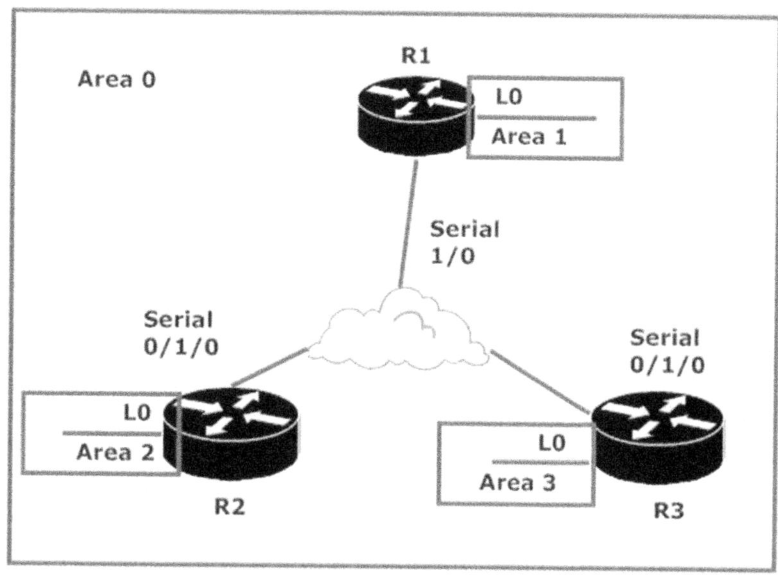

While spotting ABRs with no help from the Cisco IOS is a valuable exam-passing skill, you can verify a router's ABR role with *show ip ospf.* This command can give you screens of info, so I'll cut this output off after about eight lines.

R1:

```
Routing Process "ospf 1" with ID 1.1.1.1
Start time: 02:25:00.547, Time elapsed: 00:03:14.655
Supports only single TOS(TOS0) routes
Supports opaque LSA
Supports Link-local Signaling (LLS)
Supports area transit capability
It is an area border router
```

R2:

```
Routing Process "ospf 1" with ID 2.2.2.2
Start time: 01:08:11.020, Time elapsed: 01:22:30.000
Supports only single TOS(TOS0) routes
Supports opaque LSA
Supports Link-local Signaling (LLS)
Supports area transit capability
Event-log enabled, Maximum number of events: 1000, Mode: cyclic
It is an area border router
```

R3:

```
Routing Process "ospf 1" with ID 3.3.3.3
Start time: 01:08:29.388, Time elapsed: 01:22:54.788
Supports only single TOS(TOS0) routes
Supports opaque LSA
Supports Link-local Signaling (LLS)
Supports area transit capability
Event-log enabled, Maximum number of events: 1000, Mode: cyclic
It is an area border router
```

R3 and R4's Fast 0/0 interfaces are on the 172.12.34.0 /24 network. Let's put those interfaces in OSPF Area 34.

```
R3(config)#router ospf 1
R3(config-router)#network 172.12.34.0 0.0.0.255 area 34

R4(config)#router ospf 1
R4(config-router)#network 172.12.34.0 0.0.0.255 area 34
```

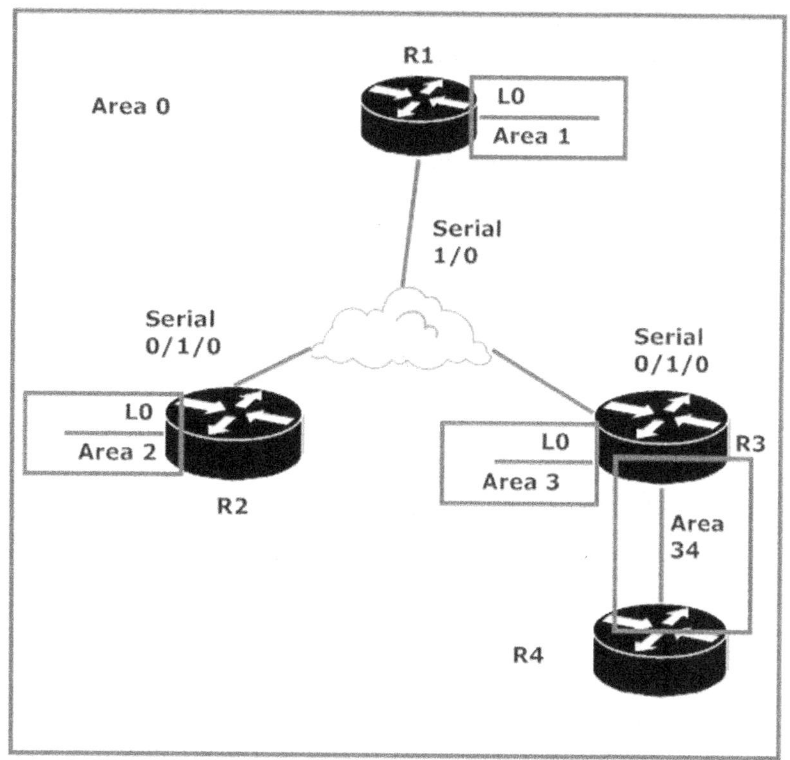

Our adjacencies check out! (R4's RID is 172.12.23.4 since there is no loopback on that router.)

```
R3#show ip ospf neighbor

Neighbor ID     Pri   State           Dead Time   Address         Interface
1.1.1.1           1   FULL/DR         00:01:34    172.12.123.1    Serial0/1/0
172.12.23.4       1   FULL/DR         00:00:39    172.12.34.4     FastEthernet0/0

R4#show ip ospf neig

Neighbor ID     Pri   State           Dead Time   Address         Interface
3.3.3.3           1   FULL/BDR        00:00:38    172.12.34.3     FastEthernet0/0
```

Let's check out R4's OSPF table.

```
R4#show ip route ospf

      1.0.0.0/32  is subnetted, 1 subnets
O IA     1.1.1.1  [110/66] via 172.12.34.3, 00:00:18, FastEthernet0/0
      2.0.0.0/32  is subnetted, 1 subnets
O IA     2.2.2.2  [110/66] via 172.12.34.3, 00:00:18, FastEthernet0/0
      3.0.0.0/32  is subnetted, 1 subnets
O IA     3.3.3.3  [110/2] via 172.12.34.3, 00:07:37, FastEthernet0/0
      172.12.0.0/16     is variably subnetted, 3 subnets, 2 masks
O IA     172.12.123.0/24 [110/65] via 172.12.34.3, 00:00:18, FastEthernet0/0
```

Looks good—but the proof is in the pinging. Let's ping each loopback along with the farthest interface on the 172.12.123.0 /24 network.

```
R4#ping 1.1.1.1
!!!!!
Success rate is 100 percent (5/5), round-trip min/avg/max = 64/65/68 ms

R4#ping 2.2.2.2
!!!!!
Success rate is 100 percent (5/5), round-trip min/avg/max = 128/129/132 ms

R4#ping 3.3.3.3
!!!!!
Success rate is 100 percent (5/5), round-trip min/avg/max = 1/2/4 ms

R4#ping 172.12.123.2
!!!!!
Success rate is 100 percent (5/5), round-trip min/avg/max = 128/131/140 ms
```

R4 has all the O IA routes we have, along with IP connectivity to each. There's nothing particularly wrong with this table, but we can make it better, faster, and stronger via the use of stub areas.

The next-hop IP address for all four routes is R3's Fast0/0 interface IP address, 172.12.34.3. That's the only next-hop address for any data leaving R4, so we could add a hundred O IA routes to R4, and the next-hop address would still be 172.12.34.3. It seems a bit inefficient to have the routing process look through a collection of specific routes when the packets are going to go to 172.12.34.3 in any case!

Let's keep that in mind while we bring some routes into OSPF via route redistribution, which is the process of taking routes and putting those routes into a protocol's domain. Routes redistributed into another protocol are said to be *injected* into that protocol's domain.

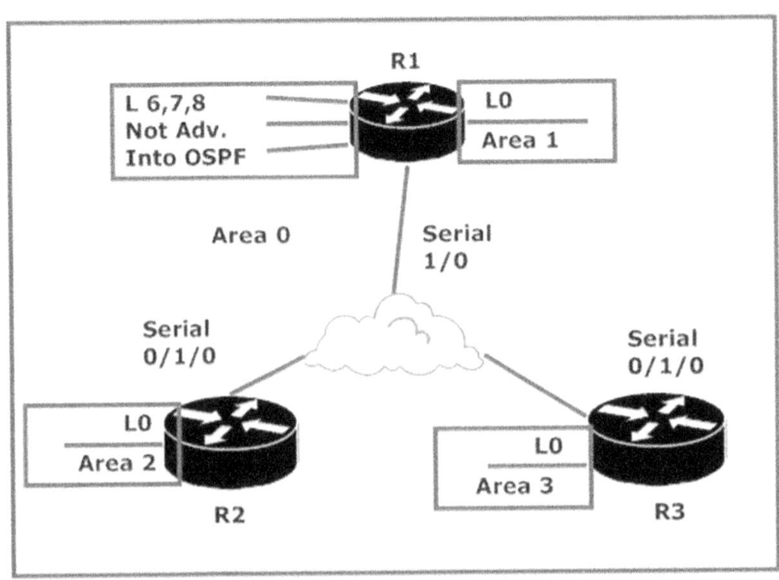

Redistributed routes can come from another routing protocol, from another process of the same routing protocol, or can be static or connected routes. We'll redistribute these three loopbacks on R1 into our existing OSPF network via the *redistribute connected* command.

```
R1(config)#router ospf 1
R1(config-router)#redistribute connected
% Only classful networks will be redistributed
R1(config-router)#redistribute connected subnets
```

It's unlikely you only want your classful network numbers to be redistributed, so you'll need the full *redistribute connected subnets* command. If you're missing subnets after redistributing routes into OSPF, the subnets option is likely missing.

Performing route redistribution on an OSPF router makes that router an Autonomous System Border Router. R1's role as an ASBR is verified with *show ip ospf.* The line right under the ASBR-related line shows the source of the redistributed routes. And yes, a router can be both an ABR and ASBR!

```
R1#show ip ospf
  Routing Process "ospf 1" with ID 1.1.1.1
  Start time: 02:25:00.547, Time elapsed: 01:24:52.925
  Supports only single TOS(TOS0) routes
  Supports opaque LSA
  Supports Link-local Signaling (LLS)
  Supports area transit capability
  It is an area border and autonomous system boundary router
  Redistributing External Routes from,
    connected, includes subnets in redistribution
```

Let's head down to R4 and check out that router's OSPF routing table, followed by a connectivity test involving the newly learned routes.

```
R4#show ip route ospf

Gateway of last resort is not set

      1.0.0.0/32  is subnetted, 1 subnets
O IA     1.1.1.1  [110/66] via 172.12.34.3, 00:58:53, FastEthernet0/0
      2.0.0.0/32  is subnetted, 1 subnets
O IA     2.2.2.2  [110/66] via 172.12.34.3, 00:58:53, FastEthernet0/0
      3.0.0.0/32  is subnetted, 1 subnets
O IA     3.3.3.3  [110/2] via 172.12.34.3, 01:06:12, FastEthernet0/0
      5.0.0.0/24  is subnetted, 1 subnets
O E2     5.1.1.0  [110/20] via 172.12.34.3, 00:03:17, FastEthernet0/0
      6.0.0.0/24  is subnetted, 1 subnets
O E2     6.1.1.0  [110/20] via 172.12.34.3, 00:03:17, FastEthernet0/0
      7.0.0.0/24  is subnetted, 1 subnets
```

```
O E2     7.1.1.0  [110/20] via 172.12.34.3, 00:03:17, FastEthernet0/0
      172.12.0.0/16 is variably subnetted, 3 subnets, 2 masks
O IA     172.12.123.0/24 [110/65] via 172.12.34.3, 00:58:53, FastEthernet0/0


R4#ping 5.1.1.1
!!!!!
Success rate is 100 percent (5/5), round-trip min/avg/max = 64/64/68 ms

R4#ping 6.1.1.1
!!!!!
Success rate is 100 percent (5/5), round-trip min/avg/max = 64/66/68 ms

R4#ping 7.1.1.1
!!!!!
Success rate is 100 percent (5/5), round-trip min/avg/max = 64/66/68 ms
```

The pingability is high, but the routing table code for those new routes is different than any codes we've seen to this point. OE2 routes are OSPF External Type 2 routes, indicating this route was originally learned by an OSPF-speaking route via route redistribution. (Teaser: yes, there is an OSPF External Type 1 route, and we'll cover those later in this section.)

One thing that hasn't changed is the next-hop IP address of those OSPF routes. Regardless of code or type, the next-hop address is still 172.12.34.3.

```
R4#show ip route ospf

      1.0.0.0/32  is subnetted, 1 subnets
O IA     1.1.1.1  [110/66] via 172.12.34.3, 01:03:39, FastEthernet0/0
      2.0.0.0/32  is subnetted, 1 subnets
O IA     2.2.2.2  [110/66] via 172.12.34.3, 01:03:39, FastEthernet0/0
      3.0.0.0/32  is subnetted, 1 subnets
O IA     3.3.3.3  [110/2] via 172.12.34.3, 01:10:58, FastEthernet0/0
      5.0.0.0/24  is subnetted, 1 subnets
O E2     5.1.1.0  [110/20] via 172.12.34.3, 00:08:03, FastEthernet0/0
      6.0.0.0/24  is subnetted, 1 subnets
O E2     6.1.1.0  [110/20] via 172.12.34.3, 00:08:03, FastEthernet0/0
      7.0.0.0/24  is subnetted, 1 subnets
O E2     7.1.1.0  [110/20] via 172.12.34.3, 00:08:03, FastEthernet0/0
      172.12.0.0/16 is variably subnetted, 3 subnets, 2 masks
O IA     172.12.123.0/24 [110/65] via 172.12.34.3, 01:03:39, FastEthernet0/0
```

It's a waste of time and router resources for R4 to look for the best match for any route, since the next-hop address is always the same. OSPF allows us to substitute a single default route for all external destinations by making Area 34 a stub area. (Configuring an area as a stub prevents LSA Type 5s from flooding that area.)

It's not enough to configure Area 34 as a stub on R3 or R4. Every router in the area must agree on the stub / no stub setting for an area, or adjacencies will start to drop. Configuring an area as a stub is called "setting the stub flag" or "setting the stub bit," and when that flag/bit is set on one router and not another, here's the end result:

```
R3(config)#router ospf 1
R3(config-router)#area 34 ?
  Authentication  Enable authentication
  Capability      Enable area specific capability
  default-cost    Set the summary default-cost of a NSSA/stub area
  filter-list     Filter networks between OSPF areas
  nssa            Specify a NSSA area
  range           Summarize routes matching address/mask (border routers only)
  sham-link       Define a sham link and its parameters
  stub            Specify a stub area
  virtual-link    Define a virtual link and its parameters

R3(config-router)#area 34 stub
R3(config-router)#
*Jun 8 16:21:50.187: %OSPF-5-ADJCHG: Process 1, Nbr 172.12.23.4 on FastEthernet
0/0 from FULL to DOWN, Neighbor Down: Adjacency forced to reset
```

Configuring Area 34 as a stub on R4 will being the adjacency right back up.

```
R4(config)#router ospf 1
R4(config-router)#area 34 stub
R4(config-router)#^Z
R4#
*Jan 1 06:00:46.302: %SYS-5-CONFIG_I: Configured from console by console
R4#
*Jan 1 06:00:48.426: %OSPF-5-ADJCHG: Process 1, Nbr 3.3.3.3 on FastEthernet0/0
from LOADING to FULL, Loading Done
```

Area 34 is now a stub. The effect on R4's routing table is immediate:

```
R4#show ip route ospf

Gateway of last resort is 172.12.34.3 to network 0.0.0.0

O*IA   0.0.0.0/0   [110/2] via 172.12.34.3, 00:00:34, FastEthernet0/0
       1.0.0.0/32  is subnetted, 1 subnets
O IA     1.1.1.1   [110/66] via 172.12.34.3, 00:00:34, FastEthernet0/0
       2.0.0.0/32  is subnetted, 1 subnets
O IA     2.2.2.2   [110/66] via 172.12.34.3, 00:00:34, FastEthernet0/0
       3.0.0.0/32  is subnetted, 1 subnets
O IA     3.3.3.3   [110/2] via 172.12.34.3, 00:00:34, FastEthernet0/0
       172.12.0.0/16 is variably subnetted, 3 subnets, 2 masks
```

```
O IA     172.12.123.0/24 [110/65] via 172.12.34.3, 00:00:34, FastEthernet0/0

R4#ping 5.1.1.1
!!!!!
Success rate is 100 percent (5/5), round-trip min/avg/max = 64/65/68 ms

R4#ping 6.1.1.1
!!!!!
Success rate is 100 percent (5/5), round-trip min/avg/max = 64/66/68 ms

R4#ping 7.1.1.1
!!!!!
Success rate is 100 percent (5/5), round-trip min/avg/max = 64/65/68 ms
```

With that simple config, the size of the OSPF routing table has been cut nearly in half. The individual E2 routes have been replaced by a single default route, marked O*IA. The best news of all—the three external loopbacks can still be pinged!

Since the four nondefault interarea routes have the same next-hop IP address, we can take this one step further and make Area 34 a total stub. In OSPF total stub areas, all external and interarea routes are replaced with a single default route. One single addition to R3's config will accomplish this. Adding the *no-summary* option to the ABR of the stub area makes this happen by preventing LSA types 3, 4, and 5 from flooding the area.

The ABR is the only router that needs *no-summary*. In our lab, putting that command on R4 doesn't hurt anything, but it also doesn't shrink our routing table. Note the router doesn't tell you any of that (but I will).

```
R4(config-router)#area 34 stub no-summary

R4#show ip route ospf

Gateway of last resort is 172.12.34.3 to network 0.0.0.0

O*IA   0.0.0.0/0   [110/21] via 172.12.34.3, 00:00:09, FastEthernet0/0
       1.0.0.0/32  is subnetted, 1 subnets
O IA     1.1.1.1   [110/66] via 172.12.34.3, 00:00:09, FastEthernet0/0
       2.0.0.0/32  is subnetted, 1 subnets
O IA     2.2.2.2   [110/66] via 172.12.34.3, 00:00:09, FastEthernet0/0
       3.0.0.0/32  is subnetted, 1 subnets
O IA     3.3.3.3   [110/2] via 172.12.34.3, 00:00:09, FastEthernet0/0
       172.12.0.0/16 is variably subnetted, 3 subnets, 2 masks
O IA     172.12.123.0/24 [110/65] via 172.12.34.3, 00:00:09, FastEthernet0/0
```

Let's try it on R3 after removing the errant command on R4.

```
R4(config-router)#no area 34 stub no-summary
```

```
R3(config)#router ospf 1
R3(config-router)#area 34 stub ?
  no-ext-capability  Do not send domain specific capabilities into stub area
  no-summary         Do not send summary LSA into stub area
  <cr>

R3(config-router)#area 34 stub no-summary

R4#show ip route ospf

Gateway of last resort is 172.12.34.3 to network 0.0.0.0

O*IA 0.0.0.0/0 [110/21] via 172.12.34.3, 00:01:24, FastEthernet0/0
```

Now *that's* shrinkage, baby! The OSPF routing table has been taken all the way down to one default route. Can R4 still ping external and interarea destinations? Let's ping R2's loopback and one of the external loopbacks on R1 and find out!

```
R4#ping 2.2.2.2
!!!!!
Success rate is 100 percent (5/5), round-trip min/avg/max = 128/128/132 ms

R4#ping 5.1.1.1
!!!!!
Success rate is 100 percent (5/5), round-trip min/avg/max = 64/65/68 ms
```

A quick review of stub versus total stub areas:

With an OSPF stub area, your OSPF routing table can contain routes to networks in the same area (O), inter-area routes (O IA), and a default inter-area route to reach external destinations (O *IA).

A total stub area's OSPF routing table can contain only routes to other networks in the total stub area (O) and a single default route for all other routes (O*IA). If we add a network to Area 34 on R3 and advertise it via the *network* command, R4 will see it as an interarea route, and as such it will have a specific entry in the OSPF table.

```
R3(config-if)#router ospf 1
R3(config-router)#network 33.3.3.3 0.0.0.0 area 34

R4#show ip route ospf

Gateway of last resort is 172.12.34.3 to network 0.0.0.0

O*IA    0.0.0.0/0   [110/21] via 172.12.34.3, 00:07:38, FastEthernet0/0
      33.0.0.0/32   is subnetted, 1 subnets
O        33.3.3.3   [110/2] via 172.12.34.3, 00:00:06, FastEthernet0/0
```

As always, you can take a good idea too far. R2 only has several OSPF routes but only one possible next-hop address, so why not make it a stub?

```
        1.0.0.0/32   is subnetted, 1 subnets
O IA      1.1.1.1    [110/65] via 172.12.123.1, 01:39:50, Serial0/1/0
        3.0.0.0/32   is subnetted, 1 subnets
O IA      3.3.3.3    [110/65] via 172.12.123.3, 01:39:50, Serial0/1/0
        5.0.0.0/24   is subnetted, 1 subnets
O E2      5.1.1.0    [110/20] via 172.12.123.1, 00:44:14, Serial0/1/0
        6.0.0.0/24   is subnetted, 1 subnets
O E2      6.1.1.0    [110/20] via 172.12.123.1, 00:44:14, Serial0/1/0
        7.0.0.0/24   is subnetted, 1 subnets
O E2      7.1.1.0    [110/20] via 172.12.123.1, 00:44:14, Serial0/1/0
        33.0.0.0/32 is subnetted, 1 subnets
O IA      33.3.3.3 [110/65] via 172.12.123.3, 00:02:59, Serial0/1/0
        172.12.0.0/16 is variably subnetted, 3 subnets, 2 masks
O IA      172.12.34.0/24 [110/65] via 172.12.123.3, 00:30:01, Serial0/1/0
```

Here's why:

```
R2(config)#router ospf 1
R2(config-router)#area 0 stub
% OSPF: Backbone can not be configured as stub area
```

You can't make Area 0 a stub of any kind. I told you, and the router told you. Don't expect the CCNP Route exam to tell you! Now, here's a stub area type you might not believe exists...

Not-So-Stubby Stub Areas

I'm not kidding. An NSSA is a stub area that contains a limited number of external routes. An NSSA is the only stub area type allowed to use Type 7 LSAs. It's a highly specialized stub area type that you won't run into every day, but you will run into it.

Using the previous lab topology, I'll add another loopback to R3 and inject it into OSPF via *redistribute connected subnets.* (The 33.0.0.0 network from the end of the previous lab has been removed from the network.)

```
R3(config)#int loopback 14
R3(config-if)#ip address 14.1.1.1 255.255.255.0

R3(config-if)#router ospf 1
R3(config-router)#redis conn subnets
```

R1 will see the route as an E2 route...

```
R1#show ip route ospf
     2.0.0.0/3 is subnetted, 1 subnets
O IA    2.2.2.2  [110/782] via 172.12.123.2, 00:00:38, Serial1/0
     33.0.0.0/32  is subnetted, 1 subnets
O IA    3.3.3.3  [110/782] via 172.12.123.3, 00:00:38, Serial1/0
     172.12.0.0/24 is subnetted, 2 subnets
O IA    172.12.34.0 [110/782] via 172.12.123.3, 00:00:38, Serial1/0
     14.0.0.0/24 is subnetted, 1 subnets
O E2    14.1.1.0 [110/20] via 172.12.123.3, 00:00:38, Serial1/0
```

...but R4 will not, since our total stub area is still in place.

```
R4#show ip route ospf

Gateway of last resort is 172.12.34.3 to network 0.0.0.0

O*IA 0.0.0.0/0 [110/21] via 172.12.34.3, 00:17:55, FastEthernet0/0
```

We'll remove the stub area setting on R3 and R4 and then configure Area 34 as an NSSA.

```
R3(config)#router ospf 1
R3(config-router)#no area 34 stub
*Jun 8 17:03:16.727: %OSPF-5-ADJCHG: Process 1, Nbr 172.12.23.4 on FastEther
0/0 from FULL to DOWN, Neighbor Down: Adjacency forced to reset
R3(config-router)#area 34 nssa

R4(config)#router ospf 1
R4(config-router)#no area 34 stub
R4(config-router)#area 34 nssa

R4#show ip route ospf

Gateway of last resort is not set

      1.0.0.0/32  is subnetted, 1 subnets
O IA    1.1.1.1  [110/66] via 172.12.34.3, 00:00:10, FastEthernet0/0
      2.0.0.0/32  is subnetted, 1 subnets
O IA    2.2.2.2  [110/66] via 172.12.34.3, 00:00:10, FastEthernet0/0
      3.0.0.0/32  is subnetted, 1 subnets
O IA    3.3.3.3  [110/2] via 172.12.34.3, 00:00:10, FastEthernet0/0
     14.0.0.0/24  is subnetted, 1 subnets
O N2   14.1.1.0  [110/20] via 172.12.34.3, 00:00:10, FastEthernet0/0
     33.0.0.0/32  is subnetted, 1 subnets
O      33.3.3.3  [110/2] via 172.12.34.3, 00:00:10, FastEthernet0/0
     172.12.0.0/16 is variably subnetted, 3 subnets, 2 masks
O IA   172.12.123.0/24 [110/65] via 172.12.34.3, 00:00:10, FastEthernet0
```

R4 sees the new route as N2, an NSSA external route. Note there is no default route in a regular NSSA! Enabling the *no-summary* option on R3's NSSA statement gets that default route back while removing the specific O IA entries.

```
R3(config-router)#area 34 nssa no-summary

R4#show ip route ospf

Gateway of last resort is 172.12.34.3 to network 0.0.0.0

O*IA    0.0.0.0/0 [110/21] via 172.12.34.3, 00:00:07, FastEthernet0/0
     14.0.0.0/24 is subnetted, 1 subnets
O N2     14.1.1.0 [110/20] via 172.12.34.3, 00:05:40, FastEthernet0/0
```

Before we move to OSPF route summarization techniques, let's review the OSPF codes and route types while taking a closer look at some of the new route types we've met! We'll look at this network through the eyes of R4.

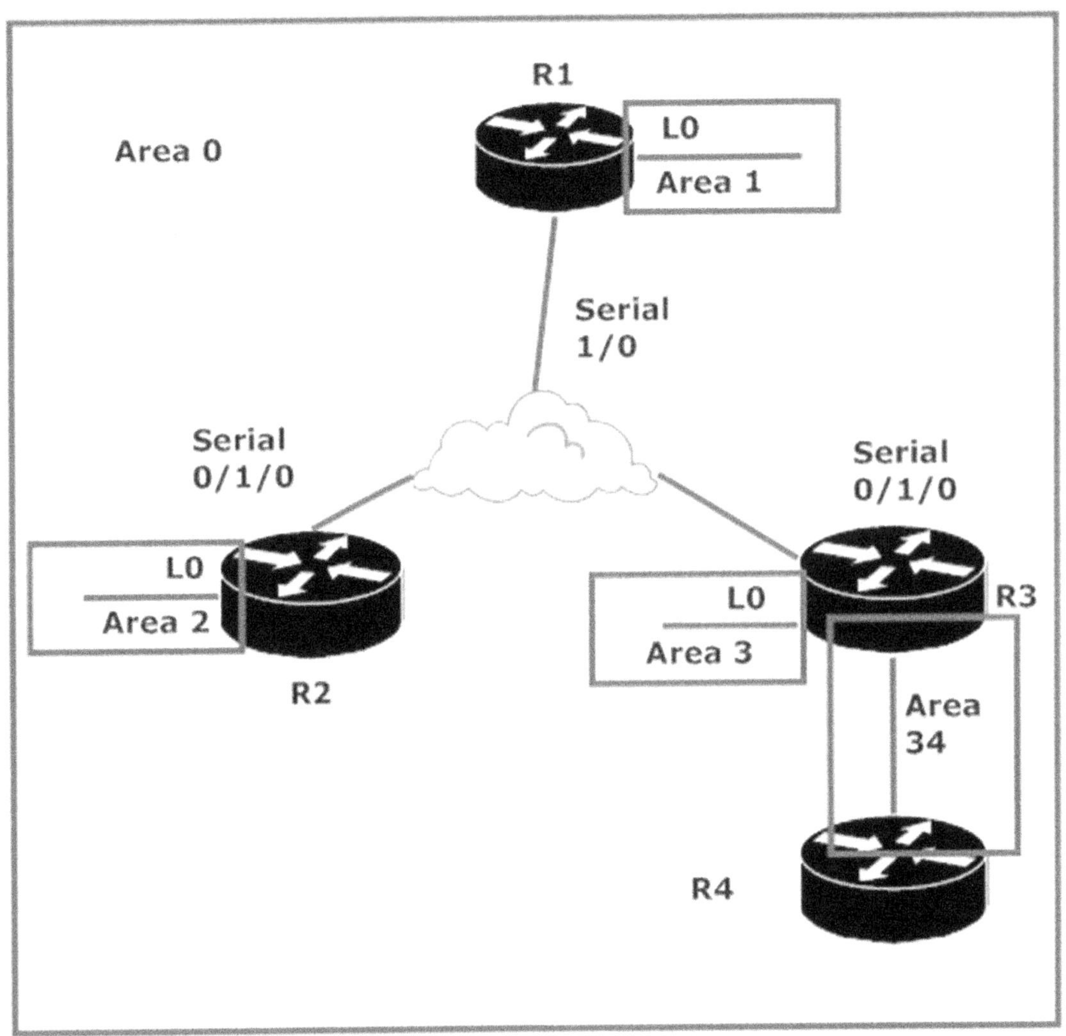

R4's OSPF routing table:

```
     1.0.0.0/32 is subnetted, 1 subnets
O IA    1.1.1.1 [110/66] via 172.12.34.3, 00:01:04, FastEthernet0/0
     2.0.0.0/32 is subnetted, 1 subnets
O IA    2.2.2.2 [110/66] via 172.12.34.3, 00:01:04, FastEthernet0/0
     3.0.0.0/32 is subnetted, 1 subnets
O IA    3.3.3.3 [110/2] via 172.12.34.3, 00:01:04, FastEthernet0/0
     33.0.0.0/32 is subnetted, 1 subnets
O       33.3.3.3 [110/2] via 172.12.34.3, 00:00:06, FastEthernet0/0
     172.12.0.0/16 is variably subnetted, 3 subnets, 2 masks
O IA    172.12.123.0/24 [110/65] via 172.12.34.3, 00:01:04, FastEthernet0/0
```

O indicates that the local router has an interface in the area containing the destination. R3's 33.3.3.0 /24 network is in Area 34, an area shared by an interface on R4, making it an OSPF internal route.

```
O       33.3.3.3 [110/2] via 172.12.34.3, 00:09:40, FastEthernet0/0
```

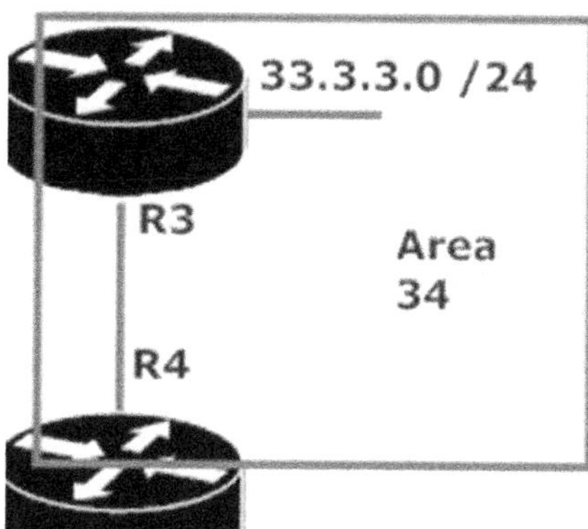

O IA indicates that the local router does not have an interface in the area containing the destination. R4's routing table is mostly O IA routes.

```
     1.0.0.0/32 is subnetted, 1 subnets
O IA    1.1.1.1 [110/66] via 172.12.34.3, 00:01:04, FastEthernet0/0
     2.0.0.0/32 is subnetted, 1 subnets
O IA    2.2.2.2 [110/66] via 172.12.34.3, 00:01:04, FastEthernet0/0
     3.0.0.0/32 is subnetted, 1 subnets
O IA    3.3.3.3 [110/2] via 172.12.34.3, 00:01:04, FastEthernet0/0
     33.0.0.0/32 is subnetted, 1 subnets
O       33.3.3.3 [110/2] via 172.12.34.3, 00:00:06, FastEthernet0/0
     172.12.0.0/16 is variably subnetted, 3 subnets, 2 masks
O IA    172.12.123.0/24 [110/65] via 172.12.34.3, 00:01:04, FastEthernet0/0
```

Let's reintroduce some external routes to our network by redistributing a new loopback on R1 into our OSPF domain.

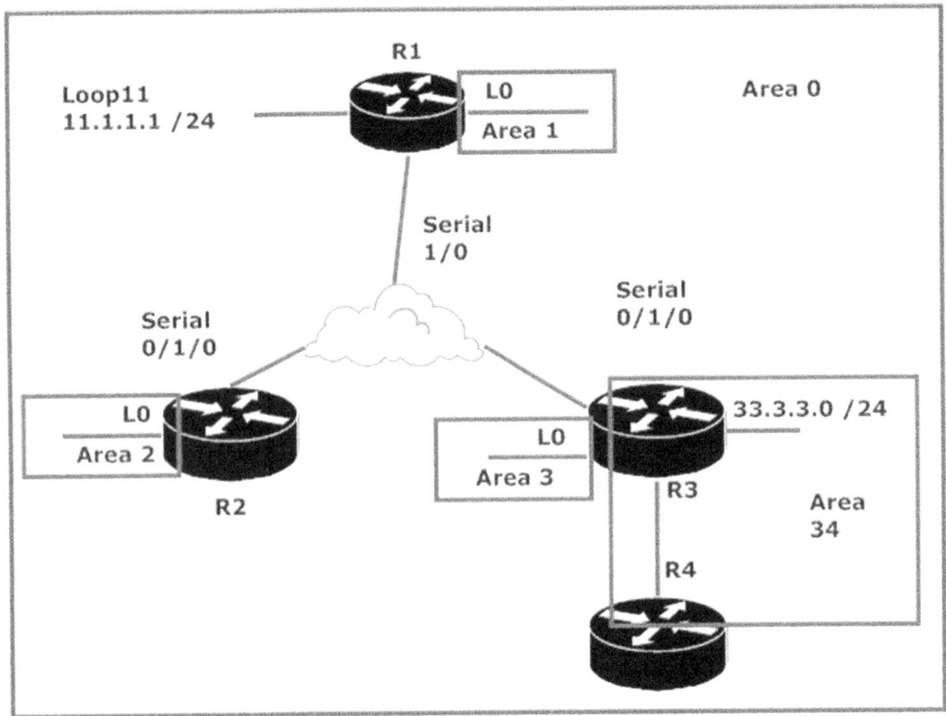


```
R1(config)#router ospf 1
R1(config-router)#redistribute connected subnets
```

The resulting route entry on R4:

```
R4#show ip route ospf | include E2
      E1 - OSPF external type 1, E2 - OSPF external type 2
O E2    11.1.1.0 [110/20] via 172.12.34.3, 00:02:34, FastEthernet0/0
```

The route table's codes include two types of external OSPF routes, helpfully named "E1" and "E2." The 11.1.1.0 /24 route is shown as an E2, so we can safely assume that's the default—but what the heck is the difference between E1 and E2 routes?

The difference is in the metrics. The metric of an E2 route reflects only the cost of the path between the ASBR and the destination network. The cost from R4 to R1 is not included in the metric! In this case, the default seed metric of 20 is the cost of the E2 route.

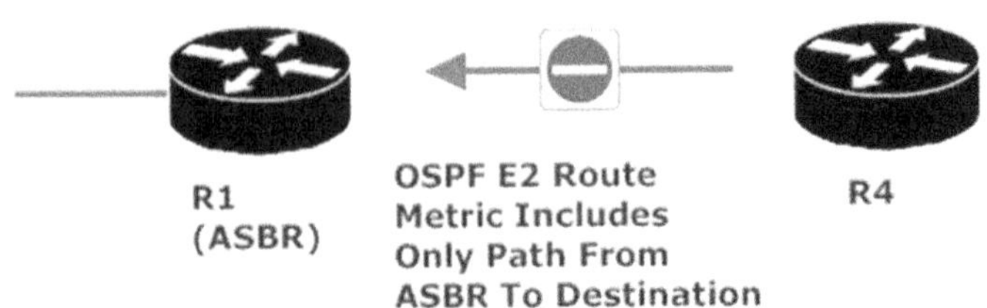

The metric of an E1 route reflects the cost of the *entire* path from the local router to the destination network.

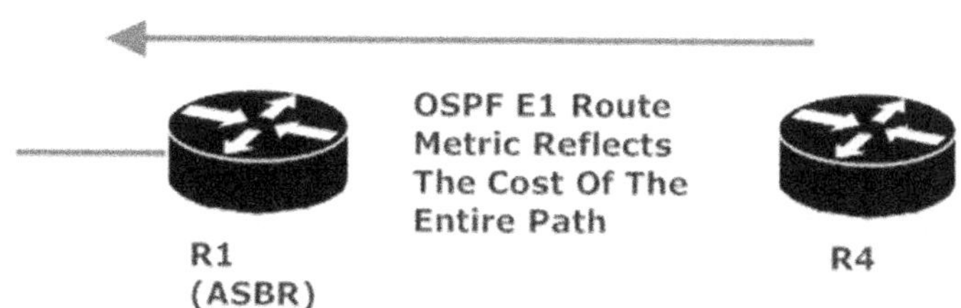

Personally, I like my route metrics to reflect the entire cost of the path, which means I prefer E1 routes. To have E1 routes rather than the default E2 routes, we need to go back to the point of redistribution and use the *metric-type* option during route redistribution. I'll remove the original route redistribution segment and then apply the same statement with the *metric-type* option.

```
R1(config)#router ospf 1
R1(config-router)#no redis conn subnets
R1(config-router)#redistribute connected subnets ?
  metric         Metric for redistributed routes
  metric-type    OSPF/IS-IS exterior metric type for redistributed routes
  route-map      Route map reference
  tag            Set tag for routes redistributed into OSPF
  <cr>

R1(config-router)#redistribute connected subnets metric-type ?
  1  Set OSPF External Type 1 metrics
  2  Set OSPF External Type 2 metrics

R1(config-router)#redistribute connected subnets metric-type 1 ?
  metric         Metric for redistributed routes
  route-map      Route map reference
  tag            Set tag for routes redistributed into OSPF
  <cr>

R1(config-router)#redistribute connected subnets metric-type 1
```

The result on R4 is an E1 route that shows the cost of the path from R4 all the way to the destination network.

```
O E1    11.1.1.0 [110/85] via 172.12.34.3, 00:01:10, FastEthernet0/0
```

There are two other OSPF external route types mentioned in the code table:

```
D - EIGRP, EX - EIGRP external, O - OSPF, IA - OSPF inter area
N1 - OSPF NSSA external type 1, N2 - OSPF NSSA external type 2
E1 - OSPF external type 1, E2 - OSPF external type 2
```

As you'd expect from the descriptions, N1 and N2 routes are found only in NSSAs. The difference between these two routes is the same as the difference between E1 and E2 routes, as N2 route metrics reflect only the cost from the ASBR to the destination, and N1 metrics show the cost of the path from the local route to the destination.

OSPF Router Types

There are several OSPF router types you should be able to identify, and we've seen two of those—the ABR and ASBR—in action throughout our labs. There are other classifications that we generally don't give the same level of attention, but since they may pop up on your CCNP Route exam, let's review them.

An OSPF internal router has all its interfaces in a single area. In our network, R4 is the only internal router. If we added a loopback to R4 and then put it into an area other than Area 34, R4 would no longer be an internal router.

Backbone routers have at least one interface in Area 0. In our network, every router except R4 is a backbone router.

Just as a router can be both an ABR and ASBR, an OSPF router can be an internal router and a backbone router at the same time, as shown here:

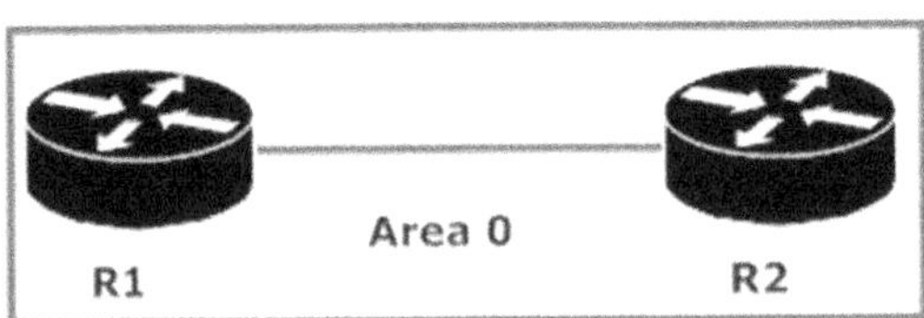

We've seen ABRs and ASBRs in action, but let's review them one more time. An Area Border Router is a router with at least one interface in Area 0 and another in a nonbackbone area. Throughout our labs, R1, R2, and R3 are all ABRs. All ABRs are backbone routers, but not all backbone routers are ABRs.

An ASBR is a router injecting routes into the OSPF domain via route redistribution. We performed route redistribution on R1 a couple of times, making that router an ASBR. To verify the ABR and ASBR status of the local router, run *show ip ospf.*

```
R1#show ip ospf
 Routing Process "ospf 1" with ID 172.12.123.1
 Start time: 02:01:03.214, Time elapsed: 00:55:10.023
 Supports only single TOS(TOS0) routes
 Supports opaque LSA
 Supports Link-local Signaling (LLS)
 Supports area transit capability
```

```
 It is an area border and autonomous system boundary router
 Redistributing External Routes from,
   connected, includes subnets in redistribution
```

To see what ABRs and ASBRs the local router knows of, run *show ip ospf border-routers*. The following output indicates that R2 sees R1 as both an ABR and ASBR and R3 as an ABR.

```
R2#show ip ospf border-routers

            OSPF Router with ID (172.12.123.2) (Process ID 1)


               Base Topology (MTID 0)

Internal Router Routing Table
Codes: i - Intra-area route, I - Inter-area route

i 172.12.123.1 [64] via 172.12.123.1, Serial0/1/0, ABR/ASBR, Area 0, SPF 7
i 3.3.3.3 [64] via 172.12.123.3, Serial0/1/0, ABR, Area 0, SPF 7
```

The LSA Types

Let's have a look at the LSA types with *show ip ospf database* on R3, starting with Type 1 LSAs.

```
R3#show ip ospf database

          OSPF Router with ID (3.3.3.3) (Process ID 1)

              Router Link States (Area 0)

Link ID      ADV Router     Age     Seq#          Checksum   Link count
1.1.1.1      1.1.1.1        34      0x80000002    0x007C31   1
2.2.2.2      2.2.2.2        34      0x80000002    0x009ED7   1
3.3.3.3      3.3.3.3        33      0x80000002    0x00600D   1
```

Type 1s ("Router Link States") are generated by each router for every area the router has a link in. These are flooded to a single area only. The name is the recipe, as LSA Type 1s contain the "router link states" for this particular router.

Type 2:

```
  Net Link States (Area 0)

Link ID        ADV Router     Age     Seq#          Checksum
172.12.123.1   1.1.1.1        34      0x80000001    0x0029BB
```

Type 2 LSAs are sent out only by DRs. The only Type 2 LSA in R3's OSPF database for Area 0 is from Advertising Router 1.1.1.1, the OSPF RID of R1.

LSA Types 1 and 2 are confined to a single area, which helps multi-area OSPF reduce the load on router resources. If you had only one large OSPF area, every router in the area would receive every single Type 1 and Type 2 LSA!

Type 3:

```
                Summary Net Link States (Area 0)

Link ID         ADV Router      Age     Seq#            Checksum
1.1.1.1         1.1.1.1         149     0x80000001      0x0047EC
2.2.2.2         2.2.2.2         132     0x80000001      0x00FA31
3.3.3.3         3.3.3.3         113     0x80000001      0x00AE75
33.3.3.3        3.3.3.3         113     0x80000001      0x0027DE
172.12.34.0     3.3.3.3         113     0x80000001      0x006CE8
```

These summary link advertisements are generated by ABRs and describe interarea routes. They summarize the networks from one area to another and are not flooded into a total stub area.

Type 4:

```
                Summary ASB Link States (Area 3)

Link ID         ADV Router      Age     Seq#            Checksum
1.1.1.1         3.3.3.3         28      0x80000001      0x007576
```

Type 4s are generated only by ABRs and describe the path to the ASBR. Type 4 LSAs are not flooded into a total stub area.

Type 5:

```
        Type-5 AS External Link States

Link ID         ADV Router      Age     Seq#            Checksum Tag
11.1.1.0        1.1.1.1         153     0x80000001      0x009F70 0
```

Type 5 LSAs describe links external to the OSPF domain. This link describes the network injected into the OSPF domain via route redistribution on R1, verified by the address listed as the advertising router. Type 5 LSAs are generated only by ASBRs, and they're flooded to all areas except stub and total stub areas.

Let's see the impact of a stub area on an OSPF database. After viewing R4's OSPF database, I'll make Area 34 a total stub.

```
R4#show ip ospf database

            OSPF Router with ID (172.12.34.4) (Process ID 1)

                Router Link States (Area 34)

Link ID         ADV Router      Age         Seq#            Checksum    Link count
3.3.3.3         3.3.3.3         40          0x80000008      0x00E535    2
172.12.34.4     172.12.34.4     39          0x80000008      0x00D3DC    1

                Net Link States (Area 34)

Link ID         ADV Router      Age         Seq#            Checksum
172.12.34.4     172.12.34.4     34          0x80000007      0x00305B

                Summary Net Link States (Area 34)

Link ID         ADV Router      Age         Seq#            Checksum
1.1.1.1         3.3.3.3         48          0x80000001      0x008D5E
2.2.2.2         3.3.3.3         48          0x80000001      0x005F88
3.3.3.3         3.3.3.3         48          0x80000001      0x00AE75
172.12.123.0    3.3.3.3         48          0x80000001      0x000EAE

                Summary ASB Link States (Area 34)

Link ID         ADV Router      Age         Seq#            Checksum
1.1.1.1         3.3.3.3         48          0x80000001      0x007576

                Type-5 AS External Link States

Link ID         ADV Router      Age         Seq#            Checksum    Tag
11.1.1.0        1.1.1.1         1284        0x80000001      0x009F70    0

R3(config)#router ospf 1
R3(config-router)#area 34 stub no-summary

R4(config)#router ospf 1
R4(config-router)#area 34 stub
```

R4 now has a much smaller OSPF database, with both Type 4 and Type 5 LSAs banished as a result of the total stub area configuration.

```
R4#show ip ospf database

            OSPF Router with ID (172.12.34.4) (Process ID 1)

                Router Link States (Area 34)

Link ID         ADV Router      Age     Seq#            Checksum  Link count
3.3.3.3         3.3.3.3         24      0x8000000A      0x00FF1B  2
172.12.34.4     172.12.34.4     23      0x8000000A      0x00EDC2  1

                Net Link States (Area 34)

Link ID         ADV Router      Age     Seq#            Checksum
172.12.34.4     172.12.34.4     23      0x80000009      0x004A41

                Summary Net Link States (Area 34)

Link ID         ADV Router      Age     Seq#            Checksum
0.0.0.0         3.3.3.3         39      0x80000001      0x0057DA
```

This is a relatively small OSPF database, but it still allows R4 to reach every destination in our network. Configuring Area 34 as a total stub makes the OSPF database smaller and also shrinksshrinking the OSPF route table. That's another way multi-area OSPF makes life easier on the router's memory and CPU!

Not shown in these databases are LSA types 6 and 7. Type 6 LSAs are a specialty LSA type generated only by routers using multicast extensions to OSPF (MOSPF), while Type 7s are generated only by an ASBR and sent into a not-so-stub stub area.

NSSAs act as stub areas, but some of the more-specific routes are advertised, rather than just a default route. Type 7 LSAs are flooded throughout the NSSA, but they don't get to leave! Instead, they're converted to Type 5 LSAs and are then sent out of the NSSA.

Following is a summary of which router types send which LSA types:

- LSA Type 1: Sent by all routers.
- LSA Type 2: Sent by DRs only.
- LSA Type 3, 4: Sent by ABRs only.
- LSA Types 5, 7: Sent by ASBRs only.
- LSA Type 6: Reserved for MOSPF.

Let's move forward to route summarization!

OSPF Route Summarization Techniques

We always want our routing tables complete and concise. OSPF stub and total stub areas help us accomplish that goal by replacing external and interarea routes with default routes, but we know it's not always possible to configure stub and total stub areas. Area 0 can't be a stub or total stub, and neither can an area serving as a transit area for a virtual link.

We can further shrink our routing table via route summarization. There are two ways to perform this summarization in OSPF, and the method you choose is dependent on the OSPF router types in use. (OSPF performs no autosummarization.)

Our first route summarization lab will use our familiar hub-and-spoke network. Our hub router, R1, has four loopback networks in Area 1. The IP addresses for those four loopbacks are 8.1.1.1, 9.1.1.1, 10.1.1.1, and 11.1.1.1, all with /8 masks.

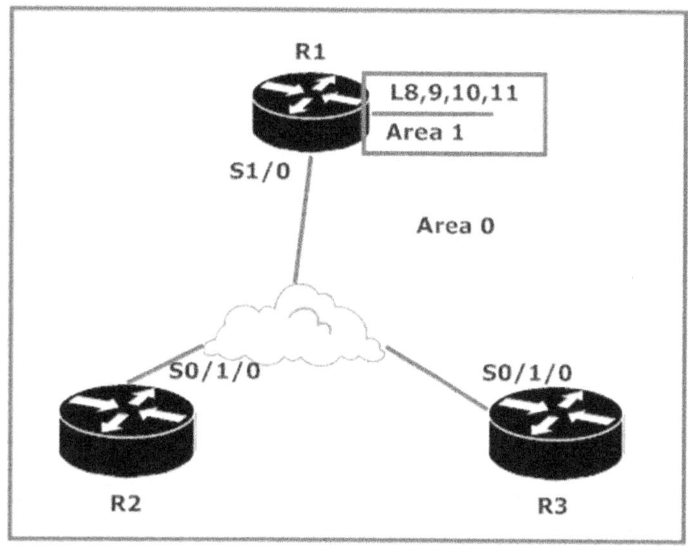


```
R1(config)#router ospf 1
R1(config-router)#network 8.0.0.0 0.255.255.255 area 1
R1(config-router)#network 9.0.0.0 0.255.255.255 area 1
R1(config-router)#network 10.0.0.0 0.255.255.255 area 1
R1(config-router)#network 11.0.0.0 0.255.255.255 area 1
```

The new routes appear on R2 and R3. Since the tables are identical, I'll show you only R2's table throughout this lab.

```
R2#show ip route ospf

      8.0.0.0/32 is subnetted, 1 subnets
O IA     8.1.1.1 [110/65] via 172.12.123.1, 00:00:54, Serial0/1/0
      9.0.0.0/32 is subnetted, 1 subnets
O IA     9.1.1.1 [110/65] via 172.12.123.1, 00:00:54, Serial0/1/0
```

```
      10.0.0.0/32 is subnetted, 1 subnets
O IA     10.1.1.1 [110/65] via 172.12.123.1, 00:00:54, Serial0/1/0
      11.0.0.0/32 is subnetted, 1 subnets
O IA     11.1.1.1 [110/65] via 172.12.123.1, 00:00:54, Serial0/1/0
```

Nothing wrong with this table, but we can make it better, stronger, and faster by configuring a summary route. Before concerning ourselves with the exact command for this situation, we better come up with the summary! (We can't even consider a stub or total stub here since the adjacencies involved are through Area 0.)

You know the drill—just convert the addresses to binary and identify the common bits. When the bits from left to right are no longer common, stop right there, and you have your summary route and mask. We only need to write out the first octet of each address for this summarization:

8 **000010**00 (the last three octets are all zeroes for all four routes)
9 **000010**01
10 **000010**10
11 **000010**11

The common bits end after the sixth bit, since the first two addresses have a zero for the seventh bit and the last two addresses have a one in that slot. Just add the numbers in bold, and you have your summary route, which in this case is 00001000 for the first octet and all zeroes for the last three. That gives us 8.0.0.0 for the summary route, but we need a mask to go with that route! For the mask, just put a one for each common bit and a zero for all others. Since the first six bits are the common bits for these four routes, the mask is 11111100 00000000 00000000 00000000, or 252.0.0.0.

Now that we have our summary route and mask, we need to apply it! When you're configuring OSPF route summarization on an ABR, use the area range command. IOS Help lets us know this command can only be used on ABRs, but the CCNP Route exam will not likely be as kind!

The area number in this command is the area containing the routes to be summarized, not the area through which the summary route is advertised. Since all four routes are in Area 1, that's the number we'll use in the command.

```
R1(config)#router ospf 1
R1(config-router)#area 0 ?
  authentication  Enable authentication
  default-cost    Set the summary default-cost of a NSSA/stub area
  filter-list     Filter networks between OSPF areas
  nssa            Specify a NSSA area
  range           Summarize routes matching address/mask (border routers only)
  sham-link       Define a sham link and its parameters
  stub            Specify a stub area
  virtual-link    Define a virtual link and its parameters
```

```
R1(config-router)#area 1 range ?
  A.B.C.D IP address to match

R1(config-router)#area 1 range 8.0.0.0 ?
  A.B.C.D IP mask for address

R1(config-router)#area 1 range 8.0.0.0 252.0.0.0
```

R2 now has the summary route in its OSPF routing table and can ping all four loopbacks using that summary route.

```
R2#show ip route ospf

Gateway of last resort is not set

O IA 8.0.0.0/6 [110/65] via 172.12.123.1, 00:02:08, Serial0/1/0

R2#ping 8.1.1.1
!!!!!
Success rate is 100 percent (5/5), round-trip min/avg/max = 64/65/68 ms

R2#ping 9.1.1.1
!!!!!
Success rate is 100 percent (5/5), round-trip min/avg/max = 64/65/68 ms

R2#ping 10.1.1.1
!!!!!
Success rate is 100 percent (5/5), round-trip min/avg/max = 64/65/68 ms

R2#ping 11.1.1.1
!!!!!
Success rate is 100 percent (5/5), round-trip min/avg/max = 64/66/68 ms
```

We can also summarize routes as they're being redistributed into OSPF. Let's make it happen with four new loopbacks on R1—4.1.1.1, 5.1.1.1, 6.1.1.1, and 7.1.1.1, all with 32-bit masks. They'll be redistributed into OSPF with *redis connected subnets.*

```
R1(config)#router ospf 1
R1(config-router)#redis conn subnets
```

All four routes show up on R2 as OSPF E2 routes.

```
R2#show ip route ospf

      4.0.0.0/32 is subnetted, 1 subnets
O E2     4.1.1.1 [110/20] via 172.12.123.1, 00:00:27, Serial0/1/0
      5.0.0.0/32 is subnetted, 1 subnets
```

```
O E2     5.1.1.1 [110/20] via 172.12.123.1, 00:00:27, Serial0/1/0
      6.0.0.0/32 is subnetted, 1 subnets
O E2     6.1.1.1 [110/20] via 172.12.123.1, 00:00:27, Serial0/1/0
      7.0.0.0/32 is subnetted, 1 subnets
O E2     7.1.1.1 [110/20] via 172.12.123.1, 00:00:27, Serial0/1/0
O IA  8.0.0.0/6 [110/65] via 172.12.123.1, 00:11:11, Serial0/1/0
```

For the summarization, just break those four new addresses down into binary and identify the common bits.

4 **000001**00
5 **000001**01
6 **000001**10
7 **000001**11

The common bits end after bit six. Add up the value of those first six bits, and we have 4.0.0.0. Setting the first six bits to one in our mask gives us 11111100 00000000 00000000 00000000, or 252.0.0.0 in dotted decimal. Use the *summary-address* command to apply the summary route and mask, and you're gold!

```
R1(config)#router ospf 1
R1(config-router)#summary-address ?
  A.B.C.D IP summary address

R1(config-router)#summary-address 4.0.0.0 ?
  A.B.C.D Summary mask

R1(config-router)#summary-address 4.0.0.0 252.0.0.0
```

The result on R2:

```
R2#show ip route ospf

O E2   4.0.0.0/6 [110/20] via 172.12.123.1, 00:00:17, Serial0/1/0
O IA   8.0.0.0/6 [110/65] via 172.12.123.1, 00:18:25, Serial0/1/0

R2#ping 4.1.1.1
!!!!!
Success rate is 100 percent (5/5), round-trip min/avg/max = 64/65/68 ms

R2#ping 5.1.1.1
!!!!!
Success rate is 100 percent (5/5), round-trip min/avg/max = 64/65/68 ms

R2#ping 6.1.1.1
!!!!!
Success rate is 100 percent (5/5), round-trip min/avg/max = 64/66/68 ms
```

```
R2#ping 7.1.1.1
!!!!!
Success rate is 100 percent (5/5), round-trip min/avg/max = 64/65/68 ms
```

Behold the power of route summarization! Without it, our table has eight routes; with it, there are only two, and we can still ping every destination network.

Time to accept the challenge of a brand new world—BGP!

Chapter 6: BGP

The study of law is something new and unfamiliar to most of you, unlike any other schooling you have ever known before.

—Charles Kingsfield, Law Professor at One of the World's Great Colleges, *The Paper Chase*

Same goes for the study of BGP.

—Chris Bryant, Bulldog, Thrown out of Several of the World's Great Colleges

Here's the deal with BGP—it's unlike anything you've studied to this point. The rules are different, the concepts are different, everything's different. BGP throws a lot of people for a loop the first time they see it, and that included me. The key to initial BGP success is to take one concept at a time, then one attribute at a time, and before you know it, you've mastered the fundamentals of BGP. (For those of you with one eye on the CCIE, this is some of the most important studying you'll do.)

The first natural question: What the heck *is* BGP, anyway? Here's one definition, courtesy of Wikipedia:

"An internet protocol that allows groups of routers (called autonomous systems) to share routing information so that efficient, loop-free routes can be established. BGP is commonly used within and between Internet Service Providers (ISPs)."

That definition sounded like EIGRP until we got to the second sentence! Both EIGRP and BGP use autonomous systems, and both protocols use that term to refer to a logical group of routers. The difference comes in where BGP fits in the big scheme of things. BGP is an Exterior Gateway Protocol that runs between ISPs, where EIGRP is an Interior Gateway Protocol that runs in the networks connected by ISPs.

BGP shares other characteristics with EIGRP:

- BGP supports VLSM and summarization.

- BGP will send full updates when routers initially become neighbors and after that will send only partial updates reflecting the latest network changes.
- BGP creates neighbor relationships before exchanging routes, and keepalives are sent to keep the adjacencies alive. If those keepalives disappear, the adjacency is gone!

BGP neighbors will exchange *much* more extensive information about networks than our IGPs do. The additional BGP path information comes in the form of *attributes*, and these path attributes are contained in the updates sent by BGP routers. Mastering these attributes are the key to success with BGP, and that starts with knowing which attributes are well known and which are optional.

Before we dive into our labs and see these attributes in action, let's take a quick look at some general Cisco BGP best practices regarding when BGP should and shouldn't be used.

When BGP *should* be used:

- Your company is connecting to more than one AS or ISP. Decisions on the best links to use can be made by utilizing BGP path attributes.
- The routing policy of your organization and your ISP differ.
- Your company is an ISP. When traffic from other autonomous systems use your AS as a transit domain, BGP will definitely be needed.

In short, if your AS has more than one connection to other ASs, or other ASs are using your AS as a transit domain, you will definitely be running BGP.

There are also circumstances that dictate when BGP should *not* be used:

- When there's a single connection to the Internet or to another AS, and no redundant link exists.
- When you don't care which path is used to reach a route in another AS.
- When router resources are limited (memory and CPU, that is).
- When there's a low-bandwidth connection between multiple ASs. In this situation, static and default routing may be a better choice.

With those guidelines in mind, let's get a BGP adjacency started!

The BGP Peering Process

Like TCP, BGP is connection-oriented ("reliable"). An underlying connection between two BGP speakers is established before routing information is actually exchanged. This connection takes place on TCP port 179, an excellent port to leave unblocked by access lists (or anything else!). Once the connection is established, the BGP speakers exchange routes and synch their tables. After this initial exchange, a BGP speaker will send further updates only upon a change in the network.

BGP speakers do not have to be in the same AS in order to become neighbors or exchange routes, as we'll see!

BGP adjacencies are also called "peerings." A BGP peer in the same AS as the local router is an Internal BGP (iBGP) peer...

...and a BGP peer in another AS is an External BGP (eBGP) peer.

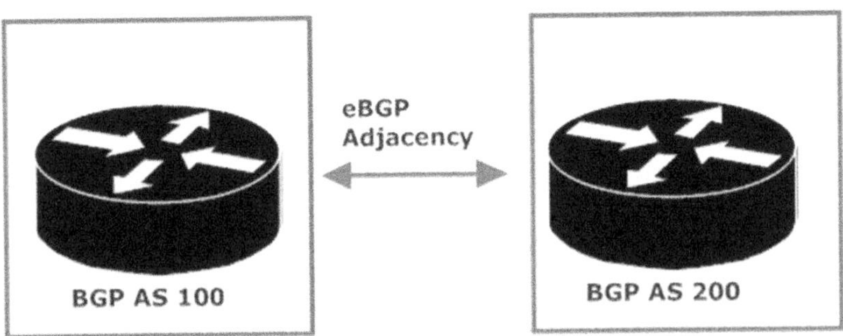

The "i" and "e" make huge differences in BGP behavior, so watch your internal versus external adjacencies! Cisco recommends that eBGP peers be directly connected; iBGP peers are not required to be so connected and generally aren't.

We'll start our first lab with the *router bgp* command, followed by a *neighbor* command to identify this BGP speaker's potential neighbors. Using IOS Help after *neighbor* gives you a hint that BGP is a bit more complex than EIGRP or OSPF:

```
R1(config)#router bgp ?
<1-65535> Autonomous system number

R1(config)#router bgp 100
R1(config-router)#neighbor ?
```

```
  A.B.C.D Neighbor address
  WORD Neighbor tag
  X:X:X:X::X Neighbor IPv6 address

R1(config-router)#neighbor 172.12.123.2 ?
  activate                  Enable the Address Family for this Neighbor
  advertise-map             specify route-map for conditional advertisement
  advertisement-interval    Minimum interval between sending BGP routing update
  allowas-in                Accept as-path with my AS present in it
  capability                Advertise capability to the peer
  default-originate         Originate default route to this neighbor
  description               Neighbor specific description
  disable-connected-check   One-hop away EBGP peer using loopback address
  distribute-list           Filter updates to/from this neighbor
  dmzlink-bw                Propagate the DMZ link bandwidth
  ebgp-multihop             Allow EBGP neighbors not on directly connected
                            networks
  fall-over                 session fall on peer route lost
  filter-list               Establish BGP filters
  inherit                   Inherit a template
  local-as                  Specify a local-as number
  maximum-prefix            Maximum number of prefixes accepted from this peer
  next-hop-self             Disable the next hop calculation for this neighbor
  next-hop-unchanged        Propagate the iBGP paths's next hop unchanged for
                            this neighbor
  password                  Set a password
  peer-group                Member of the peer-group
  prefix-list               Filter updates to/from this neighbor
  remote-as                 Specify a BGP neighbor
  remove-private-as         Remove private AS number from outbound updates
  route-map                 Apply route map to neighbor
  route-reflector-client    Configure a neighbor as Route Reflector client
  send-community            Send Community attribute to this neighbor
  shutdown                  Administratively shut down this neighbor
  soft-reconfiguration      Per neighbor soft reconfiguration
  timers                    BGP per neighbor timers
  translate-update          Translate Update to MBGP format
  transport                 Transport options
  ttl-security              BGP ttl security check
  unsuppress-map            Route-map to selectively unsuppress suppressed routes
  update-source             Source of routing updates
  version                   Set the BGP version to match a neighbor
  weight                    Set default weight for routes from this neighbor
```

Do not panic! We don't need to know them all for the CCNP Route exam, and the key to learning the ones we need to know? Mastering one at a time. It's that simple.

We'll begin our mastery by configuring R1 and R3 as eBGP peers, placing R1 into AS 100 and R3 into AS 200. The IP addresses in use in this lab are from the 172.12.123.0/24 subnet.

```
R1(config-router)#neighbor 172.12.123.2
% Incomplete command.

R1(config-router)#neighbor 172.12.123.3 remote-as ?
<1-65535> AS of remote neighbor

R1(config-router)#neighbor 172.12.123.3 remote-as 200
```

Almost all *neighbor* options we saw earlier are optional, but *remote-as* is required.

To verify BGP adjacencies, run *show ip bgp neighbor*. I'm showing you only the first few lines of this output—for now.

```
R1#show ip bgp neighbor
BGP neighbor is 172.12.123.3, remote AS 200, external link
  BGP version 4, remote router ID 0.0.0.0
  BGP state = Active
  Last read 00:01:02, last write 00:01:02, hold time is 180, keepalive interval
is 60 seconds
```

The output here can be a little misleading the first time around. The first line says a BGP neighbor is at 172.12.123.3, it's in AS 200, and it's an external link. So far, so good—but what about that BGP state of *Active*? We know from our EIGRP studies that "active" isn't always good. Is it good here?

Actually, it's not. The BGP state *Active* indicates a BGP peer connection that does not yet fully exist. Let's have a look at all the BGP states before continuing with this lab.

Idle is the initial state of a BGP peering. Should you note a connection that went to *Idle* and stayed there, check these values:

- Make sure the IP address in the neighbor statement is the correct address to use.
- Be sure the local router knows how to get to that particular IP address.

Connect follows *Idle*. In *Connect* state, a TCP connection request has been sent, but a response has not yet been received. If the TCP connection completes, BGP will move to *OpenSent*. If the connection does not complete, the state goes to *Active*.

Active indicates the BGP speaker is continuing to create a peering with the intended neighbor. Basically, this is the halfway point of the connection. The local router has successfully sent a BGP Open packet to the potential neighbor, but hasn't heard anything in return. As with Idle, there's nothing wrong with this state unless your connection stays there. In that case, check the remote router's neighbor statement and make sure the AS numbers are correct. (You'd be surprised how often wrong AS numbers are the reason for a peering not forming.)

OpenSent indicates the BGP speaker has received an *Open* message from the peer. In this state, BGP determines whether the peer is in the same AS (iBGP) or a different AS (eBGP).

OpenConfirm state has the BGP speaker waiting for a keepalive. If one is received, the state moves to *Established*, and the peering is complete. It's in the *Established* state that update packets are finally exchanged.

We know the reason the peering between our two routers hasn't completed, so let's complete the config and see if that does the trick!

```
R3(config)#router bgp 200
R3(config-router)#neighbor 172.12.123.1 remote-as 100

*Jun 12 13:52:01.835: %BGP-5-ADJCHANGE: neighbor 172.12.123.1 Up
```

Looks good! Let's verify!

```
R3#sho ip bgp neighbor 172.12.123.1
BGP neighbor is 172.12.123.1, remote AS 100, external link
  BGP version 4, remote router ID 1.1.1.1
  BGP state = Established, up for 00:01:37
```

Looks even better! Our neighbor relationship is *Established* and has been up for about a minute and a half. Let's add an iBGP peering to the mix while bringing R2 into the picture. We'll also see what happens if we try to create a peering between the local router and, well, the local router!

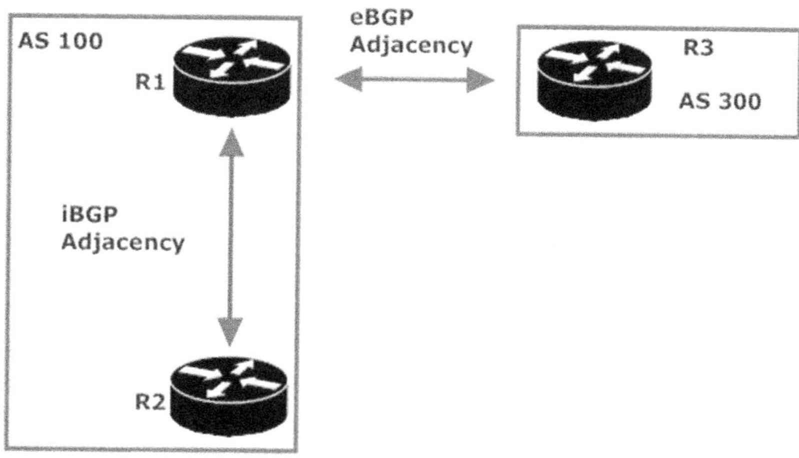

```
R1(config)#router bgp 100
R1(config-router)#neighbor 172.12.123.1 remote-as 100
% Cannot configure the local system as neighbor
R1(config-router)#oops! (Note from Chris, not an IOS command)
                    ^
% Invalid input detected at '^' marker.

R1(config-router)#neighbor 172.12.123.2 remote-as 100

R2(config)#router bgp 100
R2(config-router)#neighbor 172.12.123.1 remote-as 100
*Jun 12 14:12:39.943: %SYS-5-CONFIG_I: Configured from console by console
*Jun 12 14:12:40.363: %BGP-5-ADJCHANGE: neighbor 172.12.123.1 Up
```

With multiple adjacencies on R1, along with multiple ASs being involved, let's use a different command to verify the BGP peerings.

```
R1#show ip bgp summary
BGP router identifier 1.1.1.1, local AS number 100
BGP table version is 1, main routing table version 1

Neighbor        V  AS   MsgRcvd  MsgSent  TblVer  InQ  OutQ  Up/Down   State/PfxRcd
172.12.123.2    4  100        5        5       1    0     0  00:01:26             0
172.12.123.3    4  200       13       12       1    0     0  00:08:43             0
```

You get a lot less information with *show ip bgp summary*, but I do like this one for a quick adjacency check. The only values we're concerned with in this output right now are *neighbor, AS*, and *Up/Down*. Everything looks good so far!

Using Loopbacks for BGP Adjacencies

We used the IP addresses on R1 and R3's physical interfaces to create our first eBGP adjacency. Nothing wrong with that, but we're more likely to use IP addresses from loopback interfaces for such an adjacency. Those physical interfaces can go down for a number of reasons, but the only way a logical interface goes down is if someone intentionally deletes it or the entire router is unavailable—and in that case you have much bigger problems than lost adjacencies!

Loopback interfaces are not considered directly connected even if they share a common subnet. You'll need the *ebgp-multihop* command when configuring eBGP adjacencies with addresses that aren't on the same subnet. When those addresses are on loopback interfaces, you'll also need the *update-source loopback* command.

If you use loopback addresses for eBGP adjacencies, you may need to configure a static route on each router that points to the remote router's loopback. If your local router doesn't know how to get to the address specified by *neighbor*, we're pretty much stuck before we begin!

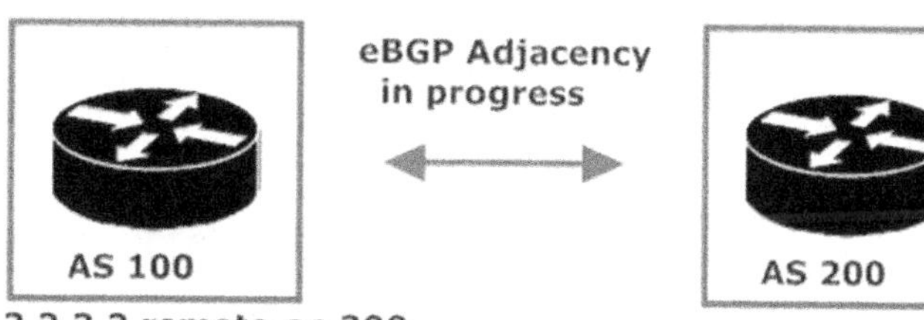

Let's drive all these concepts home by creating an adjacency between R1 and R3 using their respective loopback interfaces. The previous BGP configurations have been removed.

```
R1(config)#router bgp 100
R1(config-router)#neighbor 3.3.3.3 ?
  activate                  Enable the Address Family for this Neighbor
  advertise-map             specify route-map for conditional advertisement
  advertisement-interval    Minimum interval between sending BGP routing
                            updates
  allowas-in                Accept as-path with my AS present in it
  capability                Advertise capability to the peer
  default-originate         Originate default route to this neighbor
  description               Neighbor specific description
  disable-connected-check   One-hop away EBGP peer using loopback address
  distribute-list           Filter updates to/from this neighbor
  dmzlink-bw                Propagate the DMZ link bandwidth
  ebgp-multihop             Allow EBGP neighbors not on directly connected
                            networks
  fall-over                 session fall on peer route lost
  filter-list               Establish BGP filters
  inherit                   Inherit a template
  local-as                  Specify a local-as number
  maximum-prefix            Maximum number of prefixes accepted from this
                            peer
  next-hop-self             Disable the next hop calculation for this neighbor
  next-hop-unchanged        Propagate the iBGP paths's next hop unchanged for
                            this neighbor
  password                  Set a password
  peer-group                Member of the peer-group
  prefix-list               Filter updates to/from this neighbor
  remote-as                 Specify a BGP neighbor
  remove-private-as         Remove private AS number from outbound updates
  route-map                 Apply route map to neighbor
  route-reflector-client    Configure a neighbor as Route Reflector client
  send-community            Send Community attribute to this neighbor
  shutdown                  Administratively shut down this neighbor
```

```
  soft-reconfiguration       Per neighbor soft reconfiguration
  timers                     BGP per neighbor timers
  translate-update           Translate Update to MBGP format
  transport                  Transport options
  ttl-security               BGP ttl security check
  unsuppress-map             Route-map to selectively unsuppress suppressed
                             routes
  update-source              Source of routing updates
  version                    Set the BGP version to match a neighbor
  weight                     Set default weight for routes from this neighbor

R1(config-router)#neighbor 3.3.3.3 remote-as 200
R1(config-router)#neighbor 3.3.3.3 ebgp-multihop ?
<1-255> maximum hop count
<cr>

R1(config-router)#neighbor 3.3.3.3 ebgp-multihop 2
R1(config-router)#neighbor 3.3.3.3 update-source ?
  Async                Async interface
  BVI                  Bridge-Group Virtual Interface
  CDMA-Ix              CDMA Ix interface
  CTunnel              CTunnel interface
  Dialer               Dialer interface
  FastEthernet         FastEthernet IEEE 802.3
  Lex                  Lex interface
  Loopback             Loopback interface
  MFR                  Multilink Frame Relay bundle interface
  Multilink            Multilink-group interface
  Null                 Null interface
  Port-channel         Ethernet Channel of interfaces
  Serial               Serial
  Tunnel               Tunnel interface
  Vif                  PGM Multicast Host interface
  Virtual-PPP          Virtual PPP interface
  Virtual-Template     Virtual Template interface
  Virtual-TokenRing    Virtual TokenRing

R1(config-router)#neighbor 3.3.3.3 update-source loopback0

R3(config)#router bgp 200
R3(config-router)#neighbor 1.1.1.1 remote-as 100
R3(config-router)#neighbor 1.1.1.1 ebgp-multihop 2
R3(config-router)#neighbor 1.1.1.1 update-source loopback0
```

The *remote-as* looks good, the *ebgp-multihop* command is in place, and the *update-source* command is there as well. How about the adjacency?

```
R3#show ip bgp summ
BGP router identifier 3.3.3.3, local AS number 200
BGP table version is 1, main routing table version 1

Neighbor  V   AS  MsgRcvd  MsgSent   TblVer  InQ   OutQ  Up/Down   State/PfxRcd
1.1.1.1    4  100        0        0        1    0      0  never     Idle
R3#
BRYANT _ ADV _ 1#1
R1#show ip bgp summ
BGP router identifier 1.1.1.1, local AS number 100
BGP table version is 1, main routing table version 1

Neighbor  V   AS  MsgRcvd  MsgSent   TblVer  InQ   OutQ  Up/Down   State/PfxRcd
3.3.3.3    4  200        0        0        0    0      0  never     Active
```

One's *Active*, one's *Idle,* and neither is *Established.* The problem is that neither router has a route to the loopback address on the remote router. Let's put those static routes in place and see what happens.

```
R1(config)#ip route 3.3.3.3 255.255.255.255 172.12.123.3

R3(config)#ip route 1.1.1.1 255.255.255.255 172.12.123.1
```

A few seconds later, on R3:

```
*Jun 12 16:58:53.114: %BGP-5-ADJCHANGE: neighbor 1.1.1.1 Up
```

Looks good:

```
R1#show ip bgp summ
BGP router identifier 1.1.1.1, local AS number 100
BGP table version is 1, main routing table version 1

Neighbor  V   AS  MsgRcvd  MsgSent   TblVer  InQ   OutQ  Up/Down   State/PfxRcd
3.3.3.3    4  200        6        6        1    0      0  00:02:46  0


R3#show ip bgp summ
BGP router identifier 3.3.3.3, local AS number 200
BGP table version is 1, main routing table version 1

Neighbor  V   AS  MsgRcvd  MsgSent   TblVer  InQ   OutQ  Up/Down   State/PfxRcd
1.1.1.1    4  100        6        7        1    0      0  00:02:52
```

Looks even better! Our adjacency is in place, and we're ready to start advertising some routes!

Advertising Routes With BGP

We'll use the *network* command in BGP, but not in quite the same fashion as we do with OSPF and EIGRP. The command will look the same, but where IGPs identify the interfaces to be enabled with the protocol in question, BGP uses this command to identify the networks to be advertised by BGP.

The network specified by the BGP *network* command must be an *exact* match for a network contained in the IP routing table, and that includes the mask, should you include it. Using the mask in the BGP *network* command is not required, but it's highly recommended. If you're called upon to troubleshoot a BGP configuration and that config is missing the masks on the *network* statements, that's likely the issue. Use the masks, or you'll end up with only the classful networks.

Let's get this lab started! We're using the adjacencies we just built.

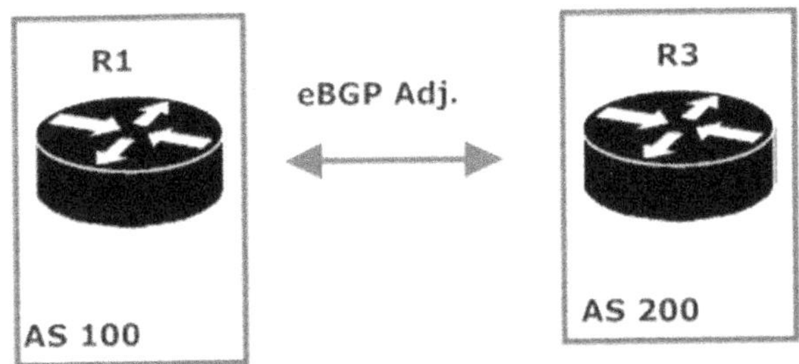

We'll advertise R3's loopback via BGP and then check out that same router's BGP route table.

```
R3(config)#router bgp 200
R3(config-router)#network ?
  A.B.C.D   Network number

R3(config-router)#network 3.3.3.3 ?
  backdoor    Specify a BGP backdoor route
  mask        Network mask
  route-map   Route-map to modify the attributes
  <cr>

R3(config-router)#network 3.3.3.3 mask ?
  A.B.C.D   Network mask

R3(config-router)#network 3.3.3.3 mask 255.255.255.255

R3#show ip bgp
BGP table version is 2, local router ID is 3.3.3.3
```

```
Status codes: s suppressed, d damped, h history, * valid, > best, i - internal,
              r RIB-failure, S Stale, m multipath, b backup-path, x best-external
Origin codes: i - IGP, e - EGP, ? - incomplete

   Network          Next Hop            Metric  LocPrf Weight  Path
*> 3.3.3.3/32       0.0.0.0                  0          32768  i
```

Note the combination of an asterisk and arrowhead (*>) next to the route. In BGP, for the route to be usable, you must see both the symbol representing "valid" and the one representing "best." Let's see how R1 sees that route, if at all:

```
R1#show ip bgp
BGP table version is 4, local router ID is 1.1.1.1
Status codes: s suppressed, d damped, h history, * valid, > best, i - internal,
r RIB-failure, S Stale
Origin codes: i - IGP, e - EGP, ? - incomplete

   Network          Next Hop            Metric  LocPrf Weight  Path
*> 3.3.3.3/32       172.12.123.3             0              0  200 i
```

A couple of values have changed, but the route still shows the asterisk and arrowhead. That's what we need! (Much more about those other values throughout this section.)

Just for fun, let's create another loopback on R3 and advertise it with a *network* statement where the mask is just a bit off.

```
R3(config)#int loopback33
R3(config-if)#ip address 33.3.3.3 255.255.255.0

R3(config-if)#router bgp 200
R3(config-router)#network 33.3.3.3 mask 255.255.255.255

R3#show ip bgp
BGP table version is 2, local router ID is 3.3.3.3
Status codes: s suppressed, d damped, h history, * valid, > best, i - internal,
              r RIB-failure, S Stale, m multipath, b backup-path, x best-external
Origin codes: i - IGP, e - EGP, ? - incomplete

   Network          Next Hop      Metric LocPrf         Weight  Path
*> 3.3.3.3/32       0.0.0.0                  0           32768  i

R1#show ip bgp
BGP table version is 4, local router ID is 1.1.1.1
Status codes: s suppressed, d damped, h history, * valid, > best, i - internal,
              r RIB-failure, S Stale
Origin codes: i - IGP, e - EGP, ? - incomplete
```

```
   Network          Next Hop            Metric LocPrf Weight Path
*> 3.3.3.3/32       172.12.123.3             0             0 200 i
```

With that slight misconfiguration in the *network* statement, neither R3 nor R1 sees the route. Fixing that misconfiguration results in both routers having an entry for the route.

```
R3(config)#router bgp 200
R3(config-router)#no network 33.3.3.3 mask 255.255.255.255
R3(config-router)#network 33.3.3.0 mask 255.255.255.0

R3#show ip bgp
BGP table version is 3, local router ID is 3.3.3.3
Status codes: s suppressed, d damped, h history, * valid, > best, i - internal,
              r RIB-failure, S Stale, m multipath, b backup-path, x best-externl
Origin codes: i - IGP, e - EGP, ? - incomplete

   Network          Next Hop            Metric LocPrf Weight Path
*> 3.3.3.3/32       0.0.0.0                  0         32768 i
*> 33.3.3.0/24      0.0.0.0                  0         32768 i
R3#

R1#show ip bgp
BGP table version is 5, local router ID is 1.1.1.1
Status codes: s suppressed, d damped, h history, * valid, > best, i - internal,
              r RIB-failure, S Stale
Origin codes: i - IGP, e - EGP, ? - incomplete

   Network          Next Hop            Metric LocPrf Weight Path
*> 3.3.3.3/32       172.12.123.3             0             0 200 i
*> 33.3.3.0/24      172.12.123.3             0             0 200 i
```

With our first two routes in the bank, let's turn our attention to the all-important BGP path attributes. To truly understand BGP and earn your CCNP, you have to know exactly what these attributes do and how they affect your BGP deployment. Let's jump right in!

The well-known mandatory attributes: AS_PATH, origin, next-hop.

The well-known discretionary attributes: local preference (LOCAL PREF), atomic aggregate.

Optional, transitive attributes: aggregator, community.

The optional nontransitive attribute: MED, the multi-exit discriminator.

The three mandatory attributes will appear in all BGP update messages sent to neighbors. These are the only three attributes all BGP speakers must understand.

The optional attributes can be a bit of a pain in the royal tuckus for BGP operation, since not every BGP speaker is going to understand every optional attribute. That's where the difference between "optional transitive" and "optional nontransitive" comes into play. A BGP path carrying an unrecognized transitive optional attribute will be accepted, and should this path be advertised to other routers, the *Partial* bit will be set and the attribute advertised to the neighbor.

Marking an attribute as *Partial* is the equivalent of the advertising router saying, "I didn't understand this attribute, but maybe you will, so here it is."

An unrecognized nontransitive optional attribute will not be passed on to other BGP speakers. With that said, let's start examining the individual attributes.

The Origin Attribute

You'll see this attribute at the far right of the output of *show ip bgp*. The actual origin codes are shown as well, but I'd have them memorized for the CCNP exams.

```
R1#show ip bgp
BGP table version is 5, local router ID is 1.1.1.1
Status codes: s suppressed, d damped, h history, * valid, > best, i - internal,
              r RIB-failure, S Stale
Origin codes: i - IGP, e - EGP, ? - incomplete

   Network          Next Hop            Metric  LocPrf Weight  Path
*> 3.3.3.3/32       172.12.123.3             0              0  200 i
*> 33.3.3.0/24      172.12.123.3             0              0  200 i
```

The letter "i" indicates a route that originated from an IGP via the *network* command, where the letter "e" indicates a path that originated from an External Gateway Protocol. The question mark tells us the true origin of the route is unclear, since it was learned via route redistribution.

In the best-path selection process, "i" is preferred over "e," which in turn is preferred over the question mark. Much more about this process later in this section.

The AS_PATH Attribute and the Best Path Selection Process

The AS_PATH attribute shows the autonomous systems along the path to the destination network, including the AS the destination network resides in. The shorter the path, the more preferred the path is during the best-path selection process.

The AS_PATH attribute helps to prevent routing loops. Should a BGP speaker receive an update that has its own AS number in the path to a destination, that route is discarded. In this example, the only AS shown in the path is the AS containing the networks. Note that on R1, the Path column shows an AS of 200, followed by the origin code...

```
R1#show ip bg
BRYANT _ ADV _ 1#1
[Resuming connection 1 to r1 ... ]

BGP table version is 5, local router ID is 1.1.1.1
Status codes: s suppressed, d damped, h history, * valid, > best, i - internal,
              r RIB-failure, S Stale
Origin codes: i - IGP, e - EGP, ? - incomplete

   Network          Next Hop            Metric LocPrf Weight Path
*> 3.3.3.3/32       172.12.123.3             0             0 200 i
*> 33.3.3.0/24      172.12.123.3             0             0 200 i
```

...while the same command on R3 shows only the origin code. There's no AS_PATH for the networks on R3, since R3 is in the same AS as the destinations.

```
R3#show ip bgp
BGP table version is 3, local router ID is 3.3.3.3
Status codes: s suppressed, d damped, h history, * valid, > best, i - internal,
              r RIB-failure, S Stale, m multipath, b backup-path, x best-external
Origin codes: i - IGP, e - EGP, ? - incomplete

   Network          Next Hop            Metric LocPrf Weight Path
*> 3.3.3.3/32       0.0.0.0                  0         32768 i
*> 33.3.3.0/24      0.0.0.0                  0         32768 i
```

Let's run a lab that allows us to see the best-path selection process in action. In this lab, every router will advertise its loopback address into BGP, and every router's loopback is its router number for each octet.

The physical network setup follows. For the sake of clarity and sanity (yours and mine), the physical interfaces and switches will not be included in the BGP diagrams. Also note that R2 is on the right side of the diagram; I mention that only because it's on the left in most of the other diagrams in the book.

The networks:

R1—R5 Ethernet: 10.1.1.0 /24

R1—R2—R3 Serial: 172.12.123.0 /24

R2—R3—R4 Ethernet: 172.12.234.0 /24

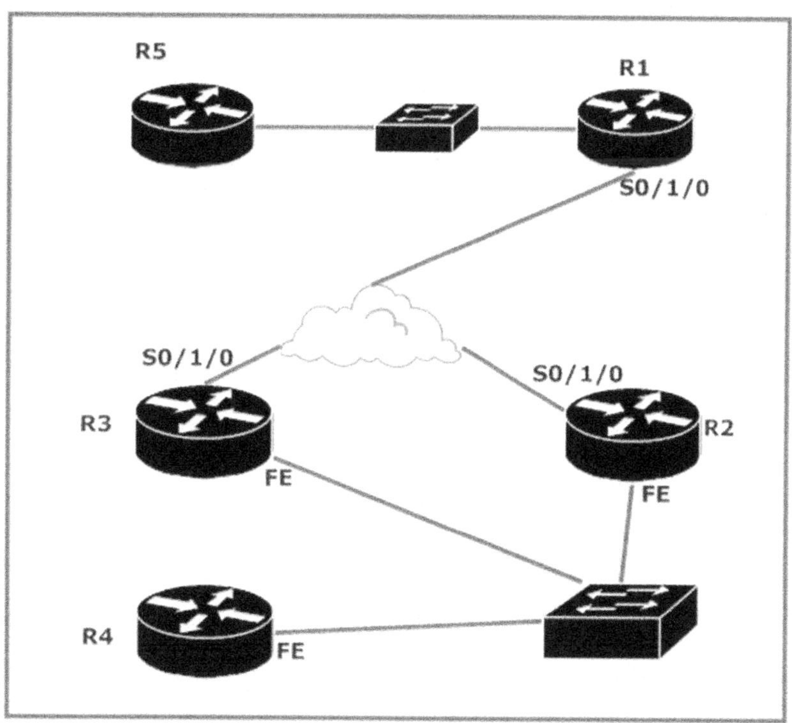

Additionally, each router has a loopback, using the router number for each octet. We're not using those for the adjacencies but will be advertising them into BGP.

The BGP ASs and adjacencies follow.

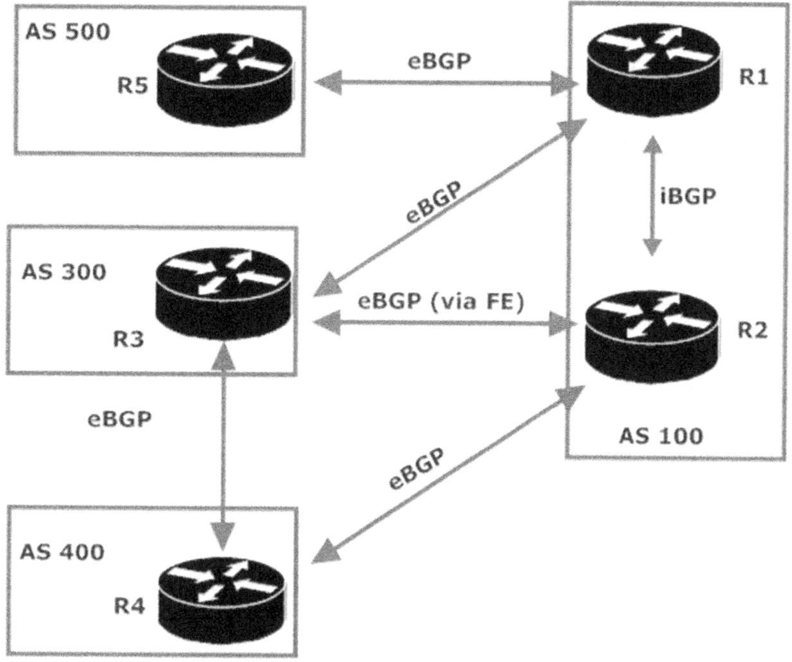

R1 has at least one entry for each loopback in our network and multiple paths for the loopbacks on R3 and R4.

```
R1#show ip bgp
BGP table version is 6, local router ID is 1.1.1.1
Status codes: s suppressed, d damped, h history, * valid, > best, i - internal,
              r RIB-failure, S Stale
Origin codes: i - IGP, e - EGP, ? - incomplete

   Network          Next Hop         Metric LocPrf Weight   Path
*> 1.1.1.1/32       0.0.0.0               0         32768  i
*>i2.2.2.2/32       172.12.123.2          0     100     0  i
* i3.3.3.3/32       172.12.234.3          0     100     0  300 i
*>                  172.12.123.3          0             0  300 i
*> 4.4.4.4/32       172.12.123.3                        0  300 400 i
* i                 172.12.234.4          0     100     0  400 i
*> 5.5.5.5/32       10.1.1.5              0             0  500 i
```

Every path is marked with an asterisk, and in BGP-speak that means every path is valid. BGP had some decisions to make as to which paths were valid and best when it came to the loopbacks on R3 and R4, and here's the rather long-winded decision-making process in all its splendor. When deciding between multiple paths for the same destination, we start at the top of this list and keep going until the tie is broken.

1. Highest weight (BGP weight is a Cisco-proprietary attribute)
2. If there is a tie or non-Cisco routers are involved, highest local preference
3. Locally originated path preferred
4. Shortest AS_PATH preferred.
5. Best origin code. (i, then e, then ?)
6. Lowest MED.
7. eBGP path preferred over iBGP path.
8. Lowest IGP metric to BGP next-hop address.
9. Oldest path.
10. Path from BGP router with lowest BGP RID.

With this list in mind, let's have another look at R1's BGP table.

```
R1#show ip bgp
BGP table version is 6, local router ID is 1.1.1.1
Status codes: s suppressed, d damped, h history, * valid, > best, i - internal,
```

```
              r RIB-failure, S Stale
Origin codes: i - IGP, e - EGP, ? - incomplete

   Network          Next Hop            Metric LocPrf Weight Path
*> 1.1.1.1/32       0.0.0.0                  0         32768 i
*>i2.2.2.2/32       172.12.123.2             0    100      0 i
* i3.3.3.3/32       172.12.234.3             0    100      0 300 i
*>                  172.12.123.3             0             0 300 i
*> 4.4.4.4/32       172.12.123.3                           0 300 400 i
* i                 172.12.234.3             0    100      0 300 400 i
*> 5.5.5.5/32       10.1.1.5                 0             0 500 i
```

The two networks with multiple paths in the table are 3.3.3.3 /32 and 4.4.4.4 /32. Let's take a closer look at those two paths and how BGP determined the best path for each, starting with 3.3.3.3 /32.

```
R1#show ip bgp

   Network          Next Hop            Metric LocPrf Weight Path
* i3.3.3.3/32       172.12.234.3             0    100      0 300 i
*>                  172.12.123.3             0             0 300 i
```

The first value BGP considers in best path selection is *weight*, and both paths have a weight of zero. The second value considered is *local preference*, with the highest local preference preferred. The path chosen as valid and best has no local preference listed, and the path not chosen has a local preference of 100. The Cisco default value for local pref is 100, so why was one path chosen over the other when it looks like all other values are the same? (Hint: it doesn't have anything to do with the RID.)

We'll come back to that after taking a closer look at the paths for 4.4.4.4 /32.

```
   Network          Next Hop            Metric LocPrf Weight Path
*> 4.4.4.4/32       172.12.123.3                           0 300 400 i
* I                 172.12.234.4             0    100      0 400 i
```

We have much the same situation as we did with 3.3.3.3 /32. The weights are both zero, so the local preference is the next value considered. The path chosen has no local preference shown, so it's at the default of 100. Since the other path *also* has a local preference of 100, why did BGP choose the path with the next-hop address of 172.12.123.3?

Those two decisions were made because of one magic word: "inaccessible."

```
R1#show ip bgp 3.3.3.3
BGP routing table entry for 3.3.3.3/32, version 4
Paths: (2 available, best #2, table Default-IP-Routing-Table)
  Advertised to update-groups:
    1          2
  300
```

```
    172.12.234.3 (inaccessible) from 172.12.123.2 (2.2.2.2)
Origin IGP, metric 0, localpref 100, valid, internal
  300
    172.12.123.3 from 172.12.123.3 (3.3.3.3)
      Origin IGP, metric 0, localpref 100, valid, external, best

R1#show ip bgp 4.4.4.4
BGP routing table entry for 4.4.4.4/32, version 6
Paths: (2 available, best #1, table Default-IP-Routing-Table)
Advertised to update-groups:
    1         2
  300 400
    172.12.123.3 from 172.12.123.3 (33.3.3.3)
      Origin IGP, localpref 100, valid, external, best
  400
    172.12.234.4 (inaccessible) from 172.12.123.2 (2.2.2.2)
    Origin IGP, metric 0, localpref 100, valid, internal
```

For a route to be marked valid and best by BGP, the next-hop address must be accessible to the local router. R1 can't reach the 172.12.234.3 and 172.12.234.4 addresses, so they're marked inaccessible, which in turn means the routes can't be marked valid and best.

```
* i3.3.3.3/32       172.12.234.3          0     100     0  300 i
*>                  172.12.123.3          0             0  300 i
*> 4.4.4.4/32       172.12.123.3                        0  300 400 i
* i                 172.12.234.4          0     100       0400 i

R1#ping 172.12.234.3

Type escape sequence to abort.
Sending 5, 100-byte ICMP Echos to 172.12.234.3, timeout is 2 seconds:
.....
Success rate is 0 percent (0/5)
R1#ping 172.12.234.4

Type escape sequence to abort.
Sending 5, 100-byte ICMP Echos to 172.12.234.4, timeout is 2 seconds:
.....
Success rate is 0 percent (0/5)
```

The next-hop addresses of the routes learned from R2 seem a bit odd. For the route to 3.3.3.3 /32, the next hop is 172.12.234.3, which is the FE interface on R3. Why didn't that next hop change to 172.12.123.2 when R2 advertised it to R1?

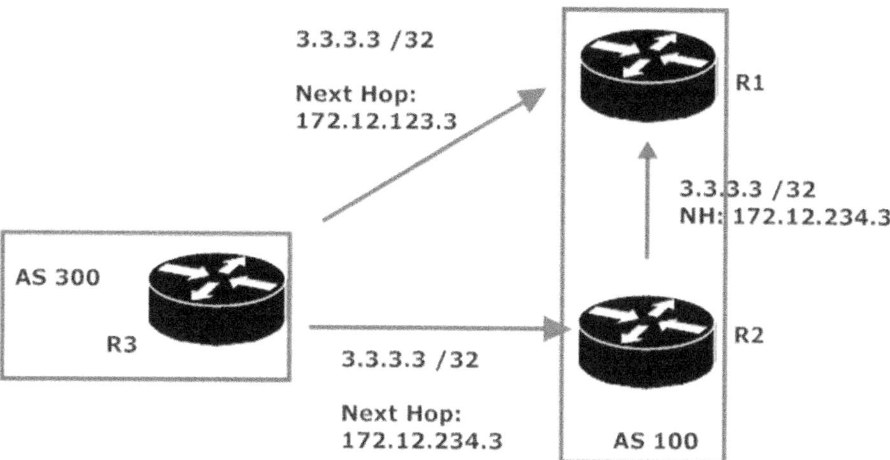

Same goes for the route to 4.4.4.4. When R2 learns that route from R4, the next hop is 172.12.234.4. When R1 learns that route from R2, the next-hop address is still 172.12.234.4. Why didn't the next-hop address change to R2's advertising interface (172.12.123.2)?

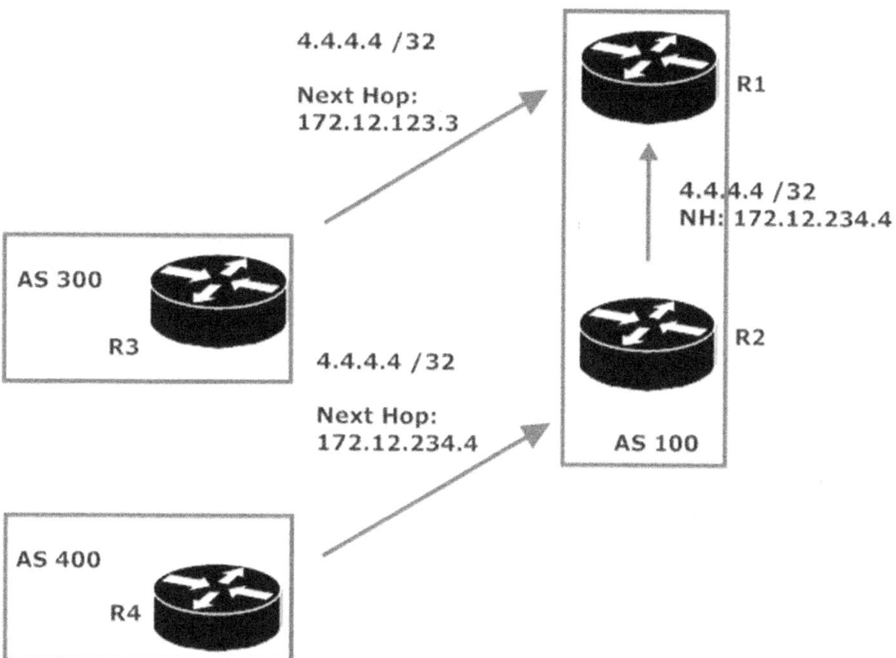

I'm going to show you why that happens in the very next lab. The reason I don't show you now is that I want to introduce you to the *next-hop-self* command. This command forces the local router to announce itself as the next hop of all paths advertised to the specified neighbor. We're not going to configure R1 and try to tweak next-hop addresses; instead, we'll configure this on R2. This command has no options.

```
R2(config-router)#neighbor 172.12.123.1 next-hop-self ?
<cr>

R2(config-router)#neighbor 172.12.123.1 next-hop-self

R2#clear ip bgp * soft out
```

The results on R1:

```
R1#show ip bgp
BGP table version is 7, local router ID is 1.1.1.1
Status codes: s suppressed, d damped, h history, * valid, > best, i - internal,
              r RIB-failure, S Stale
Origin codes: i - IGP, e - EGP, ? - incomplete

   Network          Next Hop            Metric  LocPrf Weight  Path
*> 1.1.1.1/32       0.0.0.0                  0         32768  i
*>i2.2.2.2/32       172.12.123.2             0     100         0i
* i3.3.3.3/32       172.12.123.2             0     100         0300 i
*>                  172.12.123.3             0                0  300 i
* 4.4.4.4/32        172.12.123.3                              0  300 400 i
*>I                 172.12.123.2             0     100         0400 i
*> 5.5.5.5/32       10.1.1.5                 0                0  500 i
```

R1's BGP table now shows 172.12.123.2 as the next-hop address for all paths that formerly had 172.12.234.3 or 172.12.234.4 for that value. Since R1 has no accessibility problem with 172.12.123.2, those paths can now be considered as valid and best by BGP. The route to 4.4.4.4 now has a next hop of 172.12.123.2.

```
R1#show ip bgp 4.4.4.4
BGP routing table entry for 4.4.4.4/32, version 7
Paths: (2 available, best #2, table Default-IP-Routing-Table)
Flag: 0x820
  Advertised to update-groups:
    1
  300 400
    172.12.123.3 from 172.12.123.3 (33.3.3.3)
      Origin IGP, localpref 100, valid, external
  400
    172.12.123.2 from 172.12.123.2 (2.2.2.2)
      Origin IGP, metric 0, localpref 100, valid, internal, best
```

The valid and best route to 3.3.3.3 still has a next hop of 172.12.123.3, but the next hop for the other route has changed to 172.12.123.2.

```
R1#show ip bgp 3.3.3.3
BGP routing table entry for 3.3.3.3/32, version 4
```

```
Paths: (2 available, best #2, table Default-IP-Routing-Table)
  Advertised to update-groups:
    1 2
  300
    172.12.123.2 from 172.12.123.2 (2.2.2.2)
      Origin IGP, metric 0, localpref 100, valid, internal
  300
    172.12.123.3 from 172.12.123.3 (33.3.3.3)
      Origin IGP, metric 0, localpref 100, valid, external, best
```

For 4.4.4.4 /32, the path now in use is the one with the next hop of 172.12.123.2, since its AS_PATH is shorter than the other valid path.

The best-path selection process was just a little longer for 3.3.3.3 /32. The weights are the same, the local preference is the same, none of the routes originated on R1, the AS_PATH length is the same, the origin code is the same (IGP), and the MED is the same ("metric"). Next on the list is eBGP routes being preferred over iBGP routes, and that's why the path with a next hop of 172.12.123.3 was chosen as the best path—external over internal!

Let's go back to the *original* next-hop addresses of the routes advertised by R2 to R1 by removing the *next-hop* command from R2.

```
R2(config-router)#no neighbor 172.12.123.1 next-hop-self

R2#clear ip bgp * soft out
```

Both routes are advertised via the 172.12.123.2 /24 IP address on R2, but when the routes get to R1, they have the next-hop addresses of 172.12.234.3 and 172.12.234.4, which were the next-hop addresses when R2 received them.

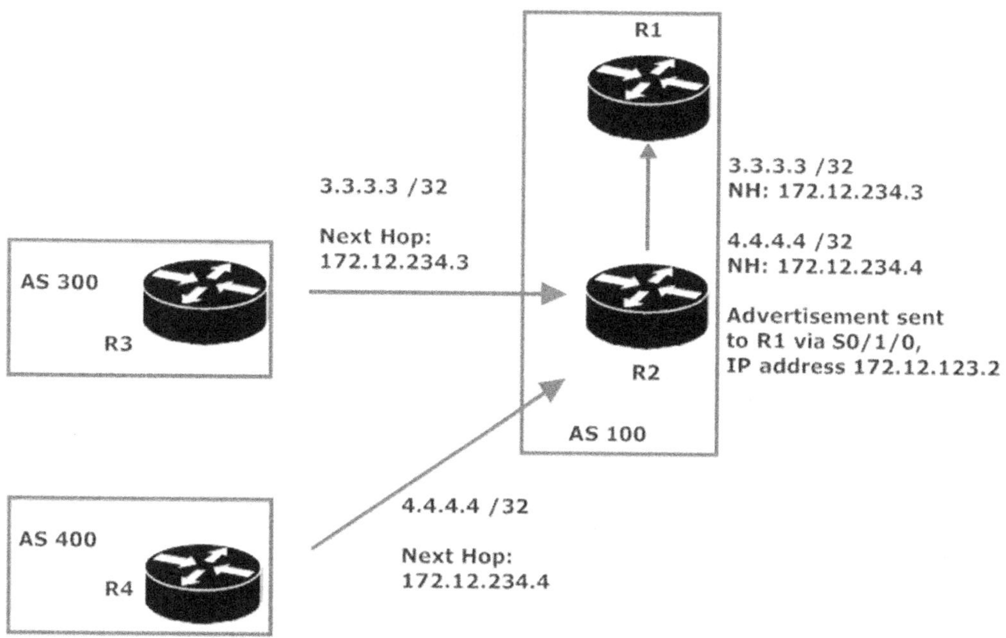

Why didn't the next-hop addresses change? Let's find out with a closer look at the rules for the default BGP next-hop address.

The Next-Hop Attribute Defaults

Let's go back to a simpler time and a simpler network. R3 is advertising its two loopback interfaces, 3.3.3.3 /32 and 33.3.3.3 /32, via an eBGP adjacency with R1. All adjacencies in this lab are over the 172.12.123.0 /24 network.

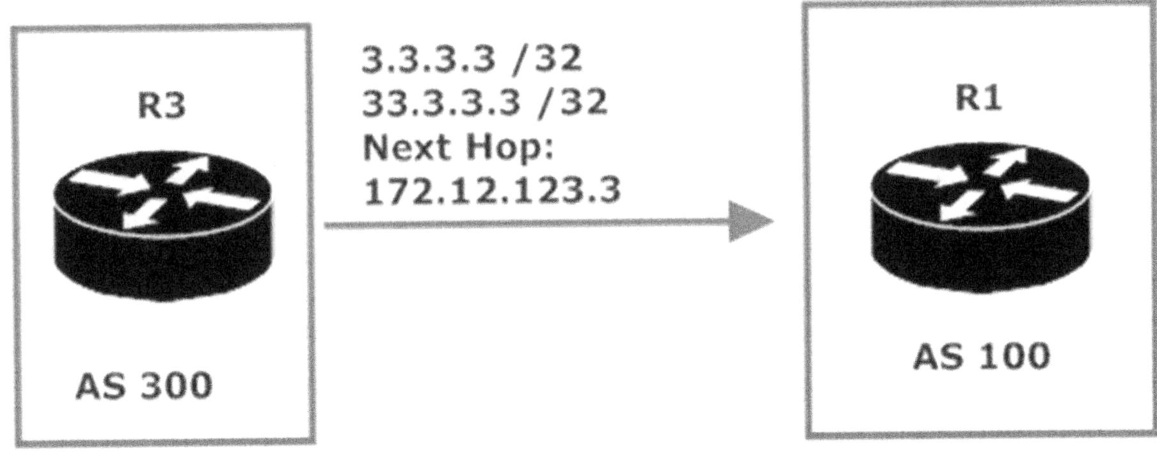

When a BGP speaker advertises a route to an eBGP neighbor, the next-hop address is that of the advertising interface. R1's BGP table shows the address of the Serial interface on R3 (172.12.123.3) as the next-hop address for both of those routes.

```
R1#show ip bgp
BGP table version is 5, local router ID is 1.1.1.1
Status codes: s suppressed, d damped, h history, * valid, > best, i - internal,
              r RIB-failure, S Stale
Origin codes: i - IGP, e - EGP, ? - incomplete

   Network          Next Hop            Metric  LocPrf Weight  Path
*> 3.3.3.3/32       172.12.123.3             0             0  200 i
*> 33.3.3.0/24      172.12.123.3             0             0  200 i
```

Makes perfect sense, right? Right! Now, here's the *slightly* odd rule. With iBGP route updates, if the route was originated outside the local AS, the next-hop address is *still* the source address of the router in the remote AS.

Weird, right? Right!

Let's prove this theory by adding R2 back to AS 100 and then advertising those two routes from R1 to R2.

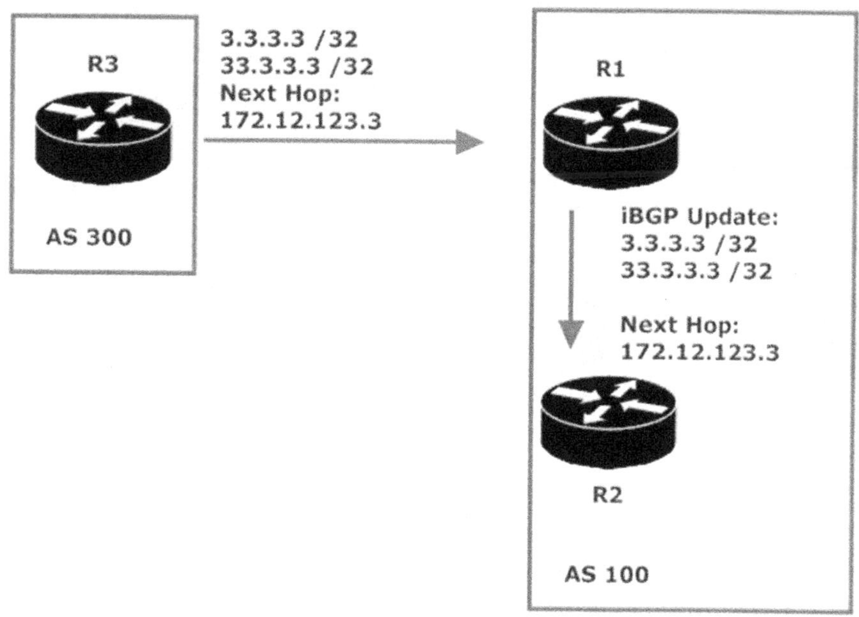


```
R2#show ip bgp
BGP table version is 3, local router ID is 2.2.2.2
Status codes: s suppressed, d damped, h history, * valid, > best, i - internal,
              r RIB-failure, S Stale, m multipath, b backup-path, x best-external
Origin codes: i - IGP, e - EGP, ? - incomplete

   Network          Next Hop            Metric LocPrf Weight Path
*>i3.3.3.3/32       172.12.123.3             0    100      0 200 i
*>i33.3.3.0/24      172.12.123.3             0    100      0 200 i
```

On R2, the next-hop address for both routes is still 172.12.123.3, just as the theory holds. Both routes are still marked valid and best since R2 has no problem reaching 172.12.123.3. This default next-hop address behavior *can* cause some trouble for us, as we saw in the previous lab. For me, the bottom line has always been to check the next-hop addresses first when I'm not getting the "valid and best route" behavior I expect. Always check your routes with *show ip bgp x.x.x.x*!

The Multi-Exit Discriminator (MED)

It sounds like something we tried to stop Godzilla with back in the day ("Fire the Multi-Exit Discriminator!"), but this optional attribute really comes in handy when there are multiple entrance points for a single AS, as in the following lab. Note the direct connections between R1 and R3 as well as R2 and R3; the frame network is not in use in this lab.

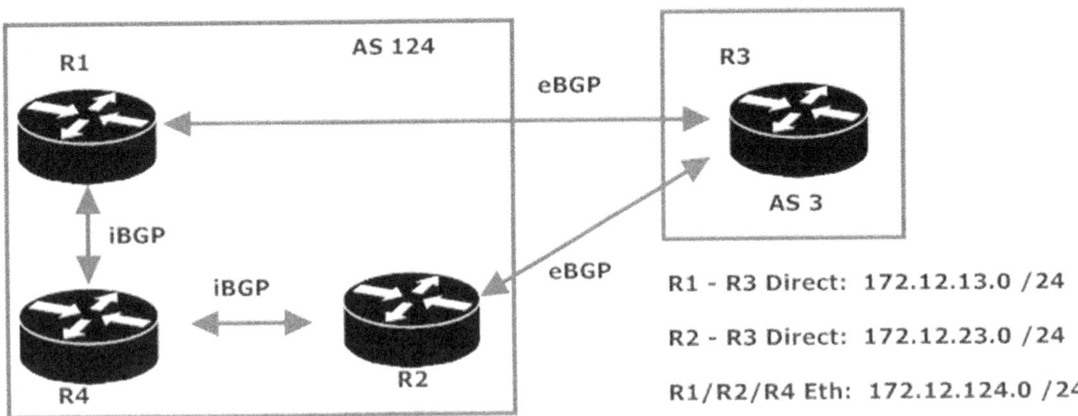

R3 can enter AS 124 via R1 or R2, and there may be one path in particular we *really* want R3 to use to reach 172.12.124.0 /24. We can use the MED to tell R3 which of those two paths is the one we'd prefer it to use. The path with the lowest MED is preferred. The MED goes from one AS to another and is *not* passed on to any other AS.

For this lab, I'll advertise two loopbacks that just happen to be sitting on R4.

```
R4(config)#router bgp 124
R4(config-router)#network 4.4.4.4 mask 255.255.255.255
R4(config-router)#network 44.4.4.4 mask 255.255.255.255
```

R3 should be able to reach either network through either R1 or R2, and while both paths show up in R3's BGP table as valid, the next hop for both paths ("valid *and* best") is 172.12.123.1.

```
R3#show ip bgp
BGP table version is 3, local router ID is 172.12.23.3
Status codes: s suppressed, d damped, h history, * valid, > best, i - internal,
              r RIB-failure, S Stale
Origin codes: i - IGP, e - EGP, ? - incomplete

   Network          Next Hop            Metric  LocPrf Weight  Path
*  4.4.4.4/32       172.12.23.2                             0  124 i
*>                  172.12.13.1                             0  124 i
*  44.4.4.4/32      172.12.23.2                             0  124 i
*>                  172.12.13.1                             0  124 i
```

Why? Let's take a detailed look at each path on R3.

```
R3#show ip bgp 4.4.4.4
BGP routing table entry for 4.4.4.4/32, version 2
Paths: (2 available, best #2, table Default-IP-Routing-Table)
  Advertised to update-groups:
     1
  124
```

```
      172.12.23.2 from 172.12.23.2 (172.12.124.2)
        Origin IGP, localpref 100, valid, external
    124
      172.12.13.1 from 172.12.13.1 (172.12.124.1)
        Origin IGP, localpref 100, valid, external, best
R3#show ip bgp 44.4.4.4
BGP routing table entry for 44.4.4.4/32, version 3
Paths: (2 available, best #2, table Default-IP-Routing-Table)
  Advertised to update-groups:
     1
  124
    172.12.23.2 from 172.12.23.2 (172.12.124.2)
      Origin IGP, localpref 100, valid, external
  124
    172.12.13.1 from 172.12.13.1 (172.12.124.1)
      Origin IGP, localpref 100, valid, external, best
```

With everything else equal, it all comes down to those BGP IDs. The paths through R1 are being selected as best because R1's ID is lower than R2's. Let's balance that load a bit by having R3 use 172.12.13.1 as the next hop for traffic headed for 4.4.4.4 and 172.12.23.2 as the next hop for 44.4.4.4.

We want R3 to go through R1 to reach 4.4.4.4, so we'll have R1 advertise a MED of 100 for that route while R2 advertises a MED of 200. Lowest MED wins!

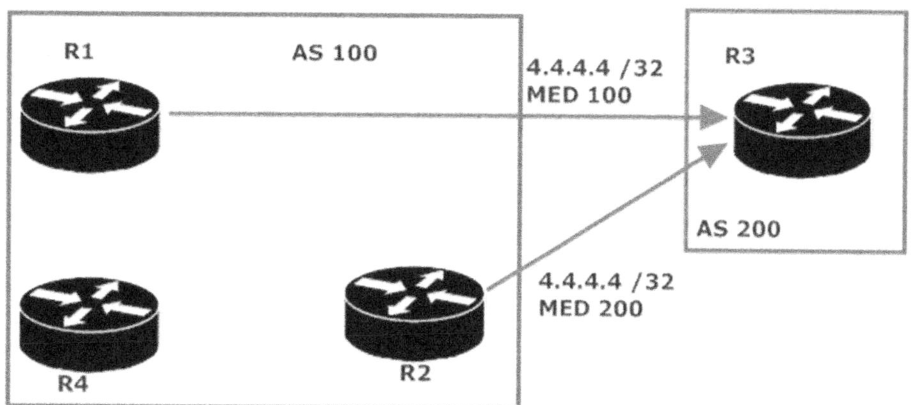

We'll do the reverse/inverse/universe for the other path, with R2 advertising the lowest MED for the 44.4.4.4 network.

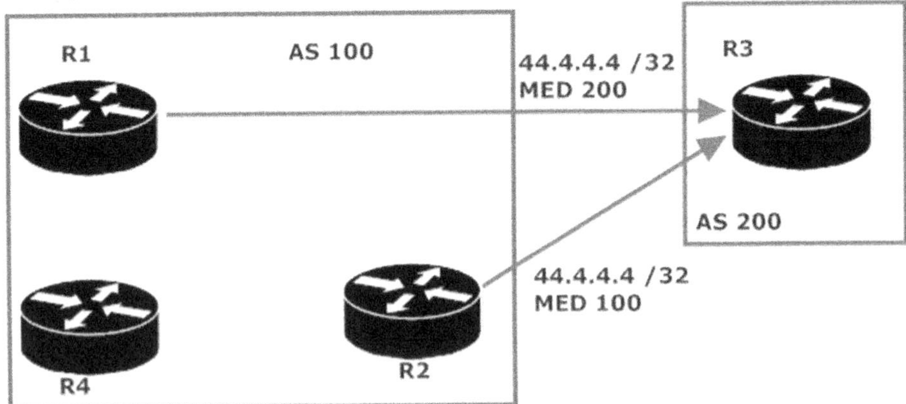

We'll make this happen with a simple access list and a route map to apply the MEDs, first on R1. There is no MED available to set—the value we want to set is *metric.*

```
R1(config)#access-list 4 permit 4.4.4.4

R1(config)#access-list 44 permit 44.4.4.4

R1(config)#route-map SETMED permit 10
R1(config-route-map)#match ip address 4
R1(config-route-map)#set metric 100
R1(config-route-map)#route-map SETMED permit 20
R1(config-route-map)#match ip address 44
R1(config-route-map)#set metric 200
```

On R2:

```
R2(config)#access-list 4 permit 4.4.4.4
R2(config)#access-list 44 permit 44.4.4.4
R2(config)#route-map SETMED permit 10
R2(config-route-map)#match ip address 4
R2(config-route-map)#set metric 200
R2(config-route-map)#route-map SETMED permit 20
R2(config-route-map)#match ip address 44
R2(config-route-map)#set metric 100
```

Almost there! With BGP, we'll apply our route maps via *neighbor.*

```
R1(config)#router bgp 124
R1(config-router)#neighbor 172.12.13.3 route-map SETMED ?
in Apply map to incoming routes
out Apply map to outbound routes

R1(config-router)#neighbor 172.12.13.3 route-map SETMED out
```

```
R2(config)#router bgp 124
R2(config-router)#neighbor 172.12.23.3 route-map SETMED out
```

A little soft reset to apply the changes...

```
R1#clear ip bgp * soft out

R2#clear ip bgp * soft out
```

...and we see the result on R3.

```
R3#show ip bgp
BGP table version is 5, local router ID is 172.12.23.3
Status codes: s suppressed, d damped, h history, * valid, > best, i - internal,
              r RIB-failure, S Stale
Origin codes: i - IGP, e - EGP, ? - incomplete

   Network          Next Hop            Metric LocPrf Weight Path
*> 4.4.4.4/32       172.12.13.1            100             0 124 i
*                   172.12.23.2            200             0 124 i
* 44.4.4.4/32       172.12.13.1            200             0 124 i
*>                  172.12.23.2            100             0 124 i
```

The two routes with a metric of 100 have been selected as the best routes. That gives R3 a next hop of 172.12.13.1 to reach 4.4.4.4 and a next hop of 172.12.23.2 to reach 44.4.4.4. Just what we wanted! You can see the metrics in the extended version of this command as well.

```
R3#show ip bgp 4.4.4.4
BGP routing table entry for 4.4.4.4/32, version 5
Paths: (2 available, best #1, table Default-IP-Routing-Table)
  Advertised to update-groups:
     1
  124
    172.12.13.1 from 172.12.13.1 (172.12.124.1)
      Origin IGP, metric 100, localpref 100, valid, external, best
  124
    172.12.23.2 from 172.12.23.2 (172.12.124.2)
      Origin IGP, metric 200, localpref 100, valid, external

R3#show ip bgp 44.4.4.4
BGP routing table entry for 44.4.4.4/32, version 4
Paths: (2 available, best #2, table Default-IP-Routing-Table)
  Advertised to update-groups:
     1
  124
    172.12.13.1 from 172.12.13.1 (172.12.124.1)
      Origin IGP, metric 200, localpref 100, valid, external
```

```
  124
    172.12.23.2 from 172.12.23.2 (172.12.124.2)
      Origin IGP, metric 100, localpref 100, valid, external, best
```

I think that's enough next-hopping for now. Let's do some local preffing!

The Local Preference Attribute

Also known as LOCAL_PREF, this well-known attribute also comes into play when multiple paths between ASs exist. However, the local pref attribute is just that...*local*. Where the MED tells routers outside the AS what entrance path is preferred, local preference tells routes inside the local AS which exit path to use when multiple paths exist. The path with the highest local preference is preferred.

The local preference value is passed only between iBGP peers, and local preference is never advertised outside the AS. Yes, the dreaded phrase "locally significant only" is back!

We'll tweak the local preference in our next lab. Just for fun, all four routers are on the same ethernet segment (10.0.0.0 /24), and all adjacencies are formed using addresses from that segment.

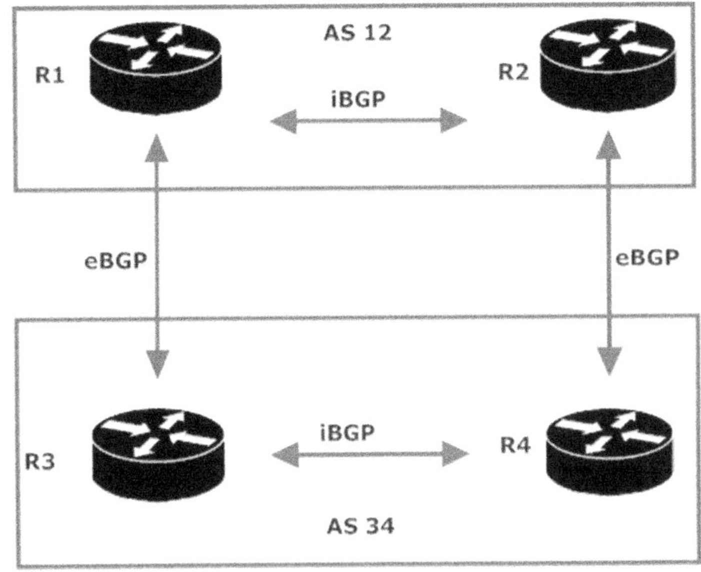

R1:

```
router bgp 12
 no synchronization
 bgp log-neighbor-changes
 neighbor 10.1.1.2 remote-as 12
 neighbor 10.1.1.3 remote-as 34
 no auto-summary
```

R2:

```
router bgp 12
 no synch
 bgp log-neighbor-changes
 neighbor 10.1.1.1 remote-as 12
 neighbor 10.1.1.4 remote-as 34
 no auto-summary
```

R3:

```
router bgp 34
 bgp log-neighbor-changes
 network 172.12.34.0 mask 255.255.255.0
 neighbor 10.1.1.1 remote-as 12
 neighbor 10.1.1.4 remote-as 34
 no auto-summary
```

R4:

```
router bgp 34
 bgp log-neighbor-changes
 network 172.12.34.0 mask 255.255.255.0
 neighbor 10.1.1.2 remote-as 12
 neighbor 10.1.1.3 remote-as 34
 no auto-summary
```

R3 and R4 are also connected via a direct serial link using the 172.12.34.0 /24 network. We're not using addresses from that link for adjacencies, but we are going to advertise the network into BGP on both R3 and R4.

```
R3(config)#router bgp 34
R3(config-router)#network 172.12.34.0 mask 255.255.255.0

R4(config)#router bgp 34
R4(config-router)#network 172.12.34.0 mask 255.255.255.0
```

R1 and R2 both have two paths to that network in their BGP tables, but there's a different next-hop address for each.

```
R1#show ip bgp
BGP table version is 2, local router ID is 10.1.1.1
Status codes: s suppressed, d damped, h history, * valid, > best, i - internal,
              r RIB-failure, S Stale
Origin codes: i - IGP, e - EGP, ? - incomplete

   Network          Next Hop            Metric LocPrf Weight Path
*> 172.12.34.0/24   10.1.1.3                 0             0 34 i
* I                 10.1.1.4                 0    100        034 i
```

```
R2#show ip bgp
BGP table version is 6, local router ID is 10.1.1.2
Status codes: s suppressed, d damped, h history, * valid, > best, i - internal,
              r RIB-failure, S Stale, m multipath, b backup-path, x best-external
Origin codes: i - IGP, e - EGP, ? - incomplete

   Network          Next Hop            Metric LocPrf Weight Path
* i172.12.34.0/24   10.1.1.3                 0    100      0 34 i
*>                  10.1.1.4                 0             0 34 i
```

R1 has chosen the path with the next-hop address 10.1.1.3 to reach 172.12.34.0 /24, while R2 is using the path with the next-hop address 10.1.1.4. Should we need R2 to use the same path as R1 to reach 172.12.34.0, we can manipulate the local preference attribute to make that happen. Run *show ip bgp x.x.x.x* to have a look at all local preferences for a given route.

```
R2#show ip bgp
BGP table version is 6, local router ID is 10.1.1.2
Status codes: s suppressed, d damped, h history, * valid, > best, i - internal,
              r RIB-failure, S Stale, m multipath, b backup-path, x best-external
Origin codes: i - IGP, e - EGP, ? - incomplete

   Network          Next Hop            Metric LocPrf Weight Path
* i172.12.34.0/24   10.1.1.3                 0    100      0 34 i
*>                  10.1.1.4                 0             0 34 i
```

The local preference for both routes is 100, so raising the local preference on R2 for the path with the next hop of 10.1.1.3 should change the route selection. We can either raise the local preference for all routes advertised by a given router, or we can change the local preference of a particular router. First, we'll look at the all-or-nothing approach.

From R2's BGP table, we know the route for 172.12.34.0 /24 with the next-hop of 10.1.1.3 is coming from R1...

```
R2#show ip bgp 172.12.34.0
BGP routing table entry for 172.12.34.0/24, version 6
Paths: (2 available, best #2, table default)
  Advertised to update-groups:
     3
  34
    10.1.1.3 from 10.1.1.1 (10.1.1.1)
      Origin IGP, metric 0, localpref 100, valid, internal
  34
    10.1.1.4 from 10.1.1.4 (172.12.34.4)
      Origin IGP, metric 0, localpref 100, valid, external, best
```

So the all-or-nothing approach requires us to change the BGP default local preference on R1 with *bgp default local-preference.*

```
R1(config-router)#bgp default ?
  ipv4-unicast Activate ipv4-unicast for a peer by default
  local-preference local preference (higher=more preferred)
  route-target Control behavior based on Route-Target attributes

R1(config-router)#bgp default local-preference ?
  <0-4294967295> Configure default local preference value

R1(config-router)#bgp default local-preference 200
R1(config-router)#^Z
R1#clear ip
*Jun 12 21:22:01.421: %SYS-5-CONFIG_I: Configured from console by console

R1#clear ip bgp * soft out
```

R2 now has a local preference of 200 for the path advertised by R1 and has now selected that path to reach 172.12.34.0 /24.

```
R2#show ip bgp
BGP table version is 7, local router ID is 10.1.1.2
Status codes: s suppressed, d damped, h history, * valid, > best, i - internal,
              r RIB-failure, S Stale, m multipath, b backup-path, x best-external
Origin codes: i - IGP, e - EGP, ? - incomplete

   Network          Next Hop            Metric  LocPrf Weight  Path
*>i172.12.34.0/24   10.1.1.3                 0     200      0  34 i
*                   10.1.1.4                 0              0  34 i
```

The only issue with this solution is that it changes all local preferences on BGP routes advertised by R1. If R1 had other routes to advertise to R2 or R1 had other iBGP neighbors, this might not be the optimal solution. Let's remove the previous local preference command and verify that R2 is again using the path with the next hop 10.1.1.4.

```
R1(config)#router bgp 12
R1(config-router)#no bgp default local-preference 200

R1#clear ip bgp * soft out

R2#show ip bgp
BGP table version is 8, local router ID is 10.1.1.2
Status codes: s suppressed, d damped, h history, * valid, > best, i - internal,
              r RIB-failure, S Stale, m multipath, b backup-path, x best-external
Origin codes: i - IGP, e - EGP, ? - incomplete
```

```
   Network          Next Hop            Metric  LocPrf Weight  Path
* i172.12.34.0/24   10.1.1.3                 0     100      0  34 i
*>                  10.1.1.4                 0              0  34 i
```

We can change the local preference of an individual route with a route map. To illustrate, I've added the 210.3.3.0 /24 network to our lab, and I'm advertising it on both R3 and R4. Let's take a look at the current BGP tables on R1 and R2.

```
R1#show ip bgp
BGP table version is 6, local router ID is 10.1.1.1
Status codes: s suppressed, d damped, h history, * valid, > best, i - internal,
              r RIB-failure, S Stale
Origin codes: i - IGP, e - EGP, ? - incomplete

   Network          Next Hop            Metric  LocPrf Weight  Path
* i172.12.34.0/24   10.1.1.4                 0     100      0  34 i
*>                  10.1.1.3                 0              0  34 i
* i210.3.3.0        10.1.1.4                 0     100      0  34 i
*>                  10.1.1.3                 0              0  34 i

R2#show ip bgp
BGP table version is 9, local router ID is 10.1.1.2
Status codes: s suppressed, d damped, h history, * valid, > best, i - internal,
              r RIB-failure, S Stale, m multipath, b backup-path, x best-external
Origin codes: i - IGP, e - EGP, ? - incomplete

   Network          Next Hop            Metric  LocPrf Weight  Path
* i172.12.34.0/24   10.1.1.3                 0     100      0  34 i
*>                  10.1.1.4                 0              0  34 i
* i210.3.3.0        10.1.1.3                 0     100      0  34 i
*>                  10.1.1.4                 0              0  34 i
```

As we'd expect, R1 is using 10.1.1.3 for the next hop for both routes, and R2 is using 10.1.1.4 for both routes. If we want to change the route selection on R2 for only the 172.12.34.0 /24 network while leaving the next-hop address intact for the new route, we couldn't use *bgp default local-preference* on R1. That would change the local preference on R2 for both routes. Instead, we'll need to configure an ACL and a route map on the advertising router.

```
R1(config)#access-list 7 permit 172.12.34.0 0.0.0.255
R1(config)#
R1(config)#route-map DOUBLEYOURPREF permit 10
R1(config-route-map)#match ip address 7
R1(config-route-map)#set local-pref 200
R1(config-route-map)#route-map DOUBLEYOURPREF permit 20
R1(config-route-map)#set local-pref 100
```

The ACL identifies 172.12.34.0 /24, and that identification is called in the first clause of the route map. The first clause sets the BGP local preference of the 172.12.34.0 /24 network to 200. The second clause sets the local preference of any other route to 100 (note there is no match statement). After a soft reset, we see the results on R2.

```
R1#clear ip bgp * soft out

R2#show ip bgp
BGP table version is 10, local router ID is 10.1.1.2
Status codes: s suppressed, d damped, h history, * valid, > best, i - internal,
              r RIB-failure, S Stale, m multipath, b backup-path, x best-external
Origin codes: i - IGP, e - EGP, ? - incomplete

   Network          Next Hop            Metric  LocPrf Weight  Path
*>i172.12.34.0/24   10.1.1.3                 0     200      0  34 i
*                   10.1.1.4                 0              0  34 i
* i210.3.3.0        10.1.1.3                 0     100      0  34 i
*>                  10.1.1.4                 0              0  34 i
```

Perfect! The next-hop address for 172.12.34.0 /24 is 10.1.1.3, while the next hop for the newer network is still 10.1.1.4. Before we move to the next attribute, let's have a look at IOS Help for *set* in route maps.

```
R2(config-route-map)#set ?
  as-path           Prepend string for a BGP AS-path attribute
  automatic-tag     Automatically compute TAG value
  clns              OSI summary address
  comm-list         set BGP community list (for deletion)
  community         BGP community attribute
  dampening         Set BGP route flap dampening parameters
  default           Set default information
  extcomm-list      Set BGP/VPN extended community list (for deletion)
  extcommunity      BGP extended community attribute
  global            Set to global routing table
  interface         Output interface
  ip                IP specific information
  ipv6              IPv6 specific information
  level             Where to import route
  local-preference  BGP local preference path attribute
  metric            Metric value for destination routing protocol
  metric-type       Type of metric for destination routing protocol
  mpls-label        Set MPLS label for prefix
  origin            BGP origin code
  tag               Tag value for destination routing protocol
  traffic-index     BGP traffic classification number for accounting
  vrf               Define VRF name
  weight            BGP weight for routing table
```

A word to the wise: you can manipulate just about *any* BGP attribute with a route map.

Time to have a look at the very first attribute considered in the BGP path selection process!

The Weight Attribute

Quick weight facts: this attribute is proprietary to Cisco, is locally significant only, and is never advertised to any other router (iBGP or eBGP). The path with the larger weight is preferred. The default for this attribute is a bit odd. The default weight for a route originated on the local router is 32768, and for all other routes, it's zero.

We'll manipulate the weight attribute in the following lab, which has two networks. The first is the very familiar 172.12.123.0 /24 network, connecting R1, R2, and R3. In this lab, R2, R3, and R4 are on the 172.12.234.0 /24 network.

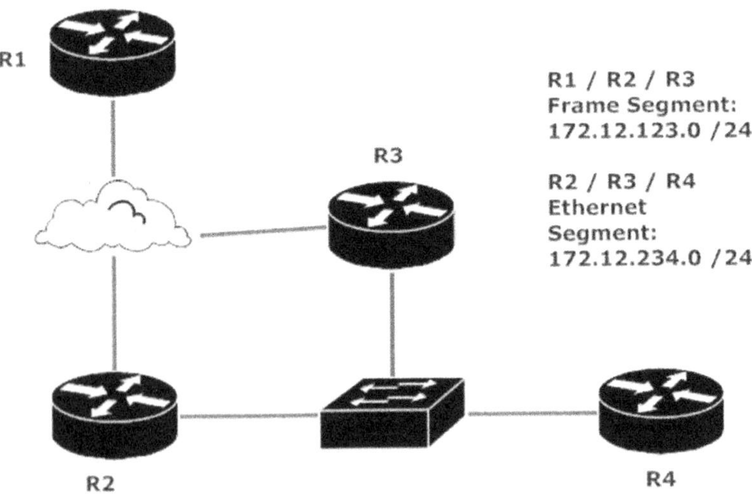

The ASs:

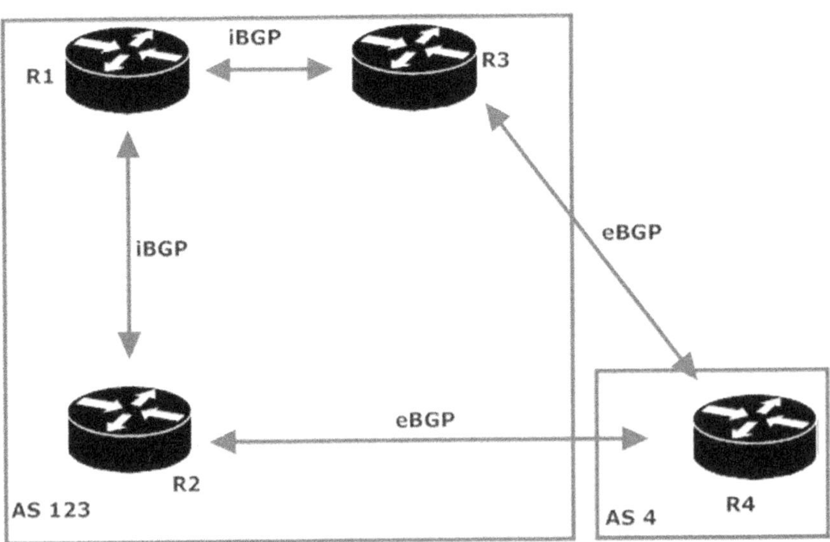

R1:

```
router bgp 123
no synchronization
bgp log-neighbor-changes
neighbor 172.12.123.2 remote-as 123
neighbor 172.12.123.3 remote-as 123
no auto-summary
```

R2:

```
router bgp 123
no synch
bgp log-neighbor-changes
neighbor 172.12.123.1 remote-as 123
neighbor 172.12.234.4 remote-as 4
no auto-summary
```

R3:

```
router bgp 123
no synch
bgp log-neighbor-changes
neighbor 172.12.123.1 remote-as 123
neighbor 172.12.234.4 remote-as 4
no auto-summary
```

R4:

```
router bgp 4
 no synch
 bgp log-neighbor-changes
 neighbor 172.12.234.2 remote-as 123
 neighbor 172.12.234.3 remote-as 123
 no auto-summary
```

With our peerings in place, let's advertise R4's loopback and then visit some routing tables!

```
R4(config)#router bgp 4
R4(config-router)#network 4.4.4.4 mask 255.255.255.255
```

Both R3 and R2 have a valid and best entry for this network:

```
R2#show ip bgp
BGP table version is 2, local router ID is 172.12.234.2
Status codes: s suppressed, d damped, h history, * valid, > best, i - internal,
              r RIB-failure, S Stale, m multipath, b backup-path, x best-external
Origin codes: i - IGP, e - EGP, ? - incomplete

   Network          Next Hop            Metric LocPrf Weight Path
*> 4.4.4.4/32       172.12.234.4             0             0 4 i
```

```
R3#show ip bgp
BGP table version is 2, local router ID is 210.3.3.3
Status codes: s suppressed, d damped, h history, * valid, > best, i - internal,
              r RIB-failure, S Stale, m multipath, b backup-path, x best-external
Origin codes: i - IGP, e - EGP, ? - incomplete

   Network          Next Hop            Metric LocPrf Weight Path
*> 4.4.4.4/32       172.12.234.4             0             0 4 i
```

We have a bit of a problem on R1, as that router has two entries for that network, and neither of them have been marked "valid and best."

```
R3#show ip bgp
BGP table version is 2, local router ID is 210.3.3.3
Status codes: s suppressed, d damped, h history, * valid, > best, i - internal,
              r RIB-failure, S Stale, m multipath, b backup-path, x best-external
Origin codes: i - IGP, e - EGP, ? - incomplete

   Network          Next Hop            Metric LocPrf Weight Path
*> 4.4.4.4/32       172.12.234.4             0             0 4 i

The problem? R1 has no idea where 172.12.234.4 is.

R1#show ip bgp
BGP table version is 1, local router ID is 172.12.123.1
Status codes: s suppressed, d damped, h history, * valid, > best, i - internal,
              r RIB-failure, S Stale
Origin codes: i - IGP, e - EGP, ? - incomplete

   Network          Next Hop            Metric LocPrf Weight Path
* i4.4.4.4/32       172.12.234.4             0    100      0 4 i
* I                 172.12.234.4             0    100      0 4 i

R1#show ip bgp 4.4.4.4
BGP routing table entry for 4.4.4.4/32, version 0
Paths: (2 available, no best path)
  Not advertised to any peer
  4
    172.12.234.4 (inaccessible) from 172.12.123.3 (210.3.3.3)
      Origin IGP, metric 0, localpref 100, valid, internal
  4
    172.12.234.4 (inaccessible) from 172.12.123.2 (172.12.234.2)
      Origin IGP, metric 0, localpref 100, valid, internal
```

I'll use *next-hop-self* on both R2 and R3 for their peerings with R1 and then check that table on R1 again.

```
R2(config)#router bgp 123
R2(config-router)#neighbor 172.12.123.1 next-hop-self

R3(config)#router bgp 123
R3(config-router)#neighbor 172.12.123.1 next-hop-self

R1#clear ip bgp * soft in
R1#show ip bgp
BGP table version is 2, local router ID is 172.12.123.1
Status codes: s suppressed, d damped, h history, * valid, > best, i - internal,
              r RIB-failure, S Stale
Origin codes: i - IGP, e - EGP, ? - incomplete

   Network          Next Hop            Metric LocPrf Weight Path
* i4.4.4.4/32       172.12.123.3             0    100      0 4 i
*>I                 172.12.123.2             0    100      0 4 i
```

The *next-hop-self* commands took effect with a soft inbound reset in R1, and we're all set! R1's BGP process has chosen the path with the next hop of 172.12.123.2 as the valid and best route. The reason? R2's BGP RID is currently lower than that of R3, as highlighted in this output:

```
R1#show ip bgp 4.4.4.4
BGP routing table entry for 4.4.4.4/32, version 2
Paths: (2 available, best #2, table Default-IP-Routing-Table)
Flag: 0x820
  Not advertised to any peer
  4
    172.12.123.3 from 172.12.123.3 (210.3.3.3)
    (Note from Chris: This address left on router from a previous lab.)
      Origin IGP, metric 0, localpref 100, valid, internal
  4
    172.12.123.2 from 172.12.123.2 (172.12.234.2)
      Origin IGP, metric 0, localpref 100, valid, internal, best
```

Using *weight* to change that path selection is simple. We can change the weight of all routes arriving from 172.12.123.3 with the neighbor command. Following a reset, the change in weight and the change in next-hop address takes effect!

```
R1(config)#router bgp 123
R1(config-router)#neighbor 172.12.123.3 weight 200

R1#show ip bgp
BGP table version is 2, local router ID is 172.12.123.1
Status codes: s suppressed, d damped, h history, * valid, > best, i - internal,
              r RIB-failure, S Stale
Origin codes: i - IGP, e - EGP, ? - incomplete
```

```
   Network          Next Hop            Metric  LocPrf Weight  Path
* i4.4.4.4/32       172.12.123.2             0     100      0  4 i
*>I                 172.12.123.3             0     100    200  4 i
```

The change in the weight attribute is local to R1. Let's add R5 to our network and give it an iBGP adjacency with R1.

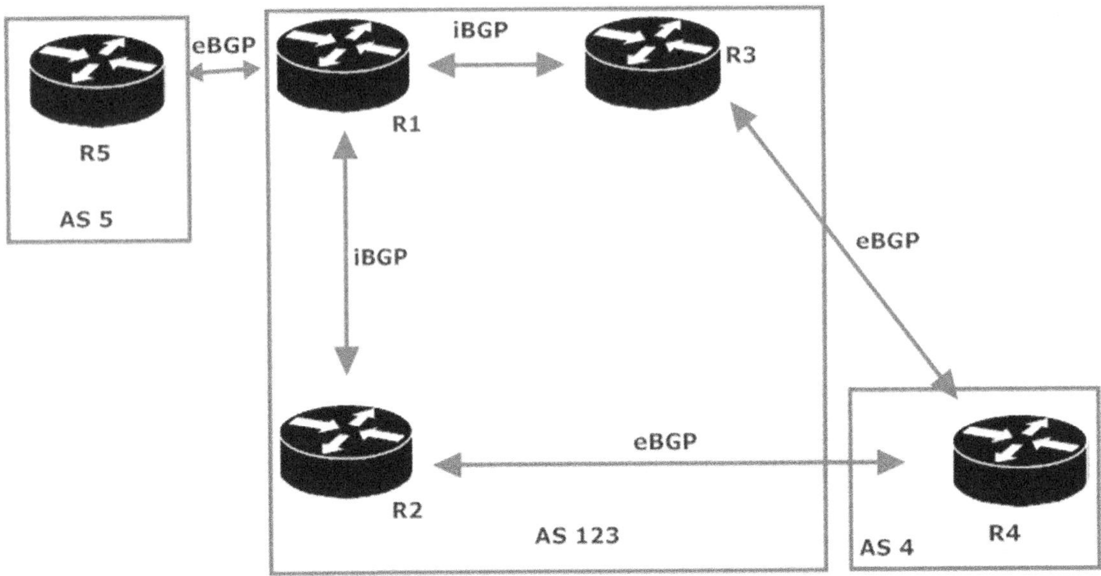

R5 has received a BGP route ad from R1 regarding 4.4.4.4 /32, but the weight is not carried in that route ad. R5 shows the route with a weight of zero.

```
R5#show ip bgp
BGP table version is 2, local router ID is 5.5.5.5
Status codes: s suppressed, d damped, h history, * valid, > best, i - internal,
              r RIB-failure, S Stale
Origin codes: i - IGP, e - EGP, ? - incomplete

   Network          Next Hop            Metric  LocPrf Weight  Path
*> 4.4.4.4/32       10.1.1.1                                0  123 4 i
```

Let's give the attributes a break for now and get some route aggregation done!

Summarizing/Aggregating BGP Routes

The "ones and zeroes" part of summarizing BGP routes works exactly the same way as does summarization with EIGRP and OSPF. We just need to write the routes out in binary, identify the common bits, and add those bits up to get the route and mask.

There are some choices with BGP route aggregation that aren't present with OSPF and EIGRP. When we configured summarization with OSPF and EIGRP, the interface sent out only the summary route and mask. We can do just that with BGP, or we can send out the aggregate route *and* the more-specific routes. We'll see that in action in the following lab, using the link between R1 and R5 from the previous lab.

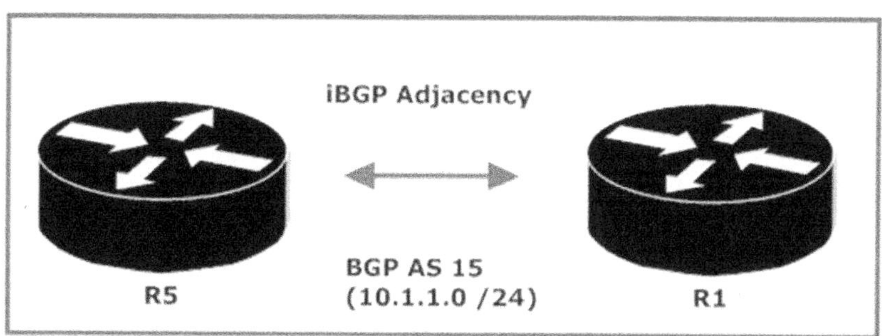

The only routes advertised in this lab are from R5—16.0.0.0, 17.0.0.0, 18.0.0.0, and 19.0.0.0, all with /8 masks. Let's check R1's table for those routes.

```
R1#show ip bgp
BGP table version is 5, local router ID is 172.12.123.1
Status codes: s suppressed, d damped, h history, * valid, > best, i - inter
              r RIB-failure, S Stale
Origin codes: i - IGP, e - EGP, ? - incomplete

   Network          Next Hop            Metric  LocPrf Weight  Path
*> 16.0.0.0         10.1.1.5                 0              0  5 i
*> 17.0.0.0         10.1.1.5                 0              0  5 i
*> 18.0.0.0         10.1.1.5                 0              0  5 i
*> 19.0.0.0         10.1.1.5                 0              0  5 i
```

Nothing wrong with this, but how do we like our routing tables? *Complete and concise!* We can easily aggregate these four routes into one summary route. You've likely done it in your head already, but let's do it on paper anyhoo. Common bits are highlighted, but you knew that, too. The common bits end in the first octet, so no need to break any other octets down.

16 **000100**00

17 **000100**01

18 **000100**10

19 **000100**11

We know the drill to get the summary route—just add the common bits, which gives us 16. The summary route is 16.0.0.0, but what of the mask? Just put a one in the mask for every common bit and a zero for the others, which gives us 11111100 00000000 00000000 00000000. In dotted decimal, that's 252.0.0.0. Now we just need to introduce the aggregate route into our BGP domain, and we're gold. We'll do that on R5 with the *aggregate-address* command.

```
R5(config-router)#aggregate-address ?
  A.B.C.D   Aggregate address

R5(config-router)#aggregate-address 16.0.0.0 ?
  A.B.C.D   Aggregate mask

R5(config-router)#aggregate-address 16.0.0.0 252.0.0.0 ?
  advertise-map Set condition to advertise attribute
  as-confed-set Generate AS confed set path information
  as-set        Generate AS set path information
  attribute-map Set attributes of aggregate
  route-map     Set parameters of aggregate
  summary-only  Filter more specific routes from updates
  suppress-map  Conditionally filter more specific routes from updates
  <cr>

R5(config-router)#aggregate-address 16.0.0.0 252.0.0.0
```

We head to R1, and...whaaaaaaaat?

```
R1#show ip bgp
BGP table version is 6, local router ID is 172.12.123.1
Status codes: s suppressed, d damped, h history, * valid, > best, i - inte
              r RIB-failure, S Stale
Origin codes: i - IGP, e - EGP, ? - incomplete

   Network          Next Hop            Metric LocPrf Weight Path
*> 16.0.0.0         10.1.1.5                 0             0 5 i
*> 16.0.0.0/6       10.1.1.5                 0             0 5 i
*> 17.0.0.0         10.1.1.5                 0             0 5 i
*> 18.0.0.0         10.1.1.5                 0             0 5 i
*> 19.0.0.0         10.1.1.5                 0             0 5 i
```

This is the default behavior of BGP route summarization—the summary route is advertised, but so are the more-specific routes. To suppress all individual routes from being advertised, use *aggregate-address* with *summary-only*.

```
R5(config)#router bgp 5
R5(config-router)#no aggregate-address 16.0.0.0 252.0.0.0
R5(config-router)#aggregate-address 16.0.0.0 252.0.0.0 ?
  advertise-map Set condition to advertise attribute
  as-confed-set Generate AS confed set path information
  as-set        Generate AS set path information
  attribute-map Set attributes of aggregate
```

```
  route-map     Set parameters of aggregate
  summary-only  Filter more specific routes from updates
  suppress-map  Conditionally filter more specific routes from updates
  <cr>

R5(config-router)#aggregate-address 16.0.0.0 252.0.0.0 summary-only
```

R1 now sees only the aggregate route.

```
R1#show ip bgp
BGP table version is 12, local router ID is 172.12.123.1
Status codes: s suppressed, d damped, h history, * valid, > best, i - internal,
              r RIB-failure, S Stale
Origin codes: i - IGP, e - EGP, ? - incomplete

   Network          Next Hop            Metric  LocPrf Weight Path
*> 16.0.0.0/6       10.1.1.5                 0             0 5 i
```

Onward!

Internal BGP: Synchronization, Route Reflectors, Full Meshes, and Lack Thereof

The only circumstances under which a BGP speaker will advertise a route to an internal neighbor is if the route was created by the advertising router via the *network* command, static route redistribution, or IGP route redistribution, or if the advertised route is a connected route.

That sounds like a lot of circumstances, but one common circumstance is missing from that list. When a BGP router learns a route from an internal neighbor, *that same router cannot advertise the route to another internal neighbor.*

Let's put that theory to the test with this simple network. R5 is advertising 5.5.5.0 /24 to R1...

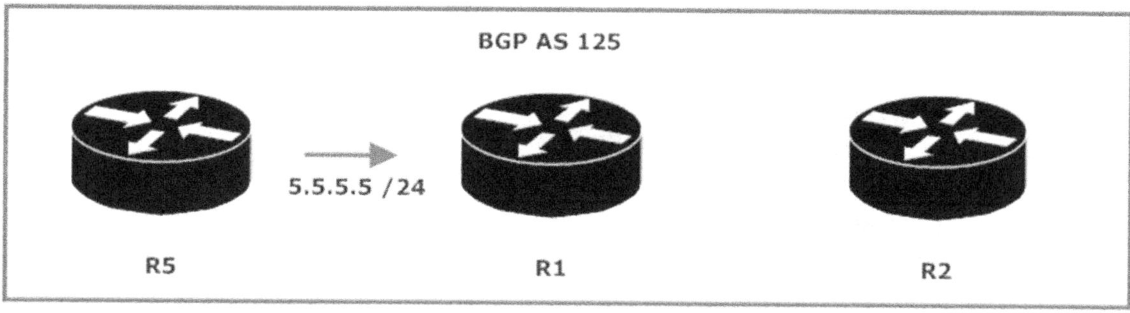

...verified with *show ip bgp 5.5.5.0* on R1.

```
R1#show ip bgp 5.5.5.0
BGP routing table entry for 5.5.5.0/24, version 2
Paths: (1 available, best #1, table Default-IP-Routing-Table)
Flag: 0x208
  Not advertised to any peer
  Local
    10.1.1.5 from 10.1.1.5 (19.5.5.5)
      Origin IGP, metric 0, localpref 100, valid, internal, best
```

Looks like the theory is correct—check out "not advertised to any peer," verified by *show ip bgp 5.5.5.0* on R2.

```
R2#show ip bgp 5.5.5.0
% Network not in table
```

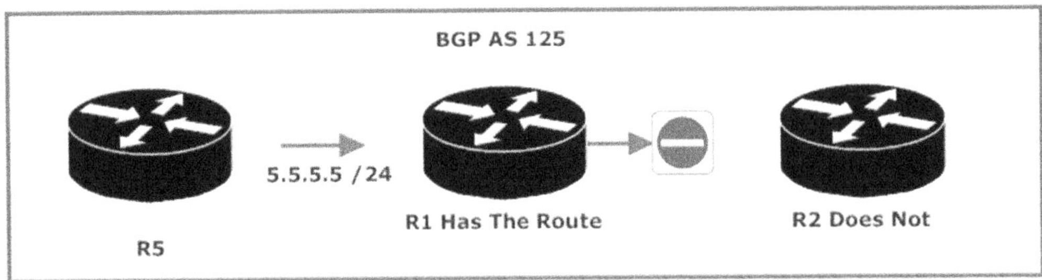

This looks to be an *extremely* restrictive rule. In theory, this would mean we'd need a full mesh in every AS in order for routes to be propagated properly and punctually. (Period.) In real-world networking, that would be an unbelievable amount of overhead. Luckily, BGP gives us a way around that logical nightmare. We'll see that solution in action shortly.

Right now, let's have a look at BGP's *rule of synchronization*. This rule only comes into play when an AS is a transit area and if there are non-BGP speakers in the transit area, like this:

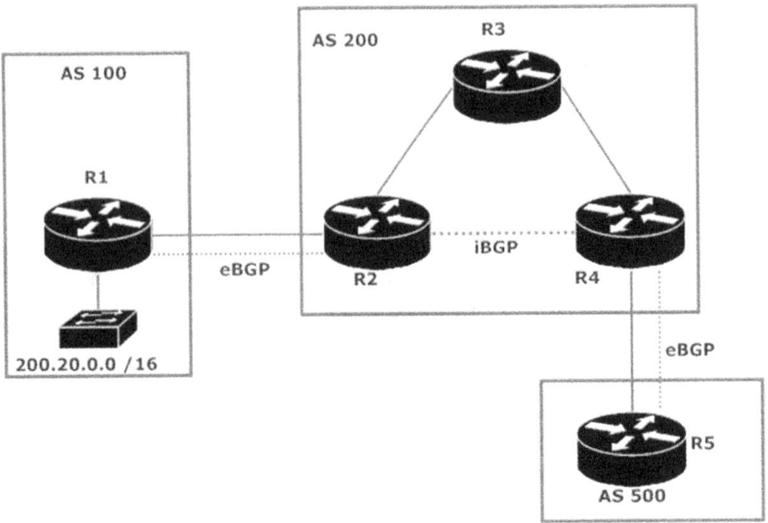

AS 200 is serving as a transit area between AS 100 and AS 500; the only iBGP neighbor relationship in AS 200 is between R2 and R4. Problem is, AS 200 is a classic hub-and-spoke config where all data sent from spoke to spoke (R2-R4, R4-R2) must go through the hub (R3). Since R3 is not running BGP, it can't possibly know about that network, so R3 will drop packets destined for 200.20.0.0 /16.

Without the synch rule, R4 would advertise a path to 200.20.0.0 over its eBGP connection to R5. As you'd expect, packets sent by R5 to 200.20.0.0 would be dropped at R3.

The BGP rule of synchronization: a transit AS will not advertise a route until every router in the transit AS has that same route in its IGP routing table. In this case, R4 will not send an advertisement for 200.20.0.0 /16 to R5 until R4 hears an advertisement for that network from R3 via an IGP. That advertisement indicates the non-BGP-speaking R3 has a route for that network.

Synchronization's major benefit is that packets that can't possibly reach the desired destination will not even be sent, reducing both the amount of unnecessary traffic and the unnecessary strain on router resources. Why send packets if they can't get where they need to go?

As you've likely noticed, BGP synchronization has been turned off by default in our configs. That's the case as of IOS 12.2(8). If BGP synch is on, it's safe to turn it off if all the routers in the AS are running BGP, if there's a full mesh in the AS, or if the AS in question isn't a transit AS. To disable BGP synch, just run the *no synch* command.

```
R5(config)#router bgp 5
R5(config-router)#no synch
```

BGP Split Horizon and Full-Mesh Deployments

You'd expect BGP split horizon to work just a little differently than EIGRP split horizon. You'd be right. BGP split horizon states that a BGP speaker cannot learn a route from an iBGP peer and then advertise it to another iBGP peer. (Sounds familiar!) To work with that rule, we'd need a logical full mesh among all iBGP peers in every BGP AS, which is not a practical idea.

The reason we don't see many BGP full meshes is really the same reason we don't see many Frame Relay full-mesh networks, and that's one simple word—*overhead.* Any full-mesh deployment of BGP is going to hammer your router resources. A full mesh will also need a ton of TCP connections, and the more routers you have, the more connections you'll need. Here's the formula for determining the number of TCP connections needed for a full mesh:

X (X–1) / 2, with "x" being the number of routers

Consider an AS with 20 routers: 20 (20–1) / 2 = 190. BGP requires 190 separate TCP connections for a 20-router AS. Add that to the administrative nightmare involved in creating and maintaining the full mesh, and you have quite the labor-intensive situation. In short, there are three really good reasons to avoid full-mesh iBGP deployments:

- An unnecessarily large number of TCP connections are needed.
- Those sessions suck up a lot of bandwidth.
- Creating and maintaining the full mesh is time intensive and a logical landmine, which is likely to result in a lot more troubleshooting than you or I would care to do.

Having analyzed the problem, let's apply the solution...*route reflectors!*

Route Reflectors

A router configured as a BGP route reflector can take a route learned from an iBGP peer and advertise it to another iBGP peer. Take *that*, split horizon!

The iBGP peers that send routes to the route reflector are *clients*. When the RR receives a route from a client, the RR does just what you think it would do—it reflects the route to the other clients. The clients have no idea this is going on. The clients don't even know they are clients, and they require no additional configuration to make this happen. The only config you'll write is on the route reflector itself. Clients will have a peering with the RR but not with each other, avoiding the full-mesh mess.

A BGP speaker with a peering to a route reflector does not have to be a client. These speakers that are not clients are technically referred to as "nonclients." Nonclients *do* need a TCP connection to every other router in the AS.

Enough talk—let's reflect some routes!

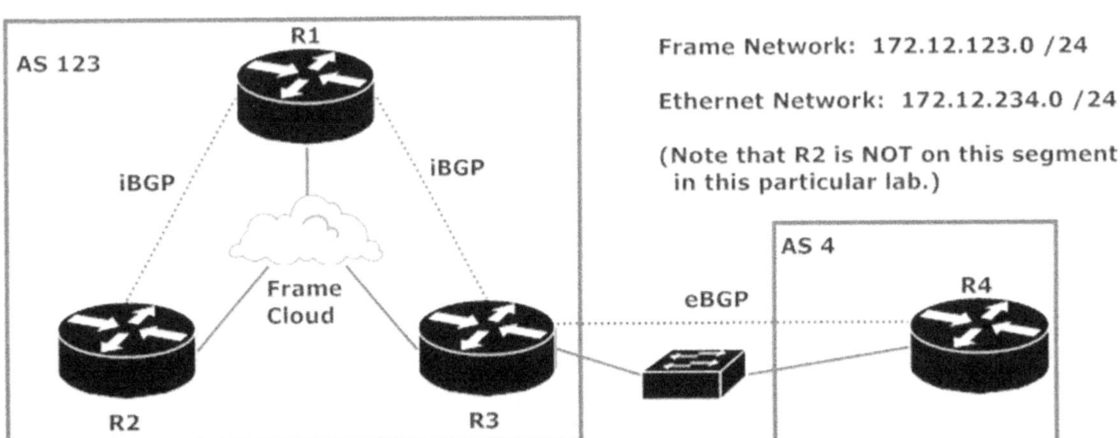

To test route reflection, we need a route to reflect! Let's advertise R4's loopback.

```
R4(config-if)#router bgp 4
R4(config-router)#network 4.4.4.4 mask 255.255.255.255
```

Does R3 have the route?

```
R3#show ip bgp
BGP table version is 2, local router ID is 172.12.234.3
Status codes: s suppressed, d damped, h history, * valid, > best, i - internal,
              r RIB-failure, S Stale, m multipath, b backup-path, x best-external
Origin codes: i - IGP, e - EGP, ? - incomplete

   Network          Next Hop            Metric  LocPrf Weight  Path
*> 4.4.4.4/32       172.12.234.4             0              0  4 i
```

Sure does, and it's marked valid and best. Let's go to the next router down the road, R1.

```
R1#show ip bgp
BGP table version is 1, local router ID is 172.12.123.1
Status codes: s suppressed, d damped, h history, * valid, > best, i - internal,
              r RIB-failure, S Stale
Origin codes: i - IGP, e - EGP, ? - incomplete

   Network          Next Hop            Metric  LocPrf Weight  Path
* i4.4.4.4/32       172.12.234.4             0     100      0  4 i
```

Got a little problem here. R1 has the route, and it's marked valid but hasn't been chosen as valid and best. I bet you know why without *show ip bgp 4.4.4.4*, but here 'tis!

```
R1#show ip bgp 4.4.4.4
BGP routing table entry for 4.4.4.4/32, version 0
Paths: (1 available, no best path)
  Not advertised to any peer
  4
    172.12.234.4 (inaccessible) from 172.12.123.3 (172.12.234.3)
      Origin IGP, metric 0, localpref 100, valid, internal
```

It's all about inaccessibility! R1 has no idea how to reach 172.12.234.4. Let's change that next-hop address via *next-hop-self* on R3.

```
R3(config)#router bgp 123
R3(config-router)#neighbor 172.12.123.1 next-hop-self

R3#clear ip bgp * soft out
```

The result on R1: an accessible next-hop address and a valid and best route!

```
R1#show ip bgp
BGP table version is 2, local router ID is 172.12.123.1
Status codes: s suppressed, d damped, h history, * valid, > best, i - internal,
              r RIB-failure, S Stale
```

```
Origin codes: i - IGP, e - EGP, ? - incomplete

   Network          Next Hop            Metric LocPrf Weight Path
*>i4.4.4.4/32       172.12.123.3             0    100      0 4 i
```

Let's head on down the road to R2.

```
R2#show ip bgp

R2#
```

This is the first time *show ip bgp* hasn't shown us anything, and BGP split horizon is the reason. The only route in play is 4.4.4.4/32. R1 learned that from an iBGP peer, R3, and now cannot advertise it to another iBGP peer. That's why R2 has nothing to show us!

Just for fun, let's add R2's loopback to the BGP network and then check the BGP tables of the other two routers in the AS.

```
R2(config-if)#router bgp 123
R2(config-router)#network 2.2.2.2 mask 255.255.255.255

R1#show ip bgp
BGP table version is 3, local router ID is 172.12.123.1
Status codes: s suppressed, d damped, h history, * valid, > best, i - internal,
              r RIB-failure, S Stale
Origin codes: i - IGP, e - EGP, ? - incomplete

   Network          Next Hop            Metric LocPrf Weight Path
*>i2.2.2.2/32       172.12.123.2             0    100      0 i
*>i4.4.4.4/32       172.12.123.3             0    100      0 4 i

R3#show ip bgp
BGP table version is 2, local router ID is 172.12.234.3
Status codes: s suppressed, d damped, h history, * valid, > best, i - internal,
              r RIB-failure, S Stale, m multipath, b backup-path, x best-external
Origin codes: i - IGP, e - EGP, ? - incomplete

   Network          Next Hop            Metric LocPrf Weight Path
*> 4.4.4.4/32       172.12.234.4             0             0 4 i
```

R1 has a valid and best entry for R2's loopback, but R3 has no route for that network. R1 learned the route from one iBGP peer (R2) and therefore cannot advertise that route to another iBGP peer (R3).

Let us banish split horizon by configuring R1 as a route reflector. R2 and R3 will be route reflector clients, and the clients require no additional configuration. The RR itself doesn't need much config!

```
R1(config)#router bgp 123
R1(config-router)#neighbor 172.12.123.1 ?
  activate                 Enable the Address Family for this Neighbor
  advertise-map            specify route-map for conditional advertisement
  advertisement-interval   Minimum interval between sending BGP routing updates
  allowas-in               Accept as-path with my AS present in it
  capability               Advertise capability to the peer
  default-originate        Originate default route to this neighbor
  description              Neighbor specific description
  disable-connected-check  One-hop away EBGP peer using loopback address
  distribute-list          Filter updates to/from this neighbor
  dmzlink-bw               Propagate the DMZ link bandwidth
  ebgp-multihop            Allow EBGP neighbors not on directly connected
                           networks
  fall-over                session fall on peer route lost
  filter-list              Establish BGP filters
  inherit                  Inherit a template
  local-as                 Specify a local-as number
  maximum-prefix           Maximum number of prefixes accepted from this peer
  next-hop-self            Disable the next hop calculation for this neighbor
  next-hop-unchanged       Propagate the iBGP paths's next hop unchanged for
                           this neighbor
  password                 Set a password
  peer-group               Member of the peer-group
  prefix-list              Filter updates to/from this neighbor
  remote-as                Specify a BGP neighbor
  remove-private-as        Remove private AS number from outbound updates
  route-map                Apply route map to neighbor
  route-reflector-client   Configure a neighbor as Route Reflector client
  send-community           Send Community attribute to this neighbor
  shutdown                 Administratively shut down this neighbor
  soft-reconfiguration     Per neighbor soft reconfiguration
  timers                   BGP per neighbor timers
  translate-update         Translate Update to MBGP format
  transport                Transport options
  ttl-security             BGP ttl security check
  unsuppress-map           Route-map to selectively unsuppress suppressed routes
  update-source            Source of routing updates
  version                  Set the BGP version to match a neighbor
  weight                   Set default weight for routes from this neighbor

R1(config-router)#neighbor 172.12.123.2 route-reflector-client
*Jun 13 18:04:13.248: %BGP-5-ADJCHANGE: neighbor 172.12.123.2 Down RR client con
fig change
*Jun 13 18:04:15.472: %BGP-5-ADJCHANGE: neighbor 172.12.123.2 Up
R1(config-router)#neighbor 172.12.123.3 route-reflector-client
```

```
*Jun 13 18:04:19.651: %BGP-5-ADJCHANGE: neighbor 172.12.123.3 Down RR client con
fig change
*Jun 13 18:04:21.874: %BGP-5-ADJCHANGE: neighbor 172.12.123.3 Up
```

You will have some adjacency bouncing as you're writing the config! Let's see the results on R2 and R3 now that our adjacencies are back up:

```
R2#show ip bgp
BGP table version is 5, local router ID is 172.12.234.2
Status codes: s suppressed, d damped, h history, * valid, > best, i - internal,
              r RIB-failure, S Stale, m multipath, b backup-path, x best-external
Origin codes: i - IGP, e - EGP, ? - incomplete

   Network          Next Hop            Metric  LocPrf Weight  Path
*> 2.2.2.2/32       0.0.0.0                  0          32768  i
*>i4.4.4.4/32       172.12.123.3             0     100      0  4 i

R3#show ip bgp
BGP table version is 5, local router ID is 172.12.234.3
Status codes: s suppressed, d damped, h history, * valid, > best, i - internal,
              r RIB-failure, S Stale, m multipath, b backup-path, x best-external
Origin codes: i - IGP, e - EGP, ? - incomplete

   Network          Next Hop            Metric  LocPrf Weight  Path
*>i2.2.2.2/32       172.12.123.2             0     100      0  i
*> 4.4.4.4/32       172.12.234.4             0              0  4 i
```

R2 now has a valid and best entry for 4.4.4.4/32, and R3 has an entry for R2's loopback. The route reflector configuration is a success!

You can verify RR clients with *show ip bgp neighbor*. This command now gives you literally three screens of information, and in the middle of it all, you'll see the RR client verification.

```
R1#show ip bgp neighbor
BGP neighbor is 172.12.123.2, remote AS 123, internal link
  BGP version 4, remote router ID 172.12.234.2
  BGP state = Established, up for 00:00:24
  Last read 00:00:24, hold time is 180, keepalive interval is 60 seconds
  Neighbor capabilities:
    Route refresh: advertised and received(old & new)
    Address family IPv4 Unicast: advertised and received
  Received 28 messages, 0 notifications, 0 in queue
  Sent 26 messages, 0 notifications, 0 in queue
  Route refresh request: received 0, sent 0
  Default minimum time between advertisement runs is 5 seconds
```

```
For address family: IPv4 Unicast
  BGP table version 7, neighbor version 7
  Index 1, Offset 0, Mask 0x2
  Route-Reflector Client
  1 accepted prefixes consume 36 bytes
  Prefix advertised 1, suppressed 0, withdrawn 0
  Number of NLRIs in the update sent: max 1, min 0

  Connections established 2; dropped 1
  Last reset 00:00:35, due to RR client config change
```

Now, route reflectors don't just reflect to *everyone*, mind you. How a route reflector handles a routing update depends on the type of BGP router that sent that update. Save yourself some serious headaches from unnecessary troubleshooting, and memorize this list!

- Updates from RR clients are sent to all client and nonclient peers.
- Updates from eBGP peers are sent to all client and nonclient peers. (I detect a pattern.)
- Updates from nonclient peers are sent to all clients.

Once you have your BGP config in place, you may want to fine-tune the routes to be advertised. Or, perhaps, the routes *not* to be advertised. Either way, prefix lists really help—and they're coming up next!

Prefix Lists And BGP

Cisco loves prefix lists for their high flexibility, their support for incremental updates, and the fact that writing BGP prefix lists is much more efficient than writing ACLs that filter BGP updates. (They're sure right on that last point!) BGP tables can be *much* larger than any IGP table you'll ever see, and since prefix lists match only on the prefix of the address, the overall process is much faster than using ACLs.

A prefix list has several things in common with an ACL:

- With both, if a route is not expressly permitted, it's denied.
- At the bottom of both a prefix list and an ACL, you'll find the implicit deny.
- Explicit deny statements do not override the implicit deny.

Prefix lists work from top to bottom, and when a match is found, the process stops. It's vital the lines are in the correct order to do the job you want the prefix list to do.

Prefix list lines are numbered, with the lowest numbers at the top. Even if you and I (the network admins!) don't number the statements manually, the IOS will number them for you, incrementing by five. This makes it easy for you to go back and add lines exactly where you need them.

Let's see prefix lists in action with the following network.

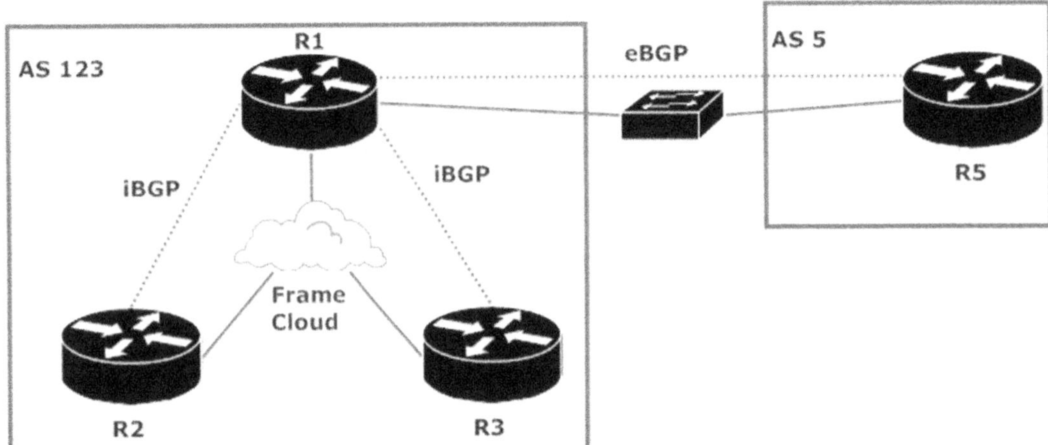

On R5, we'll advertise the usual loopback of 5.5.5.5 /32 along with four other networks.

```
router bgp 5
 no synchronization
 bgp log-neighbor-changes
 network 5.5.5.5 mask 255.255.255.255
 network 16.0.0.0
 network 17.0.0.0
 network 18.0.0.0
 network 19.0.0.0
 neighbor 10.1.1.1 remote-as 123
 no auto-summary
```

Will R1, R2, and R3 each see those routes? Will they be marked valid and best on each?

```
R1#show ip bgp
BGP table version is 8, local router ID is 172.12.123.1
Status codes: s suppressed, d damped, h history, * valid, > best, i - internal,
              r RIB-failure, S Stale
Origin codes: i - IGP, e - EGP, ? - incomplete

   Network          Next Hop            Metric  LocPrf Weight  Path
*> 5.5.5.5/32       10.1.1.5                 0              0  5 i
*> 16.0.0.0         10.1.1.5                 0              0  5 i
*> 17.0.0.0         10.1.1.5                 0              0  5 i
*> 18.0.0.0         10.1.1.5                 0              0  5 i
*> 19.0.0.0         10.1.1.5                 0              0  5 i
```

```
R2#show ip bgp
BGP table version is 1, local router ID is 2.2.2.2
Status codes: s suppressed, d damped, h history, * valid, > best, i - internal,
              r RIB-failure, S Stale, m multipath, b backup-path, x best-external

Origin codes: i - IGP, e - EGP, ? - incomplete

Network            Next Hop      Metric LocPrf  Weight   Path
* i5.5.5.5/32      10.1.1.5           0     100       0  5 i
* i16.0.0.0        10.1.1.5           0     100       0  5 i
* i17.0.0.0        10.1.1.5           0     100       0  5 i
* i18.0.0.0        10.1.1.5           0     100       0  5 i
* i19.0.0.0        10.1.1.5           0     100       0  5 i

R3#show ip bgp
BGP table version is 1, local router ID is 172.12.234.3
Status codes: s suppressed, d damped, h history, * valid, > best, i - internal,
              r RIB-failure, S Stale, m multipath, b backup-path, x best-external
Origin codes: i - IGP, e - EGP, ? - incomplete

   Network         Next Hop            Metric  LocPrf Weight  Path
* i5.5.5.5/32      10.1.1.5                 0     100      0  5 i
* i16.0.0.0        10.1.1.5                 0     100      0  5 i
* i17.0.0.0        10.1.1.5                 0     100      0  5 i
* i18.0.0.0        10.1.1.5                 0     100      0  5 i
* i19.0.0.0        10.1.1.5                 0     100      0  5 i
```

Everything's good on R1, but that next-hop address of 10.1.1.5 isn't reachable by either R2 or R3. Let's fix those entries with *next-hop-self* and move forward.

```
R1(config)#router bgp 123
R1(config-router)#neighbor 172.12.123.2 next-hop-self
R1(config-router)#neighbor 172.12.123.3 next-hop-self

R2#show ip bgp
BGP table version is 6, local router ID is 2.2.2.2
Status codes: s suppressed, d damped, h history, * valid, > best, i - internal,
              r RIB-failure, S Stale, m multipath, b backup-path, x best-external
Origin codes: i - IGP, e - EGP, ? - incomplete

   Network         Next Hop            Metric  LocPrf Weight  Path
*>i5.5.5.5/32      172.12.123.1             0     100      0  5 i
*>i16.0.0.0        172.12.123.1             0     100      0  5 i
*>i17.0.0.0        172.12.123.1             0     100      0  5 i
*>i18.0.0.0        172.12.123.1             0     100      0  5 i
*>i19.0.0.0        172.12.123.1             0     100      0  5 i
```

```
R3#show ip bgp
BGP table version is 6, local router ID is 172.12.234.3
Status codes: s suppressed, d damped, h history, * valid, > best, i - internal,
              r RIB-failure, S Stale, m multipath, b backup-path, x best-external
Origin codes: i - IGP, e - EGP, ? - incomplete

   Network          Next Hop            Metric LocPrf Weight Path
*>i5.5.5.5/32       172.12.123.1             0    100      0 5 i
*>i16.0.0.0         172.12.123.1             0    100      0 5 i
*>i17.0.0.0         172.12.123.1             0    100      0 5 i
*>i18.0.0.0         172.12.123.1             0    100      0 5 i
*>i19.0.0.0         172.12.123.1             0    100      0 5 i
```

Done and done!

We just got word that neither R2 nor R3 should know about the 16–19 networks but should know of the 5.5.5.5/32 entry and any networks added in the future. Sounds like a daunting task, but the right prefix list on R1 will get the job done.

```
R1(config)#ip prefix-list ?
  WORD              Name of a prefix list
  sequence-number   Include/exclude sequence numbers in NVGEN

R1(config)#ip prefix-list NET5ONLY ?
  deny          Specify packets to reject
  description   Prefix-list specific description
  permit        Specify packets to forward
  seq           sequence number of an entry

R1(config)#ip prefix-list NET5ONLY deny ?
A.B.C.D IP prefix <network>/<length>, e.g., 35.0.0.0/8

R1(config)#ip prefix-list NET5ONLY deny 16.0.0.0/8
R1(config)#ip prefix-list NET5ONLY deny 17.0.0.0/8
R1(config)#ip prefix-list NET5ONLY deny 18.0.0.0/8
R1(config)#ip prefix-list NET5ONLY deny 19.0.0.0/8
R1(config)#ip prefix-list NET5ONLY permit 0.0.0.0/0 le 32
```

That last line looks a little odd, but it's just the prefix list equivalent of an ACL's "permit any" statement. The "le" stands for "less than or equal to," verified by IOS Help:

```
R1(config)#ip prefix-list NET5ONLY permit 0.0.0.0/0 ?
  ge  Minimum prefix length to be matched
  le  Maximum prefix length to be matched
  <cr>
```

Now let's apply this prefix list to R2 and R3, which requires indicating the direction in which the prefix list should be applied. After applying the filter, we'll check the tables on R2 and R3.

```
R1(config)#router bgp 123
R1(config-router)#neighbor 172.12.123.2 prefix-list NET5ONLY ?
  in  Filter incoming updates
  out Filter outgoing updates

R1(config-router)#neighbor 172.12.123.2 prefix-list NET5ONLY out
R1(config-router)#neighbor 172.12.123.3 prefix-list NET5ONLY out

R1#clear ip bgp * soft out

R2#show ip bgp
BGP table version is 10, local router ID is 2.2.2.2
Status codes: s suppressed, d damped, h history, * valid, > best, i - internal,
              r RIB-failure, S Stale, m multipath, b backup-path, x best-external
Origin codes: i - IGP, e - EGP, ? - incomplete

   Network          Next Hop            Metric LocPrf Weight Path
*>i5.5.5.5/32       172.12.123.1             0    100      0 5 i

R3#show ip bgp
BGP table version is 10, local router ID is 172.12.234.3
Status codes: s suppressed, d damped, h history, * valid, > best, i - internal,
              r RIB-failure, S Stale, m multipath, b backup-path, x best-external
Origin codes: i - IGP, e - EGP, ? - incomplete

   Network          Next Hop            Metric LocPrf Weight Path
*>i5.5.5.5/32       172.12.123.1             0    100      0 5 i
```

Looks good! We were asked to allow 5.5.5.5/32 and any networks added in the future, though. Welcome to the future!

```
R5(config-if)#router bgp 5
R5(config-router)#network 55.55.55.55 mask 255.255.255.255
```

Let's verify the route on R1 and then see if the route got through the filter on the way to R2 and R3.

```
R1#show ip bgp
BGP table version is 9, local router ID is 172.12.123.1
Status codes: s suppressed, d damped, h history, * valid, > best, i - internal,
              r RIB-failure, S Stale
Origin codes: i - IGP, e - EGP, ? - incomplete
```

```
   Network          Next Hop            Metric LocPrf Weight Path
*> 5.5.5.5/32       10.1.1.5                 0             0 5 i
*> 16.0.0.0         10.1.1.5                 0             0 5 i
*> 17.0.0.0         10.1.1.5                 0             0 5 i
*> 18.0.0.0         10.1.1.5                 0             0 5 i
*> 19.0.0.0         10.1.1.5                 0             0 5 i
*> 55.55.55.55/32   10.1.1.5                 0             0 5 i

R2#show ip bgp
BGP table version is 11, local router ID is 2.2.2.2
Status codes: s suppressed, d damped, h history, * valid, > best, i - internal,
              r RIB-failure, S Stale, m multipath, b backup-path, x best-external

Origin codes: i - IGP, e - EGP, ? - incomplete

   Network          Next Hop            Metric LocPrf Weight Path
*>i5.5.5.5/32       172.12.123.1             0    100      0 5 i
*>i55.55.55.55/32   172.12.123.1             0    100      0 5 i

R3#show ip bgp
BGP table version is 11, local router ID is 172.12.234.3
Status codes: s suppressed, d damped, h history, * valid, > best, i - internal,
              r RIB-failure, S Stale, m multipath, b backup-path, x best-external

Origin codes: i - IGP, e - EGP, ? - incomplete

   Network          Next Hop            Metric LocPrf Weight Path
*>i5.5.5.5/32       172.12.123.1             0    100      0 5 i
*>i55.55.55.55/32   172.12.123.1             0    100      0 5 i
```

Success! The 55.55.55.55 /32 network didn't match any of the first five lines of our prefix list, but it did match the sixth, which allows any route through. To review the lines of any and all prefix lists, run *show ip prefix-list.*

```
R1#show ip prefix-list
ip prefix-list NET5ONLY: 5 entries
   seq 5 deny 16.0.0.0/8
   seq 10 deny 17.0.0.0/8
   seq 15 deny 18.0.0.0/8
   seq 20 deny 19.0.0.0/8
   seq 25 permit 0.0.0.0/0 le 32
```

Just for fun, let's say the word just came down that we do need to filter that 55.55.55.55 /32 entry. After praising our boss (not really), we'll add a line to that list that filters that particular address. Any sequence number not already in use and less than twenty-five will do the job. After applying the change, we'll check the tables on R2 and R3.

```
R1(config)#ip prefix-list NET5ONLY ?
  deny          Specify packets to reject
  description   Prefix-list specific description
  permit        Specify packets to forward
  seq           sequence number of an entry

R1(config)#ip prefix-list NET5ONLY seq ?
  <1-4294967294>   Sequence number

R1(config)#ip prefix-list NET5ONLY seq 24 ?
  deny    Specify packets to reject
  permit  Specify packets to forward

R1(config)#ip prefix-list NET5ONLY seq 24 deny 55.55.55.55/32
```

I'll verify the change before doing a soft outbound reset.

```
R1#show ip prefix-list
ip prefix-list NET5ONLY: 6 entries
   seq 5 deny 16.0.0.0/8
   seq 10 deny 17.0.0.0/8
   seq 15 deny 18.0.0.0/8
   seq 20 deny 19.0.0.0/8
   seq 24 deny 55.55.55.55/32
   seq 25 permit 0.0.0.0/0 le 32

R1#clear ip bgp * soft out

R2#show ip bgp
BGP table version is 12, local router ID is 2.2.2.2
Status codes: s suppressed, d damped, h history, * valid, > best, i - internal,
              r RIB-failure, S Stale, m multipath, b backup-path, x best-external
Origin codes: i - IGP, e - EGP, ? - incomplete

Network Next Hop Metric LocPrf Weight Path
*>i5.5.5.5/32 172.12.123.1 0 100 0 5 i

R3#show ip bgp
BGP table version is 12, local router ID is 172.12.234.3
Status codes: s suppressed, d damped, h history, * valid, > best, i - internal,
              r RIB-failure, S Stale, m multipath, b backup-path, x best-external
Origin codes: i - IGP, e - EGP, ? - incomplete

   Network          Next Hop            Metric LocPrf Weight Path
*>i5.5.5.5/32       172.12.123.1             0    100      0 5 i
```

The line was successfully added to the prefix list, and the 55.55.55.55 /32 route has been filtered!

Private AS Numbers

You've surely noticed the rather large range of numbers available to us for an AS:

```
R1(config)#router bgp ?
  <1-65535> Autonomous system number
```

Some of those numbers are private AS numbers or reserved for other reasons. The numbers 64496–65535 are considered private ASs, and just as private IP addresses should not be advertised to external networks, neither should private AS numbers. And no matter how hard you try, you can't assign AS a zero.

```
R1(config)#router bgp  0
                       ^
% Invalid input detected at '^' marker.
```

By the way, some Cisco documentation uses the term "ASN" to refer to an AS number, and some doesn't. Be prepared to see the term "ASN" on your exam as well as just plain ol' "AS number."

The BGP RID

You can spot the local router's BGP RID in *show ip bgp*:

```
R1#show ip bgp
BGP table version is 2, local router ID is 172.12.123.1
Status codes: s suppressed, d damped, h history, * valid, > best, i - internal,
              r RIB-failure, S Stale
Origin codes: i - IGP, e - EGP, ? - incomplete

   Network          Next Hop            Metric LocPrf Weight Path
*>i5.5.5.5/32       10.1.1.5                 0    100      0 i
```

The RID of the advertising router for a particular route can be seen with *show ip bgp x.x.x.x*.

```
R1#show ip bgp 5.5.5.5
BGP routing table entry for 5.5.5.5/32, version 2
Paths: (1 available, best #1, table Default-IP-Routing-Table)
```

```
Flag: 0x820
   Not advertised to any peer
   Local
      10.1.1.5 from 10.1.1.5 (55.55.55.55)
        Origin IGP, metric 0, localpref 100, valid, internal, best
```

The BGP RID follows much the same rules as the EIGRP and OSPF RIDs. The highest IP address assigned to a loopback is used as the BGP RID. If there's no loopback, the highest IP address assigned to an *up/up* physical interface is used. To hardcode the BGP RID, use the *bgp router-id* command. Yes, even though you're in BGP configuration mode, you still have to specify *bgp* in this command.

```
R1(config)#router bgp 1235
R1(config-router)#router-id ?
% Unrecognized command
R1(config-router)#bgp router-id ?
  A.B.C.D   Manually configured router identifier

R1(config-router)#bgp router-id 11.11.11.11 ?
  <cr>
```

Your router's adjacencies will go down and back up after this change.

```
*Jun 13 21:52:59.253: %BGP-5-ADJCHANGE: neighbor 10.1.1.5 Down Router ID changed
*Jun 13 21:52:59.257: %BGP-5-ADJCHANGE: neighbor 172.12.123.2 Down Router ID cha
nged
*Jun 13 21:52:59.257: %BGP-5-ADJCHANGE: neighbor 172.12.123.3 Down Router ID cha
nged
*Jun 13 21:52:59.281: %BGP-5-ADJCHANGE: neighbor 10.1.1.5 Up
*Jun 13 21:52:59.397: %BGP-5-ADJCHANGE: neighbor 172.12.123.2 Up
*Jun 13 21:52:59.425: %BGP-5-ADJCHANGE: neighbor 172.12.123.3 Up
```

Be careful about changing the RID, because routers with the same RID cannot form or maintain an adjacency. Here's the output on R1 after I changed the RID to match that of the neighboring R5.

```
R1(config)#router bgp 1235
R1(config-router)#bgp router-id 55.55.55.55
R1(config-router)#^Z
*Jun 13 21:55:17.620: %BGP-5-ADJCHANGE: neighbor 10.1.1.5 Down Router ID changed
*Jun 13 21:55:17.624: %BGP-5-ADJCHANGE: neighbor 172.12.123.2 Down Router ID cha
nged
*Jun 13 21:55:17.624: %BGP-5-ADJCHANGE: neighbor 172.12.123.3 Down Router ID cha
nged
*Jun 13 21:55:17.648: %BGP-3-NOTIFICATION: received from neighbor 10.1.1.5 2/3 (
BGP identifier wrong) 4 bytes 37373737
```

```
R1#
*Jun 13 21:55:17.772: %BGP-5-ADJCHANGE: neighbor 172.12.123.2 Up
*Jun 13 21:55:17.800: %BGP-5-ADJCHANGE: neighbor 172.12.123.3 Up
*Jun 13 21:55:18.032: %SYS-5-CONFIG _ I: Configured from console by console
R1#
*Jun 13 21:55:27.348: %BGP-3-NOTIFICATION: sent to neighbor 10.1.1.5 2/3 (BGP id
entifier wrong) 4 bytes 37373737
R1# FFFF FFFF FFFF FFFF FFFF FFFF FFFF FFFF 003A 0104 04D3 00B4 3737 3737 1D02 0
601 0400 0100 0102 0280 0002 0202 0002 0383 0100 0206 4104 0000 04D3
R1#
*Jun 13 21:55:34.515: %BGP-3-NOTIFICATION: sent to neighbor 10.1.1.5 2/3 (BGP id
entifier wrong) 4 bytes 37373737
```

The adjacencies with R2 and R3 came right back up, but the adjacency with R5 will not come back up until I change the RID to anything other than 55.55.55.55.

```
R1(config-router)#bgp router-id 11.11.11.11
R1(config-router)#^Z
R1#sho
*Jun 13 21:56:09.585: %BGP-5-ADJCHANGE: neighbor 172.12.123.2 Down Router ID
changed
*Jun 13 21:56:09.585: %BGP-5-ADJCHANGE: neighbor 172.12.123.3 Down Router ID
changed
*Jun 13 21:56:09.725: %BGP-5-ADJCHANGE: neighbor 172.12.123.2 Up
*Jun 13 21:56:09.749: %BGP-5-ADJCHANGE: neighbor 172.12.123.3 Up
*Jun 13 21:56:09.962: %SYS-5-CONFIG _ I: Configured from console by console
R1#show ip
*Jun 13 21:56:11.384: %BGP-5-ADJCHANGE: neighbor 10.1.1.5 Up
```

A Word about Route Redistribution between an IGP and a BGP

Route redistribution isn't always bidirectional. You can redistribute EIGRP routes into an OSPF area without necessarily taking OSPF routes and putting them into EIGRP. That's fine, you say, but what does this have to do with BGP? Well, on rare occasions, you may need to redistribute IGP routes into BGP, and we know there are three ways to make that happen—the *network* command, static route redistribution, and redistribution of routes discovered by an IGP.

Cisco strongly recommends you avoid that last choice whenever possible. That form of redistribution can easily lead to routing loops. The network command is almost always your best bet.

What of taking BGP routes and redistributing them into IGP, you ask? There's rarely a really good reason to do so, and doing so incorrectly can lead to a lot of trouble. A full

BGP routing table can have ove a hundred thousand routes. Never redistribute routes from BGP to an IGP unless you're really, really sure of what you're doing—and maybe not even then!

Speaking of route redistribution...that's our next topic!

Chapter 7: ROUTE REDISTRIBUTION

Route redistribution is simply the process of taking routes from one source and placing them into a separate routing process. The route source doesn't have to be a dynamic routing protocol—we can redistribute directly connected networks and static routes as well.

The word "simply" may be a tad misleading. The basic configurations involved with route redistribution are pretty darn simple, but there are two things to watch out for:

The more route redistribution you have, the greater the chance of routing loops. That's particularly true when you're redistributing between networks with multiple entrance and exit points, as in the following illustration. If we allowed R4 to advertise those same routes back to R2, we'd greatly increase the chance of a routing loop.

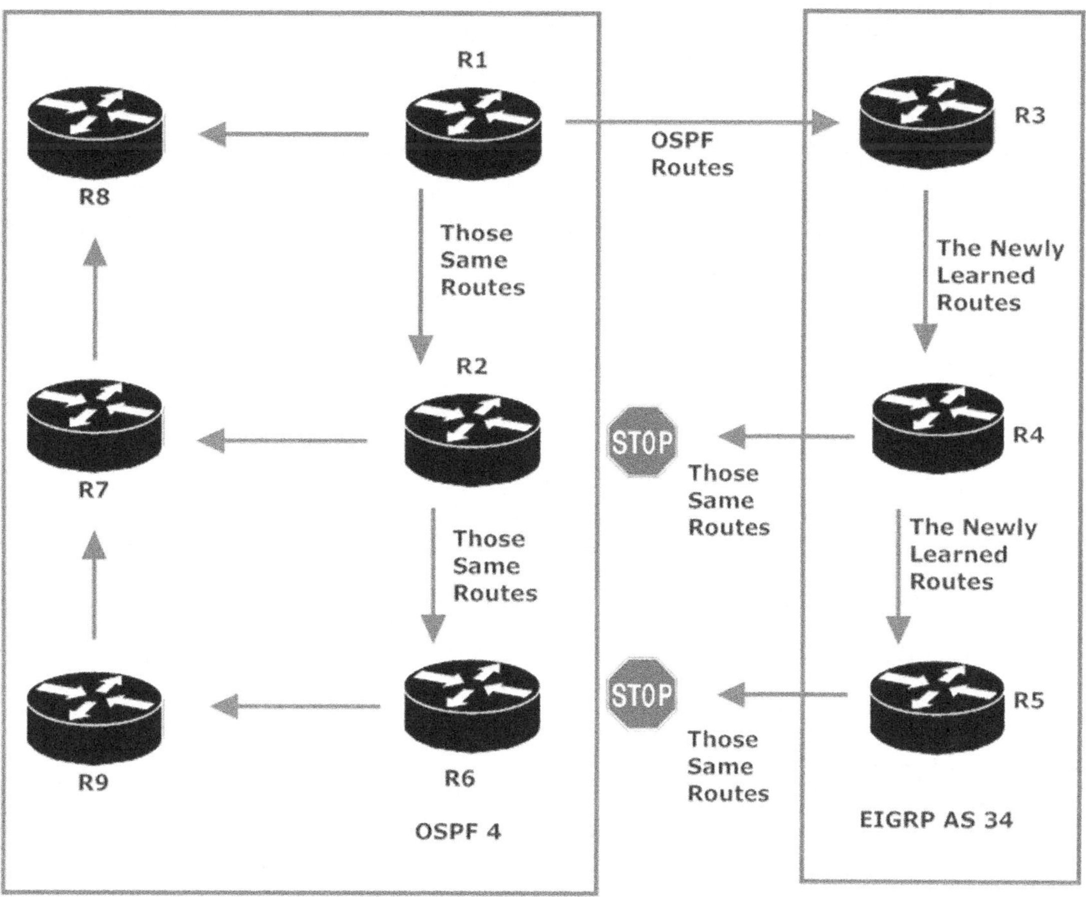

Also watch for route redistribution details regarding *seed metrics,* a default value given to a redistributed route. Some protocols require the network admins (you know who) to set the seed metric. Another protocol has that metric built in to the redistribution process. As you'll see, these rules are not complex, but they're vital.

One of those rules involves running multiple instances of EIGRP on a single router. Routes in one EIGRP AS on that router will *not* be automatically redistributed to the other AS.

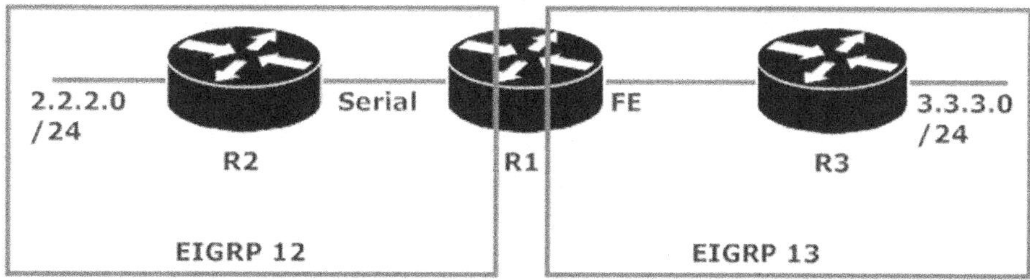

R1 has an adjacency with R2 in AS 12 and with R3 in AS 13. You can see the interfaces and subnets in use in the output of *show ip eigrp neighbor.*

```
R1#show ip eigrp neigh
IP-EIGRP neighbors for process 13
H   Address                 Interface      Hold Uptime    SRTT   RTO   Q    Seq
                                           (sec)          (ms)         Cnt  Num
0   10.1.1.3                Fa0/0          11  00:15:13   1      300   0    3
IP-EIGRP neighbors for process 12
H   Address                 Interface      Hold Uptime    SRTT   RTO   Q    Seq
                                           (sec)          (ms)         Cnt  Num
0   172.12.123.2            Se1/0          152 00:14:37   277    1662  0    3
```

R1 sees the loopbacks its neighbors are advertising...

```
R1#show ip route eigrp
       2.0.0.0/24 is subnetted, 1 subnets
D         2.2.2.0 [90/20640000] via 172.12.123.2, 00:14:42, Serial1/0
       3.0.0.0/24 is subnetted, 1 subnets
D         3.3.3.0 [90/156160] via 10.1.1.3, 00:14:21, FastEthernet0/0
```

...but the EIGRP tables of R2 and R3 are totally empty.

```
R2#show ip route eigrp
Gateway of last resort is not set

R2#

R3#show ip route eigrp
Gateway of last resort is not set

R3#
```

There's also no autoredistribution between multiple OSPF processes on the same router.

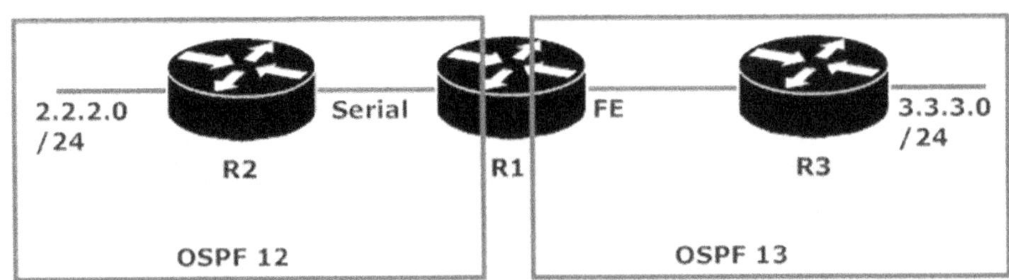

R1 has the adjacencies and the routes, but R2 and R3 can't see each other's loopback.

```
R1#show ip ospf neighbor

Neighbor ID   Pri   State          Dead Time   Address         Interface
3.3.3.3         1   FULL/BDR       00:00:33    10.1.1.3        FastEthernet0/0
2.2.2.2         0   FULL/DROTHER   00:01:39    172.12.123.2    Serial1/0
```

```
R1#show ip route ospf
       2.0.0.0/32 is subnetted, 1 subnets
O IA      2.2.2.2 [110/782] via 172.12.123.2, 00:04:02, Serial1/0
       3.0.0.0/32 is subnetted, 1 subnets
O IA      3.3.3.3 [110/2] via 10.1.1.3, 00:03:50, FastEthernet0/0

R2#show ip route ospf
(I got nothin')

R3#show ip route ospf
(I got nothin' too)
```

Since you and I have to make route redistribution happen, let's do just that!

Note: Both RIP IPv4 versions (RIPv1 and RIPv2) were removed from the CCNP ROUTE exam in 2015. Since its Admin Distance of 120 makes it perfect to illustrate route redistribution details regarding OSPF and EIGRP, *and* since RIP is still in use in real-world networking, *and* since RIPv3 (RIP for IPV6) is still on the ROUTE exam, I've included RIPv2 in this section's labs.

Using RIPv2 also allows me to introduce you to the seed metric.

RIP and the Seed Metric

See?

Seriously, folks, configuring RIPv2 is as simple as it gets, and redistributing routes into RIP is just as simple—as long as you remember the seed metric!

```
R1(config)#router rip
R1(config-router)#redistribute static ?
  metric      Metric for redistributed routes
  route-map   Route map reference
  <cr>
```

Technically, *redistribute static* is a legal command. Practically, you're not going to get much done, since no seed metric for RIP was defined. RIP's sole metric is hop count. If we redistribute an OSPF route with a cost of 74 into RIP, RIP will not accept the route, since RIP considers a metric of 16 to be unreachable. Anything higher than that is *really* unreachable, and not many OSPF routes have a metric of less than 16.

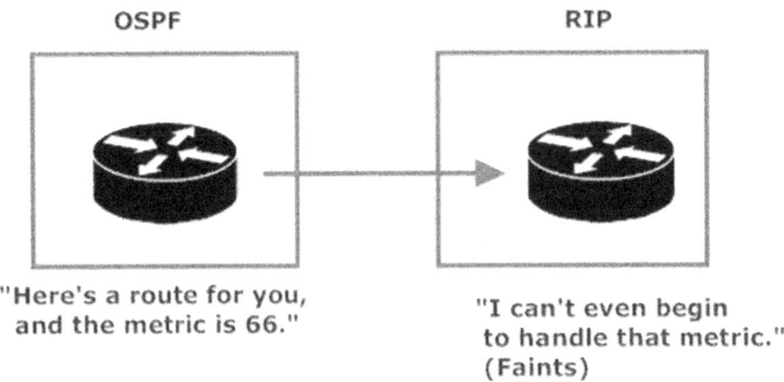

We have to give RIP a value it understands, and that's where the seed metric comes in. That seed metric will increment as the route travels through its new domain, just as it would for a route not learned via route redistribution.

Let's see all of this in action on live Cisco routers!

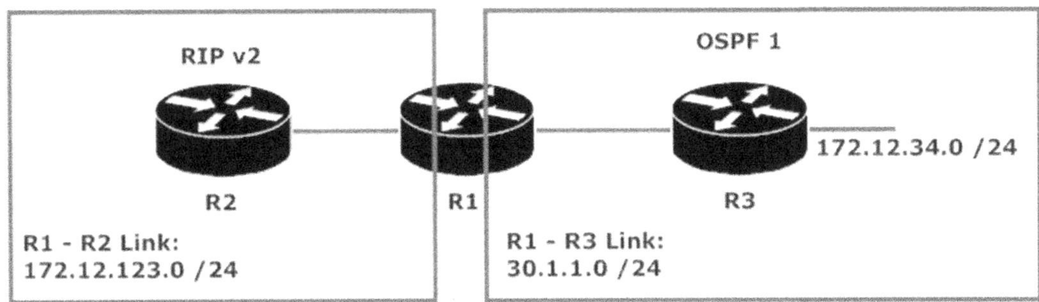

The config on R1:

```
R1(config)#router rip
R1(config-router)#version 2
R1(config-router)#no auto
R1(config-router)#network 172.12.123.0

R1(config)#router ospf 1
R1(config-router)#network 30.1.1.0 0.0.0.255 area 0
```

R2:

```
R2(config)#router rip
R2(config-router)#ver 2
R2(config-router)#no auto
R2(config-router)#network 172.12.123.0
```

And R3:

```
R3(config)#router ospf 1
R3(config-router)#network 30.1.1.0 0.0.0.255 area 0
R3(config-router)#network 172.12.34.0 0.0.0.255 area 0
```

R1 has the 172.12.34.0 /24 network in its OSPF routing table via its adjacency with R3.

```
R1#show ip route ospf
      172.12.0.0/24 is subnetted, 2 subnets
O        172.12.34.0 [110/2] via 30.1.1.3, 00:00:00, FastEthernet0/0
```

We'll try to redistribute that route into the RIP domain without specifying a seed metric, along with R1's connected route of 30.1.1.0 /24.

```
R1(config)#router rip
R1(config-router)#redistribute ospf ?
  <1-65535>   Process ID

R1(config-router)#redistribute ospf 1 ?
  match       Redistribution of OSPF routes
  metric      Metric for redistributed routes
  route-map   Route map reference
  vrf         VPN Routing/Forwarding Instance
  <cr>

R1(config-router)#redistribute ospf 1
R1(config-router)#redistribute connected
```

While the IOS made us put in the OSPF process number with the routes to be redistributed, we were not required to enter a seed metric. The result on R2?

```
R2#show ip route rip

(nothin')

R2#
```

This is one of those rare occasions where the IOS didn't let us know that the config we just entered isn't actually going to accomplish anything. No seed metric, no redistribution into RIP!

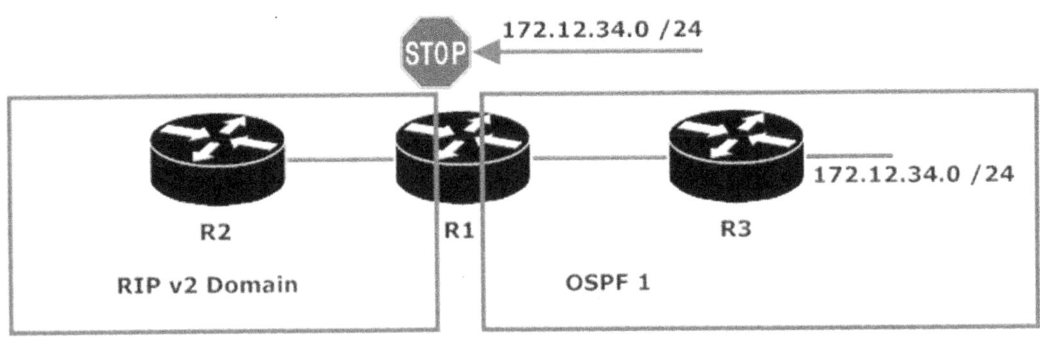

Let's try that same redistribution while adding a seed metric to each *redistribute* statement.

```
R1(config)#router rip
R1(config-router)#no redistribute ospf 1
R1(config-router)#no redistribute connected
R1(config-router)#redistribute ospf 1 ?
  match       Redistribution of OSPF routes
  metric      Metric for redistributed routes
  route-map   Route map reference
  vrf         VPN Routing/Forwarding Instance
  <cr>

R1(config-router)#redistribute ospf 1 metric ?
  <0-16>        Default metric
  Transparent   Transparently redistribute metric

R1(config-router)#redistribute ospf 1 metric 2
R1(config-router)#redistribute connected metric 2
```

The result on R2?

172.12.34.0 /24, Seed Metric 2

R2

R1

R3

172.12.34.0 /24

RIP v2 Domain

OSPF 1

```
R2#show ip route rip

        30.0.0.0/24 is subnetted, 1 subnets
R          30.1.1.0 [120/2] via 172.12.123.1, 00:00:08, Serial0/1/0
```

```
      172.12.0.0/16 is variably subnetted, 3 subnets, 2 masks
R        172.12.34.0/24 [120/2] via 172.12.123.1, 00:00:08, Serial0/1/0
```

Ta-da!

Well, almost "ta-da." I'm about to give you one of the most important pieces of networking advice you'll ever receive from me or anyone else—just because you see a network in the routing table, it doesn't mean you have two-way connectivity to hosts in that destination network. To show you what I mean, let's send pings to both interfaces on the segment connecting R1 and R3, along with R3's interface on the 172.12.34.0 /24 network.

```
R2#ping 30.1.1.1
!!!!!
Success rate is 100 percent (5/5), round-trip min/avg/max = 64/65/68 ms

R2#ping 30.1.1.3
.....
Success rate is 0 percent (0/5)

R2#ping 172.12.34.3
Success rate is 0 percent (0/5)
```

R2 can ping R1's interface on the 30.1.1.0 /24 network but can't ping either of R3's interfaces.

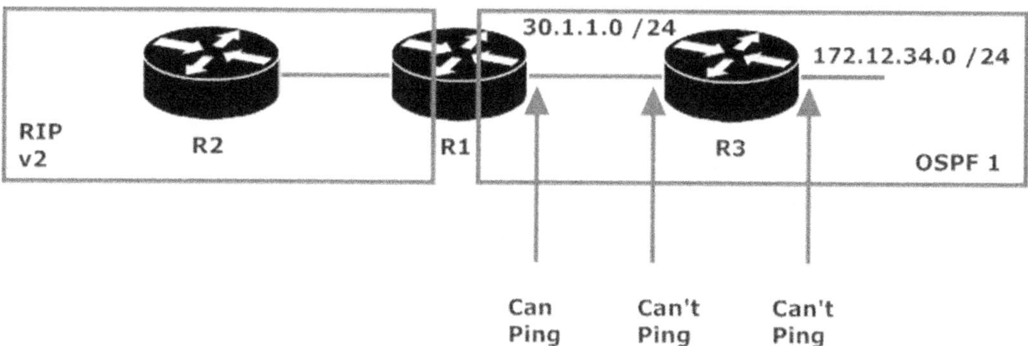

We'll see what's up by using extended ping to send ten thousand pings from R2 to 172.12.34.3 and then go to R3 to run *debug ip packet* to see what happens with those incoming packets.

```
R2#ping
Protocol [ip]:
Target IP address: 172.12.34.3
Repeat count [5]: 10000
Datagram size [100]:
Timeout in seconds [2]:
Extended commands [n]:
Sweep range of sizes [n]:
Type escape sequence to abort.
```

```
Sending 10000, 100-byte ICMP Echos to 172.12.34.3, timeout is 2 seconds:
...............................

R3#debug ip packet
IP packet debugging is on
```

I received several screens of output from that command before turning the debug off (and going back to R2 to turn the extended ping off by hitting ctrl-shift-6 *twice*). This information showed up over and over:

```
*Jul  1 13:39:35.843: IP: s=172.12.123.2 (FastEthernet0/0), d=172.12.34.3, len 1
00, rcvd 4
*Jul  1 13:39:35.843: IP: s=172.12.34.3 (local), d=172.12.123.2, len 100, unrout
able
```

unroutable is the tipoff. The packets are coming in just fine from 172.12.123.2, but R3 has no idea how to send the echo replies *back* to that address. Those replies are unroutable because there's no entry in the IP routing table for that network.

```
R3#show ip route
Gateway of last resort is not set

      30.0.0.0/8 is variably subnetted, 2 subnets, 2 masks
C        30.1.1.0/24 is directly connected, FastEthernet0/0
L        30.1.1.3/32 is directly connected, FastEthernet0/0
      172.12.0.0/16 is variably subnetted, 2 subnets, 2 masks
C        172.12.34.0/24 is directly connected, FastEthernet0/1
L        172.12.34.3/32 is directly connected, FastEthernet0/1
```

We could put a static route on R3 to resolve that issue, but since we're in the redistribution business right now, let's do that instead! R3 needs to see the 172.12.123.0 /24 network, and that route is a *connected* route on R1. No seed metric needs to be specified; we'll stick with OSPF's default seed metric of 20.

```
R1(config)#router ospf 1
R1(config-router)#redistribute connected
% Only classful networks will be redistributed

R1(config-router)#redistribute connected ?
  metric       Metric for redistributed routes
  metric-type  OSPF/IS-IS exterior metric type for redistributed routes
  route-map    Route map reference
  subnets      Consider subnets for redistribution into OSPF
  tag          Set tag for routes redistributed into OSPF
  <cr>

R1(config-router)#redistribute connected subnets
```

What OSPF does require is the inclusion of the *subnets* option if you want subnets to be redistributed! (And it's likely you do.)

R3's OSPF table:

```
R3#show ip route ospf

      172.12.0.0/16 is variably subnetted, 3 subnets, 2 masks
O E2     172.12.123.0/24 [110/20] via 30.1.1.1, 00:00:04, FastEthernet0/0
```

There are two important OSPF defaults in that single route, one of which we already know. The default seed metric of 20 is right behind the AD in those brackets, and the other is that curious *O E2* code. That's the default code for a route redistributed into OSPF. An E2 metric reflects only the cost from the ASBR (R1) to the destination (R2). It does not include the cost from the local router to the ASBR.

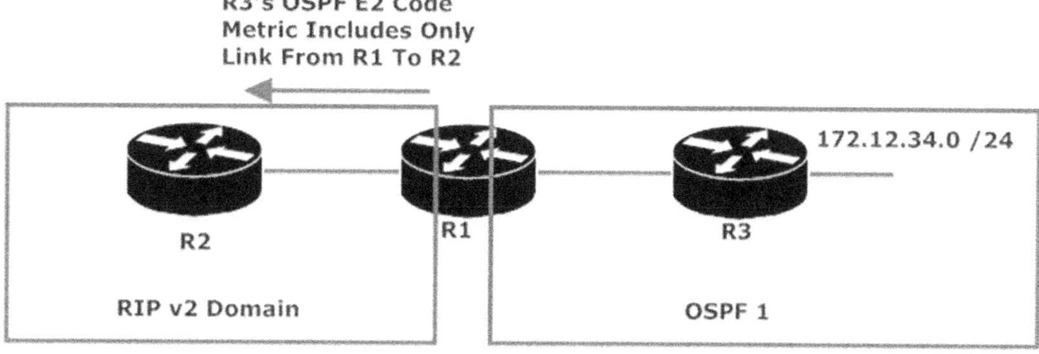

Let's do a little pinging here:

```
R3#ping 172.12.123.2
!!!!!
Success rate is 100 percent (5/5), round-trip min/avg/max = 64/64/68 ms



R2#ping 30.1.1.3
!!!!!
Success rate is 100 percent (5/5), round-trip min/avg/max = 64/65/68 ms

R2#ping 172.12.34.3
!!!!!
Success rate is 100 percent (5/5), round-trip min/avg/max = 64/64/68 ms
```

R3 can ping R2's interface, and R2 can ping both of R3's interfaces. We're in business!

Before we proceed, here's a quick review of the default seed metrics (or lack of same) for our dynamic routing protocols:

EIGRP and RIP have a seed metric of "infinity," and no route with a metric of "infinity" is ever going to make it into our routing table. Both RIP and EIGRP require a default seed metric.

OSPF has a default seed metric of 20 and a default route type of E2. Exception: BGP routes redistributed into OSPF are given a seed metric of 1.

The link state protocol ISIS has a default seed metric of zero, but it does allow a route to be redistributed into an ISIS domain without a defined seed metric. (You won't see ISIS on the Routing and Switching Cisco exam tracks.)

OSPF's default seed metric can be changed in the *redistribution* command itself. To illustrate, I'll double the OSPF default seed metric for the 20.1.1.0 /24 route in the previous lab.

```
R1(config)#router ospf 1
R1(config-router)#no redistribute connected subnets
R1(config-router)#redistribute connected subnets ?
  metric        Metric for redistributed routes
  metric-type   OSPF/IS-IS exterior metric type for redistributed routes
  route-map     Route map reference
  tag           Set tag for routes redistributed into OSPF
  <cr>

R1(config-router)#redistribute connected subnets metric ?
  <0-16777214>    OSPF default metric

R1(config-router)#redistribute connected subnets metric 40
```

The result on R3:

```
R3#show ip route ospf
        20.0.0.0/24 is subnetted, 1 subnets
O E2       20.1.1.0 [110/40] via 172.12.13.1, 00:00:46, Serial0/1/0
```

That's not something you'll do terribly often, but it can come in handy to tweak route selection on occasion. And speaking of tweaking...

Know the Enemy: Suboptimal Routing and Routing Loops

When route distribution is working, it's a beautiful thing. When it's not working correctly, it can be a major pain in obvious and less-than-obvious ways. The two most common pains are suboptimal routing (bad) and routing loops (veddy bad). With suboptimal routing, packets eventually get where they're supposed to go, but they're just not getting there as efficiently as they should. As in...

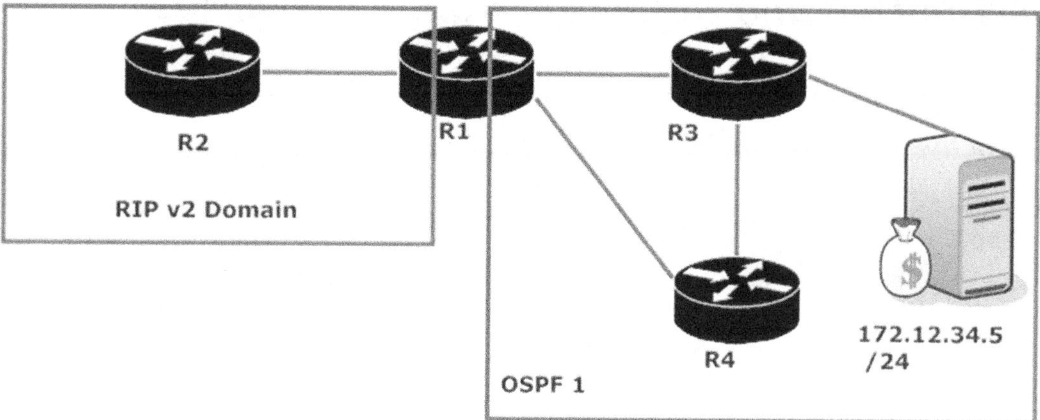

Note: only the *important* servers have giant money bags next to them.

There are two valid paths that R2 can use to get packets to that server, R1-R4-R3 and R1-R3. The physically shortest path isn't necessarily the logically shortest path, but for this discussion we'll assume it is. In the case of suboptimal routing, R2 would end up using the longer path. The packets would still get to 172.12.34.5, but not as quickly as they should. Using the longer path would put an unnecessary strain on R4 as well, since it would end up handling packets it shouldn't be handling.

Packets that enter a routing loop have a much rougher time of it, as do we. Packets in a routing loop will be sent back and forth between the same routers over and over (and over) without ever reaching their destination. *Traceroute* is an excellent tool for spotting a routing loop. If you see the same IP addresses over and over with a traceroute, you, my friend, have a routing loop on your hands.

```
R2#traceroute 4.4.4.4

Type escape sequence to abort. (Same as for pings - CB)
Tracing the route to 4.4.4.4

  1 172.12.23.3 4 msec
    172.12.123.1 36 msec 32 msec
  2 172.12.123.1 36 msec
    172.12.123.3 24 msec 28 msec
  3 172.12.123.3 24 msec
    172.12.123.1 56 msec 56 msec
  4 172.12.123.1 56 msec
    172.12.123.3 48 msec 48 msec
```

Redistribution and Adjusting Admin Distances

You know what the AD is, and you know the common and not-so-common ADs. That's a good thing, since we're going to need that knowledge in our next lab!

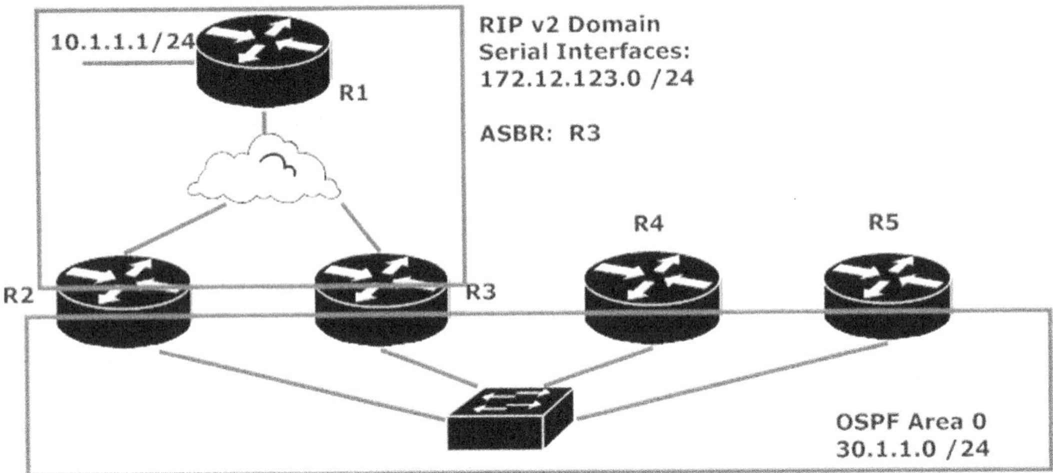

Our objective is for all routers to have the 10.1.1.0 /24 network in their routing tables. The ASBR in this lab is R3. Our first step is *always* to make sure the ASBR has the route to be redistributed!

```
R3#show ip route rip

         10.0.0.0/24  is subnetted, 1 subnets
R           10.1.1.0  [120/1] via 172.12.123.1, 00:00:20, Serial0/1/0

R2#show ip route rip
         10.0.0.0/24  is subnetted, 1 subnets
R           10.1.1.0     [120/1] via 172.12.123.1, 00:00:27, Serial0/1/0
```

Just for fun, I included the RIP routing table of R2. Both R2 and R3 are border routers, so it's a good idea to watch the effects of this lab on both routers. R3 will be the only router on which we perform redistribution. Let's redistribute the RIP subnet and the connected subnet (172.12.123.0 /24) into OSPF...

```
R3(config)#router ospf 1
R3(config-router)#redistribute rip subnets
R3(config-router)#redistribute connected subnets
```

...and the connected route 30.1.1.0 /24 into RIP, along with a seed metric of 2.

```
R3(config)#router rip
R3(config-router)#redistribute connected metric 2
```

Both R4 and R5 see the newly redistributed routes, and both can ping R1's interface on each segment. No problems here!

```
R4#show ip route ospf
     10.0.0.0/24 is subnetted, 1 subnets
O E2    10.1.1.0 [110/20] via 30.1.1.3, 00:01:00, FastEthernet0/0
     172.12.0.0/24 is subnetted, 1 subnets
O E2    172.12.123.0 [110/20] via 30.1.1.3, 00:01:00, FastEthernet0/0

R4#ping 10.1.1.1
!!!!!
Success rate is 100 percent (5/5), round-trip min/avg/max = 64/66/68 ms

R4#ping 172.12.123.1
!!!!!
Success rate is 100 percent (5/5), round-trip min/avg/max = 64/65/68 ms

R5#show ip route ospf
     10.0.0.0/24 is subnetted, 1 subnets
O E2    10.1.1.0 [110/20] via 30.1.1.3, 00:01:06, GigabitEthernet0/0
     172.12.0.0/24 is subnetted, 1 subnets
O E2    172.12.123.0 [110/20] via 30.1.1.3, 00:01:06, GigabitEthernet0/0

R5#ping 10.1.1.1
!!!!!
Success rate is 100 percent (5/5), round-trip min/avg/max = 64/64/68 ms

R5#ping 172.12.123.1
!!!!!
Success rate is 100 percent (5/5), round-trip min/avg/max = 64/64/68 ms
```

Looks good! Before we leave, let's have a look at R2's RIP table.

```
R2#show ip route rip
<empty>
```

Hmm. Maybe we better stick around awhile. What about the OSPF table?

```
R2#show ip route ospf
     10.0.0.0/24 is subnetted, 1 subnets
O E2    10.1.1.0 [110/20] via 30.1.1.3, 00:04:24, FastEthernet0/0
```

R2 is now showing an OSPF route where it once had a RIP route, and that "once had" time was before route redistribution. Why the change? R2 is now hearing about the 10.1.1.0 route from two sources. R1 is advertising that route over the RIP domain, and R3 is advertising it via OSPF.

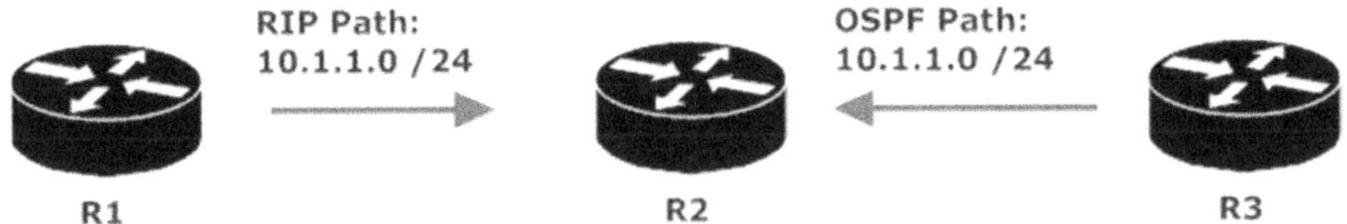

The prefix length is exactly the same in both ads, and that's where admin distance comes in. The OSPF route is preferred over the RIP route, since OSPF's AD is 110 and RIP's is 120. Before redistribution, packets from R2 to 10.1.1.0 /24 would go straight to R1, using 172.12.123.1 as the next-hop IP address...

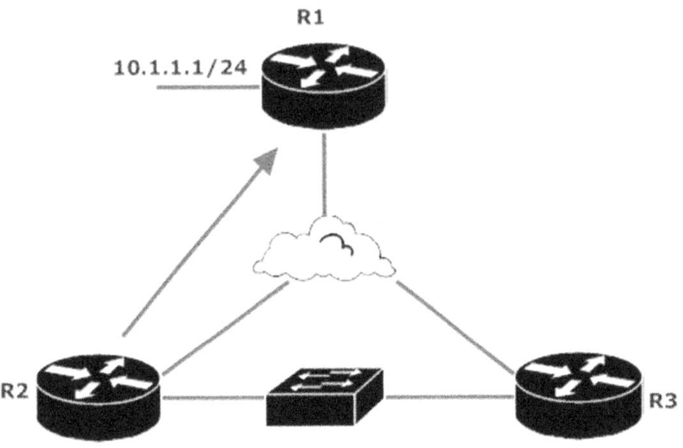


```
R2#show ip route rip
      10.0.0.0/24 is subnetted, 1 subnets
R        10.1.1.0 [120/1] via 172.12.123.1, 00:00:27, Serial0/1/0
```

...but that route is now an OSPF route using 30.1.1.3 as the next-hop address. Packets from R2 must now go through the Ethernet segment before being sent across the cloud to R1.

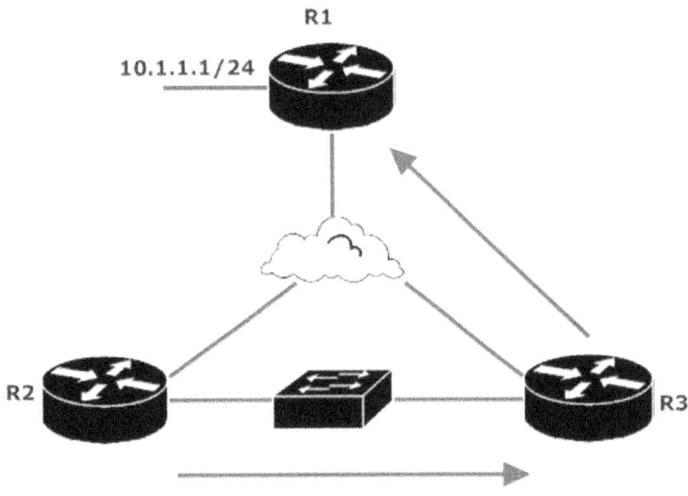

```
R2#show ip route ospf
     10.0.0.0/24 is subnetted, 1 subnets
O E2    10.1.1.0 [110/20] via 30.1.1.3, 00:04:24, FastEthernet0/0
```

That suboptimal path is verified by *traceroute.*

```
R2#traceroute 10.1.1.1

Type escape sequence to abort.
Tracing the route to 10.1.1.1

  1 30.1.1.3 0 msec 0 msec 0 msec
  2 172.12.123.1 32 msec * 32 msec
```

We'd prefer traffic leaving R2 headed for 10.1.1.0 /24 go straight across the cloud to R1, and changing the admin distance of our OSPF route just might help us out here. With OSPF, we have two major options to choose from when it comes to changing the AD. Right now, we'll use the *distance* command.

```
R2(config)#router ospf 1
R2(config-router)#distance ?
  <1-255>  Administrative distance
  Ospf     OSPF distance

R2(config-router)#distance 121
```

The effect is immediate. The RIP route is again used to reach 10.1.1.0, verified by two *show ip route* commands, followed by *traceroute.*

```
R2#show ip route ospf

R2#show ip route rip

       10.0.0.0/24  is subnetted, 1 subnets
R         10.1.1.0  [120/1] via 172.12.123.1, 00:00:18, Serial0/1/0

R2#traceroute 10.1.1.1

Type escape sequence to abort.
Tracing the route to 10.1.1.1

     1 172.12.123.1 32 msec * 32 msec
```

Should that RIP route leave the table, the OSPF route should reenter it. To test that, let's close R2's serial interface to get rid of the RIP route and then check the OSPF table.

```
R2(config)#int serial 0/1/0
R2(config-if)#shut
*Jun 17 23:56:10.126: %SYS-5-CONFIG _ I: Configured from console by console
*Jun 17 23:56:11.486: %LINK-5-CHANGED: Interface Serial0/1/0, changed state to
administratively down
*Jun 17 23:56:12.486: %LINEPROTO-5-UPDOWN: Line protocol on Interface Serial0/
0, changed state to down

R2#show ip route ospf
        10.0.0.0/24 is subnetted, 1 subnets
O E2       10.1.1.0 [121/20] via 30.1.1.3, 00:00:08, FastEthernet0/0
      172.12.0.0/24 is subnetted, 1 subnets
O E2      172.12.123.0 [121/20] via 30.1.1.3, 00:00:08, FastEthernet0/0
```

Note the admin distance of both OSPF routes. (172.12.123.0 is now shown as an OSPF route since it's no longer directly connected to R2 after we shut that serial interface down.) The path is again verified by *traceroute*, and connectivity is verified with *ping*.

```
R2#traceroute 10.1.1.0

Type escape sequence to abort.
Tracing the route to 10.1.1.0

  1 30.1.1.3 4 msec 0 msec 0 msec
  2 172.12.123.1 36 msec 32 msec 32 msec


R2#ping 10.1.1.1
!!!!!
Success rate is 100 percent (5/5), round-trip min/avg/max = 64/65/68 ms
```

We've turned the OSPF route to 10.1.1.0 /24 into something like a floating static route. The higher AD guarantees that OSPF routes for a given route will enter the routing table only if the RIP routes for the exact same route disappear.

The only drawback to *distance* is the all-or-nothing admin distance change. With larger OSPF tables (and larger networks), you may want to change the AD of particular routes rather than all routes discovered by a particular protocol. I'll show you how to do that after I add two additional routes to R1, reopen R2's serial interface, and remove the *distance* command from R2's OSPF configuration.

```
R1(config)#int loopback 5
R1(config-if)#ip address 5.5.5.5 255.255.255.0

R1(config-if)#int loopback6
R1(config-if)#ip address 6.6.6.6 255.255.255.0
```

```
R1(config-if)#router rip
R1(config-router)#network 5.0.0.0
R1(config-router)#network 6.0.0.0

R2(config)#int serial 0/1/0
R2(config-if)#no shut

*Jun 18 00:03:53.598: %LINK-3-UPDOWN: Interface Serial0/1/0, changed state to up
*Jun 18 00:03:54.598: %LINEPROTO-5-UPDOWN: Line protocol on Interface Serial0/1/
0, changed state to up

R2(config-if)#router ospf 1
R2(config-router)#no distance 121
```

R2 sees all three routes now redistributed into OSPF, the AD for all three routes is 110, and 30.1.1.3 is the next-hop address for each route.

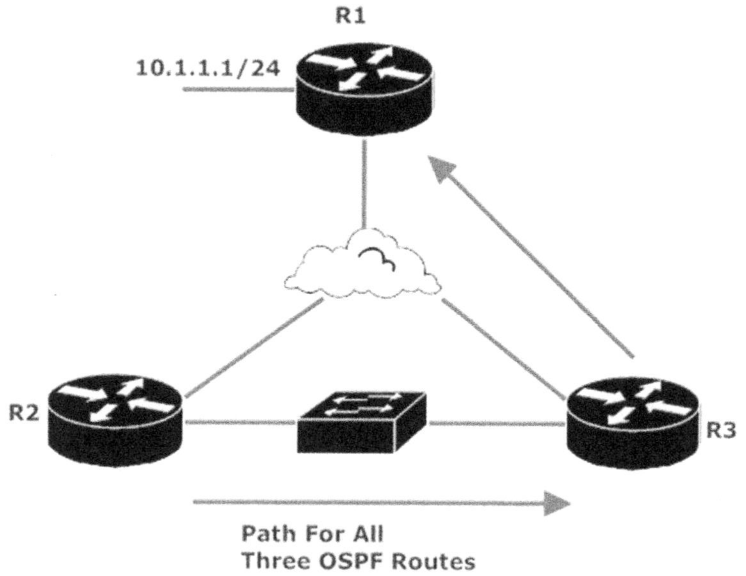


```
R2#show ip route ospf
        5.0.0.0/24 is subnetted, 1 subnets
O E2       5.5.5.0 [110/20] via 30.1.1.3, 00:00:37, FastEthernet0/0
        6.0.0.0/24 is subnetted, 1 subnets
O E2       6.6.6.0 [110/20] via 30.1.1.3, 00:00:37, FastEthernet0/0
        10.0.0.0/24  is subnetted, 1 subnets
O E2       10.1.1.0  [110/20] via 30.1.1.3, 00:00:37, FastEthernet0/0
```

We'd like traffic leaving R2 and headed for 10.1.1.0 /24 to take the direct path to R1 while leaving the other two routes alone to take the longer path. (This is for practice. Just pretend it's an order from a clueless department head.)

Just as before, we identify the traffic to have its distance changed with an ACL.

```
R2(config)#access-list 77 permit 10.1.1.0 0.0.0.255
```

We'll use the *distance* command and a few of its handy options along with this ACL to make it happen. I could tie the source address down in the *distance* command, but instead I'll make it apply to *any* source with the source address of 0.0.0.0 and a wildcard mask of all ones. (If you enter a specific source address here, it must be the OSPF RID of the source, even if that RID is not the IP address of the interface sending the updates.)

```
R2(config)#router ospf 1
R2(config-router)#distance 121 ?
  A.B.C.D   IP Source address
  <cr>

R2(config-router)#distance 121 0.0.0.0 ?
  A.B.C.D   Wildcard bits

R2(config-router)#distance 121 0.0.0.0 255.255.255.255 ?
  <1-99>        IP Standard access list number
  <1300-1999>   IP Standard expanded access list number
  WORD          Standard access-list name
  <cr>

R2(config-router)#distance 121 0.0.0.0 255.255.255.255 77
```

The result is immediate! The full IP routing table shows the RIP route to 10.1.1.0 /24 is now preferred, and the OSPF routes for the two newest routes are still in that table. Only the AD for the OSPF 10.1.1.0 /24 route was changed.

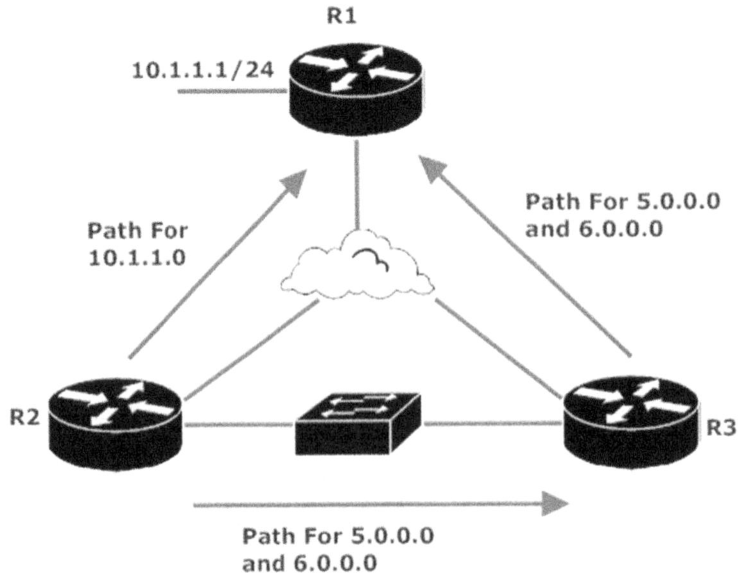

```
R2#show ip route

        5.0.0.0/24 is subnetted, 1 subnets
O E2       5.5.5.0 [110/20] via 30.1.1.3, 00:00:11, FastEthernet0/0
        6.0.0.0/24 is subnetted, 1 subnets
O E2       6.6.6.0 [110/20] via 30.1.1.3, 00:00:11, FastEthernet0/0
        10.0.0.0/24  is subnetted, 1 subnets
R          10.1.1.0  [120/1] via 172.12.123.1, 00:00:08, Serial0/1/0
```

Shutting down R2's serial interface again puts the OSPF route for 10.1.1.0/24 back in the table. Note the AD of that route is indeed 121 while the others stay at 110.

```
R2(config)#int serial 0/1/0
R2(config-if)#shut
*Jun 18 00:18:01.394: %LINK-5-CHANGED: Interface Serial0/1/0, changed state to
administratively down
*Jun 18 00:18:02.394: %LINEPROTO-5-UPDOWN: Line protocol on Interface Serial0/1/
0, changed state to down

R2#show ip route

        5.0.0.0/24 is subnetted, 1 subnets
O E2       5.5.5.0 [110/20] via 30.1.1.3, 00:04:02, FastEthernet0/0
        6.0.0.0/24 is subnetted, 1 subnets
O E2       6.6.6.0 [110/20] via 30.1.1.3, 00:04:02, FastEthernet0/0
        10.0.0.0/24  is subnetted, 1 subnets
O E2       10.1.1.0  [121/20] via 30.1.1.3, 00:00:06, FastEthernet0/0
```

Before we move on to EIGRP route redistribution, let's have a look at the distance option you might have thought we'd use first—*distance ospf.*

```
R2(config-router)#distance ospf ?
  external     External type 5 and type 7 routes
  inter-area   Inter-area routes
  intra-area   Intra-area routes
```

It's intuitive to think *distance ospf* command is the command to use to change OSPF admin distance, right? Right! And while it might be the one to use, you're likely to use the *distance* command as we've used it so far. The *distance ospf* command does come in handy if you want to change the AD of a particular type of route or routes, as in the following route table. This table is not from the prior labs, and OSPF is the only routing protocol running.

```
R2#show ip route ospf
        3.0.0.0/32 is subnetted, 1 subnets
O IA       3.3.3.3 [110/2] via 30.1.1.3, 00:13:16, FastEthernet0/0
       10.0.0.0/24 is subnetted, 1 subnets
O E2       10.1.1.0 [110/20] via 30.1.1.3, 00:09:21, FastEthernet0/0
```

```
       33.0.0.0/32 is subnetted, 1 subnets
O         33.3.3.3 [110/2] via 30.1.1.3, 00:12:41, FastEthernet0/0
      172.12.0.0/24 is subnetted, 1 subnets
O E2      172.12.123.0 [110/20] via 30.1.1.3, 00:09:49, FastEthernet0/0
```

There's a little of everything in this table! R2 has two external routes, an interarea route, and an intra-area route. Let's use distance ospf to change all of those ADs.

```
R2(config)#router ospf 1
R2(config-router)#distance ospf ?
  external     External type 5 and type 7 routes
  inter-area   Inter-area routes
  intra-area   Intra-area routes

R2(config-router)#distance ospf external ?
  <1-255>   Distance for external type 5 and type 7 routes

R2(config-router)#distance ospf external 200 ?
  inter-area   Inter-area routes
  intra-area   Intra-area routes
  <cr>

R2(config-router)#distance ospf external 200 inter-area ?
  <1-255>   Distance for inter-area routes

R2(config-router)#distance ospf external 200 inter-area 150 ?
  intra-area   Intra-area routes
  <cr>

R2(config-router)#distance ospf external 200 inter-area 150 intra-area ?
  <1-255> Distance for intra-area routes

R2(config-router)#distance ospf external 200 inter-area 150 intra-area 140
```

You could certainly enter three separate *distance ospf* commands, one for each route type, instead of this one long command. The important thing is that the command works...

```
R2#show ip route ospf

        3.0.0.0/32 is subnetted, 1 subnets
O IA      3.3.3.3 [150/2] via 30.1.1.3, 00:01:00, FastEthernet0/0
        10.0.0.0/24  is subnetted, 1 subnets
O E2      10.1.1.0  [200/20] via 30.1.1.3, 00:01:00, FastEthernet0/0
        33.0.0.0/32  is subnetted, 1 subnets
O          33.3.3.3 [140/2] via 30.1.1.3, 00:01:00, FastEthernet0/0
         172.12.0.0/24 is subnetted, 1 subnets
O E2      172.12.123.0 [200/20] via 30.1.1.3, 00:01:00, FastEthernet0/0
```

...and it does! The real problem with *distance ospf* is that it does not allow the use of ACLs to filter out some routes. If we wanted to change the AD of only one of the external routes in that table, we'd have to use *distance <AD>* instead and use an ACL to indicate which route to change. As IOS Help showed us, there's no ACL option with *distance ospf.*

EIGRP and Route Redistribution

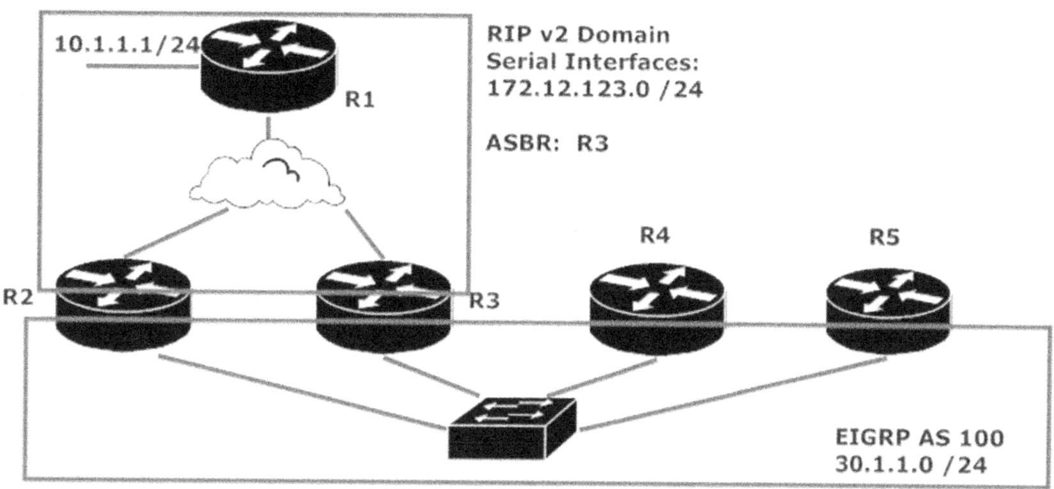

The addressing is the same as in the previous lab. Only the dynamic routing protocol has been changed (to protect the innocent). I've also removed the 5.0.0.0 and 6.0.0.0 networks from R1 that were added at the end of the previous lab.

EIGRP requires a seed metric that's just a tad more complex than that of RIP. We can apply this metric for routes from a specific course as part of the *redistribute* command itself, or we can use *default-metric* to set that value for all routes learned via redistribution.

```
R2(config)#router eigrp 100
R2(config-router)#no auto
R2(config-router)#?
Router configuration commands:
  address-family         Enter Address Family command mode
  auto-summary           Enable automatic network number summarization
  bfd                    BFD configuration commands
  default                Set a command to its defaults
  default-information    Control distribution of default information
  default-metric         Set metric of redistributed routes
```

In this lab, we'll take the first approach. With EIGRP, the *redistribute* command is incomplete until all five metrics have been defined. Before we get started, let's make sure our ASBR-to-be has the route in its routing table:

```
R3#show ip route rip
      10.0.0.0/24 is subnetted, 1 subnets
R        10.1.1.0 [120/1] via 172.12.123.1, 00:00:23, Serial0/1/0
```

And there it is! Let's get to it!

```
R3(config)#router eigrp 100
R3(config-router)#redistribute rip ?
  metric      Metric for redistributed routes
  route-map   Route map reference
  <cr>

R3(config-router)#redistribute rip metric ?
  <1-4294967295>   Bandwidth metric in Kbits per second

R3(config-router)#redistribute rip metric 1544 ?
  <0-4294967295>   EIGRP delay metric, in 10 microsecond units

R3(config-router)#redistribute rip metric 1544 10 ?
  <0-255>   EIGRP reliability metric where 255 is 100% reliable

R3(config-router)#redistribute rip metric 1544 10 255 ?
  <1-255>   EIGRP Effective bandwidth metric (Loading) where 255 is 100% loaded

R3(config-router)#redistribute rip metric 1544 10 255 1 ?
  <1-65535>   EIGRP MTU of the path

R3(config-router)#redistribute rip metric 1544 10 255 1 1544 ?
  route-map   Route map reference
  <cr>

R3(config-router)#redistribute rip metric 1544 10 255 1 1544
```

Previous IOS versions mentioned "IGRP" where you see "EIGRP" in IOS Help above. That's just an IOS quirk—don't sweat it if you see it. Right now, let's have a look at the EIGRP tables on R4 and R5.

```
R4#show ip route eigrp 100
Codes: L - local, C - connected, S - static, R - RIP, M - mobile, B - BGP
      10.0.0.0/24 is subnetted, 1 subnets
D EX     10.1.1.0 [170/1662976] via 30.1.1.3, 00:01:25, FastEthernet0/0
      172.12.0.0/24 is subnetted, 1 subnets
D EX     172.12.123.0 [170/1662976] via 30.1.1.3, 00:01:25, FastEthernet0/0

R5#show ip route eigrp
      10.0.0.0/24 is subnetted, 1 subnets
D EX     10.1.1.0 [170/1662976] via 30.1.1.3, 00:00:26, GigabitEthernet0/0
```

```
        172.12.0.0/24  is subnetted, 1 subnets
D EX        172.12.123.0   [170/1662976] via 30.1.1.3, 00:00:26, GigabitEthernet0/0
```

Redistribution wins again! The routes are both marked *D EX*, indicating an EIGRP External route. The AD of each route is 170, as opposed to an EIGRP Internal route (90).

Let's have a look at R2's routing table, before and after redistribution.

Before:

```
R2#show ip route
        10.0.0.0/24 is subnetted, 1 subnets
R          10.1.1.0 [120/1] via 172.12.123.1, 00:00:17, Serial0/1/0
```

After:

```
R2#show ip route
        10.0.0.0/24 is subnetted, 1 subnets
R          10.1.1.0 [120/1] via 172.12.123.1, 00:00:26, Serial0/1/0
```

In the RIP-OSPF redistribution lab, R2 has this route as a RIP route before redistribution and an OSPF route afterward. In this lab, R2 has this route as a RIP route before *and* after redistribution. Why? Because the EIGRP external route AD of 170 is higher than that of RIP's 120, so the RIP route is preferred over the EIGRP external route.

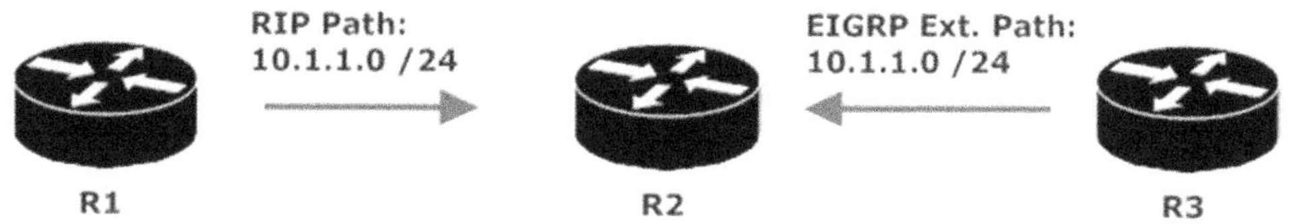

Should R2's serial interface mysteriously go down again (heh heh heh), the EIGRP external path will be put into the routing table.

```
R2(config)#int serial 0/1/0
R2(config-if)#shut

R2#show ip route

        10.0.0.0/24 is subnetted, 1 subnets
D EX       10.1.1.0 [170/1662976] via 30.1.1.3, 00:00:04, FastEthernet0/0
```

I'll reopen that interface, the route is again a RIP route, and we press on!

```
R2#show ip route
        10.0.0.0/24 is subnetted, 1 subnets
R          10.1.1.0 [120/1] via 172.12.123.1, 00:00:02, Serial0/1/0
```

Let's say we want the EIGRP route to be preferred without the messiness of closing an interface. We'll change the AD of EIGRP external routes on R2 to 119, just one less than RIP's AD. This command requires you to enter both the internal and external AD, even if you're just changing one.

```
R2(config)#router eigrp 100
R2(config-router)#distance ?
<1-255> Set route administrative distance
eigrp Set distance for internal and external routes

R2(config-router)#distance eigrp ?
<1-255> Distance for internal routes

R2(config-router)#distance eigrp 90 ?
<1-255> Distance for external routes

R2(config-router)#distance eigrp 90 119 ?
<cr>

R2(config-router)#distance eigrp 90 119
R2#clear ip route *

*Jun 18 13:04:53.207: %DUAL-5-NBRCHANGE: EIGRP-IPv4 100: Neighbor 30.1.1.5
(FastEthernet0/0) is down: route configuration changed
*Jun 18 13:04:53.207: %DUAL-5-NBRCHANGE: EIGRP-IPv4 100: Neighbor 30.1.1.3
(FastEthernet0/0) is down: route configuration changed
*Jun 18 13:04:53.207: %DUAL-5-NBRCHANGE: EIGRP-IPv4 100: Neighbor 30.1.1.4
(FastEthernet0/0) is down: route configuration changed
*Jun 18 13:04:55.075: %DUAL-5-NBRCHANGE: EIGRP-IPv4 100: Neighbor 30.1.1.5
(FastEthernet0/0) is up: new adjacency
*Jun 18 13:04:55.083: %DUAL-5-NBRCHANGE: EIGRP-IPv4 100: Neighbor 30.1.1.4
(FastEthernet0/0) is up: new adjacency
*Jun 18 13:04:55.083: %DUAL-5-NBRCHANGE: EIGRP-IPv4 100: Neighbor 30.1.1.3
(FastEthernet0/0) is up: new adjacency

R2#show ip route

      10.0.0.0/24 is subnetted, 1 subnets
D EX     10.1.1.0 [119/1662976] via 30.1.1.3, 00:00:07, FastEthernet0/0
```

Fine-Tuning Route Redistribution

You'll often run into route redistribution situations where you want some routes to be fully redistributed and others to be only partially so. A great way to fine-tune redistribution is with distribute lists. Distribute lists use ACLs (there they are again!) to define the routes to be redistributed. They also define the routes to *not* be redistributed, whether that denial be explicit or implicit.

You'll see what I mean as we work through this lab!

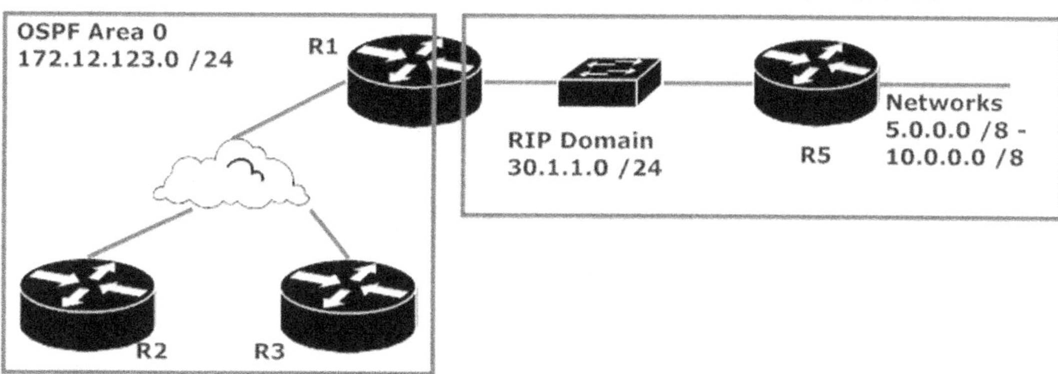

R1 is receiving six routes from R5.

```
R1#show ip route rip
R     5.0.0.0/8 [120/1] via 30.1.1.5, 00:00:06, FastEthernet0/0
R     6.0.0.0/8 [120/1] via 30.1.1.5, 00:00:13, FastEthernet0/0
R     7.0.0.0/8 [120/1] via 30.1.1.5, 00:00:13, FastEthernet0/0
R     8.0.0.0/8 [120/1] via 30.1.1.5, 00:00:13, FastEthernet0/0
R     9.0.0.0/8 [120/1] via 30.1.1.5, 00:00:13, FastEthernet0/0
R     10.0.0.0/8 [120/1] via 30.1.1.5, 00:00:13, FastEthernet0/0
```

If we perform redistribution as we have up to this point, the OSPF routers would receive all six of those routes.

```
R1(config)#router ospf 1
R1(config-router)#redistribute rip subnets
R1(config-router)#redistribute connected subnets

R2#show ip route ospf

O E2  5.0.0.0/8 [110/20] via 172.12.123.1, 00:00:09, Serial0/1/0
O E2  6.0.0.0/8 [110/20] via 172.12.123.1, 00:00:09, Serial0/1/0
O E2  7.0.0.0/8 [110/20] via 172.12.123.1, 00:00:09, Serial0/1/0
O E2  8.0.0.0/8 [110/20] via 172.12.123.1, 00:00:09, Serial0/1/0
O E2  9.0.0.0/8 [110/20] via 172.12.123.1, 00:00:09, Serial0/1/0
O E2  10.0.0.0/8 [110/20] via 172.12.123.1, 00:00:09, Serial0/1/0

R3#show ip route ospf

O E2  5.0.0.0/8 [110/20] via 172.12.123.1, 00:00:15, Serial0/1/0
O E2  6.0.0.0/8 [110/20] via 172.12.123.1, 00:00:15, Serial0/1/0
O E2  7.0.0.0/8 [110/20] via 172.12.123.1, 00:00:15, Serial0/1/0
```

```
O E2   8.0.0.0/8 [110/20] via 172.12.123.1, 00:00:15, Serial0/1/0
O E2   9.0.0.0/8 [110/20] via 172.12.123.1, 00:00:15, Serial0/1/0
O E2   10.0.0.0/8 [110/20] via 172.12.123.1, 00:00:15, Serial0/1/0
```

Our bosses want only the routers in the RIP domain to know of 8.0.0.0 /8 and 9.0.0.0 /8, meaning we have to prevent their redistribution into the OSPF domain while allowing the other routes to be redistributed successfully.

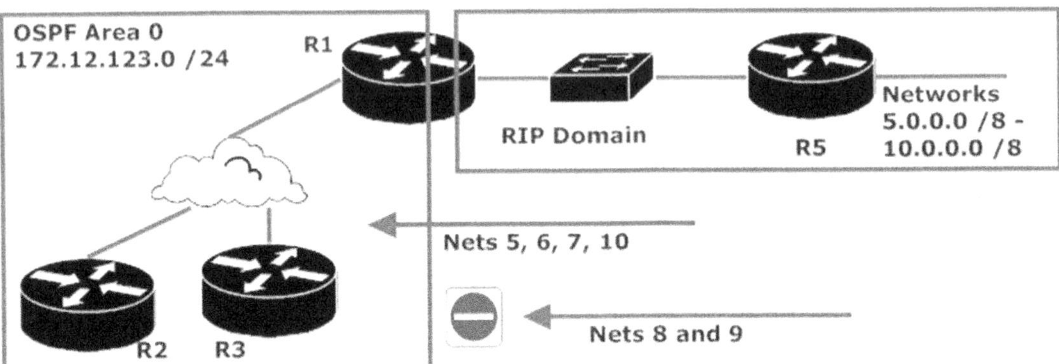

Let's make it happen! We can write an ACL identifying those two networks as networks to be denied and then apply that ACL to the redistribute process with *distribute-list*.

```
R1(config)#access-list 17 deny 8.0.0.0 0.255.255.255
R1(config)#access-list 17 deny 9.0.0.0 0.255.255.255
R1(config)#access-list 17 permit any

R1(config)#router ospf 1
R1(config-router)#distribute-list ?
  <1-199>       IP access list number
  <1300-2699>   IP expanded access list number
  WORD          Access-list name
  gateway       Filtering incoming updates based on gateway
  prefix        Filter prefixes in routing updates
  route-map     Filter prefixes based on the route-map

R1(config-router)#distribute-list 17 ?
  in Filter incoming routing updates
  out Filter outgoing routing updates

R1(config-router)#distribute-list 17 out ?
  Async                  Async interface
  BVI                    Bridge-Group Virtual Interface
  CDMA-Ix                CDMA Ix interface
  CTunnel                CTunnel interface
  Dialer                 Dialer interface
  FastEthernet           FastEthernet IEEE 802.3
```

```
Lex                   Lex interface
Loopback              Loopback interface
MFR                   Multilink Frame Relay bundle interface
Multilink             Multilink-group interface
Null                  Null interface
Port-channel          Ethernet Channel of interfaces
Serial                Serial
Tunnel                Tunnel interface
Vif                   PGM Multicast Host interface
Virtual-PPP           Virtual PPP interface
Virtual-Template      Virtual Template interface
Virtual-TokenRing     Virtual TokenRing
Bgp                   Border Gateway Protocol (BGP)
Connected             Connected
eigrp                 Enhanced Interior Gateway Routing Protocol (EIGRP)
ospf                  Open Shortest Path First (OSPF)
rip                   Routing Information Protocol (RIP)
static                Static routes
<cr>
```

The interesting thing here is that we can specify an interface or a protocol to be filtered. Let's filter updates going out of R1's serial interface.

```
R1(config-router)#distribute-list 17 out serial 1/0
% Interface not allowed with OUT for OSPF
```

Or not! Let's try specifying a protocol instead of an interface.

```
R1(config-router)#distribute-list 17 out rip
```

We didn't get an error message, so let's check the OSPF tables on R2 and R3.

```
R2#show ip route ospf
O E2  5.0.0.0/8 [110/20] via 172.12.123.1, 00:05:31, Serial0/1/0
O E2  6.0.0.0/8 [110/20] via 172.12.123.1, 00:05:31, Serial0/1/0
O E2  7.0.0.0/8 [110/20] via 172.12.123.1, 00:05:31, Serial0/1/0
O E2  10.0.0.0/8 [110/20] via 172.12.123.1, 00:05:31, Serial0/1/0

R3#show ip route ospf
O E2  5.0.0.0/8 [110/20] via 172.12.123.1, 00:08:05, Serial0/1/0
O E2  6.0.0.0/8 [110/20] via 172.12.123.1, 00:08:05, Serial0/1/0
O E2  7.0.0.0/8 [110/20] via 172.12.123.1, 00:08:05, Serial0/1/0
O E2  10.0.0.0/8 [110/20] via 172.12.123.1, 00:08:05, Serial0/1/0
```

If we didn't even want R1 to know of those two filtered networks, we could apply a distribute list to RIP and specify the fast0/0 interface.

```
R1(config)#router rip
  Async              Async interface
  BVI                Bridge-Group Virtual Interface
  CDMA-Ix            CDMA Ix interface
  CTunnel            CTunnel interface
  Dialer             Dialer interface
  FastEthernet       FastEthernet IEEE 802.3
  Lex                Lex interface
  Loopback           Loopback interface
  MFR                Multilink Frame Relay bundle interface
  Multilink          Multilink-group interface
  Null               Null interface
  Port-channel       Ethernet Channel of interfaces
  Serial             Serial
  Tunnel             Tunnel interface
  Vif                PGM Multicast Host interface
  Virtual-PPP        Virtual PPP interface
  Virtual-Template   Virtual Template interface
  Virtual-TokenRing  Virtual TokenRing
  <cr>

R1(config)#router rip
R1(config-router)#distribute-list 17 in    rip
                                            ^
% Invalid input detected at '^' marker.

R1(config-router)#distribute-list 17 in fast0/0
```

After clearing R1's routing table of dynamically learned routes (this is RIP, after all, and it needs a little help in hurrying), R1's routing table no longer shows the two filtered routes.

```
R1#clear ip route *

R1#show ip route rip
R     5.0.0.0/8 [120/1] via 30.1.1.5, 00:00:01, FastEthernet0/0
R     6.0.0.0/8 [120/1] via 30.1.1.5, 00:00:01, FastEthernet0/0
R     7.0.0.0/8 [120/1] via 30.1.1.5, 00:00:01, FastEthernet0/0
R     10.0.0.0/8 [120/1] via 30.1.1.5, 00:00:01, FastEthernet0/0
```

Distribute lists can filter all routes from being advertised via a given interface without making that interface passive and losing the adjacency, as you'll see in our next lab! The addressing over the R1-R2-R3 and R1-R5 networks is the same as the previous lab.

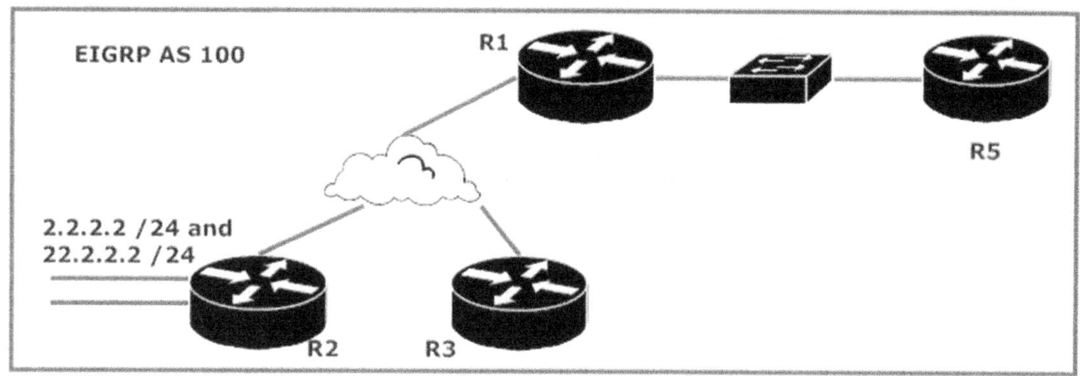

R2 is advertising two routes into EIGRP. R1 sees them, as does R5.

```
R1#show ip route eigrp
       2.0.0.0/24 is subnetted, 1 subnets
D         2.2.2.0 [90/20640000] via 172.12.123.2, 00:00:09, Serial1/0
      22.0.0.0/24  is subnetted, 1 subnets
D        22.2.2.0  [90/20640000] via 172.12.123.2, 00:00:04, Serial1/0

R5#show ip route eigrp
       2.0.0.0/24 is subnetted, 1 subnets
D         2.2.2.0 [90/20642560] via 30.1.1.1, 00:00:14, GigabitEthernet0/0
       22.0.0.0/24 is subnetted, 1 subnets
D         22.2.2.0 [90/20642560] via 30.1.1.1, 00:00:09, GigabitEthernet0/0
         172.12.0.0/24 is subnetted, 1 subnets
D           172.12.123.0 [90/20514560] via 30.1.1.1, 00:01:21, GigabitEthernet0/0
```

We'd like to prevent R5 from seeing those routes. We could make the FastEthernet interface on R1 passive, but that means we lose the adjacency.

```
R1(config)#router eigrp 100
R1(config-router)#passive-int fast0/0

*Jun 15 23:29:52.100: %DUAL-5-NBRCHANGE: IP-EIGRP(0) 100: Neighbor 30.1.1.5
FastEthernet0/0) is down: interface passive
```

Let's get the interface back up and consider other options.

```
R12

*Jun 15 23:31:34.752: %DUAL-5-NBRCHANGE: IP-EIGRP(0) 100: Neighbor 30.1.1.5
(FastEthernet0/0) is up: new adjacency
```

We could write an ACL that denies all traffic and then apply it to R1—or *can* we? Let's find out!

```
R1(config)#access-list 35 deny any

R1(config)#router eigrp 100
R1(config-router)#distribute-list 35 out fast0/0

*Jun 14 06:38:30.992: %DUAL-5-NBRCHANGE: IP-EIGRP(0) 100: Neighbor 30.1.1.5
(FastEthernet0/0) is resync: route configuration changed
```

The routes have been successfully filtered. R5 no longer has the routes, but it still has the adjacency to R1.

```
R5#show ip route eigrp
< no routes >

R5#show ip eigrp neighbor
EIGRP-IPv4 Neighbors for AS(100)
H   Address          Interface         Hold    Uptime  SRTT   RTO   Q    Seq
                                       (sec)           (ms)         Cnt  Num
0   30.1.1.1         Gi0/0               11    00:12:20   3   200   0    15
```

You can verify your distribute list with *show ip protocols.*

```
R1#show ip protocols
Routing Protocol is "eigrp 100"
  Outgoing update filter list for all interfaces is not set
    FastEthernet0/0 filtered by 35, default is 35
  Incoming update filter list for all interfaces is not set
```

We can also use *distribute-list* to filter EIGRP routes when redistribution is involved. This lab has a slightly different topology from the last one; R1 and R3 are connected over a separate subnet than the one used for R1 and R2. R2 is advertising the same two routes as in the previous lab.

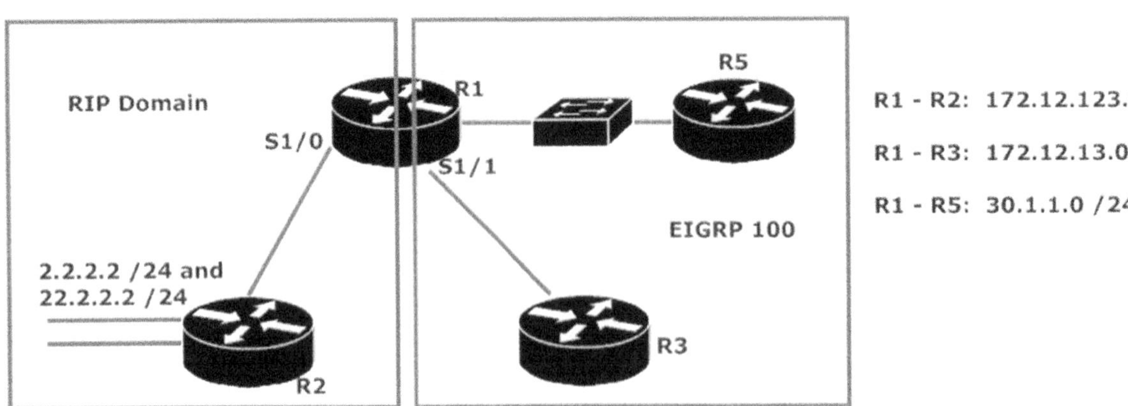

R1 sees both routes advertised by R2.

```
R1#show ip route rip
R     2.0.0.0/8 [120/1] via 172.12.123.2, 00:00:16, Serial1/0
R     22.0.0.0/8 [120/1] via 172.12.123.2, 00:00:10, Serial1/0
```

Before we redistribute the connected and RIP subnets on R1 into EIGRP AS 100, I'll use *default-metric* to set our default seed metric for EIGRP. After I enter that command, I'm no longer required to set those metrics in the *redistribute* commands, as I was in an earlier lab.

```
R1(config)#router eigrp 100
R1(config-router)#default-metric ?
  <1-4294967295>   Bandwidth in Kbits per second

R1(config-router)#default-metric 1544 ?
  <0-4294967295>   Delay metric, in 10 microsecond units

R1(config-router)#default-metric 1544 ?
  <0-4294967295>   Delay metric, in 10 microsecond units

R1(config-router)#default-metric 1544 10 ?
  <0-255>  Reliability metric where 255 is 100% reliable

R1(config-router)#default-metric 1544 10 255 ?
  <1-255>  Effective bandwidth metric (Loading) where 255 is 100% loaded

R1(config-router)#default-metric 1544 10 255 1 ?
  <1-65535>  Maximum Transmission Unit metric of the path

R1(config-router)#default-metric 1544 10 255 1 1500 ?
  <cr>

R1(config-router)#default-metric 1544 10 255 1 1500
R1(config-router)#redistribute connected ?
  Metric      Metric for redistributed routes
  route-map   Route map reference
  <cr>

R1(config-router)#redistribute connected
R1(config-router)#redistribute rip
```

Both R3 and R5 now see the two RIP routes and the 172.12.123.0 /24 network as EIGRP external routes.

```
R3#show ip route eigrp

D EX  2.0.0.0/8 [170/2172416] via 172.12.13.1, 00:01:10, Serial0/1/0
```

```
D EX   22.0.0.0/8 [170/2172416] via 172.12.13.1, 00:01:10, Serial0/1/0
       30.0.0.0/24 is subnetted, 1 subnets
D         30.1.1.0 [90/2172416] via 172.12.13.1, 00:01:02, Serial0/1/0
       172.12.0.0/16 is variably subnetted, 3 subnets, 2 masks
D EX      172.12.123.0/24 [170/21024000] via 172.12.13.1, 00:01:10, Serial0/1/0

R5#show ip route eigrp

D EX   2.0.0.0/8 [170/1662976] via 30.1.1.1, 00:00:37, GigabitEthernet0/0
D EX   22.0.0.0/8 [170/1662976] via 30.1.1.1, 00:00:37, GigabitEthernet0/0
       172.12.0.0/24 is subnetted, 2 subnets
D         172.12.13.0 [90/20514560] via 30.1.1.1, 00:00:37, GigabitEthernet0/0
D EX      172.12.123.0
            [170/20514560] via 30.1.1.1, 00:00:37, GigabitEthernet0/0
```

We just got word that R5 should not know of any of these EIGRP routes, external or internal, and R3 should continue to see all of them. Nothing to it, right? Just write a *deny any* ACL…

```
R1(config)#access-list 13 deny any
```

…and then apply it in the protocol config and on the appropriate interface.

```
R1(config)#router eigrp 100
R1(config-router)#distribute-list 13 out fast0/0
```

R3 still has the routes, but R5 no longer does. Success!

```
R3#show ip route eigrp
D EX   2.0.0.0/8 [170/2172416] via 172.12.13.1, 00:06:13, Serial0/1/0
D EX   22.0.0.0/8 [170/2172416] via 172.12.13.1, 00:06:13, Serial0/1/0
       30.0.0.0/24 is subnetted, 1 subnets
D         30.1.1.0 [90/2172416] via 172.12.13.1, 00:06:05, Serial0/1/0
       172.12.0.0/16 is variably subnetted, 3 subnets, 2 masks
D EX      172.12.123.0/24 [170/21024000] via 172.12.13.1, 00:06:13, Serial0/1/0

R5#show ip route eigrp

< no routes >

R5#
```

But (and you knew that was coming), what if we now want to filter a single route from R3's table? We'd obviously need a different ACL and a different distribute list. That brings up three questions:

- Can we use more than one distribute list on the same router?
- If so, can we use more than one distribute list in the same protocol config?

- If we can, what's the net effect to all of our routing tables?

Let's find out! We just got the word that R3 shouldn't have the 30.1.1.0 /24 network in its table, but it should continue to have the external routes. We'll write an ACL identifying the route to be filtered while allowing all others...

```
R1(config)#access-list 33 deny 30.1.1.0 0.0.0.255
R1(config)#access-list 33 permit any
```

...and we'll apply another distribute list in the EIGRP config without specifying an interface or protocol.

```
R1(config)#router eigrp 100
R1(config-router)#distribute-list 33 out

*Jun 14 07:48:20.511: %DUAL-5-NBRCHANGE: IP-EIGRP(0) 100: Neighbor 172.12.13.3
(Serial1/3) is resync: route configuration changed
*Jun 14 07:48:20.515: %DUAL-5-NBRCHANGE: IP-EIGRP(0) 100: Neighbor 30.1.1.5
(FastEthernet0/0) is resync: route configuration changed
```

The routing table on R3:

```
R3#show ip route eigrp
D EX  2.0.0.0/8 [170/2172416] via 172.12.13.1, 00:14:27, Serial0/1/0
D EX  22.0.0.0/8 [170/2172416] via 172.12.13.1, 00:14:27, Serial0/1/0
      172.12.0.0/16 is variably subnetted, 3 subnets, 2 masks
D EX     172.12.123.0/24 [170/21024000] via 172.12.13.1, 00:14:27, Serial0/1/0
```

The 30.1.1.0 /24 route has been successfully removed. What about the previous distribute list? How does R5's routing table look now?

```
R5#show ip route eigrp
<no routes>
R5#
```

The previous distribute list is still in effect, since it was specifically written to filter route updates leaving fast0/0. General distribute lists (lists that do not indicate a specific interface or protocol) do not overwrite distribute lists that specifically mention an interface or protocol.

On occasion, we'll need to do more than a simple permit or deny when it comes to redistributed routes. Sometimes we just may need to set different metrics for different routes and maybe even change an OSPF external route type or two. We can get those jobs done with route maps.

Route maps operate in a similar fashion to access lists. Both route maps and ACLs arrive at a decision of "permit" or "deny." Route maps give us power over the packets beyond that simple "send" or "don't send"; we can actually change BGP route attributes with these babies, among other things.

Let's get to our next lab, which looks just a bit like our last lab! Note the change in the routing protocol on the right side of the network. R2 is now advertising an additional route.

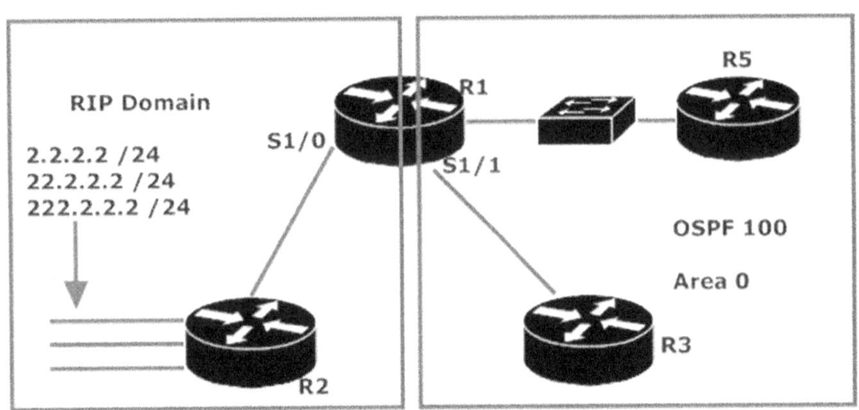

R1 - R2: 172.12.123.0 /24

R1 - R3: 172.12.13.0 /24

R1 - R5: 30.1.1.0 /24

R1 sees all three routes advertised by R2.

```
R1#show ip route rip
R     222.2.2.0/24 [120/1] via 172.12.123.2, 00:00:07, Serial1/0
R     2.0.0.0/8 [120/1] via 172.12.123.2, 00:00:07, Serial1/0
R     22.0.0.0/8 [120/1] via 172.12.123.2, 00:00:07, Serial1/0
```

We have three routes, so why not three requirements for the lab?

2.0.0.0 /8: Double the default seed metric, and set the route type to E1.

22.0.0.0 /8: Keep the default seed metric, and set the route type to E1.

222.2.2.0 /24: Don't redistribute this route at all.

Oh, just one more thing ... all routes redistributed into OSPF in the *future* should keep the default seed metric and the default route type.

That ought to keep us busy! The first step, as always, is to identify each route or group of routes with an ACL.

```
R1(config)#access-list 2 permit 2.0.0.0 0.255.255.255

R1(config)#access-list 22 permit 22.0.0.0 0.255.255.255

R1(config)#access-list 44 permit 222.2.2.0 0.0.0.255
```

Now to start on the route map. Route maps are named rather than numbered, and you should give yours at least a slightly intuitive name. And as you can see, a route map can match on a shipload of values. (A *big* ship.)

```
R1(config)#route-map RIP2OSPF permit 10
R1(config-route-map)#match ?
as-path Match BGP AS path list
clns CLNS information
community Match BGP community list
extcommunity Match BGP/VPN extended community list
interface Match first hop interface of route
ip IP specific information
ipv6 IPv6 specific information
length Packet length
local-preference Local preference for route
metric Match metric of route
mpls-label Match routes which have MPLS labels
nlri BGP NLRI type
policy-list Match IP policy list
route-type Match route-type of route
source-protocol Match source-protocol of route
tag Match tag of route

R1(config-route-map)#match ip ?
  address Match address of route or match packet
  next-hop Match next-hop address of route
  route-source Match advertising source address of route

R1(config-route-map)#match ip address ?
  <1-199> IP access-list number
  <1300-2699> IP access-list number (expanded range)
  WORD IP access-list name
  prefix-list Match entries of prefix-lists

R1(config-route-map)#match ip address 2
```

All IP addresses matching ACL 2 will match this route-map clause. (You can specify more than one ACL for a single route-map clause.) And just as quite a few values can be matched here, quite a few attributes can be set!

```
R1(config-route-map)#match ip address 2
R1(config-route-map)#set ?
  as-path           Prepend string for a BGP AS-path attribute
  automatic-tag     Automatically compute TAG value
  clns              OSI summary address
  comm-list         set BGP community list (for deletion)
  community         BGP community attribute
  dampening         Set BGP route flap dampening parameters
  default           Set default information
  extcommunity      BGP extended community attribute
  interface         Output interface
```

```
ip                  IP specific information
ipv6                IPv6 specific information
level               Where to import route
local-preference    BGP local preference path attribute
metric              Metric value for destination routing protocol
metric-type         Type of metric for destination routing protocol
mpls-label          Set MPLS label for prefix
nlri                BGP NLRI type
origin              BGP origin code
tag                 Tag value for destination routing protocol
traffic-index       BGP traffic classification number for accounting
vrf                 Define VRF name
weight              BGP weight for routing table
```

Quite a few BGP mentions here, but as we're about to see, route maps are hardly limited to BGP configurations. We'll use this clause to set both the metric and metric type for this particular route as it's being redistributed into OSPF.

```
R1(config-route-map)#set metric ?
  +/-<metric>       Add or subtract metric
  <0-4294967295>    Metric value or Bandwidth in Kbits per second

R1(config-route-map)#set metric 40
R1(config-route-map)#set metric-type ?
   External  IS-IS external metric
   Internal  IS-IS internal metric or Use IGP metric as the MED for BGP
   type-1    OSPF external type 1 metric
   type-2    OSPF external type 2 metric

R1(config-route-map)#set metric-type type-1
```

Just as you can put more than one *match* statement in a single clause, you can enter multiple *set* statements, as we just did!

The next clause will match ACL 22. We'll leave the seed metric alone with this clause, and we'll set the OSPF route type to E1.

```
R1(config-route-map)#route-map RIP2OSPF permit 20
R1(config-route-map)#match ip address 22
R1(config-route-map)#set metric-type type-1
```

The third clause will match ACL 44 and will deny the matching route from being redistributed. We won't do that with a *set* statement; rather, we'll make that happen with *deny* in the route-map clause. This particular clause will not have a *set* statement at all!

```
R1(config-route-map)#route-map RIP2OSPF deny 30
R1(config-route-map)#match ip address 44
```

That takes care of the redistributed routes we have now, but we were asked to allow future routes to be redistributed with the default seed metric and route type. For that, we'll write what I call a catch-all clause—a clause that matches any route that wasn't specifically matched earlier in the route map. This clause will have no *match* rule, and since we're not changing any attributes, it won't have any *set* rules. 'Tis an empty clause but an important one!

```
R1(config-route-map)#route-map RIP2OSPF permit 40
R1(config-route-map)#
```

These suckers can get pretty involved! Review your work before applying the route map with *show route-map.*

```
R1#show route-map
route-map RIP2OSPF, permit, sequence 10
  Match clauses:
    ip address (access-lists): 2
  Set clauses:
    metric 40
    metric-type type-1
  Policy routing matches: 0 packets, 0 bytes
route-map RIP2OSPF, permit, sequence 20
  Match clauses:
    ip address (access-lists): 22
  Set clauses:
    metric-type type-1
  Policy routing matches: 0 packets, 0 bytes
route-map RIP2OSPF, deny, sequence 30
  Match clauses:
    ip address (access-lists): 44
  Set clauses:
  Policy routing matches: 0 packets, 0 bytes
route-map RIP2OSPF, permit, sequence 40
  Match clauses:
  Set clauses:
  Policy routing matches: 0 packets, 0 bytes
```

Let's take a look at the route redistribution results before applying the route map.

```
R1(config)#router ospf 100
R1(config-router)#redistribute rip subnets
```

The tables on R3 and R5:

```
R3#show ip route ospf

O E2  2.0.0.0/8 [110/20] via 172.12.13.1, 00:04:29, Serial0/1/0
```

```
O E2   22.0.0.0/8 [110/20] via 172.12.13.1, 00:04:29, Serial0/1/0
       30.0.0.0/24 is subnetted, 1 subnets
O         30.1.1.0 [110/65] via 172.12.13.1, 00:01:23, Serial0/1/0
       172.12.0.0/16 is variably subnetted, 3 subnets, 2 masks
O E2      172.12.123.0/24 [110/20] via 172.12.13.1, 00:04:29, Serial0/1/0
O E2   222.2.2.0/24 [110/20] via 172.12.13.1, 00:04:29, Serial0/1/0

R5#show ip route ospf

O E2   2.0.0.0/8 [110/20] via 30.1.1.1, 00:01:44, GigabitEthernet0/0
O E2   22.0.0.0/8 [110/20] via 30.1.1.1, 00:01:44, GigabitEthernet0/0
       172.12.0.0/24 is subnetted, 2 subnets
O         172.12.13.0 [110/782] via 30.1.1.1, 00:01:44, GigabitEthernet0/0
O E2      172.12.123.0 [110/20] via 30.1.1.1, 00:01:44, GigabitEthernet0/0
O E2   222.2.2.0/24 [110/20] via 30.1.1.1, 00:01:44, GigabitEthernet0/0
```

Just what we expected! We'll now remove that *redistribute rip subnets* statement and replace it with one that calls the route map. We'll throw in a *redistribute connected* statement to get 172.12.123.0 /24 redistributed into OSPF.

```
R1(config)#router ospf 100
R1(config-router)#no redis rip subnets
R1(config-router)#redis rip subnets route-map RIP2OSPF
R1(config-router)#redis connected subnets

R3#show ip route ospf
O E1   2.0.0.0/8 [110/104] via 172.12.13.1, 00:00:07, Serial0/1/0
O E1   22.0.0.0/8 [110/84] via 172.12.13.1, 00:00:07, Serial0/1/0
       30.0.0.0/24 is subnetted, 1 subnets
O         30.1.1.0 [110/65] via 172.12.13.1, 00:01:46, Serial0/1/0
       172.12.0.0/16 is variably subnetted, 3 subnets, 2 masks
O E2      172.12.123.0/24 [110/20] via 172.12.13.1, 00:00:07, Serial0/1/0
```

The 2.0.0.0 /8 route is marked E1, and the seed metric was doubled to 40 during redistribution. Since E1 routes reflect the entire path to the destination, the final cost is not the doubled seed metric of 40, but 104.

The 22.0.0.0 /8 route is marked E1, and the seed metric was left alone. The cost of 84 reflects the entire cost of the path to the destination.

The 222.2.2.0 /24 route does not appear, having been filtered during redistribution.

172.12.123.0 was redistributed via *redistribute connected*, which didn't have a route map applied, so we see the usual defaults in a seed metric of 20 and a route code of E2.

Great stuff! Route maps are a powerful tool for controlling redistribution and changing route attributes, BGP or otherwise.

Before we move on, we need to test the fourth clause of our route map. Let's add a route not specifically named by the first three lines and see what happens.

```
R2(config)#int loopback 55
R2(config-if)#ip address 55.5.5.5
*Jun 18 19:10:49.306: %LINEPROTO-5-UPDOWN: Line protocol on Interface Loopback55,
changed state to up
R2(config-if)#ip address 55.5.5.5 255.255.255.0

R2(config-if)#router rip
R2(config-router)#network 55.0.0.0
```

The route is in R1's RIP routing table...

```
R1#show ip route rip
R 222.2.2.0/24 [120/1] via 172.12.123.2, 00:00:19, Serial1/0
R 2.0.0.0/8 [120/1] via 172.12.123.2, 00:00:19, Serial1/0
55.0.0.0/24 is subnetted, 1 subnets
R 55.5.5.0 [120/1] via 172.12.123.2, 00:00:19, Serial1/0
R 22.0.0.0/8 [120/1] via 172.12.123.2, 00:00:19, Serial1/0
```

...and R3 has it via route redistribution, with both the default seed metric of 20 and default code of E2, having matched clause 40 of the route map.

```
R3#show ip route ospf

O E1   2.0.0.0/8 [110/104] via 172.12.13.1, 00:10:41, Serial0/1/0
O E1   22.0.0.0/8 [110/84] via 172.12.13.1, 00:10:41, Serial0/1/0
       30.0.0.0/24 is subnetted, 1 subnets
O         30.1.1.0 [110/65] via 172.12.13.1, 00:12:20, Serial0/1/0
       55.0.0.0/24 is subnetted, 1 subnets
O E2      55.5.5.0 [110/20] via 172.12.13.1, 00:01:44, Serial0/1/0
       172.12.0.0/16 is variably subnetted, 3 subnets, 2 masks
O E2      172.12.123.0/24 [110/20] via 172.12.13.1, 00:10:41, Serial0/1/0
```

We can have multiple *match* statements in a single clause, and should we do so, both *match* statements must do just that in order for the clause to match. For example, the following clause would have to match both ACL 5 and be an OSPF E2 route in order to have its metric set to the specified value.

```
R1(config)#route-map OSPF2RIPDOMAIN permit 10
R1(config-route-map)#match ip address 5
R1(config-route-map)#match route-type external type-2
R1(config-route-map)#set metric 5
```

There's one more *set* value I want to introduce you to...

Route Redistribution and the Tag Attribute

Right in the middle of all these route attributes lies the tag.

```
R1(config)#route-map OSPF2RIPDOMAIN permit 20
R1(config-route-map)#set ?
  as-path            Prepend string for a BGP AS-path attribute
  automatic-tag      Automatically compute TAG value
  clns               OSI summary address
  comm-list          set BGP community list (for deletion)
  community          BGP community attribute
  dampening          Set BGP route flap dampening parameters
  default            Set default information
  extcommunity       BGP extended community attribute
  interface          Output interface
  ip                 IP specific information
  ipv6               IPv6 specific information
  level              Where to import route
  local-preference   BGP local preference path attribute
  metric             Metric value for destination routing protocol
  metric-type        Type of metric for destination routing protocol
  mpls-label         Set MPLS label for prefix
  nlri               BGP NLRI type
  origin             BGP origin code
  tag                Tag value for destination routing protocol
  traffic-index      BGP traffic classification number for accounting
  vrf                Define VRF name
  weight             BGP weight for routing table
```

That little value helps to prevent some big nasty routing loops, especially with two-way route redistribution in place. You can tag routes with a number as they're redistributed and then prohibit routes with that same value from being "re-redistributed" back into the original routing protocol.

Let's use the previous lab topology for a demo. Everything except the basic RIP and OSPF configurations from the previous lab has been removed, and there's a different address on the R1-R3 link.

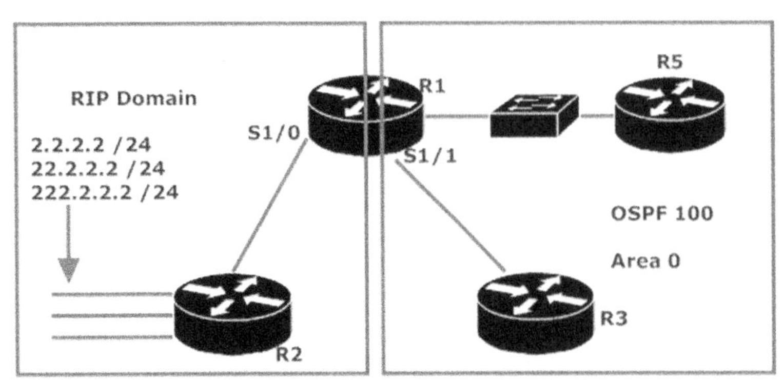

R1 - R2: 172.12.123.0 /24

R1 - R3: 199.12.13.0 /24

R1 - R5: 30.1.1.0 /24

In the previous lab, we configured one-way route redistribution (RIP into OSPF, namely). Let's say we're getting ready to configure two-way redistribution this time, and we want to make absolutely sure routes redistributed into OSPF cannot be brought back into the RIP domains and vice versa. That includes the possibility of additional border routers being added later.

As routes are redistributed into OSPF, we can tag them with a value of 10, and then deny values with that same tag from being redistributed back into the RIP domain.

R1 has the three routes advertised by R2:

```
R1#show ip route rip
R     222.2.2.0/24 [120/1] via 172.12.123.2, 00:00:02, Serial1/0
R     2.0.0.0/8 [120/1] via 172.12.123.2, 00:00:02, Serial1/0
R     22.0.0.0/8 [120/1] via 172.12.123.2, 00:00:02, Serial1/0
```

To tag all redistributed routes as they go into OSPF, no match statement is needed—just this simple route map:

```
R1(config)#route-map RIP2OSPF permit 10
R1(config-route-map)#set tag 10
R1(config-route-map)#exit

R1(config)#router ospf 1
R1(config-router)#redis rip route-map RIP2OSPF subnets
R1(config-router)#redis connected subnets
```

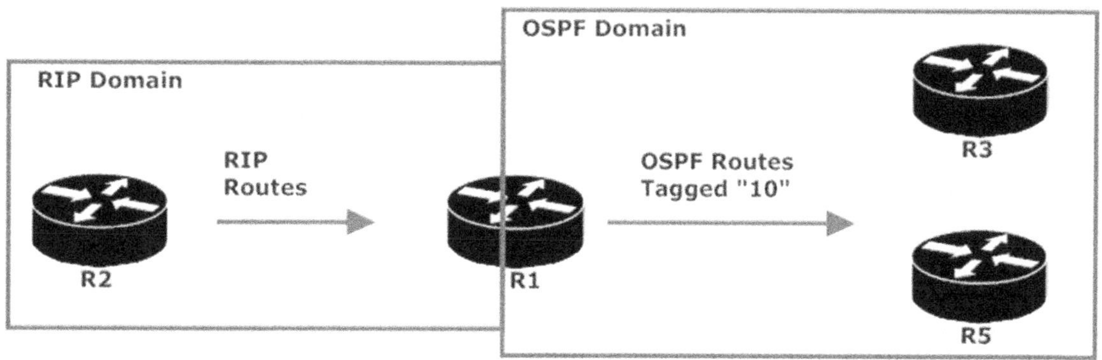

The resulting OSPF table on R3:

```
R3#show ip route ospf

O E2  2.0.0.0/8 [110/20] via 172.12.13.1, 00:00:31, Serial0/1/0
O E2  22.0.0.0/8 [110/20] via 172.12.13.1, 00:00:31, Serial0/1/0
      30.0.0.0/24 is subnetted, 1 subnets
O        30.1.1.0 [110/65] via 172.12.13.1, 00:00:26, Serial0/1/0
      172.12.0.0/16 is variably subnetted, 3 subnets, 2 masks
```

```
O E2     172.12.123.0/24 [110/20] via 172.12.13.1, 00:00:31, Serial0/1/0
O E2  222.2.2.0/24 [110/20] via 172.12.13.1, 00:00:31, Serial0/1/0
```

All three tagged routes appear along with the internal 30.1.1.0 /24 network and the connected-to-R1 network 172.12.123.0 /24. You won't see the tags in the routing table, but you will see them with the extended *show ip route* command.

```
R3#show ip route 2.2.2.0
Routing entry for 2.0.0.0/8
Known via "ospf 1", distance 110, metric 20
Tag 10, type extern 2, forward metric 64
Last update from 172.12.13.1 on Serial0/1/0, 00:02:58 ago
Routing Descriptor Blocks:
* 172.12.13.1, from 172.12.123.1, 00:02:58 ago, via Serial0/1/0
      Route metric is 20, traffic share count is 1
      Route tag 10
R3#show ip route 22.2.2.0
Routing entry for 22.0.0.0/8
Known via "ospf 1", distance 110, metric 20
Tag 10, type extern 2, forward metric 64
Last update from 172.12.13.1 on Serial0/1/0, 00:03:04 ago
Routing Descriptor Blocks:
* 172.12.13.1, from 172.12.123.1, 00:03:04 ago, via Serial0/1/0
      Route metric is 20, traffic share count is 1
      Route tag 10

R3#show ip route 222.2.2.0
Routing entry for 222.2.2.0/24
Known via "ospf 1", distance 110, metric 20
Tag 10, type extern 2, forward metric 64
Last update from 172.12.13.1 on Serial0/1/0, 00:03:09 ago
Routing Descriptor Blocks:
* 172.12.13.1, from 172.12.123.1, 00:03:09 ago, via Serial0/1/0
      Route metric is 20, traffic share count is 1
      Route tag 10

R3#show ip route 172.12.123.0
Routing entry for 172.12.123.0/24
  Known via "ospf 1", distance 110, metric 20, type extern 2, forward metric 64
  Last update from 172.12.13.1 on Serial0/1/0, 00:03:14 ago
  Routing Descriptor Blocks:
  * 172.12.13.1, from 172.12.123.1, 00:03:14 ago, via Serial0/1/0
      Route metric is 20, traffic share count is 1
```

The following config will prevent any routes tagged "10" from being redistributed from OSPF back into RIP while allowing untagged routes to be redistributed and tagged "20."

```
R1(config)#route-map OSPF2RIP deny 10
R1(config-route-map)#match tag 10
R1(config-route-map)#route-map OSPF2RIP permit 20
R1(config-route-map)#set tag 20
```

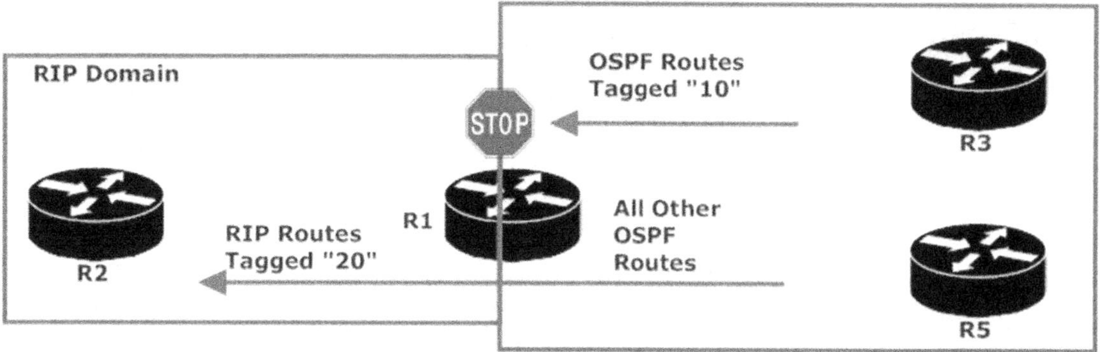

If we now want to go back to the RIP2OSPF route map and use that tag of 20 to prevent routes from being advertised back to OSPF…well, let's have a look at that route map first.

```
R1#show route-map RIP2OSPF
route-map RIP2OSPF, permit, sequence 10
  Match clauses:
  Set clauses:
    tag 10
  Policy routing matches: 0 packets, 0 bytes
```

We need the new clause to have a sequence number of less than 10, since we need this deny clause in front of this clause, which allows all routes and tags them with 10. We'll write the new clause with a sequence number of five and then verify with *show route-map RIP2OSPF.*

```
R1(config)#route-map RIP2OSPF deny 5
R1(config-route-map)#match tag 20

R1#show route-map RIP2OSPF
route-map RIP2OSPF, deny, sequence 5
  Match clauses:
    tag 20
  Set clauses:
  Policy routing matches: 0 packets, 0 bytes
route-map RIP2OSPF, permit, sequence 10
  Match clauses:
  Set clauses:
    tag 10
  Policy routing matches: 0 packets, 0 bytes
```

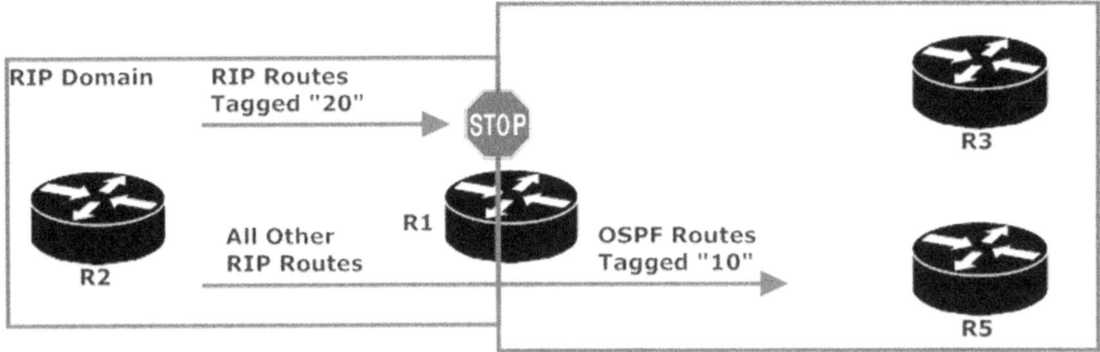

Just as with ACLs, the order of the lines in a route map is vital. Sequence numbers make it easy to keep your lines in line!

Policy Routing

Policy-based routing, generally referred to as "policy routing," uses route maps to apply certain values to incoming traffic. We'll have a look at those values in just a moment, but right now, let's have a look at some basic policy routing rules.

- Policy routing doesn't affect the destination of the packet, but it can affect the path the traffic takes to get there, including the next-hop IP address. (Spoiler alert!)
- Policy routing can forward traffic based on the source or destination IP address with the use of an extended ACL. (Spoiler alert number two!)
- Applying policy routing on an interface affects only packets arriving on that interface.
- Applying policy routing locally applies the policy to packets generated on that router.
- If a packet doesn't match any of the specific criteria in a route map or does match a line that has an explicit *deny* statement, the data is sent to the routing process and is processed normally.
- If you don't want to route packets that have no match for a route-map clause in policy routing, the *set* command must be used to send those packets to the null0 interface. Naturally, this *set* command should be the final set command in the route map.

Let's see these rules in action with this lab! We'll pay special attention to R4's loopback throughout the next two labs.

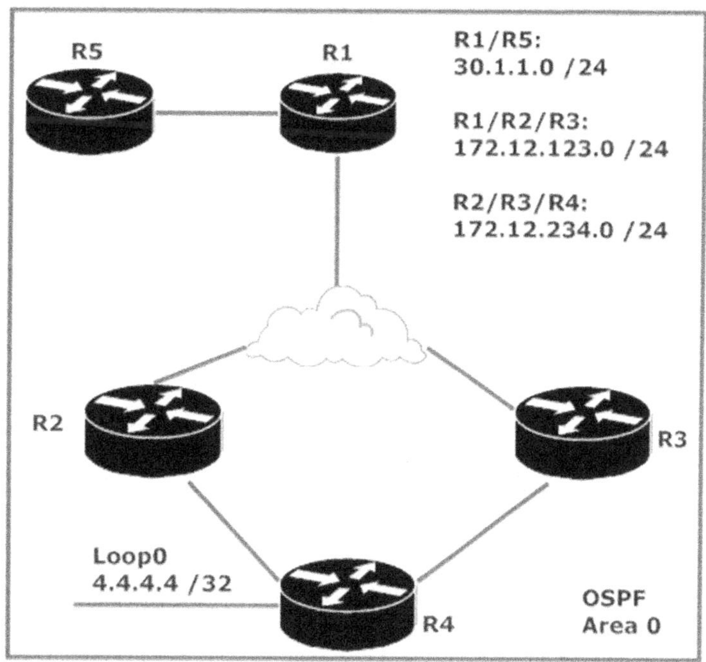

traceroute reveals the path packets take from R5 to R4's loopback.

```
R5#traceroute 4.4.4.4
Tracing the route to 4.4.4.4

  1 30.1.1.1 0 msec 0 msec 4 msec
  2 172.12.123.2 32 msec 32 msec 32 msec
  3 172.12.234.4 32 msec * 32 msec
```

We'll use policy routing to have packets originating on R5 and headed for 4.4.4.4 to leave R1 and use 172.12.123.3 as the next-hop IP address. We'll start with an ACL identifying the source of the traffic to be policy routed, followed by a route map that changes the next-hop IP address of packets whose source matches the ACL we just wrote.

```
R1(config)#access-list 5 permit host 30.1.1.5

R1(config)#route-map NEXTHOP permit 10
R1(config-route-map)#match ip address 5
R1(config-route-map)#set ip next-hop 172.12.123.3

R1(config-route-map)#int fast 0/0
R1(config-if)#ip policy ?
  route-map Policy route map

R1(config-if)#ip policy route-map ?
  WORD Route map name
```

```
R1(config-if)#ip policy route-map NEXTHOP ?
  <cr>

R1(config-if)#ip policy route-map NEXTHOP
```

We didn't need to specify *in* or *out* when applying policy routing. We weren't even given the option to do so, since policy routing is applied only to incoming traffic. With that said, let's head back to R5 and *traceroute* again.

```
R5#traceroute 4.4.4.4
Tracing the route to 4.4.4.4

  1 30.1.1.1 4 msec 0 msec 0 msec
  2 172.12.123.3 36 msec 32 msec 32 msec
  3 172.12.234.4 36 msec *    32 msec
```

Packets from R5 destined for 4.4.4.4 are successfully policy routed to use 172.12.123.3 as the next-hop IP address, which is great! The only problem with this method is that *all* traffic from R5 will be policy routed, including traffic unicast to 172.12.123.2. Check out this *traceroute*:

```
R5#traceroute 172.12.123.2
Tracing the route to 172.12.123.2

  1 30.1.1.1 0 msec 4 msec 0 msec
  2 172.12.123.3 32 msec 36 msec 32 msec
  3 172.12.123.1 24 msec 24 msec 24 msec
  4 172.12.123.2 56 msec *    52 msec
```

Pings from R5 to 172.12.123.2 are actually crossing the WAN three times! First, those pings arrive on R1 and are policy routed to 172.12.123.3.

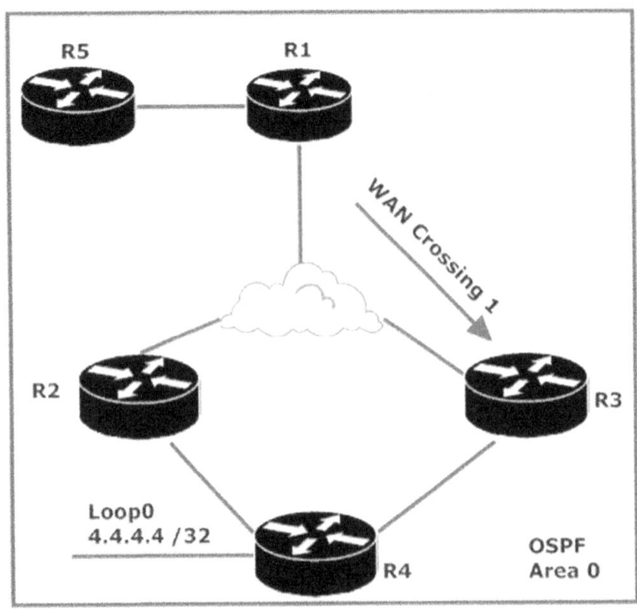

R3 sees the packets are destined for 172.12.123.2, and the best match for that network in R3's routing table is the directly connected network that uses R1 as the next hop!

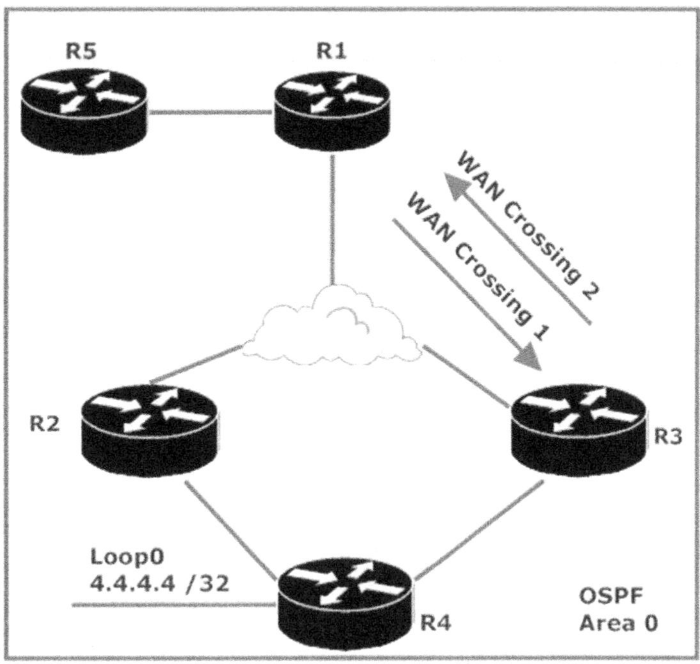

When R1 gets those packets, they no longer have the source IP address that matches the ACL, so the packets are routed normally to R2. This is suboptimal routing, and it's a situation that calls for policy routing that uses an extended ACL rather than a standard one.

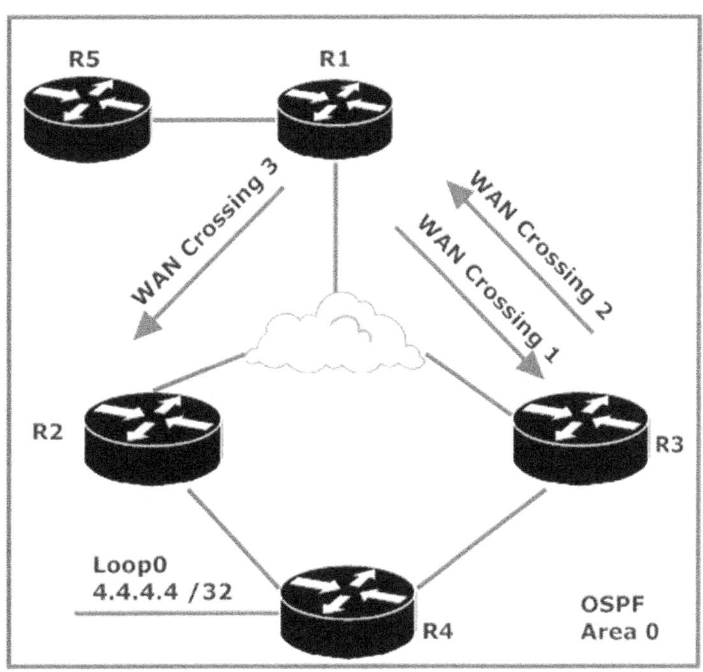

Let's remove the route map and ACL and give that another shot!

```
R1(config)#no route-map NEXTHOP
R1(config)#int fast 0/0
R1(config-if)#no ip policy route-map NEXTHOP
R1(config-if)#exit
R1(config)#no access-list 5
```

Our extended ACL will match traffic sourced from 30.1.1.5 and destined for 4.4.4.4.

```
R1(config)#access-list 105 permit ip host 30.1.1.5 host 4.4.4.4
```

Traffic matching that route map will use the next-hop address 172.12.123.3.

```
R1(config)#route-map NEXTHOP permit 10
R1(config-route-map)#match ip address 105
R1(config-route-map)#set ip next-hop 172.12.123.3
```

We'll apply that route map and send two *traceroutes* from R5.

```
R1(config)#int fast 0/0
R1(config-if)#ip policy route-map NEXTHOP

R5#traceroute 4.4.4.4

Tracing the route to 4.4.4.4

  1 30.1.1.1 4 msec 4 msec 0 msec
  2 172.12.123.3 36 msec 36 msec 32 msec
  3 172.12.234.4 32 msec *    32 msec

R5#traceroute 172.12.123.2

Tracing the route to 172.12.123.2

  1 30.1.1.1 4 msec 0 msec 0 msec
  2 172.12.123.2 32 msec *    32 msec
```

Success! The packets to 4.4.4.4 are using 172.12.123.3 as the next-hop address when leaving R1, while packets destined for 172.12.123.2 go straight there. That's what an extended ACL can do for your policy routing!

Local Policy Routing

Once in a while, you might just want to policy route packets that originate on the local router. That's what we'll do in our next lab! I've added three loopbacks to R1 and added them to OSPF Area 0.

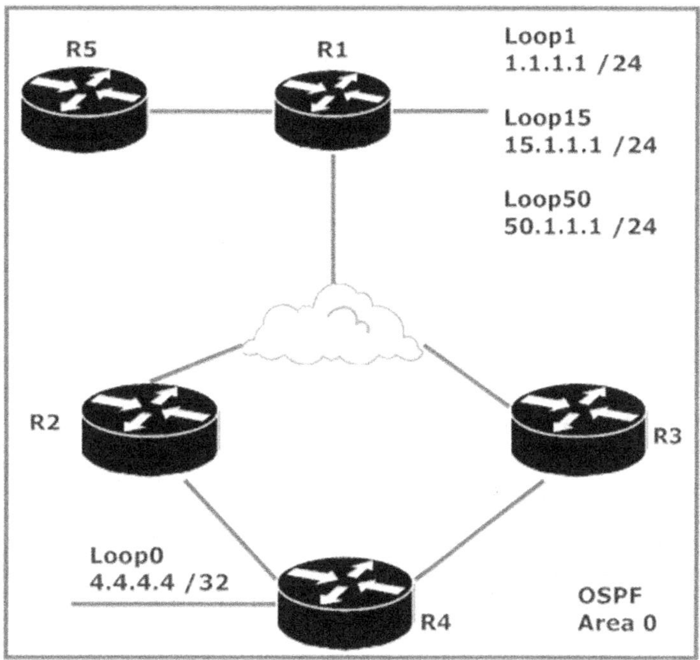

traceroute reveals that packets sent from any of those interfaces are using R2 as the next hop.

```
R1#traceroute 4.4.4.4 source 1.1.1.1
Tracing the route to 4.4.4.4

  1 172.12.123.2 32 msec 32 msec 32 msec
  2 172.12.234.4 32 msec *     32 msec

R1#traceroute 4.4.4.4 source 15.1.1.1
Tracing the route to 4.4.4.4

  1 172.12.123.2 32 msec 32 msec 32 msec
  2 172.12.234.4 32 msec *     32 msec

R1#traceroute 4.4.4.4 source 50.1.1.1
Tracing the route to 4.4.4.4

  1 172.12.123.2 32 msec 32 msec 32 msec
  2 172.12.234.4 32 msec *     32 msec
```

We need a policy that sends traffic originating from the first two loopbacks to use 172.12.123.3 as the next hop when that traffic is destined for 4.4.4.4, while loopback50 should continue to use 172.12.123.2.

Writing an ACL identifying the source addresses to use R3 as the next hop—*no problem!*

```
R1(config)#access-list 101 permit ip host 1.1.1.1 host 4.4.4.4
R1(config)#
R1(config)#access-list 101 permit ip host 15.1.1.1 host 4.4.4.4
```

Writing the route map that will use that ACL—*no problem!*

```
R1(config)#route-map NEXTHOP _ R3 permit 10
R1(config-route-map)#match ip address 101
R1(config-route-map)#set ip next-hop 172.12.123.3
```

Applying policy routing to the interfaces—*problem!*

We know that policy routing is applied to inbound packets, so how do we apply it to packets originating on the local router? The first point at which these packets would be "inbound" is on R2 or R3, and then it's too late to get the result we want in an effective manner. For packets originating on the local router, we need *local policy routing.* The effect on the packets is the same as with the policy routing we performed in the previous lab, but the commands are different. Local policy routing is applied with the *ip local policy* command in global configuration mode.

```
R1(config)#ip local policy ?
  route-map Policy route map

R1(config)#ip local policy route-map ?
  WORD Route map name

R1(config)#ip local policy route-map NEXTHOP _ R3 ?
  <cr>

R1(config)#ip local policy route-map NEXTHOP _ R3
```

Let's test our policy!

```
R1#traceroute 4.4.4.4 source 1.1.1.1
Tracing the route to 4.4.4.4

  1 172.12.123.3 32 msec 36 msec 32 msec
  2 172.12.234.4 36 msec * 32 msec

R1#traceroute 4.4.4.4 source 15.1.1.1
Tracing the route to 4.4.4.4
```

```
  1 172.12.123.3 32 msec 36 msec 32 msec
  2 172.12.234.4 32 msec * 32 msec

R1#traceroute 4.4.4.4 source 50.1.1.1
Tracing the route to 4.4.4.4

  1 172.12.123.2 32 msec 32 msec 32 msec
  2 172.12.234.4 32 msec * 32 msec
```

Success! Traffic originating from 1.1.1.1 and 15.1.1.1 and headed for 4.4.4.4 uses 172.12.123.3 as the next hop, while traffic originating from 50.1.1.1 and headed for 4.4.4.4 continues to use 172.12.123.2 as the next hop.

Configuring local policy routing has no effect on previously configured policy routing. The policy routing config from the previous lab is still in effect, as we see with a *traceroute* from R5.

```
R5#traceroute 4.4.4.4
Tracing the route to 4.4.4.4

  1 30.1.1.1 4 msec 0 msec 0 msec
  2 172.12.123.3 36 msec 32 msec 32 msec
  3 172.12.234.4 32 msec *    32 msec
```

No matter how long and seemingly complex policies become, they all operate according to these fundamentals. Keep these in mind, and you'll succeed with policy routing every time!

That's enough IPv4 for now. Let's head to IPv6!

Chapter 8:

IP VERSION 6

The good news: the 128-bit addresses used in IPv6 give us a tremendous number of addresses, and IPv6 was designed specifically with route summarization in mind.

The temporarily bad news: those 128-bit addresses. The ones that are 128 bits long. That's a lonnnng address to type, especially for those of us who hate entering 32-bit addresses.

I say "temporarily bad" because there is a bit of shock factor in just hearing about 128-bit addresses when you're used to IPv4's 32-bit addresses. Once you get used to the IPv6 address format (and you will), working with IPv6 will become second nature.

IPv6 brings us quite a few improvements over IPv4:

- Those broadcasts we're always trying to limit are things of the past. IPv6 doesn't use broadcasts.
- NAT isn't gone yet, but it will be as IPv6 continues to replace IPv4. (NAT is not a thing of the past when it comes to the CCNP Route exam, and we'll discuss NAT in another part of the course.)
- It bears repeating that IPv6 was designed with route aggregation in mind, which makes aggregation easier and more effective and in turn keeps our routing tables—say it with me!—*complete and concise.*
- DHCP is still around, but IPv6 nodes can assign themselves an address without the help of a DHCP server through a little process called *autoconfiguration*. More on that soon.
- Quality of Service (QoS) capabilities are greater with the IPv6 header values.

Moving your entire network from IPv4 to IPv6 is a little tricky and requires careful planning. (Two massive understatements for one low price!) Knowing the fundamentals of IPv6 makes that migration a lot easier, and we'll jump right into those fundamentals now with a comparison of the IPv4 and IPv6 headers.

IPv6 Header Fields

There are quite a few changes in the headers as we move from IPv4 to IPv6. There are eight header fields overall in IPv6:

- *Version:* Set to "6." And yes, I know you know that.
- *Traffic Class:* In IPv4, this was the *Type of Service* field. The name "traffic class" comes from this field's ability to allow us to assign levels of importance to packets via QoS.
- *Flow Label:* This field allows a packet to be labeled as part of a particular flow. This also helps with QoS, allowing us to prioritize traffic flows rather than individual packets. This header has no equivalent in IPv4.
- *Payload Length:* Same thing as the *Total Length* field in IPv4.
- *Hop Limit:* Roughly equivalent to IPv4's *Time to Live* field. Every hop decrements this counter by one. When this counter hits zero, the *Time to Live* becomes the *Time to Be Discarded.*
- *Next Header*: Equivalent to IPv4's *Protocol* field.
- *Source Address, Destination Address:* Same function, just larger. 128 bits each, to be exact!
- A few IPv4 fields didn't make the cut to IPv6: *Header Length, Identification, Flags, Fragment Offset,* and *Header Checksum.*

Now, about those 128 bits…

The IPv6 Address Format, Zero Compression, and Leading Zero Compression

Sample IPv4 address: 129.14.12.200

Sample IPv6 address: 1029:9183:81AE:0000:0000:0AC1:2143:019B

A noncompressed IPv6 address has eight sections of four hex values, separated by a total of seven colons. Luckily for you and me (the you-know-whos), there are ways to compress these addresses so not so many numbers and letters are involved. This helps in the field, and it'll really help the day you pass your CCNP Route exam.

From your CCNA studies, you remember there's no difference between an uppercase letter and a lowercase letter in hex. Simple rule, right? Right! The other simple rules deal with all the zeroes you'll deal with in IPv6 addressing.

If you have consecutive fields of zeroes, they can be expressed with two colons. It doesn't matter if you have two fields of zeroes or eight (really!), you can simply type two colons, and you're done. The key here with this *zero compression* is that you can only do it once per address. Here's an example:

Original IPv6 address: 1234:1234:0000:0000:0000:0000:3456:3434

Same address with zero compression: 1234:1234::3456:3434

Thought you'd like that! I also know you'll like *leading zero compression*, which allows us to drop the leading zeroes in any field. Here are the key rules with leading zero compression:

- You have to leave at least one number in each field, even if the field is all zeroes.
- You can perform leading zero compression as often as needed in a single address.

And here's an example of leading zero compression:

Original address: 1234:0000:1234:0000:1234:0000:1234:0123

Same address using only leading zero compression: 1234:0:1234:0:1234:0:1234:123

One more leading zero / zero compression rule: you're allowed to use both in a single address. Just remember the frequency rules, and you're all set! Let's see what we can do using both methods:

Original address: 1111:0000:0000:1234:0011:0022:0033:0044

Newly compressed address: 1111::1234:11:22:33:44

We used zero compression to use a double colon to replace the second and third fields, which were both all zeroes. Leading zero compression replaced the two zeroes at the beginning of each of the last four fields.

Watch out for incorrectly expressed IPv6 addresses, both on your exam and in the field. If you're looking at an IPv6 address with more than two consecutive colons, or you see more than one set of consecutive colons, you're looking at an illegally expressed IPv6 address. The following two addresses are illegal just on the base of the colons, so you don't have to look at anything else—they're *immediately illegal* expressions.

Immediately Illegal: 1111::::2222:3333:4444:5555

Immediately Illegal: 1111::2222:3333::

Interface Identifiers and EUI-64

Every interface on any given IPv6 link needs a unique identifier, cleverly called the *interface identifier.* The interface identifier is a 64-bit value that you and I don't have to manually enter, but we do need to know how it's created and how it's assigned.

RFC 2373 defines the 64-bit Extended Unique Identifier (EUI-64). This allows the interface to assign an interface identifier to itself, using the interface's MAC address. Sounds like we need a few extra bits from somewhere, since the MAC address is only 48 bits long! We get those extra bits by dropping "FFFE" right in the middle of the address, between the OUI and the vendor code. If you see "FFFE" in the middle of an interface identifier, you know it's an EUI-64 assigned identifier.

A quick MAC address review: in the MAC address 00-01-02-aa-bb-cc, the Organizationally Unique Identifier (OUI) is 00-01-02, and the vendor code is aa-bb-cc. That makes it easy enough to come up with the interface identifier for this address:

00-01-02-FF-FE-aa-bb-cc

And that's right…*almost.* There's just one little detail we need to take care of, and that detail is the seventh bit of the first octet (00000000). The seventh bit is the Universal/Local bit, which kind of describes what this bit is all about. This bit tells us whether this address is universally unique or just locally unique (unique only to this link, that is). It's assumed a MAC address is universally unique, so we'll set that the U/L bit is set to 1…

00000010

…giving us a final interface identifier of 02-01-02-FF-FE-aa-bb-cc.

Let's walk through this interface identifier creation process on a live Cisco router. Here's the MAC address of Fast0/0 on R1. What's the interface identifier?

```
R1#show int fast 0/0
FastEthernet0/0 is up, line protocol is up
  Hardware is AmdFE, address is 000f.f7c4.09c0 (bia 000f.f7c4.09c0)
```

The MAC is 000f.f7c4.09c0. Here's how we get to the interface identifier:

- Put "FFFE" smack in the middle of the MAC, giving us 000f.f7ff.fec4.09c0.
- Take the first digit in the result—in this case, 0—write it in binary, and change the seventh bit to a 1. The result is 00000010, which converts to the decimal "2."

That gives us 200f.f7ff.fec4.09c0. Does it match the router's result? I've already enabled ipv6 on that interface, and *show ipv6 interface fast 0/0* displays the link local address, with the interface identifier portion of that address in bold.

```
R1#show ipv6 int fast 0/0
FastEthernet0/0 is up, line protocol is up
  IPv6 is enabled, link-local address is FE80::20F:F7FF:FEC4:9C0
```

Success! The Cisco router obviously performed some zero and leading zero compression on its own, but the link-local address is exactly what we thought it would be. (More on that FE80 address portion shortly!)

IPv6 Address Types

You know the drill with IPv4 address types! *Unicasts* represent a single host, *multicasts* represent a group of hosts, and *broadcasts* represent all hosts. We still have unicasts and multicasts with IPv6, but broadcasts are gone, and we have a *new* address type. *Anycasts* are addresses that represent multiple interfaces, as does a multicast. The difference is that when an anycast is sent to a group of interfaces, it's sent to the interface that's considered *closest to the sender.*

How is "closest" defined for anycasts? It depends...

- If there *are* directly connected neighbors, the closest one is the first one learned.
- If there are *no* directly connected neighbors, the closest neighbor is determined by the routing protocol metric.

When an IPv6 *multicast* is sent to a group of interfaces, it's received by every member of the group, just as an IPv4 multicast would be.

IPv6 brings us different types of unicast IP addresses as well, including the *global unicast address*. This address is equivalent to the public IPv4 address class. These addresses are fully routable and can be used for Internet access. This range is 2000::/3, meaning any address that begins with 001 is a global unicast address.

The link-local address is an address that's kept on the local link. These addresses have a prefix of Fe80 (1111 1110 10)::/10, followed by the interface identifier.

Two more address types you can spot by their initial bits are multicasts (1111 1111) and *IPv4-compatible addresses*. Any IPv6 address with the first 96 bits set to zero is an IPv4-compatible address. Expressed with zero compression, that's ::x.x.x.x. Using only leading zero compression, that's 0:0:0:0:0:0:x.x.x.x.

The Reserved IPv6 Addresses

Just as IPv4 has 127.0.0.1 reserved for testing, IPv6 reserves 0000:0000:0000:0000:0000:0000:0000:0001. Thankfully, we can express that address as 0:0:0:0:0:0:0:1 (with leading zero compression only) or ::1 (using a combination of leading zero and zero compression). Compression's looking pretty good right now!

Unique to IPv6 is the *unspecified address*, used to express an unknown address. The full address is 0000:0000:0000:0000:0000:0000:0000:0000, which thankfully we can express as 0:0:0:0:0:0:0:0 or ::/128. ("::/0" is the IPv6 default route.)

A Little More about IPv4-Compatible IPv6 Addresses

Addresses beginning with ninety-six zeroes are IPv4-compatible address. We know the full IPv6 address is 128 bits, and if the first 96 bits are zeroes, that leaves 32 bits. That number of bits should sound familiar! The remaining 32 bits in the address are simply a hex expression of the IPv4 address.

Let's say we need to convert the IPv6 address ::D190:4E71 to its IPv4 equivalent. We know the double colon is zero compression in action, so we just need to convert the remaining bits into decimal.

Hex D1= 13 ("D") units of 16 + 1 unit of 1 = 208 + 1 = 209

Hex 90= 9 units of 16 + 0 units of 1 = 144

Hex 4E= 4 units of 16 + 14 ("E") units of 1 = 64 + 14 = 78

Hex 71= 7 units of 16 + 1 unit of 1 = 112 + 1 = 113

The IPv4 address embedded into that IPv6 address is 209.144.78.113. Practice your hex-to-decimal and decimal-to-hex skills so they're both second nature on exam day!

Multicasts and Anycasts

IPv4 multicast addresses are Class D addresses with a first octet of 224–239. The IPv6 multicast range is much larger but easier to remember. Any address that begins with 1111 1111, or "FF" in hex, is a multicast address. The full prefix is FF00::/8.

There are some local-link-only addresses in that range worth noting:

FF02::1—All nodes on the local link

FF02::2—All routers on the local link

FF02::5—All OSPF routers

FF02::6—All OSPF DRs

FF02::9—All RIP routers

FF02::A—All EIGRP routers

FF02::1:FFzz:zzzz/104—*Solicited-node addresses.* These are used in Neighbor Solicitation messages, which we'll examine in detail shortly. The "z"s represent the rightmost 24 bits of the unicast/address of the node.

To see the multicast and anycast groups joined by an interface, run *show ipv6 interface.*

```
R1#show ipv6 int fast 0/0
FastEthernet0/0 is up, line protocol is up
  IPv6 is enabled, link-local address is FE80::20F:F7FF:FEC4:9C0
  Global unicast address(es):
    2014::1, subnet is 2014::/64
  Joined group address(es):
    FF02::1
    FF02::2
    FF02::5
    FF02::6
    FF02::1:FF00:1
    FF02::1:FFC4:9C0
```

The IPv6 Autoconfiguration Process

IPv6 offers two types of autoconfiguration, *stateless* and *stateful.* Stateful autoconfiguration has a host obtain an IPv6 address (along with other info) from a server. That likely sounds a lot like DHCP to you, and for good reason. Stateful autoconfiguration *is* DHCPv6! The key phrase here is "from a server." If the DHCPv6 server goes down, we're out of luck.

Stateless Address Autoconfiguration (SLAAC) has no such dependence, and that entire process starts with an IPv6 host configuring its *own* link-local address.

The first 64 bits of this self-generated address are 1111 1110 10 (FE80) followed by fifty-four zeroes. The last 64 bits are the interface identifier. This self-created address needs a little testing before we allow its use, though.

The *Duplicate Address Detection* (DAD) test consists of the host sending a *Neighbor Solicitation* (NS) message to see if any other host on the same link is using that same link-local address. You can see the NS leaving the interface and the DAD status by running *debug ipv6 nd* before opening an interface (or closing it, running the debug, and reopening it, as I did here).

```
ICMPv6-ND: Sending NS for FE80::20F:F7FF:FEC4:9C0 on FastEthernet0/0
ICMPv6-ND: DAD: FE80::20F:F7FF:FEC4:9C0 is unique.
Sending NA for FE80::20F:F7FF:FEC4:9C0 on FastEthernet0/0
Address FE80::20F:F7FF:FEC4:9C0/10 is up on FastEthernet0/0

ICMPv6-ND: Sending NS for 2001:1::1 on FastEthernet0/0
ICMPv6-ND: DAD: 2001:1::1 is unique.
ICMPv6-ND: Sending NA for 2001:1::1 on FastEthernet0/0
ICMPv6-ND: Address 2001:1::1/64 is up on FastEthernet0/0
```

I removed the timestamps to make this easier to read, so take my word that all this happened in about twelve milliseconds. First, the router sent an NS for its own link-local address.

Had R1 received a *Neighbor Advertisement* (NA) in response to that NS, alerting R1 the link-local address in question was already in use, R1 would have disabled that address. Since no such message was received, DAD determined the link-local address was unique, and R1 sent an NA of its own claiming that address.

R1 then went through the same process with its global address. R1 sent an NS with that address...

...and when no NA was received in response, DAD determined the global address to be unique, and R1 sent an NA of its own for this address.

The host now sends a Router Solicitation (RS) to FF02::2, the "all-routers" multicast address. The host is soliciting additional configuration information from a router in the form of a Router Advertisement (RA), shown coming in here:

```
ICMPv6-ND: Received RA from FE80::21B:D4FF:FEC2:990 on FastEthernet0/0
```

Routers send these RAs periodically without being prodded by a client request, but even though the host would only have to wait ten seconds or so, polling the router immediately upon need with an RS does speed the process up! The information in the Router Advertisement includes the following:

- Flags indicating whether the host should use DHCP for addressing information.
- If DHCP is in use, the RA tells the host where the DHCP Server is.
- If DHCP is not in use, the RA contains the prefix and prefix lifetime information. The router will attach the network prefix to the host's link-local address, resulting in the host's full IPv6 address, complete with network prefix.

IPv6 Routing on Cisco Routers

To go along with our new address types, we have new variations of RIP (RIP New Generation, or RIPng), EIGRP, ISIS, OSPF (OSPF v3), and Multiprotocol BGP. We're hitting OSPFv3, EIGRP for IPv6, and RIPng in this section. The first step is always enabling the router's nondefault IPv6 routing capabilities with *ipv6 unicast-routing.*

```
Enter configuration commands, one per line. End with CNTL/Z.
R1(config)#ipv6 unicast-routing
```

Let's dive in to OSPF for IPv6, otherwise known as OSPFv3!

OSPFv3 on Cisco Routers

OSPF for IPv6 is also called OSPFv3, and since OSPFv3 is the term is used throughout Cisco documentation, it's likely the term you'll see on the exam. Be ready for either, and you're gold. Before we start configuring this protocol, let's see how it compares to OSPF for IPv4 (OSPFv2).

During a production network migration from v2 to v3, you may run both versions of OSPF on the same router. The two OSPF instances are kept as separate, as they would be if you ran two instances of v2 on the same router.

With OSPFv3, you won't necessarily start a config with *ipv6 router ospf.* One major difference between v2 and v3 is that v3 is enabled on a per-interface basis, rather than the router config mode of v2. The following command actually starts an OSPF process in v3:

```
R1(config)#int fast 0/0
R1(config-if)#ipv6 ospf 1 area 0
```

There are similarities between the versions, starting with the RID. V3 will use the exact same set of rules as V2 does in RID determination, going as far as using an IPv4 address! If there is no IPv4 address on the router, you'll need to use *router-id* to create the RID. The RID must be entered in IPv4 format, even if you're only running IPv6 on the router.

The basic theory of v3 is quite similar to that of v2. Hellos, LSAs, and good ol' Area 0 are still around, as are stub, total stub, and not-so-stub stub areas. The general rules for neighbor discovery and adjacencies are the same, including the rule that the hub or hubs in an NBMA network require a neighbor statement.

Neither v3 nor v2 point-to-point and point-to-multipoint networks elect DRs or BDRs.

A major version difference is v3 allowing a single link to be part of multiple OSPF instances, where v2 would allow a link to be a part of only one.

The v2 reserved address 224.0.0.5 is represented in v3 by FF02::5.

The v2 reserved address 224.0.0.6 is represented in v3 by FF02::6.

While we certainly have new addresses and slightly different commands to get used to, the theory remains much the same. Let's start working with those addresses and commands right now!

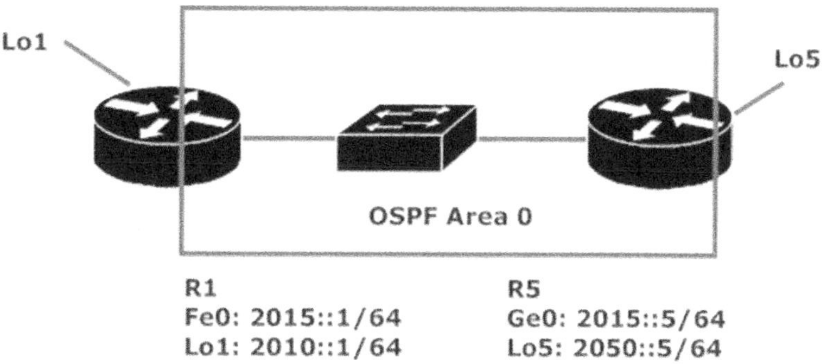

These two routers have zero IPv4 addresses at present, so we'll get this little reminder when we enable OSPFv3:

```
R1(config)#ipv6 router ospf 1
*Jun 16 02:18:46.822: %OSPFv3-4-NORTRID: OSPFv3 process 1 could not pick a route
r-id, please configure manually
```

```
R5(config)#ipv6 router ospf 1
*Jul 5 15:42:01: %OSPFv3-4-NORTRID: OSPFv3 process 1 could not pick a router-id
,please configure manually
R5(config-rtr)#router-id 5.5.5.5
```

We'll verify with *show ipv6 ospf.* Note the bandwidth reference unit is the same default value as v2.

```
R1#show ipv6 ospf
 Routing Process "ospfv3 1" with ID 1.1.1.1
 SPF schedule delay 5 secs, Hold time between two SPFs 10 secs
 Minimum LSA interval 5 secs. Minimum LSA arrival 1 secs
 LSA group pacing timer 240 secs
 Interface flood pacing timer 33 msecs
 Retransmission pacing timer 66 msecs
 Number of external LSA 0. Checksum Sum 0x000000
 Number of areas in this router is 0. 0 normal 0 stub 0 nssa
 Reference bandwidth unit is 100 mbps


R5#show ipv6 ospf
 Routing Process "ospfv3 1" with ID 5.5.5.5
 Event-log enabled, Maximum number of events: 1000, Mode: cyclic
 Initial SPF schedule delay 5000 msecs
 Minimum hold time between two consecutive SPFs 10000 msecs
 Maximum wait time between two consecutive SPFs 10000 msecs
 Minimum LSA interval 5 secs
 Minimum LSA arrival 1000 msecs
 LSA group pacing timer 240 secs
 Interface flood pacing timer 33 msecs
 Retransmission pacing timer 66 msecs
 Number of external LSA 0. Checksum Sum 0x000000
 Number of areas in this router is 0. 0 normal 0 stub 0 nssa
 Graceful restart helper support enabled
 Reference bandwidth unit is 100 mbps
```

We'll send a few pings before starting the OSPF config.

```
R1#ping 2015::5
!!!!!
Success rate is 100 percent (5/5), round-trip min/avg/max = 0/1/4 ms

R1#ping 2050::5
.....
Success rate is 0 percent (0/5)
```

```
R5#ping 2015::1
!!!!!
Success rate is 100 percent (5/5), round-trip min/avg/max = 0/0/4 ms

R5#ping 2010::1
% No valid source address for destination
Success rate is 0 percent (0/1)
```

As you'd expect with either IPv4 or IPv6, each router can ping the other router's address on the connecting subnet, but not the loopbacks. Let's enable OSPF all the way around and change that!

```
R1(config)#int fast 0/0
R1(config-if)#ipv6 ospf ?
  <1-65535>             Process ID
  authentication        Enable authentication
  cost                  Interface cost
  database-filter       Filter OSPF LSA during synchronization and flood
  dead-interval         Interval after which a neighbor is declared dead
  demand-circuit        OSPF demand circuit
  flood-reduction       OSPF Flood Reduction
  hello-interval        Time between HELLO packets
  mtu-ignore            Ignores the MTU in DBD packets
  neighbor              OSPF neighbor
  network               Network type
  priority              Router priority
  retransmit-interval   Time between retransmitting lost link state advertisements
  transmit-delay        Link state transmit delay

R1(config-if)#ipv6 ospf 1 ?
  area Set the OSPF area ID

R1(config-if)#ipv6 ospf 1 area ?
  <0-4294967295>   OSPF area ID as a decimal value
  A.B.C.D          OSPF area ID in IP address format

R1(config-if)#ipv6 ospf 1 area 0 ?
  instance Set the OSPF instance
  <cr>

R1(config-if)#ipv6 ospf 1 area 0

R5(config)#int gig 0/0
R5(config-if)#ipv6 ospf 1 area 0

*Jul 5 16:00:24: %OSPFv3-5-ADJCHG: Process 1, Nbr 1.1.1.1 on GigabitEthernet
from LOADING to FULL, Loading Done
```

Looks good! Let's verify with *show ipv6 ospf neighbor.* (The hardest part of the v3 commands is remembering to put "v6" in there.)

```
R1#show ipv6 ospf neighbor

Neighbor ID     Pri   State           Dead Time   Interface ID Interface
5.5.5.5           1   FULL/DR         00:00:38    2            FastEthernet0/0

R5#show ipv6 ospf neighbor

Neighbor ID     Pri   State           Dead Time   Interface ID Interface
1.1.1.1           1   FULL/BDR        00:00:39    4            GigabitEthernet0/0
```

To gather extra intelligence on your neighbor, add *detail* to that command.

```
R1#show ipv6 ospf neighbor detail
 Neighbor 5.5.5.5
     In the area 0 via interface FastEthernet0/0
     Neighbor: interface-id 2, link-local address FE80::216:9DFF:FEE5:F500
     Neighbor priority is 1, State is FULL, 6 state changes
     DR is 5.5.5.5 BDR is 1.1.1.1
     Options is 0x000013 in Hello (V6-Bit E-Bit R-bit )
     Options is 0x000013 in DBD (V6-Bit E-Bit R-bit )
     Dead timer due in 00:00:33
     Neighbor is up for 00:02:17
     Index 1/1/1, retransmission queue length 0, number of retransmission 1
     First 0x0(0)/0x0(0)/0x0(0) Next 0x0(0)/0x0(0)/0x0(0)
     Last retransmission scan length is 2, maximum is 2
     Last retransmission scan time is 0 msec, maximum is 0 msec

R1#show ipv6 ospf neighbor detail
 Neighbor 5.5.5.5
     In the area 0 via interface FastEthernet0/0
     Neighbor: interface-id 2, link-local address FE80::216:9DFF:FEE5:F500
     Neighbor priority is 1, State is FULL, 6 state changes
     DR is 5.5.5.5 BDR is 1.1.1.1
     Options is 0x000013 in Hello (V6-Bit E-Bit R-bit )
     Options is 0x000013 in DBD (V6-Bit E-Bit R-bit )
     Dead timer due in 00:00:33
     Neighbor is up for 00:02:17
     Index 1/1/1, retransmission queue length 0, number of retransmission 1
     First 0x0(0)/0x0(0)/0x0(0) Next 0x0(0)/0x0(0)/0x0(0)
     Last retransmission scan length is 2, maximum is 2
     Last retransmission scan time is 0 msec, maximum is 0 msec
```

To gather *extra* intelligence on the local router, run *show ipv6 ospf interface.* Beyond the link-local addresses, this looks a lot like the output of the familiar *show ip ospf interface.*

```
R1#show ipv6 ospf interface
FastEthernet0/0 is up, line protocol is up
  Link Local Address FE80::20F:F7FF:FEC4:9C0, Interface ID 4
  Area 0, Process ID 1, Instance ID 0, Router ID 1.1.1.1
  Network Type BROADCAST, Cost: 1
  Transmit Delay is 1 sec, State BDR, Priority 1
  Designated Router (ID) 5.5.5.5, local address FE80::216:9DFF:FEE5:F500
  Backup Designated router (ID) 1.1.1.1, local address FE80::20F:F7FF:FEC4:9C0
  Timer intervals configured, Hello 10, Dead 40, Wait 40, Retransmit 5
    Hello due in 00:00:06
  Index 1/1/1, flood queue length 0
  Next 0x0(0)/0x0(0)/0x0(0)
  Last flood scan length is 1, maximum is 3
  Last flood scan time is 0 msec, maximum is 0 msec
  Neighbor Count is 1, Adjacent neighbor count is 1
    Adjacent with neighbor 5.5.5.5 (Designated Router)
  Suppress hello for 0 neighbor(s)

R5#show ipv6 ospf interface
GigabitEthernet0/0 is up, line protocol is up
  Link Local Address FE80::216:9DFF:FEE5:F500, Interface ID 2
  Area 0, Process ID 1, Instance ID 0, Router ID 5.5.5.5
  Network Type BROADCAST, Cost: 1
  Transmit Delay is 1 sec, State DR, Priority 1
  Designated Router (ID) 5.5.5.5, local address FE80::216:9DFF:FEE5:F500
  Backup Designated router (ID) 1.1.1.1, local address FE80::20F:F7FF:FEC4:9C0
  Timer intervals configured, Hello 10, Dead 40, Wait 40, Retransmit 5
    Hello due in 00:00:03
  Graceful restart helper support enabled
  Index 1/1/1, flood queue length 0
  Next 0x0(0)/0x0(0)/0x0(0)
  Last flood scan length is 0, maximum is 3
  Last flood scan time is 0 msec, maximum is 0 msec
  Neighbor Count is 1, Adjacent neighbor count is 1
    Adjacent with neighbor 1.1.1.1 (Backup Designated Router)
  Suppress hello for 0 neighbor(s)
```

Let's get our loopbacks involved!

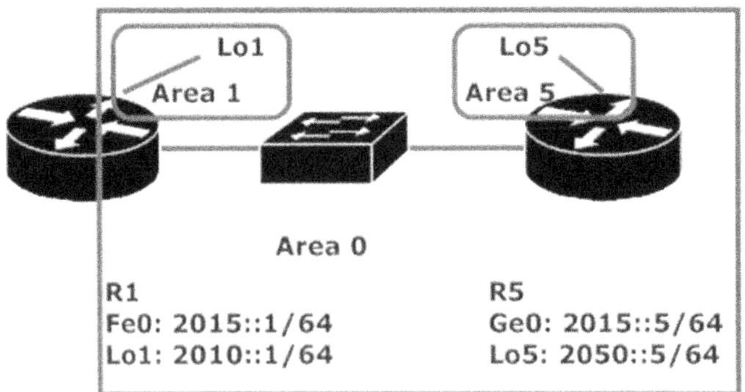


```
R1(config)#int loopback1
R1(config-if)#ipv6 ospf 1 area 1

R5(config)#int loopback5
R5(config-if)#ipv6 ospf 1 area 5
```

The resulting OSPFv3 tables:

```
R1#show ipv6 route ospf
IPv6 Routing Table - 9 entries
Codes: C - Connected, L - Local, S - Static, R - RIP, B - BGP
       U - Per-user Static route
       I1 - ISIS L1, I2 - ISIS L2, IA - ISIS interarea, IS - ISIS summary
       O - OSPF intra, OI - OSPF inter, OE1 - OSPF ext 1, OE2 - OSPF ext 2
       ON1 - OSPF NSSA ext 1, ON2 - OSPF NSSA ext 2
OI 2050::5/128 [110/1]
     via FE80::216:9DFF:FEE5:F500, FastEthernet0/0

R5#show ipv6 route ospf
IPv6 Routing Table - default - 6 entries
Codes: C - Connected, L - Local, S - Static, U - Per-user Static route
       B - BGP, HA - Home Agent, MR - Mobile Router, R - RIP
       I1 - ISIS L1, I2 - ISIS L2, IA - ISIS interarea, IS - ISIS summary
       D - EIGRP, EX - EIGRP external, ND - Neighbor Discovery
       O - OSPF Intra, OI - OSPF Inter, OE1 - OSPF ext 1, OE2 - OSPF ext 2
       ON1 - OSPF NSSA ext 1, ON2 - OSPF NSSA ext 2
OI 2010::1/128 [110/1]
     via FE80::20F:F7FF:FEC4:9C0, GigabitEthernet0/0
```

Each router now has an entry for the other's loopback. The proof is in the pinging, and we'll send some IPv6 pings this time...

```
R1#ping ipv6 2050::5
Sending 5, 100-byte ICMP Echos to 2050::5, timeout is 2 seconds:
!!!!!
Success rate is 100 percent (5/5), round-trip min/avg/max = 0/0/4 ms
```

```
R5#ping ipv6 2010::1
Sending 5, 100-byte ICMP Echos to 2010::1, timeout is 2 seconds:
!!!!!
Success rate is 100 percent (5/5), round-trip min/avg/max = 0/0/4 ms
```

...and there's the proof!

Let's add OSPF Area 14 to the network, using a direct serial link between R1 and R4.

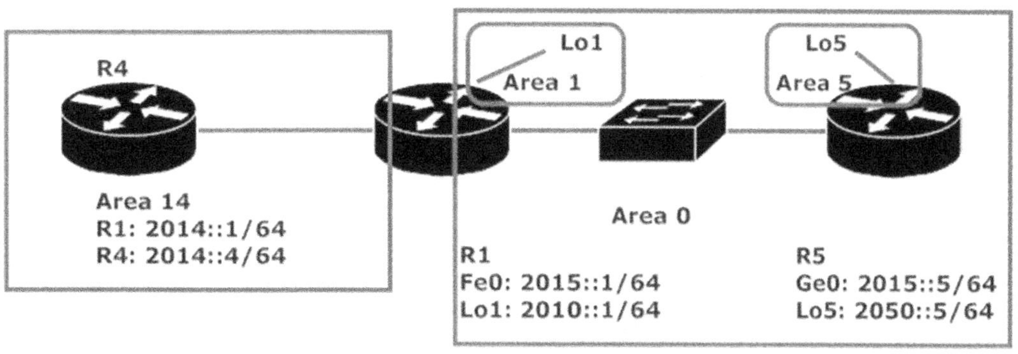


```
R4(config)#ipv6 unicast-routing

R4(config)#ipv6 router ospf 1
R4(config-rtr)#router-id 4.4.4.4

R4(config)#int serial 0/1/0
R4(config-if)#ipv6 enable
R4(config-if)#ipv6 ospf 1 area 14

R1(config)#int serial 1/1
R1(config-if)#ipv6 enable
R1(config-if)#ipv6 ospf 1 area 14


R1#show ipv6 ospf neighbor

Neighbor ID     Pri   State           Dead Time   Interface ID Interface
5.5.5.5           1   FULL/DR         00:00:39    2            FastEthernet0/0
4.4.4.4           1   FULL/           -           00:00:30     5     Serial1/1

R4#show ipv6 ospf neighbor

Neighbor ID     Pri   State           Dead Time   Interface ID Interface
1.1.1.1           0   FULL/           -           00:00:30     7     Serial0/1/0
```

The dash is back! The OSPFv3 link between R1 and R4 is a point-to-point network, verified by *show ipv6 ospf interface.*

```
R4#show ipv6 ospf interface serial 0/1/0
Serial0/1/0 is up, line protocol is up
  Link Local Address FE80::217:59FF:FEE2:474A, Interface ID 5
  Area 14, Process ID 1, Instance ID 0, Router ID 4.4.4.4
  Network Type POINT_TO_POINT, Cost: 64
  Transmit Delay is 1 sec, State POINT_TO_POINT
  Timer intervals configured, Hello 10, Dead 40, Wait 40, Retransmit 5
    Hello due in 00:00:04
  Graceful restart helper support enabled
  Index 1/1/1, flood queue length 0
  Next 0x0(0)/0x0(0)/0x0(0)
  Last flood scan length is 1, maximum is 2
  Last flood scan time is 0 msec, maximum is 0 msec
  Neighbor Count is 1, Adjacent neighbor count is 1
    Adjacent with neighbor 1.1.1.1
  Suppress hello for 0 neighbor(s)
```

Just as with OSPFv2, we'll have neither a DR nor a BDR on a point-to-point network. Let's check the OSPFv3 table on R4 and then ping all remote addresses.

```
R4#show ipv6 route ospf
IPv6 Routing Table - default - 6 entries
Codes: C - Connected, L - Local, S - Static, U - Per-user Static route
       B - BGP, HA - Home Agent, MR - Mobile Router, R - RIP
       I1 - ISIS L1, I2 - ISIS L2, IA - ISIS interarea, IS - ISIS summary
       D - EIGRP, EX - EIGRP external, NM - NEMO, ND - Neighbor Discovery
       O - OSPF Intra, OI - OSPF Inter, OE1 - OSPF ext 1, OE2 - OSPF ext 2
       ON1 - OSPF NSSA ext 1, ON2 - OSPF NSSA ext 2
OI   2010::1/128 [110/64]
      via FE80::20F:F7FF:FEC4:9C0, Serial0/1/0
OI   2015::/64 [110/65]
      via FE80::20F:F7FF:FEC4:9C0, Serial0/1/0
OI   2050::5/128 [110/65]
      via FE80::20F:F7FF:FEC4:9C0, Serial0/1/0

R4#ping 2010::1    (R1's loopback)
!!!!!
Success rate is 100 percent (5/5), round-trip min/avg/max = 32/32/36 ms

R4#ping 2015::1    (R1's interface on link with R5)
!!!!!
Success rate is 100 percent (5/5), round-trip min/avg/max = 32/32/36 ms

R4#ping 2015::5    (R5's interface on the same link as previous ping)
!!!!!
Success rate is 100 percent (5/5), round-trip min/avg/max = 32/32/32 ms
```

```
R4#ping 2050::5    (R5's loopback)
!!!!!
Success rate is 100 percent (5/5), round-trip min/avg/max = 32/32/32 ms
```

R4 can ping all destinations listed in that table, so we're gold. Let's raise the stakes and configure an NBMA network by adding R2 and R3 back to the network. To squeeze in our NBMA network, I've removed the previously listed IPv6 addresses from the diagram. No addresses have been changed in the lab.

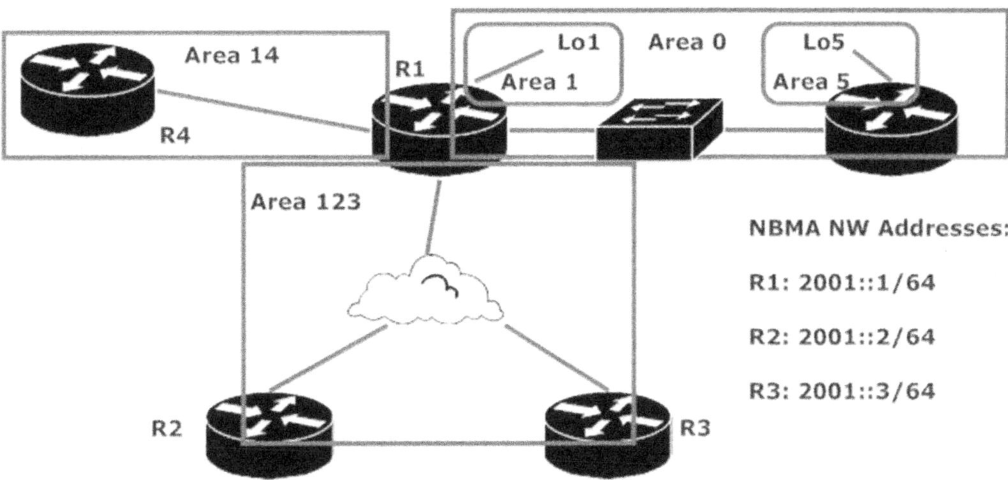

Before we put the appropriate interfaces on R1, R2, and R3 into Area 123, let's set the OSPFv3 interface priority to zero on the spoke routers.

```
R2(config)#int serial 0/1/0
R2(config-if)#ipv6 ospf priority 0

R3(config)#int serial 0/1/0
R3(config-if)#ipv6 ospf priority 0
```

We also need two *neighbor* commands on R1, just as we did in OSPFv2.

```
R1(config-rtr)#int serial 1/0
R1(config-if)#ipv6 ospf ?
  <1-65535>           Process ID
  authentication      Enable authentication
  cost                Interface cost
  database-filter     Filter OSPF LSA during synchronization and flooding
  dead-interval       Interval after which a neighbor is declared dead
  demand-circuit      OSPF demand circuit
  flood-reduction     OSPF Flood Reduction
  hello-interval      Time between HELLO packets
  mtu-ignore          Ignores the MTU in DBD packets
  neighbor            OSPF neighbor
  network             Network type
```

```
  priority              Router priority
  retransmit-interval   Time between retransmitting lost link state advertisements
  transmit-delay        Link state transmit delay

R1(config-if)#ipv6 ospf neighbor ?
X:X:X:X::X Neighbor IPv6 address

R1(config-if)#ipv6 ospf neighbor FE80::21B:D4FF:FEC2:990
R1(config-if)#ipv6 ospf neighbor FE80::21F:CAFF:FE96:2754
```

And finally, the *ipv6 ospf* statements!

```
R1(config)#int serial 1/0
R1(config-if)#ipv6 ospf 1 area 123

R2(config)#int serial 0/1/0
R2(config-if)#ipv6 ospf 1 area 123

R3(config)#int serial 0/1/0
R3(config-if)#ipv6 ospf 1 area 123
```

R1 now has four OSPFv3 adjacencies, and the information regarding the NBMA network acquired via *show ipv6 ospf interface serial1/0* all checks out.

```
R1#show ipv6 ospf neighbor

Neighbor ID     Pri  State          Dead Time  Interface ID Interface
5.5.5.5           1  FULL/DR        00:00:34   2            FastEthernet0/0
4.4.4.4           1  FULL/  -       00:00:32   5            Serial1/1
3.3.3.3           0  FULL/DROTHER   00:01:49   5            Serial1/0
2.2.2.2           0  FULL/DROTHER   00:01:43   5            Serial1/0

R1#show ipv6 ospf int serial 1/0
Serial1/0 is up, line protocol is up
  Link Local Address FE80::20F:F7FF:FEC4:9C0, Interface ID 6
  Area 123, Process ID 1, Instance ID 0, Router ID 1.1.1.1
  Network Type NON_BROADCAST, Cost: 64
  Transmit Delay is 1 sec, State DR, Priority 1
  Designated Router (ID) 1.1.1.1, local address FE80::20F:F7FF:FEC4:9C0
  No backup designated router on this network
  Timer intervals configured, Hello 30, Dead 120, Wait 120, Retransmit 5
    Hello due in 00:00:04
  Index 1/1/4, flood queue length 0
  Next 0x0(0)/0x0(0)/0x0(0)
  Last flood scan length is 1, maximum is 4
  Last flood scan time is 0 msec, maximum is 0 msec
  Neighbor Count is 2, Adjacent neighbor count is 2
```

```
    Adjacent with neighbor 3.3.3.3
    Adjacent with neighbor 2.2.2.2
  Suppress hello for 0 neighbor(s)
```

Let's check out the OSPFv3 table on R2 and send some pings!

```
R2#show ipv6 route ospf
<code table deleted for clarity>

OI  2010::1/128 [110/64]
     via FE80::20F:F7FF:FEC4:9C0, Serial0/1/0
OI  2014::/64 [110/845]
     via FE80::20F:F7FF:FEC4:9C0, Serial0/1/0
OI  2015::/64 [110/65]
     via FE80::20F:F7FF:FEC4:9C0, Serial0/1/0
OI  2050::5/128 [110/65]
     via FE80::20F:F7FF:FEC4:9C0, Serial0/1/0

R2#ping ipv6 2010::1    (R1's loopback)
!!!!!
Success rate is 100 percent (5/5), round-trip min/avg/max = 64/64/64 ms

R2#ping ipv6 2050::5    (R5's loopback)
!!!!!
Success rate is 100 percent (5/5), round-trip min/avg/max = 64/65/68 ms

R2#ping 2014::4     (R4's only interface)
!!!!!
Success rate is 100 percent (5/5), round-trip min/avg/max = 96/96/100 ms

R2#ping 2015::5    (R5's interface on segment shared with R1)
!!!!!
Success rate is 100 percent (5/5), round-trip min/avg/max = 64/64/68 ms
```

Looks good! We've now built NBMA, point-to-point, and broadcast networks in OSPFv3. Let's do just a *little* route redistribution by creating three new loopbacks on R1 and then redistributing them into OSPF. Note the v3 *redistribute connected* command doesn't require the *subnets* option. (It's not even available!)

```
interface Loopback13
 no ip address
 ipv6 address 2013::1/64
!
interface Loopback14
 no ip address
 ipv6 address 2012::1/64
!
```

```
interface Loopback16
 no ip address
 ipv6 address 2016::1/64

R1(config)#ipv6 router ospf 1
R1(config-rtr)#redistribute connected ?
  metric        Metric for redistributed routes
  metric-type   OSPF/IS-IS exterior metric type for redistributed routes
  route-map     Route map reference
  tag           Set tag for routes redistributed into OSPF
  <cr>

R1(config-rtr)#redistribute connected

R4#show ipv6 route ospf
< code table removed >

OI   2001::/64 [110/128]
      via FE80::20F:F7FF:FEC4:9C0, Serial0/1/0
OI   2010::1/128 [110/64]
      via FE80::20F:F7FF:FEC4:9C0, Serial0/1/0
OE2  2012::/64 [110/20]
      via FE80::20F:F7FF:FEC4:9C0, Serial0/1/0
OE2  2013::/64 [110/20]
      via FE80::20F:F7FF:FEC4:9C0, Serial0/1/0
OI   2015::/64 [110/65]
      via FE80::20F:F7FF:FEC4:9C0, Serial0/1/0
OE2  2016::/64 [110/20]
      via FE80::20F:F7FF:FEC4:9C0, Serial0/1/0
OI   2050::5/128 [110/65]
      via FE80::20F:F7FF:FEC4:9C0, Serial0/1/0
```

Let's ping each of the new loopbacks from R4.

```
R4#ping 2012::1
!!!!!
Success rate is 100 percent (5/5), round-trip min/avg/max = 32/32/36 ms

R4#ping 2013::1
!!!!!
Success rate is 100 percent (5/5), round-trip min/avg/max = 32/32/36 ms

R4#ping 2016::1
!!!!!
Success rate is 100 percent (5/5), round-trip min/avg/max = 32/32/32 ms
```

Looks good, but we're always looking to keep our routing tables complete and concise, right? With these three external routes all having the same next-hop v6 address...

```
OE2 2012::/64 [110/20]
     via FE80::20F:F7FF:FEC4:9C0, Serial0/1/0
OE2 2013::/64 [110/20]
     via FE80::20F:F7FF:FEC4:9C0, Serial0/1/0
OE2 2016::/64 [110/20]
     via FE80::20F:F7FF:FEC4:9C0, Serial0/1/0
```

...it's OSPF stub routing time, IPV6 style! Nothing to it—just enter OSPFv3 config mode and enter the *area 14 stub* command on each router. As you'd expect, the adjacency comes down after configuring the area as stub on R1.

```
R1(config)#ipv6 router ospf 1
R1(config-rtr)#area 14 stub

*Jun 16 13:02:00.727: %OSPFv3-5-ADJCHG: Process 1, Nbr 4.4.4.4 on Serial1/1 from
 FULL to DOWN, Neighbor Down: Adjacency forced to reset
```

That adjacency should come right back after we finish the stub config on R4.

```
R4(config)#ipv6 router ospf 1
R4(config-rtr)#area 14 stub
%OSPFv3-5-ADJCHG: Process 1, Nbr 1.1.1.1 on Serial0/1/0 from LOADING to FULL,
Loading Done
```

The *show ipv6 ospf* command verifies Area 14 as a stub.

```
R4#show ipv6 ospf
 Routing Process "ospfv3 1" with ID 4.4.4.4
 Event-log enabled, Maximum number of events: 1000, Mode: cyclic
 Initial SPF schedule delay 5000 msecs
 Minimum hold time between two consecutive SPFs 10000 msecs
 Maximum wait time between two consecutive SPFs 10000 msecs
 Minimum LSA interval 5 secs
 Minimum LSA arrival 1000 msecs
 LSA group pacing timer 240 secs
 Interface flood pacing timer 33 msecs
 Retransmission pacing timer 66 msecs
 Number of external LSA 0. Checksum Sum 0x000000
 Number of areas in this router is 1. 0 normal 1 stub 0 nssa
 Graceful restart helper support enabled
 Reference bandwidth unit is 100 mbps
    Area 14
         Number of interfaces in this area is 1
         It is a stub area
```

```
SPF algorithm executed 14 times
Number of LSA 11. Checksum Sum 0x05A8F1
Number of DCbitless LSA 0
Number of indication LSA 0
Number of DoNotAge LSA 0
Flood list length 0
```

What are the changes to R4's routing table, you ask?

```
R4#show ipv6 route ospf

OI   ::/0 [110/65]
      via FE80::20F:F7FF:FEC4:9C0, Serial0/1/0
OI   2001::/64 [110/128]
      via FE80::20F:F7FF:FEC4:9C0, Serial0/1/0
OI   2010::1/128 [110/64]
      via FE80::20F:F7FF:FEC4:9C0, Serial0/1/0
OI   2015::/64 [110/65]
      via FE80::20F:F7FF:FEC4:9C0, Serial0/1/0
OI   2050::5/128 [110/65]
      via FE80::20F:F7FF:FEC4:9C0, Serial0/1/0
```

The external OSPFv3 routes are gone, replaced by IPv6's default route, *::/0*. Can we still ping those three loopbacks?

```
R4#ping 2012::1
!!!!!
Success rate is 100 percent (5/5), round-trip min/avg/max = 32/32/36 ms

R4#ping 2013::1
!!!!!
Success rate is 100 percent (5/5), round-trip min/avg/max = 32/32/36 ms

R4#ping 2016::1
!!!!!
Success rate is 100 percent (5/5), round-trip min/avg/max = 32/32/36 ms
```

Sure can! We've done a good job on shrinking that table, and we can take it just a bit further by making Area 14 a total stub area. We'll do just that with the *no-summary* option on R1.

```
R1(config)#ipv6 router ospf 1
R1(config-rtr)#area 14 stub ?
  no-summary Do not send summary LSA into stub area
  <cr>

R1(config-rtr)#area 14 stub no-summary
```

```
R4#show ipv6 route ospf

OI   ::/0 [110/65]
  via FE80::20F:F7FF:FEC4:9C0, Serial0/1/0
```

Now *that's* shrinking a table! We can still ping other networks...

```
R4#ping 2015::5 (R5's interface on the R1-R5 segment)
!!!!!
Success rate is 100 percent (5/5), round-trip min/avg/max = 32/32/32 ms

R4#ping 2010::1 (R1's loopback)
!!!!!
Success rate is 100 percent (5/5), round-trip min/avg/max = 32/33/36 ms

R4#ping 2050::5 (R5's loopback)
!!!!!
Success rate is 100 percent (5/5), round-trip min/avg/max = 32/32/36 ms

R4#ping 2001::2 (R2's interface on the NBMA network)
!!!!!
Success rate is 100 percent (5/5), round-trip min/avg/max = 96/96/100 ms

R4#ping 2001::3 (R3's interface on the NBMA network)
!!!!!
Success rate is 100 percent (5/5), round-trip min/avg/max = 96/96/100 ms
```

...and our routing table went from seven OSPF routes to one. Great stuff!

One last OSPFv3 note—R1 is indeed an ASBR once it performs route redistribution, as verified by *show ip ospf* on R1...

```
R1#show ipv6 ospf
 Routing Process "ospfv3 1" with ID 1.1.1.1
 It is an area border and autonomous system boundary router
 Redistributing External Routes from,
      Connected
```

...and *show ipv6 ospf border-router* on R4.

```
R4#show ipv6 ospf border-router

OSPFv3 Process 1 internal Routing Table

Codes: i - Intra-area route, I - Inter-area route

i 1.1.1.1 [64] via FE80::20F:F7FF:FEC4:9C0,Serial0/1/0,ABR/ASBR,Area 14,SPF 17
```

Time to take a little break from OSPFv3. Let's do some EIGRP and RIP on IPv6!

Configuring EIGRP for IPV6 on Cisco Routers

All OSPF-related commands have been removed from all routers. The fundamental IPv6 commands are still running. We'll start by setting an EIGRP RID for R2, R3, and R4.

```
R2(config)#ipv6 router eigrp 100
R2(config-rtr)#router-id 2.2.2.2

R3(config)#ipv6 router eigrp 100
R3(config-rtr)#router-id 3.3.3.3

R4(config)#ipv6 router eigrp 100
R4(config-rtr)#router-id 4.4.4.4
```

We'll build the following network in this lab:

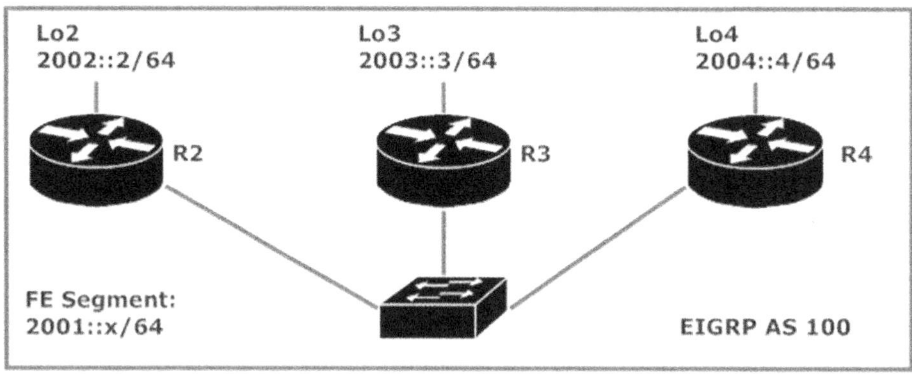

Each router can ping the other two router addresses on the 2001::x/64 network but obviously can't ping each others' loopbacks. Let's fix that right now! First, we need adjacencies over the FE interfaces.

```
R2(config)#int fast 0/0
R2(config-if)#ipv6 eigrp 100

R3(config)#int fast 0/0
R3(config-if)#ipv6 eigrp 100

R4(config)#int fast 0/0
R4(config-if)#ipv6 eigrp 100

%DUAL-5-NBRCHANGE: EIGRP-IPv6 100: Neighbor FE80::21B:D4FF:FEC2:990
(FastEthernet0/0) is up: new adjacency
%DUAL-5-NBRCHANGE: EIGRP-IPv6 100: Neighbor FE80::21F:CAFF:FE96:2754
(FastEthernet0/0) is up: new adjacency
```

I'm sure you noticed our old friend DUAL is still around! Let's verify the adjacencies:

```
R4#show ipv6 eigrp neighbor
EIGRP-IPv6 Neighbors for AS(100)
H   Address                  Interface     Hold    Uptime    SRTT   RTO   Q    Seq
                                           (sec)             (ms)         Cnt  Num
1   Link-local address:      Fa0/0           13    00:05:57     2   200   0    6
FE80::21F:CAFF:FE96:2754
0   Link-local address:      Fa0/0           11    00:05:57     1   200   0    6
FE80::21B:D4FF:FEC2:990
```

That should look *darn* familiar. Now let's get some routes into our EIGRP tables.

```
R2(config)#int loopback2
R2(config-if)#ipv6 eigrp 100 ?
  <cr>
R2(config-if)#ipv6 eigrp 100
```

No options beyond the mandatory AS number:

```
R3(config)#int loopback3
R3(config-if)#ipv6 eigrp 100

R4(config)#int loopback4
R4(config-if)#ipv6 eigrp 100

R2#show ipv6 route eigrp

D   2003::/64 [90/156160]
     via FE80::21F:CAFF:FE96:2754, FastEthernet0/0
D   2004::/64 [90/156160]
     via FE80::217:59FF:FEE2:474A, FastEthernet0/0
```

Looks good! Let's ping the loopbacks on R3 and R4 from R2.

```
R2#ping 2003::3
!!!!!
Success rate is 100 percent (5/5), round-trip min/avg/max = 0/0/4 ms

R2#ping 2004::4
!!!!!
Success rate is 100 percent (5/5), round-trip min/avg/max = 0/0/4 ms
```

Beautiful! I'm sure you noticed the AD of these EIGRPv6 internal routes is 90, the same as you'll find in EIGRPv4. Let's introduce a route via redistribution and see what's going on with EIGRPv6 external routes. We'll start with setting the default metrics. You'll see some old friends in this IOS Help readout!

```
R2(config)#ipv6 router eigrp 100
R2(config-rtr)#?
  default             Set a command to its defaults
  default-metric      Set metric of redistributed routes
  distance            Define an administrative distance
  distribute-list     Filter networks in routing updates
  eigrp               EIGRP specific commands
  exit                Exit from IPv6 routing protocol configuration mode
  maximum-paths       Forward packets over multiple paths
  metric              Modify metrics and parameters for advertisement
  neighbor            Specify a neighbor router
  no                  Negate a command or set its defaults
  passive-interface   Suppress routing updates on an interface
  redistribute        Redistribute IPv6 prefixes from another routing protocol
  shutdown            Shutdown topology
  timers              Adjust topology specific timers
  variance            Control load balancing variance

R2(config-rtr)#default-metric ?
  <1-4294967295>   Bandwidth in Kbits per second

R2(config-rtr)#default-metric 1544 ?
  <0-4294967295>   delay metric in 10 microsecond units

R2(config-rtr)#default-metric 1544 10 ?
  <0-255>   Reliability metric where 255 is 100% reliable

R2(config-rtr)#default-metric 1544 10 255 ?
  <1-255>   Effective bandwidth metric (Loading) where 255 is 100% loaded

R2(config-rtr)#default-metric 1544 10 255 1 ?
  <1-65535>   Maximum Transmission Unit metric of the path

R2(config-rtr)#default-metric 1544 10 255 1 1500

R2(config-rtr)#redistribute ?
  bgp         Border Gateway Protocol (BGP)
  connected   Connected Routes
  eigrp       Enhanced Interior Gateway Routing Protocol (EIGRP)
  isis        ISO IS-IS
  nemo        Network Mobility (NEMO)
  ospf        Open Shortest Path First (OSPF)
  rip         IPv6 Routing Information Protocol (RIPv6)
  static      Static Routes
```

```
R2(config-rtr)#redistribute connected ?
  metric      Metric for redistributed routes
  route-map   Route map reference
  <cr>

R2(config-rtr)#redistribute connected
```

Let's see what we see on R3 and R4.

```
R3#show ipv6 route eigrp

D   2002::/64 [90/156160]
     via FE80::21B:D4FF:FEC2:990, FastEthernet0/0
D   2004::/64 [90/156160]
     via FE80::217:59FF:FEE2:474A, FastEthernet0/0
EX  2022::/64 [170/1662976]
     via FE80::21B:D4FF:FEC2:990, FastEthernet0/0


R4#show ipv6 route eigrp

D   2002::/64 [90/156160]
     via FE80::21B:D4FF:FEC2:990, FastEthernet0/0
D   2003::/64 [90/156160]
     via FE80::21F:CAFF:FE96:2754, FastEthernet0/0
EX  2022::/64 [170/1662976]
     via FE80::21B:D4FF:FEC2:990, FastEthernet0/0
```

The code for EIGRPv6 external routes is *EX* rather than EIGRPv4's *D EX*, but the AD is the same. More importantly, can R3 and R4 ping the newly learned route?

```
R3#ping 2022::2
!!!!!
Success rate is 100 percent (5/5), round-trip min/avg/max = 0/0/4 ms

R4#ping 2022::2
!!!!!
Success rate is 100 percent (5/5), round-trip min/avg/max = 0/1/4 ms
```

So far, the fundamentals of OSPF and EIGRP for IPV6 are much the same as those two protocols for IPV4. Let's see if the same hold for RIP!

Configuring RIP for IPV6 on Cisco Routers

We'll use the same topology as we had in the EIGRPv6 lab.

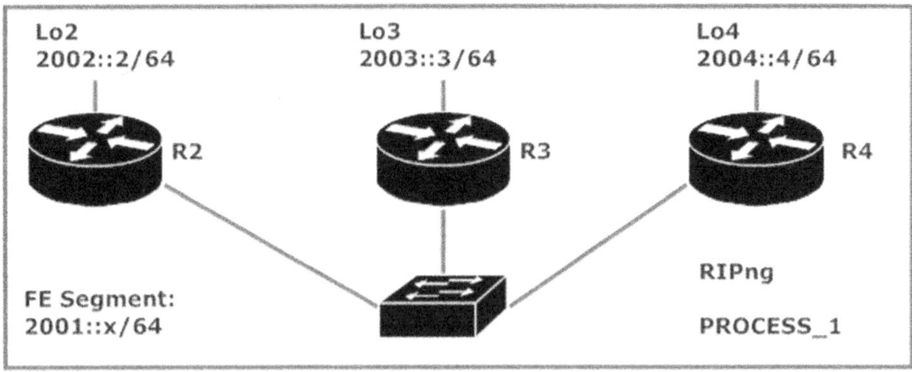

With our global IPV6 commands in place, let's enable RIPng—*RIP for the Next Generation!*

```
R2(config)#int fast 0/0
R2(config-if)#ipv6 rip ?
  WORD User selected string identifying this RIP process

R2(config-if)#ipv6 rip PROCESS _ 1 ?
  default-information   Configure handling of default route
  enable                Enable/disable RIP routing
  metric-offset         Adjust default metric increment
  summary-address       Configure address summarization

R2(config-if)#ipv6 rip PROCESS _ 1 enable


R3(config-if)#ipv6 rip PROCESS _ 1 enable


R4(config-if)#ipv6 rip PROCESS _ 1 enable
```

Well, *that* was anticlimactic. But that's how we enable RIPng! To verify the config and gather info, run *show ipv6 rip.* To see information on one particular RIP process, just specify the process name after that command.

```
R2#show ipv6 rip ?
  WORD        RIP process name
  Database    RIP local RIB
  next-hops   RIP next-hops
  |           Output modifiers
  <cr>

R2#show ipv6 rip
RIP process "PROCESS _ 1", port 521, multicast-group FF02::9, pid 305
     Administrative distance is 120. Maximum paths is 16
     Updates every 30 seconds, expire after 180
```

```
    Holddown lasts 0 seconds, garbage collect after 120
    Split horizon is on; poison reverse is off
    Default routes are not generated
    Periodic updates 16, trigger updates 0, Full Advertisement 0
  Interfaces:
    FastEthernet0/0
  Redistribution:
    None
```

Some familiar values there, including the AD and last number of the multicast group, as RIPv2 for IPv4 multicasts to 224.0.0.9. The join to multicast group FF02::9 is also confirmed by *show ipv6 interface fast 0/0.*

```
R2#show ipv6 int fast 0/0
FastEthernet0/0 is up, line protocol is up
  IPv6 is enabled, link-local address is FE80::21B:D4FF:FEC2:990
  No Virtual link-local address(es):
  Global unicast address(es):
    2001::2, subnet is 2001::/64
  Joined group address(es):
    FF02::1
    FF02::2
    FF02::9
    FF02::1:FF00:2
    FF02::1:FFC2:990
```

Let's enable all three loopbacks with RIPng.

```
R2(config)#int loopback2
R2(config-if)#ipv6 rip PROCESS_1 enable

R3(config)#int loopback3
R3(config-if)#ipv6 rip PROCESS_1 enable

R4(config)#int loopback4
R4(config-if)#ipv6 rip PROCESS_1 enable
```

Let's have a look at R2's RIP routing table and ping the other loopbacks.

```
R2#ping 2003::3
!!!!!
Success rate is 100 percent (5/5), round-trip min/avg/max = 0/0/4 ms

R2#ping 2004::4
!!!!!
   Success rate is 100 percent (5/5), round-trip min/avg/max = 0/0/4 ms
```

Success is sweet! As with RIP for IPv4, RIPng doesn't come with a lot of bells and whistles. There is one option you're familiar with but with OSPF rather than RIP.

```
R2(config)#int fast 0/0
R2(config-if)#ipv6 rip PROCESS _ 1 ?
  default-information   Configure handling of default route
  enable                Enable/disable RIP routing
  metric-offset         Adjust default metric increment
  summary-address       Configure address summarization

R2(config-if)#ipv6 rip PROCESS _ 1 default-information ?
  only        Advertise only the default route
  originate   Originate the default route

R2(config-if)#ipv6 rip PROCESS _ 1 default-information originate
```

The command looks familiar, but the options are a little different. You must choose either *only* or *originate*, and *originate* means just that. The local router will generate a default route and advertise it via the specified interface. (If the local router in turn receives a default route, that router will just ignore it in order to prevent a possible routing loop.)

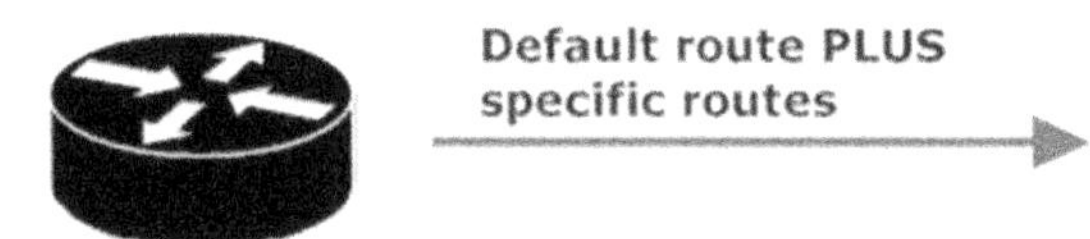

With *originate*, R3 and R4 both have a default route pointing to R2. Both routers still have the route to R2's loopback in their table as well.

```
R3#show ipv6 route rip

R ::/0 [120/2]
     via FE80::21B:D4FF:FEC2:990, FastEthernet0/0
R 2002::/64 [120/2]
     via FE80::21B:D4FF:FEC2:990, FastEthernet0/0
R 2004::/64 [120/2]
     via FE80::217:59FF:FEE2:474A, FastEthernet0/0

R4#show ipv6 route rip

R ::/0 [120/2]
     via FE80::21B:D4FF:FEC2:990, FastEthernet0/0
R 2002::/64 [120/2]
     via FE80::21B:D4FF:FEC2:990, FastEthernet0/0
R 2003::/64 [120/2]
     via FE80::21F:CAFF:FE96:2754, FastEthernet0/0
```

default-information only generates the default route and advertises it via the specified interface, but nondefault routes are no longer advertised.

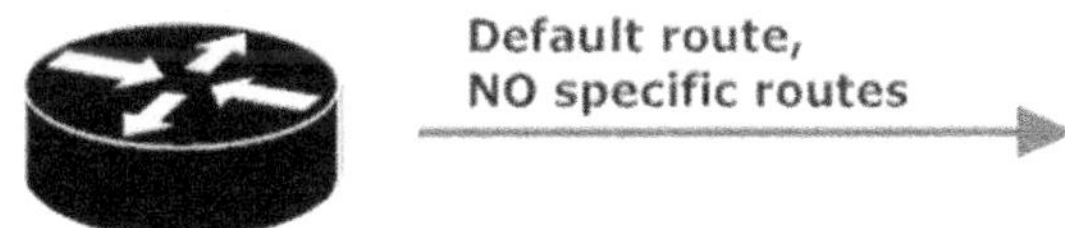


```
R2(config)#int fast 0/0
R2(config-if)#no ipv6 rip PROCESS_1 default-information originate
R2(config-if)#ipv6 rip PROCESS_1 default-information only

R3#show ipv6 route rip

R ::/0 [120/2]
     via FE80::21B:D4FF:FEC2:990, FastEthernet0/0
R 2004::/64 [120/2]
     via FE80::217:59FF:FEE2:474A, FastEthernet0/0

R4#show ipv6 route rip

R ::/0 [120/2]
     via FE80::21B:D4FF:FEC2:990, FastEthernet0/0
R 2003::/64 [120/2]
     via FE80::21F:CAFF:FE96:2754, FastEthernet0/0
```

R3 and R4 can still ping R2's loopback, since the default route points to R2.

```
R3#ping 2002::2
!!!!!
Success rate is 100 percent (5/5), round-trip min/avg/max = 0/0/4 ms

R4#ping 2002::2
!!!!!
Success rate is 100 percent (5/5), round-trip min/avg/max = 0/0/4 ms
```

To further fine-tune RIP, drop into RIPng config mode with ipv6 router rip and the process name you want to configure. You can change the AD, change the number of allowed *maximum-paths*, configure route redistribution, and a lot more. We're not going to run labs with each of these, but in case you run into RIPng in the field, you should know where these values can be changed.

```
R2(config)#ipv6 router rip PROCESS_1
R2(config-rtr)#?
  default           Set a command to its defaults
```

```
distance          Administrative distance
distribute-list   Filter networks in routing updates
exit              Exit from IPv6 routing protocol configuration mode
maximum-paths     Forward packets over multiple paths
no                Negate a command or set its defaults
poison-reverse    Poison reverse updates
port              Port and multicast address
redistribute      Redistribute IPv6 prefixes from another routing protocol
split-horizon     Split horizon updates
timers            Adjust routing timers
```

Back To OSPFv3!

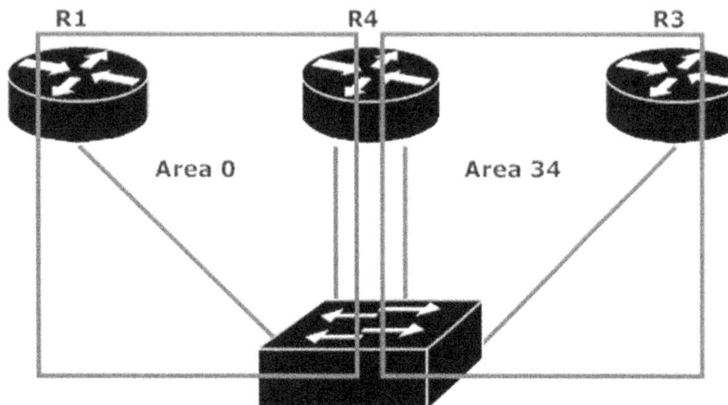


```
R1(config)#ipv6 unicast-routing
R1(config)#int loopback1
R1(config-if)#ip address 1.1.1.1 255.255.255.255 (for the RID)
R1(config-if)#int fast 0/0
R1(config-if)#ipv6 address 2014::1/64
R1(config-if)#ipv6 ospf 1 area 0
R1(config-if)#no shut

R4(config)#int loopback0
R4(config-if)#ip address 4.4.4.4 255.255.255.255

R4(config)#ipv6 unicast-routing

R4(config)#int fast 0/0
R4(config-if)#ipv6 address 2014::4/64
R4(config-if)#ipv6 ospf 1 area 0
R4(config-if)#no shut
```

The adjacency between R4 and R1 comes right up. So far, so good!

```
%OSPFv3-5-ADJCHG: Process 1, Nbr 1.1.1.1 on FastEthernet0/0 from LOADING to FULL,
Loading Done
```

```
R1#show ipv6 ospf neighbor

Neighbor ID     Pri   State           Dead Time   Interface ID Interface
4.4.4.4           1   FULL/BDR        00:00:36    3            FastEthernet0/0

R4#show ipv6 ospf neighbor

Neighbor ID     Pri   State           Dead Time   Interface ID Interface
1.1.1.1           1   FULL/DR         00:00:37    4            FastEthernet0/0
```

Let's get the adjacency up between R3 and R4 in Area 34.

```
R4(config)#int fast 0/1
R4(config-if)#ipv6 address 2034::4/64
R4(config-if)#ipv6 ospf 1 area 34

R3(config)#ipv6 unicast-routing
R3(config)#int loopback0
R3(config-if)#ip address 3.3.3.3 255.255.255.255
R3(config-if)#int fast 0/0
R3(config-if)#ipv6 address 2034::3/64
R3(config-if)#ipv6 ospf 1 area 34
R3(config-if)#no shut
```

The adjacency is up, and we're rocking and rolling!

```
R3#show ipv6 ospf neigh

Neighbor ID     Pri   State           Dead Time   Interface ID Interface
4.4.4.4           1   FULL/DR         00:00:31    4            FastEthernet0/0

R4#show ipv6 ospf neigh

Neighbor ID     Pri   State           Dead Time   Interface ID Interface
1.1.1.1           1   FULL/DR         00:00:38    4            FastEthernet0/0
3.3.3.3           1   FULL/BDR        00:00:39    3            FastEthernet0/1
```

R1 sees the 2034::x/64 network in its OSPFv3 routing table and can ping both R3 and R4 on that segment.

```
R1#show ipv6 route ospf

OI   2034::/64 [110/2]
      via FE80::217:59FF:FEE2:474A, FastEthernet0/0

R1#ping 2034::3
!!!!!
```

```
Success rate is 100 percent (5/5), round-trip min/avg/max = 0/4/16 ms

R1#ping 2034::4
!!!!!
Success rate is 100 percent (5/5), round-trip min/avg/max = 0/2/5 ms
```

Let's add an IPv6 address to the loopbacks on each router and then put them in their own individual OSPF area.

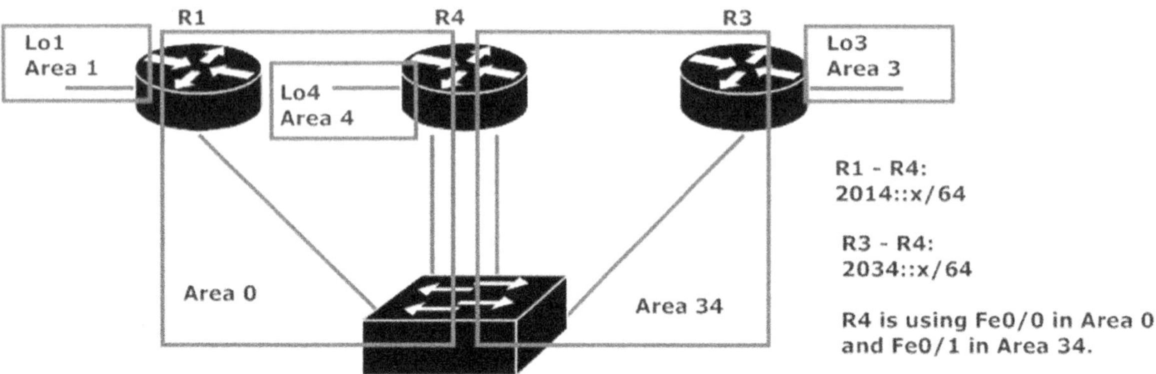


```
R1(config)#int loopback1
R1(config-if)#ipv6 address 2001::1/64
R1(config-if)#ipv6 ospf 1 area 1

R4(config)#int loopback4
R4(config-if)#ipv6 address 2004::1/64
R4(config-if)#ipv6 ospf 1 area 4

R3(config)#int loopback3
R3(config-if)#ipv6 address 2003::1/64
R3(config-if)#ipv6 ospf 1 area 3
```

Let's have a look at our OSPFv3 routing tables and check pingability while we're at it! Interestingly enough, R1 has R4's loopback in its table, but not R3's. R1 can ping R4's loopback successfully.

```
R1#show ipv6 route ospf
OI   2004::1/128 [110/1]
      via FE80::217:59FF:FEE2:474A, FastEthernet0/0
OI   2034::/64 [110/2]
      via FE80::217:59FF:FEE2:474A, FastEthernet0/0

R1#ping 2004::1
Sending 5, 100-byte ICMP Echos to 2004::1, timeout is 2 seconds:
!!!!!
```

R4 has R1's loopback in its OSPFv3 table, but not R3's loopback. R4 can ping R1's loopback.

```
R4#show ipv6 route ospf

OI   2001::1/128 [110/1]
      via FE80::20F:F7FF:FEC4:9C0, FastEthernet0/0

R4#ping 2001::1
!!!!!
Success rate is 100 percent (5/5), round-trip min/avg/max = 0/2/4 ms
```

On the third hand, R3 can see both R1's and R4's loopbacks and can ping them both.

```
R3#show ipv6 route ospf

OI   2001::1/128 [110/2]
      via FE80::217:59FF:FEE2:474B, FastEthernet0/0
OI   2004::1/128 [110/1]
      via FE80::217:59FF:FEE2:474B, FastEthernet0/0
OI   2014::/64 [110/2]
      via FE80::217:59FF:FEE2:474B, FastEthernet0/0

R3#ping 2001::1
!!!!!
Success rate is 100 percent (5/5), round-trip min/avg/max = 0/0/4 ms

R3#ping 2004::1
!!!!!
Success rate is 100 percent (5/5), round-trip min/avg/max = 0/0/4 ms
```

What's going *on* here? Have another look at our network...

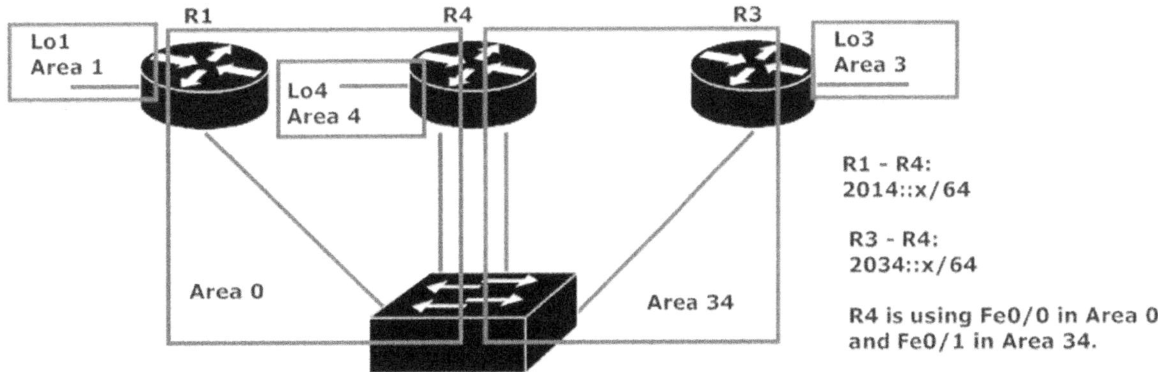

The problem is much like the one we ran into during our OSPFv2 labs. Whether you're running OSPF for IPv4 or IPv6, every nonbackbone area in our OSPF network must contain a router that has a physical or logical interface in Area 0. Areas 1 and 4 observe this rule, but

Area 3 does not, as R3 does not have a physical interface in Area 0. Let's put a logical one there—namely, a virtual link!

The only thing tricky about an OSPFv3 virtual link is remembering that the command will require the OSPF RID of the remote router, and that's *always an IPv4 address*. Save yourself a little (or a lot) of unnecessary t-shooting time and run *show ipv6 ospf neigh* before configuring the VL.

```
R3#show ipv6 ospf neighbor

Neighbor ID     Pri   State           Dead Time    Interface ID Interface
4.4.4.4           1   FULL/DR         00:00:31     4            FastEthernet0/0

R3#conf t
Enter configuration commands, one per line. End with CNTL/Z.
R3(config)#ipv6 router ospf 1
R3(config-rtr)#area 34 virtual-link 4.4.4.4

R4#show ipv6 ospf neighbor

Neighbor ID     Pri   State           Dead Time    Interface ID Interface
1.1.1.1           1   FULL/DR         00:00:38     4            FastEthernet0/0
3.3.3.3           1   FULL/BDR        00:00:34     3            FastEthernet0/1

R4(config)#ipv6 router ospf 1
R4(config-rtr)#area 34 virtual-link 3.3.3.3

*Jan 1 05:01:45.091: %OSPFv3-5-ADJCHG: Process 1, Nbr 3.3.3.3 on OSPFv3_VL0 fro
m LOADING to FULL, Loading Done
```

Looks good, but I'm verifying anyway!

```
R4# show ipv6 ospf virtual-link
Virtual Link OSPFv3_VL0 to router 3.3.3.3 is up
  Interface ID 10, IPv6 address 2034::3
  Run as demand circuit
  DoNotAge LSA allowed.
  Transit area 34, via interface FastEthernet0/1, Cost of using 1
  Transmit Delay is 1 sec, State POINT_TO_POINT,
  Timer intervals configured, Hello 10, Dead 40, Wait 40, Retransmit 5
    Adjacency State FULL (Hello suppressed)
```

The proof is in the routing, and R4 and R1 now see R3's loopback and can each ping it.

```
R4#show ipv6 route ospf

OI  2001::1/128 [110/1]
     via FE80::20F:F7FF:FEC4:9C0, FastEthernet0/0
```

```
OI   2003::1/128 [110/1]
      via FE80::21F:CAFF:FE96:2754, FastEthernet0/1
O    2034::3/128 [110/1]
      via FE80::21F:CAFF:FE96:2754, FastEthernet0/1

R4#ping 2003::1
!!!!!
Success rate is 100 percent (5/5), round-trip min/avg/max = 0/1/4 ms

R1#show ipv6 route ospf

OI   2003::1/128 [110/2]
      via FE80::217:59FF:FEE2:474A, FastEthernet0/0
OI   2004::1/128 [110/1]
      via FE80::217:59FF:FEE2:474A, FastEthernet0/0
OI   2034::/64 [110/2]
      via FE80::217:59FF:FEE2:474A, FastEthernet0/0
OI   2034::3/128 [110/2]
      via FE80::217:59FF:FEE2:474A, FastEthernet0/0
OI   2034::4/128 [110/1]
      via FE80::217:59FF:FEE2:474A, FastEthernet0/0

R1#ping 2003::1
!!!!!
Success rate is 100 percent (5/5), round-trip min/avg/max = 0/0/4 ms
```

With our OSPFv3 fundamentals mastered, let's talk migration strategies!

Migrating from V4 to V6

The real trick for all of us in the years ahead is taking an IPv4 network and making it an IPv6 network. Every migration has its challenges! (Ladies and gentlemen, the understatement of the year.)

Theory holds that an IPv6 rollout starts at the network edge and works toward the core. That means you and I (the you-know-whos) have to make IPv6 and IPv4 play together nicely as we move toward an all-IPv6 network. This migration can involve *stacking*, *tunneling*, or *translating*.

Stacking—*dual stacking*, that is—occurs when you're running IPv4 and v6 simultaneously across your entire network. You got your v6-to-v6 connections and your v4-to-v4 connections, and all is well! IPv4 hosts don't have to run IPv6 to get their job done, and IPv6 hosts don't have to run IPv4 to do their work.

The only real issue with dual stacking is likely the reason you're not doing it on your network right now, and that's the fact that your network likely needs some upgrades to hardware and/or software. The move from IPv4 to IPv6 is usually going to require a touch of network redesign for the new addressing scheme. In short, it's a rare IPv4 network that can go straight to IPv6.

The *6-to-4 tunnel* is built when needed, torn down when not needed, and is highly scalable. Sounds great so far! 6-to-4 tunneling is accomplished by taking an IPv6 packet and encapsulating it with an IPv4 packet. This allows transport of the IPv6 packet across an IPv4 section of the network. The packet is then deencapsulated when the time comes for it to be IPv6 routed. The IPv6 networks separated by an IPv4 core are sometimes called *IPv6 islands*.

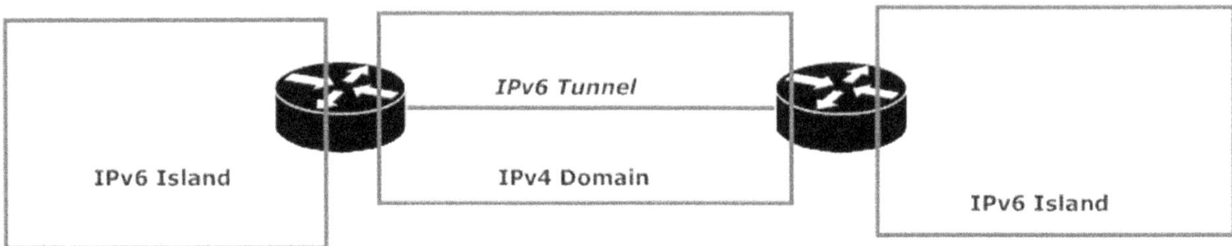

You can quickly see one major issue with tunneling—IPv6 hosts can't communicate with IPv4 hosts or access IPv4-based services unless you get dual stacking involved.

6-to-4 tunnels have a reserved IPV6 address prefix for edge routers, such as those shown in the prior illustration. The prefix begins with 2002 and is followed by the router's IPv4 address express in hex. These addresses carry a /48 mask.

NAT64

When you first learn NAT can be used for IPv6-IPv4 translation, you just might shake your head and say, "I thought we were getting *away* from NAT with IPv6!" The NAT you're going to use for IPv6-IPv4 translation isn't traditional NAT; rather, it's *Network Address Translation IPv6 to IPv4*, thankfully shortened to NAT64.

We used to use *NAT-PT* (NAT-Protocol Translation) for this translation, but NAT-PT is now a thing of the past, largely due to its integrated use of DNS. A major benefit of NAT64 is keeping the NAT64 and DNS64 functions totally separate.

NAT64 can run in stateless or stateful mode, and we know when there are two ways to run something, we better know the major differences between the two!

Stateless NAT64 embeds an IPv4 address directly into an IPv6 address, resulting in a one-to-one mapping of IPv6 addresses to IPv4 addresses. One reason for the move to IPv6 is that we're running out of IPv4 addresses, so the lack of IPv4 address conservation with stateless NAT64 is a concern.

Stateful mode doesn't suck up our IPv4 addresses as quickly, since stateful NAT64 allows multiple IPv6 addresses to use a single IPv4 address. NAT veterans may remember PAT performing a similar form of overloading. (If not, don't sweat it, I'll fill you in during another part of the course!)

Not to be confused with NAT64, *NPTv6* performs one-to-one translation of IPv6 addresses. Specifically, the address prefix is translated to another prefix. With *source translation*, the internal prefix is changed to an external prefix as packets are leaving. *Destination translation* sees an external prefix changed to the appropriate internal prefix as packets arrive on the translating device. NPTv6 can also translate one global, routable prefix to another.

NPTv6 sounds a little like NAT, but NPTv6 cannot perform any kind of port overloading, and as a result, NPTv6 is considered *stateless*. NPTv6 isn't something you run into every day, and here's some information from my pals at Wikipedia that explains why:

"It has fewer downsides than traditional IPv4 NAT; it is for example stateless and preserves the end-to-end principle. It still breaks any protocol embedding IPv6 addresses for example IPSec, and requires a more complex DNS setup (split-horizon DNS)."

And now...

Our IPV6 Conclusion: "I Know You're Not, But What Am I?"

You see the oddest things just tooling around in a lab. I was working with an IPv6 static route, using the same topology from an earlier IPv6 OSPF lab.

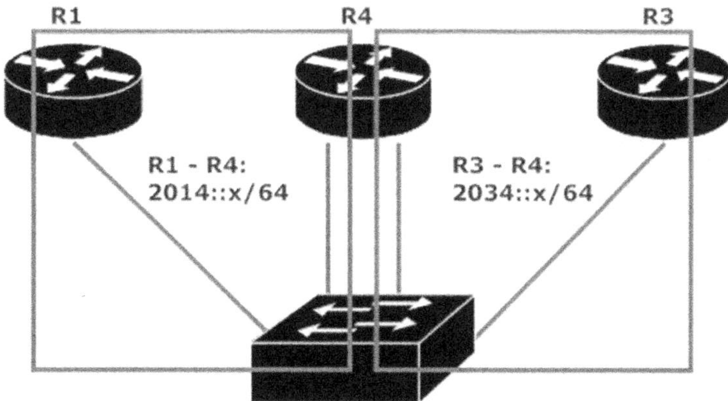

I didn't use OSPF, though. I simply entered a default route on R1, using R4 as the default gateway, and then configured another one on R3, also using R4 as the default gateway.

```
R1(config)#ipv6 route ::0/0 2014::4

R3(config)#ipv6 route ::0/0 2034::4
```

Pings from R1 wouldn't hit 2034::3, nor would pings from R3 hit 2014::1.

```
R1#ping 2034::3
Sending 5, 100-byte ICMP Echos to 2034::3, timeout is 2 seconds:
.....
Success rate is 0 percent (0/5)
```

Each router *could* hit R4's interfaces on the other subnet.

```
R1#ping 2034::4
Sending 5, 100-byte ICMP Echos to 2034::4, timeout is 2 seconds:
!!!!!
Success rate is 100 percent (5/5), round-trip min/avg/max = 0/0/0 ms
```

```
R3#ping 2014::4
Sending 5, 100-byte ICMP Echos to 2014::4, timeout is 2 seconds:
!!!!!
Success rate is 100 percent (5/5), round-trip min/avg/max = 0/1/4 ms
```

I sent a ping string from R1 of ten thousand pings, which gave me plenty of time to go over to R4 and run *debug ipv6 packet* while the pings were coming in.

```
R1#ping 2034::3 repeat 10000
Sending 10000, 100-byte ICMP Echos to 2034::3, timeout is 2 seconds:
```

Here's part of that debug output:

```
IPv6-Fwd: Destination lookup for 2034::3 : i/f=FastEthernet0/1, nexthop=2034::3
IPV6: source 2014::1 (FastEthernet0/0)
dest 2034::3 (FastEthernet0/1)
traffic class 0, flow 0x0, len 100+14, prot 58, hops 64, not a router?
```

Everything looked great right up to the time we're presented with the musical question *"not a router?"* Don't you *know* whether you're a router or not?

Well, what that phrase *really* means is *"not an IPv6 router?"*—and you already know what little command I left off R4:

```
R4(config)#ipv6 unicast-routing
```

I hopped back to R1, and where there were sad little dots there were now many happy exclamation points.

```
[Resuming connection 1 to r1 ... ]
..!!!!!
!!!!!!!!!!!!!!!!!!!!!!!!!!!!!!!!!!!!!!!!!!!!!!!!!!!!!!!!!!!!!!!!!!!!!!
!!!!!!!!!!!!!!!!!!!!!!!!!!!!!!!!!!!!!!!!!!!!!!!!!!!!!!!!!!!!!!!!!!!!!!
!!!!!!!!!!!!!!!!!!!!!!!!!!!!!!!!!!!!!!!!!!!!!!!!!!!!!!!!!!!!!!!!!!!!!!
!!!!!!!!!!!!!!!!!!!!!!!!!!!!!!!!!!!!!!!!!!!!!!!!!!!!!!!!!!!!!!!!!!!!!!
!!!!!!!!!!!!!!!!!!!!!!!!!!!!!!!!!!!!!!!!!!!!!!!!!!!!!!!!!!!!!!!!!!!!!!
!!!!!!!!!!!!!!!!!!!!!!!!!!!!!!!!!!!!!!!!!!!!!!!!!!!!!!!!!!!!!!!!!!!!!!
!!!!!!!!!!!!!!!!!!!!!!!!!!!!!!!!!!!!!!!!!!!!!!!!!!!!!!!!!!!!!!!!!!!!!!
!!!!!!!!!!!!!!!!!!!!!!!!!!!!!!!!!!!!!!!!!!!!!!!!!!!!!!!!!!!!!!!!!!!!!!
!!!!!!!!!!!!!!!!!!!!!!!!!!!!!!!!!!!!!!!!!!!!!!!!!!!!!!!!!!!!!!!!!!!!!!
!!!!!!!!!!!!!!!!!!!!!!!!!!!!!!!!!!!!!!!!!!!!!!!!!!!!!!!!!!!!!!!!!!!!!!
!!!!!!!!!!!!!!!!!!!!!!!!!!!!!!!!!!!!!!!!!!!!!!!!!!!!!!!!!!!!!!
Success rate is 97 percent (1898/1952), round-trip min/avg/max = 0/1/5 ms
```

So now you know how to write an IPv6 default static route *and* how to troubleshoot with *debug ipv6 packet*! With that, let's take an IPv6 break and take a look at some less complex but still important topics!

Chapter 9:

A TOUCH OF CEF AND SLA

An Introduction to Cisco Express Forwarding

The definition of CEF, from my friends at Wikipedia:

"CEF is an advanced layer 3 switching technology used mainly in large core networks or the Internet to enhance the overall network performance."

Whaaaaaaaaaaaat? "Layer 3 switching"? Well, really it's layer 3 *packet* switching. That's what CEF (and routing) are all about. CEF has nothing to do with frame switching, which is a pure L2 operation. With that clear, let's check out the rest of that definition.

"Although CEF is a Cisco proprietary protocol, other vendors of multi-layer switches or high-capacity routers offer a similar functionality where layer 3 switching or routing is done in hardware (in an ASIC) instead of by software and the (central) CPU."

So if you're thinking, "Hey, didn't we go over CEF in Chris's CCNP Switch course and book," you are absolutely correct. CEF shows up on multilayer switching and routers, so it's a topic for both Switch and Route.

Remember the three "main planes" of a router? No? Here's a quick review:

The management plane is involved with router management. (No kidding, right?) When we're configuring protocols, addresses, or services on a router, we're interacting with the management plane.

Routing protocols run on the control plane. The ARP and IP routing tables are built here.

CEF's two main components, the Forwarding Information Base (FIB) and the Adjacency Table (AT), are both part of the data plane. The FIB is derived from the IP routing table. (When you use *clear ip route ** to clear the IP routing table of dynamically learned entries, you're actually clearing both the IP and FIB tables.) CEF is generally on by default, but it never hurts to check with *show ip cef.* Following is the first hint CEF may not be on:

```
R1#show ip cef
%CEF not running
Prefix              Next Hop             Interface
```

Turn CEF on with *ip cef.* I left a previous lab on so we'd have a little something to look at in the FIB table.

```
R1(config)#ip cef

R1#show ip cef
Prefix              Next Hop             Interface
0.0.0.0/0           drop                 Null0 (default route handler entry)
0.0.0.0/8           drop
0.0.0.0/32          receive
2.2.2.0/24          172.12.123.2         Serial1/0
22.2.2.0/24         172.12.123.2         Serial1/0
30.1.1.0/24         attached             FastEthernet0/0
30.1.1.0/32         receive
30.1.1.1/32         receive
30.1.1.5/32         30.1.1.5             FastEthernet0/0
30.1.1.255/32       receive
55.5.5.0/24         172.12.123.2         Serial1/0
(truncated, there's two more screens of this!)
```

Not exactly the IP routing table we've come to know! The FIB of a CEF-enabled Cisco device keeps the usual routing info—destination networks, masks, next-hop IP addresses, exit interfaces—just in a different format than the IP routing table. The routing information in the FIB is updated dynamically as change notifications are received from the L3 engine.

You can also verify CEF operation with *show ip interface,* a rather verbose but helpful command. The CEF information is about 60 percent of the way down in the output.

```
R1#show ip interface serial 1/0
Serial1/0 is up, line protocol is up
  Internet address is 172.12.123.1/24
  Broadcast address is 255.255.255.255
  Address determined by non-volatile memory
  MTU is 1500 bytes
  Helper address is not set
  Directed broadcast forwarding is disabled
  Multicast reserved groups joined: 224.0.0.9
```

```
  Outgoing access list is not set
  Inbound access list is not set
  Proxy ARP is enabled
  Local Proxy ARP is disabled
  Security level is default
  Split horizon is disabled
  ICMP redirects are always sent
  ICMP unreachables are always sent
  ICMP mask replies are never sent
  IP fast switching is enabled
  IP fast switching on the same interface is enabled
  IP Flow switching is disabled
  IP CEF switching is enabled
  IP CEF Fast switching turbo vector
  IP multicast fast switching is enabled
(truncated)
```

L2 information is kept in the Adjacency Table (AT), and you can see that information with *show adjacency* and *show adjacency detail.*

```
R1#show adjacency
Protocol Interface                  Address
IP       Serial1/1                  point2point(5)
IP       FastEthernet0/0            30.1.1.5(5)
IP       Serial1/0                  172.12.123.3(5) (incomplete)
IP       Serial1/0                  172.12.123.2(13)

R1#show adjacency detail
Protocol Interface                  Address
IP       Serial1/1                  point2point(5)
                                    0 packets, 0 bytes
                                    0F000800
                                    CEF   expires: 00:02:06
                                          refresh: 00:00:06
                                    Epoch: 0
IP       FastEthernet0/0            30.1.1.5(5)
                                    0 packets, 0 bytes
                                    00169DE5F500000FF7C409C00800
                                    ARP          00:47:25
                                    Epoch: 0
IP       Serial1/0                  172.12.123.3(5) (incomplete)
                                    0 packets, 0 bytes
                                    FR-MAP      never
                                    Epoch: 0
IP       Serial1/0                  172.12.123.2(13)
                                    0 packets, 0 bytes
                                    1CA10800
```

```
                                    FR-MAP     never
                                    Epoch: 0
```

Let's take a closer look at 2.2.2.0 /24 and 22.2.2.0 /24. Thankfully, we can filter the *show ip cef* output by interface or network number.

```
R1#show ip cef 2.2.2.0
2.2.2.0/24, version 17, epoch 0, cached adjacency 172.12.123.2
0 packets, 0 bytes
  via 172.12.123.2, Serial1/0, 0 dependencies
    next hop 172.12.123.2, Serial1/0
    valid cached adjacency


R1# show adjacency
Protocol Interface                  Address
IP       Serial1/1                  point2point(5)
IP       FastEthernet0/0            30.1.1.5(5)
IP       Serial1/0                  172.12.123.3(5) (incomplete)
IP       Serial1/0                  172.12.123.2(13)
```

The path to 2.2.2.0 uses 172.12.123.2 as the next hop, and that address in turn is mapped to Serial1/0 in the AT.

I'm sure you noticed the *(incomplete)* next to 172.12.123.3. Before starting the lab that's giving us this FIB and AT information, I created a frame map statement to 172.12.123.3 on R1. Problem is, there is no 172.12.123.3 in that particular lab. Any time you see *(incomplete)* in the AT table, something's amiss regarding the ARP information for that address, since the AT is derived from ARP. Running *show ip cef* for any incomplete entry gives you a hint that there's trouble afoot.

```
R1#show ip cef 172.12.123.3
172.12.123.3/32, version 12, epoch 0, cached adjacency 172.12.123.3
0 packets, 0 bytes
  via 172.12.123.3, Serial1/0, 0 dependencies
    next hop 172.12.123.3, Serial1/0
    invalid cached adjacency
```

You can also spot a router's default route in the CEF table—as long as the router has one! The prefix 0.0.0.0/0 will always appear in the AT table, but be careful, as it's what you see under *next hop* that counts. R1 is dropping traffic destined for 0.0.0.0 /0...

```
R1#show ip cef
Prefix              Next Hop             Interface
0.0.0.0/0           drop                 Null0 (default route handler entry)
```

...and R3 has no default route.

```
R3#show ip cef
Prefix              Next Hop              Interface
0.0.0.0/0           no route
```

R2 *does* have a default route, as indicated by an address under *next hop* for the 0.0.0.0/0 entry.

```
R2#show ip cef
Prefix              Next Hop              Interface
0.0.0.0/0           172.12.123.1          Serial0/1/0
```

The absence and presence of the default route is verified by *show ip route 0.0.0.0.*

```
R1#show ip route 0.0.0.0
% Network not in table

R3#show ip route 0.0.0.0
% Network not in table

R2#show ip route 0.0.0.0
Routing entry for 0.0.0.0/0, supernet
  Known via "static", distance 1, metric 0, candidate default path
  Routing Descriptor Blocks:
  * 172.12.123.1
      Route metric is 0, traffic share count is 1
```

There are two other packet-switching methods you should be aware of: process switching and fast switching. Process switching is our least favorite, since the CPU has to be involved with the forwarding of every packet. We have better things for our CPU to do!

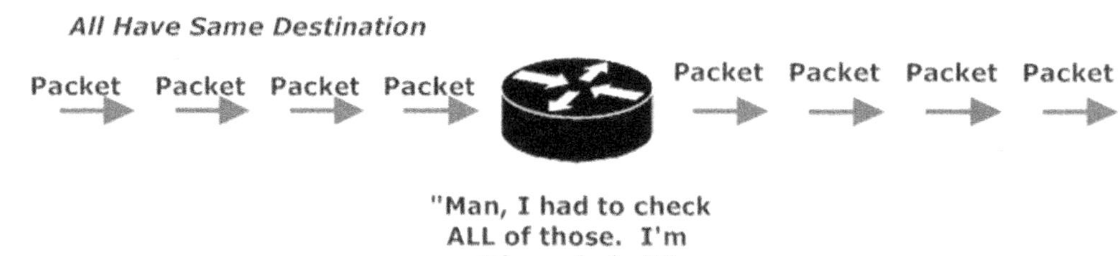

Fast switching is a major improvement since the CPU need only be involved in forwarding one packet of a given flow—the very first one. The router keeps a fast-switching cache that keeps information regarding destination IP addresses of packets it's already switched. When other packets come in, the router checks that cache to see if there's an entry for that flow. If there is, the packets are appropriately forwarded without the CPU being involved.

To enable fast switching on an interface, run *ip route-cache*. To disable it, run (you guessed it!) *no ip route-cache*.

Service-Level Agreements

During your Frame Relay studies in your CCNA days, you were introduced to the Committed Information Rate (CIR). The CIR is basically a guarantee given to the customer by the Frame Relay service provider, where the provider says, "For X dollars, we guarantee you'll get Y amount of bandwidth. You may get more, but we guarantee you won't get less." Given that guarantee of minimum performance, the customer can then plan the WAN appropriately.

The SLA is based on the concept of minimum, guaranteed performance, but this agreement is between different parties. It can be much like the CIR, where a service provider guarantees a certain level of overall network uptime and performance, or it can be between the internal clients of a company and the network team at that same company.

The SLA can involve just about any quality-measurable value in your network, from available bandwidth to acceptable levels of jitter in voice networks to DNS lookup time to trouble notification and resolution time. Here's a sneak peek of the available tests, shown in SLA operation config mode (the *5* is the assigned operation number):

```
R2(config)#ip sla 5
R2(config-ip-sla)#?
IP SLAs entry configuration commands:
  dhcp          DHCP Operation
  dns           DNS Query Operation
  ethernet      Ethernet Operations
  exit          Exit Operation Configuration
  ftp           FTP Operation
  http          HTTP Operation
  icmp-echo     ICMP Echo Operation
  icmp-jitter   ICMP Jitter Operation
  path-echo     Path Discovered ICMP Echo Operation
  path-jitter   Path Discovered ICMP Jitter Operation
  tcp-connect   TCP Connect Operation
  udp-echo      UDP Echo Operation
```

```
udp-jitter    UDP Jitter Operation
voip          Voice Over IP Operation
```

An SLA setup consists of a *source* and a *responder*. To kick off the festivities, the source sends control packets to the responder via UDP port 1967 in an attempt to create a control connection similar to that in FTP. This connection isn't the actual SLA test, but it is an agreement on the rules of communication. In this case, the rules sent to the responder are the port number to be listened to during the test and the time limit on that listening.

Should the responder be kind enough to agree, it'll send a message back to the source indicating the same, and then the responder starts listening to the indicated port. (If the responder doesn't agree, it'll send a message back indicating that decision, and our story ends prematurely.)

We now go from *controlling* to *probing*, as the source sends test packets to the responder. The source wants to see if the packets are echoed back *and* how long the overall process takes.

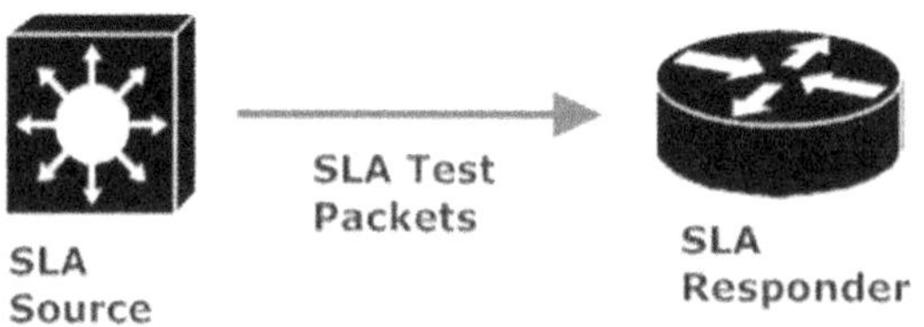

The responder adds timestamps to those packets both as the packets are accepted and as they are returned. This gives the sender a better idea of the overall time the responder took to process the packets as well as the overall round trip time. (Of course, this timestamping only helps if the devices have synched time—NTP, anyone?)

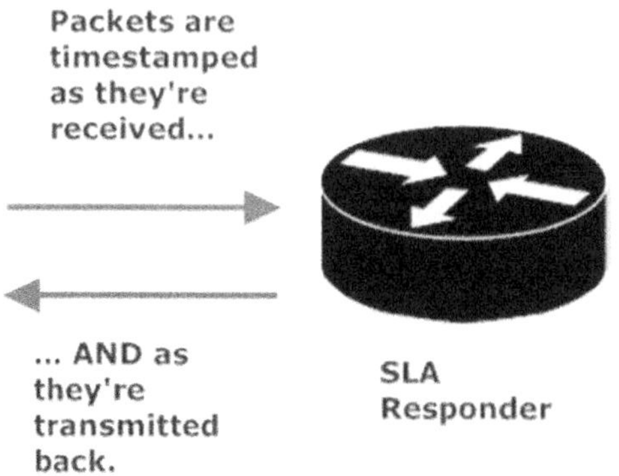

Let's tackle an SLA lab! MLS_1 will be the SLA source, with ROUTER_3 serving as the responder. Here are the first options for the *ip sla* command:

```
MLS _ 1(config)#ip sla ?
  <1-2147483647>          Entry Number
  enable                  Enable Event Notifications
  group                   Group Configuration or Group Scheduling
  key-chain               Use MD5 Authentication for IP SLAs Control Messages
  logging                 Enable Syslog
  low-memory              Configure Low Water Memory Mark
  reaction-configuration  IP SLAs Reaction-Configuration
  reaction-trigger        IP SLAs Trigger Assignment
  read                    Read data for use with IP SLA
  reset                   IP SLAs Reset
  responder               Enable IP SLAs Responder
  restart                 Restart An Active Entry
  schedule                Entry Scheduling
```

We'll go with SLA entry number five, and accepting that value drops us into SLA entry config mode. We'll then choose the *icmp-echo* test, using 10.1.1.3 as the target of the test. Note the option to configure the source interface and IP address—those options can come in handy in larger networks. Since we only have one path from source to responder, we'll leave those alone here.

```
MLS _ 1(config)#ip sla 5
MLS _ 1(config-ip-sla)#?
IP SLAs entry configuration commands:
  dhcp         DHCP Operation
  dns          DNS Query Operation
  exit         Exit Operation Configuration
  ftp          FTP Operation
  http         HTTP Operation
  icmp-echo    ICMP Echo Operation
  path-echo    Path Discovered ICMP Echo Operation
  path-jitter  Path Discovered ICMP Jitter Operation
  tcp-connect  TCP Connect Operation
  udp-echo     UDP Echo Operation
  udp-jitter   UDP Jitter Operation
  video        Video Operation

MLS _ 1(config-ip-sla)#icmp-echo ?
  Hostname or A.B.C.D Destination IP address or hostname, broadcast disallowed

MLS _ 1(config-ip-sla)#icmp-echo 10.1.1.3 ?
  source-interface    Source Interface (ingress icmp packet interface)
  source-ip           Source Address
  <cr>
```

```
MLS _ 1(config-ip-sla)#icmp-echo 10.1.1.3
```

We then drop into SLA ICMP Echo config mode (!), where I'll set a frequency of sixty seconds between tests. That also happens to be the default!

```
MLS _ 1(config-ip-sla)#icmp-echo 10.1.1.3
MLS _ 1(config-ip-sla-echo)#?
IP SLAs Icmp Echo Configuration Commands:
  default            Set a command to its defaults
  exit               Exit operation configuration
  frequency          Frequency of an operation
  history            History and Distribution Data
  no                 Negate a command or set its defaults
  owner              Owner of Entry
  request-data-size  Request data size
  tag                User defined tag
  threshold          Operation threshold in milliseconds
  timeout            Timeout of an operation
  tos                Type Of Service
  verify-data        Verify data
  vrf                Configure IP SLAs for a VPN Routing/Forwarding instance

MLS _ 1(config-ip-sla-echo)#frequency ?
  <1-604800>   Frequency in seconds

MLS _ 1(config-ip-sla-echo)#frequency 60
```

Finally, we get to schedule this sucker! I'll use IOS Help to show you the options and then start the test immediately. Note the option to grant the test eternal life.

```
MLS _ 1(config)#ip sla schedule ?
  <1-2147483647>   Entry number

MLS _ 1(config)#ip sla schedule 5 ?
  ageout      How long to keep this Entry when inactive
  life        Length of time to execute in seconds
  recurring   Probe to be scheduled automatically every day
  start-time  When to start this entry
  <cr>

MLS _ 1(config)#ip sla schedule 5 life ?
  <0-2147483647> Life seconds (default 3600)
  forever          continue running forever

MLS _ 1(config)#ip sla schedule 5 start-time ?
  after     Start after a certain amount of time from now
  hh:mm     Start time (hh:mm)
```

```
  hh:mm:ss   Start time (hh:mm:ss)
  now        Start now
  pending    Start pending

MLS _ 1(config)#ip sla schedule 5 start-time now
```

Verify your config with *show ip sla config.* I'll show you the entire output here, and the most important information to us is near the top.

```
MLS _ 1#show ip sla config
IP SLAs Infrastructure Engine-III
Entry number: 5
Owner:
Tag:
Operation timeout (milliseconds): 5000
Type of operation to perform: icmp-echo
Target address/Source address: 10.1.1.3/0.0.0.0
Type Of Service parameter: 0x0
Request size (ARR data portion): 28
Verify data: No
Vrf Name:
Schedule:
   Operation frequency (seconds): 60 (not considered if randomly scheduled)
   Next Scheduled Start Time: Start Time already passed
   Group Scheduled : FALSE
   Randomly Scheduled : FALSE
   Life (seconds): 3600
   Entry Ageout (seconds): never
   Recurring (Starting Everyday): FALSE
   Status of entry (SNMP RowStatus): Active
Threshold (milliseconds): 5000
Distribution Statistics:
   Number of statistic hours kept: 2
   Number of statistic distribution buckets kept: 1
   Statistic distribution interval (milliseconds): 20
Enhanced History:
History Statistics:
   Number of history Lives kept: 0
   Number of history Buckets kept: 15
   History Filter Type: None
```

To view SLA statistics, run *show ip sla statistics.* I ran the command twice, and we can see the tests are running a minute apart, and they've both been successful. The default TTL is 3600 seconds, and we can see that's ticking away.

```
MLS _ 1#show ip sla stat
IPSLAs Latest Operation Statistics
```

```
IPSLA operation id: 5
        Latest RTT: 1 milliseconds
Latest operation start time: 06:11:35 EST Thu Mar 26 2015
Latest operation return code: OK
Number of successes: 1
Number of failures: 0
Operation time to live: 3552 sec


MLS _ 1#show ip sla stat
IPSLAs Latest Operation Statistics

IPSLA operation id: 5
        Latest RTT: 1 milliseconds
Latest operation start time: 06:12:35 EST Thu Mar 26 2015
Latest operation return code: OK
Number of successes: 2
Number of failures: 0
Operation time to live: 3528 sec
```

An interesting thing about SLA tests—you can't edit one that's in progress. Here, I tried to go back and set this test to live forever rather than time out, and here's what happened:

```
MLS _ 1(config)#ip sla 5
Entry already running and cannot be modified
        (only can delete (no) and start over)
        (check to see if the probe has finished exiting)
```

It's always *something*!

Hey, did you notice I never configured anything on the responder? Since I was running a simple ICMP echo test, I didn't need to, since I know the responder can handle pinging. For some of those other tests, though, you may need *ip sla responder.* It doesn't hurt anything to enable SLA capabilities for the simpler tests. We have the option to set up a connection-oriented (tcp-connect) or connectionless (udp-echo) SLA session, but we'll leave that for future studies.

```
R2(config)#ip sla responder ?
  auto-register   Setup auto-register to hub
  tcp-connect     Setup tcp-connect responder
  udp-echo        Setup udp-echo responder
  <cr>

ROUTER _ 3(config)#ip sla responder
```

We can secure our SLA config with a keychain and the *ip sla key-chain* command.

```
ROUTER_3(config)#key chain CCNP
ROUTER_3(config-keychain)#key 1
ROUTER_3(config-keychain-key)#key-string SPIDERS

ROUTER_3(config)#ip sla key-chain CCNP

MLS_1(config)#key chain CCNP
MLS_1(config-keychain)#key 1
MLS_1(config-keychain-key)#key-string SPIDERS

MLS_1(config)#ip sla key-chain CCNP
```

You need to see what the *statistics* output is when something's gone wrong. Here, I shut ROUTER_3's port down that leads to the switch. Here's the result of the very next echo test:

```
MLS_1#show ip sla stat
IPSLAs Latest Operation Statistics

IPSLA operation id: 5
        Latest RTT: NoConnection/Busy/Timeout
Latest operation start time: 06:53:35 EST Thu Mar 26 2015
Latest operation return code: Timeout
Number of successes: 42
Number of failures: 1
Operation time to live: 1024 sec
```

After reopening the interface, the successes start incrementing again!

```
MLS_1#show ip sla stat
IPSLAs Latest Operation Statistics

IPSLA operation id: 5
        Latest RTT: 1 milliseconds
Latest operation start time: 06:54:35 EST Thu Mar 26 2015
Latest operation return code: OK
Number of successes: 43
Number of failures: 1
Operation time to live: 989 sec
```

Tracking an Interface with SLA

SLA tracking works quite a bit like the HSRP tracking you saw in action during my CCNP Switch course. If for some reason you didn't see that, no worries, I'll bring you right up to speed. (But shame on you!) In this lab, R2 has two paths to 172.12.34.0.

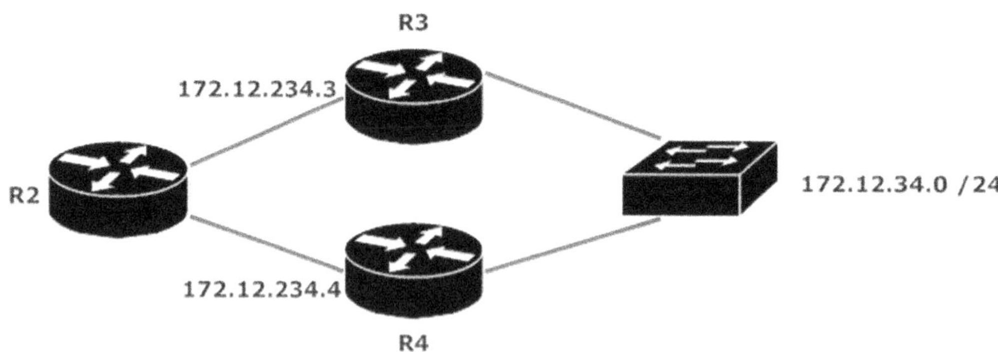

R2 has a static route pointing to each of the two possible next-hop addresses. The path through R3 is preferred due to the higher AD assigned to the path through R4, as verified by a peek at the routing table.

```
ip route 172.12.34.0 255.255.255.0 172.12.234.3
ip route 172.12.34.0 255.255.255.0 172.12.234.4 40

R2#show ip route 172.12.34.0 255.255.255.0
Routing entry for 172.12.34.0/24
Known via "static", distance 1, metric 0
Routing Descriptor Blocks:
* 172.12.234.3
      Route metric is 0, traffic share count is 1
```

R2 can indeed ping both R3 and R4's interfaces on the 172.12.34.0 /24 network.

```
R2#ping 172.12.34.3
!!!!!
Success rate is 100 percent (5/5), round-trip min/avg/max = 1/2/4 ms

R2#ping 172.12.34.4
!!!!!
Success rate is 100 percent (5/5), round-trip min/avg/max = 16/16/20 ms
```

Should 172.12.234.3 become unreachable, nothing will change on *R2* regarding the next-hop address for 172.12.34.0, and the pings will no longer go through. There's no reason for the floating static route to 172.12.34.0 /24 to go into use on R2 since the existing static route is still in the table!

```
R3(config)#int fast 0/0
R3(config-if)#shut

R2#show ip route 172.12.34.0 255.255.255.0
Routing entry for 172.12.34.0/24
  Known via "static", distance 1, metric 0
  Routing Descriptor Blocks:
```

```
  * 172.12.234.3
      Route metric is 0, traffic share count is 1

R2#ping 172.12.34.4
.....
Success rate is 0 percent (0/5)

R2# ping 172.12.34.3
.....
Success rate is 0 percent (0/5)
```

SLA tracking allows us to tie an SLA object to a static route, and should that SLA object indicate the next-hop address is not reachable, the static route will be removed from the table. It's easier to configure than to put into words, so let's configure it! We'll start with the SLA object config right after I reopen R3's Fast 0/0 interface.

```
R3(config)#int fast 0/0
R3(config-if)#no shut
```

I'm not going to change any of the *icmp-echo* defaults, but note the frequency default is sixty seconds. You may want more or less frequent testing.

```
R2(config)#ip sla 1
R2(config-ip-sla)#?
IP SLAs entry configuration commands:
  dhcp            DHCP Operation
  dns             DNS Query Operation
  ethernet        Ethernet Operations
  exit            Exit Operation Configuration
  ftp             FTP Operation
  http            HTTP Operation
  icmp-echo       ICMP Echo Operation
  icmp-jitter     ICMP Jitter Operation
  path-echo       Path Discovered ICMP Echo Operation
  path-jitter     Path Discovered ICMP Jitter Operation
  tcp-connect     TCP Connect Operation
  udp-echo        UDP Echo Operation
  udp-jitter      UDP Jitter Operation
  voip            Voice Over IP Operation

R2(config-ip-sla)#icmp-echo 172.12.234.3
R2(config-ip-sla-echo)#?
IP SLAs Icmp Echo Configuration Commands:
  default               Set a command to its defaults
  exit                  Exit operation configuration
  frequency             Frequency of an operation
  history               History and Distribution Data
```

```
  no                    Negate a command or set its defaults
  owner                 Owner of Entry
  request-data-size     Request data size
  tag                   User defined tag
  threshold             Operation threshold in milliseconds
  timeout               Timeout of an operation
  tos                   Type Of Service
  verify-data           Verify data
  vrf                   Configure IP SLAs for a VPN Routing/Forwarding instance
```

With the object created, we need to set up the start time and how far into the future we'd like this test to run.

```
R2(config)#ip sla schedule ?
  <1-2147483647> Entry number

R2(config)#ip sla schedule 1 ?
  ageout How long to keep this Entry when inactive
  life Length of time to execute in seconds
  recurring Probe to be scheduled automatically every day
  start-time When to start this entry
  <cr>
```

How long do we want it to run? *Forevah!*

```
R2(config)#ip sla schedule 1 life forever ?
  ageout How long to keep this Entry when inactive
  recurring Probe to be scheduled automatically every day
  start-time When to start this entry
  <cr>
```

When do we want it? *Now!*

```
R2(config)#ip sla schedule 1 life forever start-time ?
  after      Start after a certain amount of time from now
  hh:mm      Start time (hh:mm)
  hh:mm:ss   Start time (hh:mm:ss)
  now        Start now
  pending    Start pending

R2(config)#ip sla schedule 1 life forever start-time now
```

Now we set up the tracking...

```
R2(config)#track 1 ?
  application   Application
  interface     Select an interface to trac
```

```
  ip           IP protocol
  list         Group objects in a list
  stub-object  Stub tracking object

R2(config)#track 1 ip ?
  route   IP route
  sla     IP Service Level Agreement

R2(config)#track 1 ip sla ?
  <1-2147483647>   Entry number

R2(config)#track 1 ip sla 1 ?
  reachability  Reachability
  state         Return code state
  <cr>

R2(config)#track 1 ip sla 1 reachability ?
  <cr>

R2(config)#track 1 ip sla 1 reachability
```

...and here comes the one little thing that can really trip you up. It's not enough to add *track* at the end of the static route you want to track—you must get rid of the current static route to be tracked entirely, then add the route back with the track option at the end. If you leave the original statement in, this tracking will not work.

```
R2(config)#no ip route 172.12.34.0 255.255.255.0 172.12.234.3

R2(config)#ip route 172.12.34.0 255.255.255.0 172.12.234.3 ?
  <1-255>     Distance metric for this route
  multicast   multicast route
  name        Specify name of the next hop
  permanent   permanent route
  tag         Set tag for this route
  track       Install route depending on tracked item
  <cr>

R2(config)#ip route 172.12.34.0 255.255.255.0 172.12.234.3 track ?
  <1-500>   tracked object number

R2(config)#ip route 172.12.34.0 255.255.255.0 172.12.234.3 track 1
```

Show track tells us reachability is up, and it's been six minutes and nineteen seconds since that changed (or in this case, 6:19 since tracking started).

```
R2#show track
Track 1
```

```
  IP SLA 1 reachability
  Reachability is Up
    1 change, last change 00:07:31
  Latest operation return code: OK
  Latest RTT (millisecs) 1
  Tracked by:
    STATIC-IP-ROUTING 0
```

show ip route verifies the next-hop address in use for that network is 172.12.234.3.

```
R2#show ip route 172.12.34.0 255.255.255.0
Routing entry for 172.12.34.0/24
  Known via "static", distance 1, metric 0
  Routing Descriptor Blocks:
  * 172.12.234.3
      Route metric is 0, traffic share count is 1
```

We'll shut R3's Fast 0/0 interface down, go back to R2…and wait.

```
R3(config)#int fast 0/0
R3(config-if)#shut

*Aug 27 13:13:23.695: %TRACKING-5-STATE: 1 ip sla 1 reachability Up->Down
```

Down goes reachability! Run *show track* to confirm and see how long it's been since reachability failed. Note the operation return code is now *timeout.*

```
R2#show track
Track 1
  IP SLA 1 reachability
  Reachability is Down
    2 changes, last change 00:02:40
  Latest operation return code: Timeout
  Tracked by:
    STATIC-IP-ROUTING 0
```

The next-hop address for traffic to 172.12.34.0 is indeed 172.12.234.4!

```
R2#show ip route 172.12.34.0
Routing entry for 172.12.34.0/24
  Known via "static", distance 40, metric 0
  Routing Descriptor Blocks:
  * 172.12.234.4
      Route metric is 0, traffic share count is 1
```

Once we reopen the interface on R3 and tracking reports the reachability test has passed, the original next-hop address for that route returns to the table.

```
*Aug 27 13:21:18.695: %TRACKING-5-STATE: 1 ip sla 1 reachability Down->Up
R2#show track
Track 1
   IP SLA 1 reachability
   Reachability is Up
     4 changes, last change 00:00:05
   Latest operation return code: OK
   Latest RTT (millisecs) 1
   Tracked by:
     STATIC-IP-ROUTING 0

R2#show ip route 172.12.34.0
Routing entry for 172.12.34.0/24
   Known via "static", distance 1, metric 0
   Routing Descriptor Blocks:
   * 172.12.234.3
     Route metric is 0, traffic share count is 1
```

Let's shift our focus to protecting our network!

Chapter 10:

NETWORK SECURITY

ACL Review

Just to be sure that everyone's totally up-to-speed on ACLs, I've included this review of basic ACL logic, standard ACLs, and extended ACLs. Even if you're comfortable with ACLs, I suggest *strongly* you review this material before moving ahead. We'll also have a look at time-based ACLs. Let's get started!

ACL Logic

When a packet enters or exits an interface with an ACL applied in the direction the packet is traveling, the packet is compared against the criteria of the ACL's initial line. If the packet matches, the appropriate action is taken, and the process is over. If there is no match, the second line is examined, and if it matches, the named action is taken, and the process is done. If there's no match on the second line, the router keeps looking through the ACL's lines until a match is found.

If no explicit match is found in any line, the packet is denied via the implicit deny. If a packet is not expressly permitted, it's implicitly denied.

Configuring Standard ACLs and Extended ACLs

A standard ACL is concerned only with the source IP address of the packet. That's literally the only value that can be configured when writing a standard ACL. IOS Help will make no mention of which address you're matching on (source or destination, that is), so you better have it down cold.

```
R5(config)#access-list 5 permit ?
  Hostname or A.B.C.D   Address to match
  any                   Any source host
  host                  A single host address
```

Extended ACLs consider both the source and destination IP address and can consider the port number as well. Even if you don't care about the source and just want to match on destination, you'll have to put *any* in for the source. Plenty of practice coming up with that soon!

Standard and extended ACLs use separate numeric ranges. Standard ACLs use 1–99 and 1300–1999; extended ACLs use 100–199 and 2000–2699.

```
R5(config)#access-list ?
  <1-99>            IP standard access list
  <100-199>         IP extended access list
  <1000-1099>       IPX SAP access list
  <1100-1199>       Extended 48-bit MAC address access list
  <1200-1299>       IPX summary address access list
  <1300-1999>       IP standard access list (expanded range)
  <200-299>         Protocol type-code access list
  <2000-2699>       IP extended access list (expanded range)
  <300-399>         DECnet access list
  <600-699>         Appletalk access list
  <700-799>         48-bit MAC address access list
  <800-899>         IPX standard access list
  <900-999>         IPX extended access list
  dynamic-extended  Extend the dynamic ACL absolute timer
  rate-limit        Simple rate-limit specific access list
```

ACLs are applied to Cisco router interfaces with the *ip access-group* command, along with two important values. Let's say we've written *ACL 5*, permitting packets sourced from 172.12.12.0 /24 and denying all other sources. Here's what that ACL looks like:

```
R5(config)#access-list 5 permit 172.12.12.0 ?
  A.B.C.D  Wildcard bits
  log      Log matches against this entry
  <cr>

R5(config)#access-list 5 permit 172.12.12.0 0.0.0.255
```

When applying the ACL, you must specify the ACL number and the direction in which the packets will be checked against the ACL.

```
R5(config)#int fast 0/0
R5(config-if)#ip access-group ?
  <1-199>       IP access list (standard or extended)
  <1300-2699>   IP expanded access list (standard or extended)
  WORD          Access-list name

R5(config-if)#ip access-group 5 ?
  in   inbound packets
```

```
  out   outbound packets

R5(config-if)#ip access-group 5 out
```

And that's it! Verify with *show ip access-list*, *show access-list*, and/or *show ip interface* (a handy and often overlooked command), and you're gold!

```
R5(config)#int gig 0/0
R5(config-if)#ip access-group 5 out

R5#show ip int gig 0/0
GigabitEthernet0/0 is up, line protocol is up
  Internet address is 10.1.1.1/24
  Broadcast address is 255.255.255.255
  Address determined by setup command
  MTU is 1500 bytes
  Helper address is not set
  Directed broadcast forwarding is disabled
  Outgoing access list is 5
  Inbound access list is not set
(output truncated)
```

Using "Host" and "Any" in Wildcard Masks

A wildcard mask of all zeroes (0.0.0.0) means the address specified in the ACL line must be matched exactly in order for the specified action to be taken. You've likely used 0.0.0.0 as a wildcard mask in OSPF in order to enable only a specific address with OSPF. With ACLs, use *host* to represent a mask of 0.0.0.0 in either a standard or extended ACL.

Using *host* in a standard ACL:

```
R5(config)#access-list 7 permit ?
  Hostname or A.B.C.D   Address to match
  any                   Any source host
  host                  A single host address

R5(config)#access-list 7 permit host ?
  Hostname or A.B.C.D    Host address
```

Using *host* in an extended ACL:

```
R5(config)#access-list 7 permit host 172.12.12.3
R5(config)#access-list 177 permit ip host 172.12.12.3 ?
  A.B.C.D       Destination address
  any           Any destination host
  host          A single destination host
  object-group  Destination network object group
```

```
R5(config)#access-list 177 permit ip host 172.12.12.3
```

At the other end of the spectrum, we have 255.255.255.255, which matches any address. Lines using this address are often written to negate the implicit deny...

```
R5(config)#access-list 8 permit 0.0.0.0 255.255.255.255
```

...or to log packets that are denied.

```
R5(config)#access-list 9 deny 0.0.0.0 255.255.255.255 log
```

You can use *any* in place of that address and mask. It'll save you some typing, too! The following two ACLs do the exact same thing as ACLs 8 and 9 above.

```
R5(config)#access-list 8 permit any

R5(config)#access-list 9 deny any log
```

Watch the Order of Your ACL Lines!

Getting just one line out of place in an ACL can wreck everything you're trying to do. Let's say we need an ACL that denies traffic from 172.18.18.0 /24 while allowing traffic from any other subnet. Some enterprising soul (me) has presented you with four different ACLs. Which is correct, and exactly why are the other three wrong?

```
R5(config)#access-list 17 deny 172.18.18.0 0.0.0.255
R5(config)#access-list 17 perm any

R5(config)#access-list 18 perm any
R5(config)#access-list 18 deny 172.18.18.0 0.0.0.255

R5(config)#access-list 19 deny 172.18.18.0 255.0.0.0
R5(config)#access-list 19 perm any

R5(config)#access-list 20 perm any
R5(config)#access-list 20 deny 172.18.18.0 255.0.0.0
```

We know ACLs 19 and 20 can't be right, since the masks on each would match the last three octets while not caring what the first octet is. You're not going to want a wildcard mask like *that* often.

That leaves ACLs 17 and 18. ACL 18 will match all traffic with its very first line ("Hey, permit anything!"). The second line denying the specific traffic will never be read. The ACL we want is 17, where the specific traffic is denied and then the remaining traffic is allowed.

More on Extended ACLs

Extended ACLs not only allow matches against the IP source and destination IP addresses, but they demand both. Even if you're only matching against the destination, you still have to put something in for the source, even if it's *any*. (Yes, I told you this before. I'm just telling you again!) Matching on source port, destination port, and protocol type are optional.

Let's write an extended ACL that denies traffic sourced from 172.50.50.0 /24 if it's destined for 172.50.100.0 /24. All other packets should be allowed.

```
R5(config)#access-list 100 deny ip ?
  A.B.C.D      Source address
  any          Any source host
  host         A single source host
  object-group Source network object group

R5(config)#access-list 100 deny ip 172.50.50.0 ?
  A.B.C.D      Source wildcard bits

R5(config)#access-list 100 deny ip 172.50.50.0 0.0.0.255 ?
  A.B.C.D      Destination address
  any          Any destination host
  host         A single destination host
  object-group Destination network object group

R5(config)#access-list 100 deny ip 172.50.50.0 0.0.0.255 172.50.100.0 ?
  A.B.C.D Destination wildcard bits

R5(config)#$ 100 deny ip 172.50.50.0 0.0.0.255 172.50.100.0 0.0.0.255 ?
  dscp         Match packets with given dscp value
  fragments    Check non-initial fragments
  log          Log matches against this entry
  log-input    Log matches against this entry, including input interface
  option       Match packets with given IP Options value
  precedence   Match packets with given precedence value
  time-range   Specify a time-range
  tos          Match packets with given TOS value
  <cr>

R5(config)#$ 100 deny ip 172.50.50.0 0.0.0.255 172.50.100.0 0.0.0.255
R5(config)#access-list 100 permit ip any any
```

Did you notice the dollar sign in front of the *100*? That symbol indicates that you've typed a command longer than the console screen can show you at once. In the last line, there are two *any* statements, and that's how you get rid of the implicit deny. The *permit any* statement in an extended ACL will have two *anys*—one for the source address, and the next for the destination address. If you try to put just one *any* in, the router won't let you get away with it!

```
R5(config)#access-list 101 permit ip any
% Incomplete command.
```

Let's see extended ACLs in action! R4 has two loopbacks and has an OSPF adjacency with R5 via its FE interface. R5 sees both loopbacks in its OSPF route table and can ping both... for now!

```
R5#show ip route ospf

      4.0.0.0/32 is subnetted, 1 subnets
O        4.4.4.4 [110/2] via 30.1.1.4, 00:11:17, GigabitEthernet0/0
      44.0.0.0/32 is subnetted, 1 subnets
O        44.4.4.4 [110/2] via 30.1.1.4, 00:11:07, GigabitEthernet0/0
R5#ping 4.4.4.4
!!!!!
Success rate is 100 percent (5/5), round-trip min/avg/max = 1/1/4 ms

R5#ping 44.4.4.4
!!!!!
Success rate is 100 percent (5/5), round-trip min/avg/max = 1/1/4 ms
```

On R4, we'll write an ACL blocking traffic sourced from 30.1.1.0 /24 and destined for 4.4.4.4 /32 and apply said ACL to Fast0/0. The ACL will allow all other traffic.

```
R4(config)#access-list 144 deny ip 30.1.1.0 0.0.0.255 host 4.4.4.4
R4(config)#access-list 144 perm ip any any

R4(config)#int fast 0/0
R4(config-if)#ip access-group 144 in
```

R5 can no longer ping 4.4.4.4 but can still ping 44.4.4.4. Pings to 4.4.4.4 are blocked since both the source and destination IP addresses match the first line of the ACL, and the pings to 172.50.100.4 are permitted because only the source IP address matches the first line.

```
R5#ping 4.4.4.4
U.U.U
Success rate is 0 percent (0/5)


R5#ping 44.4.4.4
!!!!!
Success rate is 100 percent (5/5), round-trip min/avg/max = 1/1/4 ms
```

A quick *show ip access-list* on R4 verifies the reason for the stoppage.

```
R4#show ip access-list
Extended IP access list 144
       10 deny ip 30.1.1.0 0.0.0.255 host 4.4.4.4 (5 matches)
       20 permit ip any any (24 matches)
```

OSPF hello packets are permitted by this ACL, and the matches on the permit line will continue to increment as the neighbors exchange hellos. Here's the output of the same command just a few minutes later:

```
R4#show ip access-list
Extended IP access list 144
        10 deny ip 30.1.1.0 0.0.0.255 host 4.4.4.4 (5 matches)
        20 permit ip any any (34 matches)
```

And that's that!

Named ACLs

We've seen named ACLs mentioned by IOS Help throughout the course, so it's time we have a look at their configuration! The syntax of a named ACL is slightly different than that of a numbered ACL, but the logic is the same as is the use of *host* and *any*. We'll repeat the previous lab but use a named extended ACL.

```
R1(config)#ip access-list ?
      Extended   Extended Access List
      log-upda   Control access list log updates
      loggi      Control access list logging
      resequen   Resequence Access List
      standa     Standard Access List

R1(config)#ip access-list extended ?
   <100-199>     Extended IP access-list number
   <2000-2699>   Extended IP access-list number (expanded range)
   WORD          Access-list name

R1(config)#ip access-list extended NO_56_OUT
R1(config-ext-nacl)#deny ip 175.56.56.0 0.0.0.255 ?
   A.B.C.D  Destination address
   any      Any destination host
   host     A single destination host

R1(config-ext-nacl)#deny ip 175.56.56.0 0.0.0.255 any
R1(config-ext-nacl)#permit ip any any

R1(config)#int fast 0/0
R1(config-if)#ip access-group NO_56_OUT out
```

You can also write a standard named ACL. Just as with numbered standard ACLs, only the source IP address is considered.

```
R1(config)#ip access-list ?
  extended     Extended Access List
  log-update   Control access list log updates
  logging      Control access list logging
  resequence   Resequence Access List
  standard     Standard Access List

R1(config)#ip access-list standard ?
  <1-99>        Standard IP access-list number
  <1300-1999>   Standard IP access-list number (expanded range)
  WORD          Access-list name

R1(config)#ip access-list standard EXAMPLE
R1(config-std-nacl)#deny ?
  Hostname or A.B.C.D Address to match
  any                   Any source host
  host                  A single host address

R1(config-std-nacl)#deny host 10.1.1.1 ?
  log Log matches against this entry
  <cr>

R1(config-std-nacl)#deny host 10.1.1.1
```

Time-Based ACLs

You can block some of the packets all of the time, and all of the packets some of the time. But if you block all of the packets all of the time, you're in big trouble.

—Me

Time-based ACLs allow us to block the specified traffic some of the time, whether "some of the time" be a few hours or a couple of days. The ACL logic remains the same, but we must identify the time range during which the ACL will be active with the *time-range* command. In this lab, we'll allow Telnet access from R5 to R4 from 9:00 a.m. to 5:00 p.m., Monday through Friday. No weekend access!

```
R4(config)#time-range TELNET
R4(config-time-range)#?
Time range configuration commands:
    absolute absolute time and date
    default Set a command to its defaults
    exit Exit from time-range configuration mode
    no Negate a command or set its defaults
    periodic periodic time and date
```

```
R4(config-time-range)#periodic weekdays ?
  hh:mm Starting time

R4(config-time-range)#periodic weekdays 09:00 ?
  to ending day and time

R4(config-time-range)#periodic weekdays 09:00 to ?
  hh:mm Ending time - stays valid until beginning of next minute

R4(config-time-range)#periodic weekdays 09:00 to 17:00 ?
    <cr>

eR4(config-time-range)#periodic weekdays 09:00 to 17:00
```

Apply this time range to an ACL, and then apply the ACL to an interface or lines:

```
R4(config)#access-list 145 permit tcp any any eq telnet ?
  ack          Match on the ACK bit
  dscp         Match packets with given dscp value
  established  Match established connections
  fin          Match on the FIN bit
  log          Log matches against this entry
  log-input    Log matches against this entry, including input interface
  option       Match packets with given IP Options value
  precedence   Match packets with given precedence value
  psh          Match on the PSH bit
  rst          Match on the RST bit
  syn          Match on the SYN bit
  time-range   Specify a time-range
  tos          Match packets with given TOS value
  urg          Match on the URG bit
  <cr>

R4(config)#$ 145 permit tcp any any eq telnet time-range TELNET

R4(config)#line vty 0 4
R4(config-line)#password CCNP
R4(config-line)#login
R4(config-line)#privilege level 15
R4(config-line)#access-class 145 in
```

Verify with *show ip access-list.*

```
R4#show ip access-list
Extended IP access list 145
      10 permit tcp any any eq telnet time-range TELNET (inactive)
```

You might see *(inactive)* next to your time-based ACL and think something's wrong, but all is well. That just means the ACL is not currently being applied because the current time is outside the defined time range. I currently have the router set to a Sunday, so the ACL is doing its job! I'll try to connect to Telnet from R5...

```
R4#show ip access-list
Extended IP access list 145
      10 permit tcp any any eq telnet time-range TELNET (inactive)
```

...and I'll be rejected! Let's head to R4 and set the clock to a Monday.

```
R4#clock set 10:30:00 August 31 2015

R4#show ip access-list
Extended IP access list 145
      10 permit tcp any any eq telnet time-range TELNET (active)
```

The time-based ACL is now active, and the Telnet attempt from R5 is now successful.

```
R5#telnet 30.1.1.4
Trying 30.1.1.4 ... Open


User Access Verification

Password:
R4#
```

A Fundamental Review of Fundamental Passwords

Ah, the ol' *enable password* and *enable secret*! Both passwords protect enable mode, just in case we'd like users to need to know the password to go from here...

```
R1>enable
```

...to here.

```
R1#
```

You can use either, but I know you know the major difference between them!

```
enable secret 5 $1$Uy7m$7T0tTmS4YYLVn1txoRvXa0
enable password CCNA
```

The enable secret is encrypted by default. Not a particularly heavy-duty encryption, mind you, but it's enough to stop someone from looking over your shoulder and seeing the password. And when both passwords are set, which one takes precedence?

```
R1>enable
Password:
Password:
R1#
```

You'll have to take my word that the enable secret takes precedence over the enable password, because the password you enter at the prompt does not appear on the screen. The cursor doesn't even move.

We have a few lines we might like to password protect as well.

```
line con 0
exec-timeout 0 0
logging synchronous
line aux 0
line vty 0 4
```

We need to enable logins and set a password in order to allow Telnet access. The order in which you enter the *login* and *password* commands doesn't matter, so if you see the following when you enter the login command...

```
R4(config)#line vty 0 4
R4(config-line)#login
% Login disabled on line 194, until 'password' is set
% Login disabled on line 195, until 'password' is set
% Login disabled on line 196, until 'password' is set
% Login disabled on line 197, until 'password' is set
% Login disabled on line 198, until 'password' is set
```

...do not panic about *login disabled*. Just set the password, and then *you're* set! Should you enable Telnet login and then forget to set a password, any and all Telnet attempts will fail.

```
R4(config)#line vty 0 4
R4(config-line)#login
% Login disabled on line 194, until 'password' is set
% Login disabled on line 195, until 'password' is set
% Login disabled on line 196, until 'password' is set
% Login disabled on line 197, until 'password' is set
% Login disabled on line 198, until 'password' is set
R4(config-line)#

R5#telnet 30.1.1.4
Trying 30.1.1.4 ... Open
```

```
Password required, but none set

[Connection to 30.1.1.4 closed by foreign host]
```

Let's set a password on R4 and try that again!

```
R4(config-line)#password SPIDERS

R5#telnet 30.1.1.4
Trying 30.1.1.4 ... Open


User Access Verification

Password:
R4>
```

I'm sure you'll agree with me that having a one-size-fits-all password for your VTY lines is a terrible, awful, rotten idea. Instead of using a single password for those lines, we can create a username/password database and have the VTY lines refer to those lines with the *login local* command. This will negate any single password configured directly on the VTY lines. (You can use this username/password database in any number of situations; it's not confined to the VTY lines.)

```
R1(config)#username les password thatcher
R1(config)#username johnny password weaver
R1(config)#username george password becker

R1(config)#line vty 0 4
R1(config-line)#login ?
    local Local password checking
    tacacs     Use tacacs server for password checking
    <cr>

R1(config-line)#login local
```

Now instead of entering a password possibly known by many, the user will need to enter his or her individual username and matching password to gain access via Telnet. I've removed all ACLs from R1, including the one on the VTY lines, and will now attempt to connect to Telnet from 172.12.123.2.

```
line vty 0 4
 password SPIDERS
 login local

R2#telnet 172.12.123.1
Trying 172.12.123.1 ... Open
```

```
User Access Verification

Username: cbryant
Password:
% Login invalid

Username: les
Password:
R1>enable
Password:
R1#
```

I tried to access Telnet with a username/password combo that isn't in the database, and *that* sure didn't work. I then accessed Telnet successfully with a username/password combination that is valid, and I was placed into *user exec* mode. To get into enable mode, I still had to know the enable secret!

By the way, to place incoming Telnet connections straight into enable mode without having to know the enable password, add *privilege 15* to the individual's username/password entry...

```
R1(config)#username les privilege 15 password thatcher
```

...or make that happen for all incoming Telnet connections by configuring *privilege level 15* directly on the VTY lines.

```
R1(config)#line vty 0 4
R1(config-line)#privilege level 15
```

Having switched the VTY lines back to their one-password-fits-all config, I'd like to show you just one little problem with line passwords, the passwords in our username/password database, and the enable password:

```
enable password CCNA

username les privilege 15 password 0 thatcher
username johnny password 0 weaver
username george password 0 becker

line vty 0 4
 privilege level 15
 password SPIDERS
 login
```

They're just sitting there in clear text, waiting to be read right over your shoulder. We can encrypt those passwords with *service password-encryption.*

```
R1#show run
Building configuration...

enable password 7 047828282E

username les privilege 15 password 7 105A011811141A0E1E
username johnny password 7 15050E0D122F39
username george password 7 14151708070138

line vty 0 4
 privilege level 15
 password 7 0538362605697C3A
 login
```

Nice! This isn't exactly the world's strongest encryption—Cisco's own website warns you that it's easily cracked—but it's certainly better than having them sitting there in clear text!

Putting the "Secure" in Secure Shell

There's a huge problem with Telnet in that it sends all data in an unencrypted format, including any and all passwords involved.

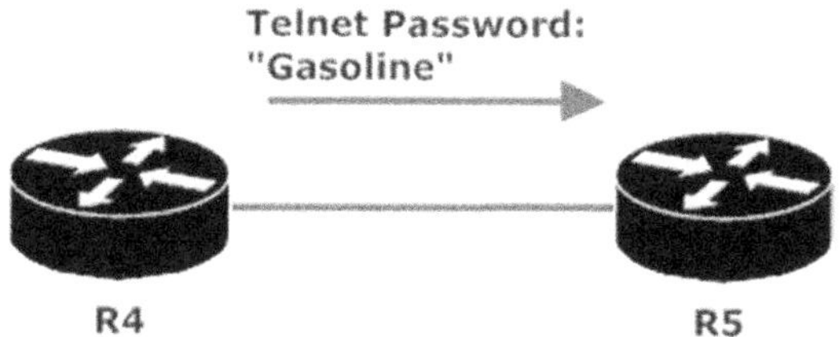

Any would-be network intruder who gets his or her hands on that information is then a "will-be" network intruder, and the trouble has just begun. Secure Shell is basically encrypted Telnet. The basic operation of each is similar, but Secure Shell encrypts all the data involved in the transaction, including the password.

The obvious question is, "Why do we still use Telnet?" Telnet is easier to set up, and that's part of its appeal, but the real issue tends to be with hardware. SSH takes a little more work, which we don't mind, but it may require a hardware upgrade that's not in your budget. Should your routers be up to speed on SSH, you can allow only SSH logins with the *transport input ssh* command on your VTY lines.

```
R1(config-line)#transport input ?
  all       All protocols
  lat       DEC LAT protocol
  mop       DEC MOP Remote Console Protocol
  none      No protocols
  pad       X.3 PAD
  rlogin    Unix rlogin protocol
  ssh       TCP/IP SSH protocol
  telnet    TCP/IP Telnet protocol
  udptn     UDPTN async via UDP protocol
  v120      Async over ISDN

R1(config-line)#transport input ssh
```

At the very least, your SSH config will require a username/password database on the local router. You can set up exterior devices to handle this authentication, including an AAA server. If you're using the local database, configure *login local* on your VTY lines.

You'll also need to specify the router's domain name with *ip domain-name*. Once that's in place, run *crypto key generate rsa*, and you're gold when you see the message regarding SSH being enabled.

```
R1(config)#ip domain-name BRYANTADVANTAGE.COM

R1(config)#crypto key generate rsa
The name for the keys will be: R1.BRYANTADVANTAGE.COM
Choose the size of the key modulus in the range of 360 to 2048 for your
  General Purpose Keys. Choosing a key modulus greater than 512 may take
  a few minutes.

Jul 12 18:59:29.355: %SSH-5-ENABLED: SSH 1.99 has been enabled
```

A quick note before we proceed: There's some cutover between the Switch and Route exams when it comes to SNMP and the Network Time Protocol (NTP). When it comes to NTP, the Route exam seems to be only concerned with securing it. Instead of just telling you how to secure NTP, I've included my full NTP lesson from my Switch book, which is more than enough for Route. I'd rather you knew all about NTP than just how to secure it. Both of the following sections will show configs on L3 switches, and the commands are exactly the same on routers.

In short, I'd rather give you full information on a topic than just a little. Having said that, let's have at it!

Simple Network Management Protocol

The Simple Network Management Protocol (SNMP) is used to carry network management information from one network device to another, and you'll find it in just about every network out there today. An SNMP deployment has three main parts:

- The *SNMP Manager,* the actual monitoring device
- The *SNMP Agents,* the devices being monitored (and running an SNMP instance)
- The *Management Information Base* (MIB), the database on the Agent that contains important information ("variables") about the Agent

SNMP Managers *poll* Agents over UDP port 161, and these messages take the form of GETs and SETs. A "GET" is a request for information...

...and a "SET" is a request from the Manager to the Agent, requesting that a certain variable be set to the value indicated in the SET.

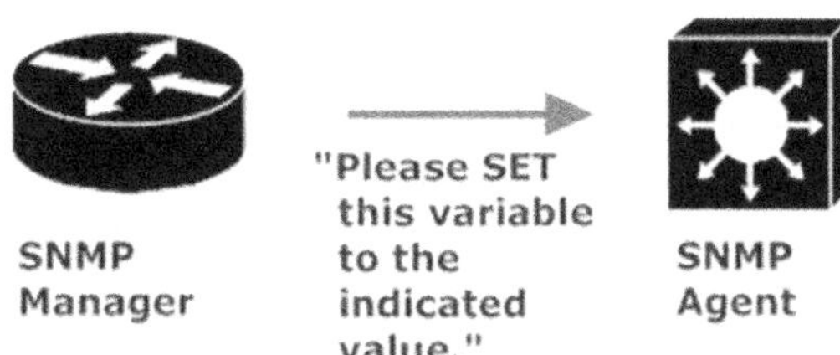

Seems like a good approach, but there's one glaring issue. The only way for the Manager to receive immediate or even near-immediate notice of a critical network event is to poll the Agents quite often, which in turn sucks up bandwidth and is a hit on the Manager's CPU.

Let's say our Manager is polling our Agent every ten minutes regarding one particular variable. Three seconds after the Agent answers one such GET, that variable undergoes a critical change. It would then take nine minutes and fifty-seven seconds for the Manager to find out about the change!

To get a quick notification on such an event without overloading the Manager, we configure *SNMP traps* on the managed devices, allowing the Agents to send a message to the Manager when such a variable changes.

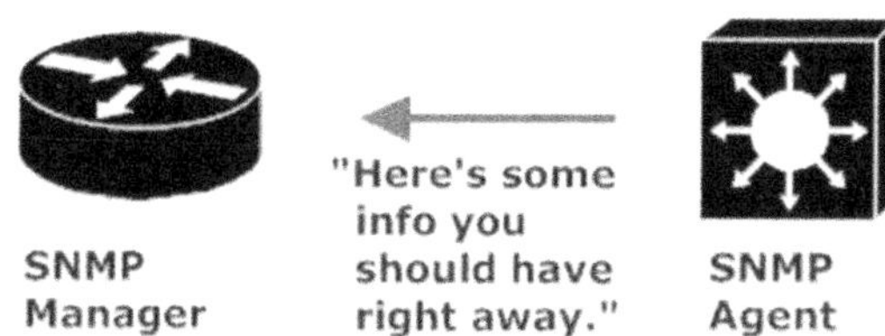

We still have three versions of SNMP out there—versions 1, 2c, and 3—and there are some serious security concerns with the earlier versions. V3 has both authentication and encryption capabilities; the earlier versions do not. For that reason alone, you should use V3 whenever possible, and the use of the other versions should be restricted to allowing read-only access via the use of *community strings.*

SNMP community strings, found in SNMP v1 and 2c, are a kind of password / authority level combination that allow you to set the strings as *read-only* or *read-write.*

```
MLS_1(config)#snmp-server community ?
WORD SNMP community string

MLS_1(config)#snmp-server community CCNP ?
  <1-99>        Std IP accesslist allowing access with this community string
  <1300-1999>   Expanded IP accesslist allowing access with this community
                string
  WORD          Access-list name
  ro            Read-only access with this community string
  rw            Read-write access with this community string
  view          Restrict this community to a named MIB view
  <cr>

MLS_1(config)#snmp-server community CCNP ro ?
    <1-99>      Std IP accesslist allowing access with this community string
    <1300-1999> Expanded IP accesslist allowing access with this community
                string
    WORD        Access-list name
    ipv6        Specify IPv6 Named Access-List
    <cr>

MLS_1(config)#snmp-server community CCNP ro 15
```

This configuration would allow hosts identified by ACL 15 to have read-only access to all SNMP objects specified by this community string.

With SNMP v3, things are much more secure and just a tad more complex. Let's use IOS Help to venture through some of the most long-winded commands you're ever going to see. Let's start with creating an SNMP group and then assigning a user to that group.

```
MLS _ 1(config)#snmp-server group BULLDOGS ?
  v1    group using the v1 security model
  v2c   group using the v2c security model
  v3    group using the User Security Model (SNMPv3)

MLS _ 1(config)#snmp-server group BULLDOGS v3 ?
  auth    group using the authNoPriv Security Level
  noauth  group using the noAuthNoPriv Security Level
  priv    group using SNMPv3 authPriv security level
```

A quick word about those three security levels—they look intimidating, but when you break them down, they're easy to remember.

authNoPriv—You have **auth**entication but no **priv**acy (no encryption).

noAuthNoPriv—You're really asking for it. You have no **auth**entication and no **priv**acy (encryption).

authPriv—Your SNMP packets are **auth**enticated, and **priv**acy is assured via encryption.

```
MLS _ 1(config)#snmp-server group BULLDOGS v3 priv ?
  access    specify an access-list associated with this group
  context   specify a context to associate these views for the group
  match     context name match criteria
  notify    specify a notify view for the group
  read      specify a read view for the group
  write     specify a write view for the group
  <cr>

MLS _ 1(config)#snmp-server group BULLDOGS v3 priv
```

The views mentioned in the last IOS Help readout aren't required, and creating them is out of the exam scope, but I do want you to know the defaults:

- If no read view is defined, all objects can be read.
- If no write view is defined, no objects can be written.
- If no notify view is defined, group members are not sent notifications.

Now let's create our user, using SHA for authentication and AES 128-bit encryption, both excellent choices when your hardware allows them.

```
MLS _ 1(config)#snmp-server user CHRIS ?
  WORD Group to which the user belongs

MLS _ 1(config)#snmp-server user CHRIS BULLDOGS ?
  remote    Specify a remote SNMP entity to which the user belongs
  v1        user using the v1 security model
```

```
  v2c       user using the v2c security model
  v3        user using the v3 security model

MLS _ 1(config)#snmp-server user CHRIS BULLDOGS v3 ?
  access      specify an access-list associated with this group
  auth        authentication parameters for the user
  encrypted   specifying passwords as MD5 or SHA digests
  <cr>

MLS _ 1(config)#snmp-server user CHRIS BULLDOGS v3 auth ?
  md5  Use HMAC MD5 algorithm for authentication
  sha  Use HMAC SHA algorithm for authentication

MLS _ 1(config)#snmp-server user CHRIS BULLDOGS v3 auth sha ?
  WORD  authentication pasword for user

MLS _ 1(config)#snmp-server user CHRIS BULLDOGS v3 auth sha CCNP ?
  access   specify an access-list associated with this group
  priv     encryption parameters for the user
  <cr>

MLS _ 1(config)#snmp-server user CHRIS BULLDOGS v3 auth sha CCNP priv ?
  3des  Use 168 bit 3DES algorithm for encryption
  aes   Use AES algorithm for encryption
  des   Use 56 bit DES algorithm for encryption

MLS _ 1(config)#snmp-server user CHRIS BULLDOGS v3 auth sha CCNP priv aes ?
  128  Use 128 bit AES algorithm for encryption
  192  Use 192 bit AES algorithm for encryption
  256  Use 256 bit AES algorithm for encryption

MLS _ 1(config)#snmp-server user CHRIS BULLDOGS v3 auth sha CCNP priv aes 128 ?
  WORD  privacy pasword for user

MLS _ 1(config)#$S BULLDOGS v3 auth sha CCNP priv aes 128 TIREDOFTYPING ?
  Access   specify an access-list associated with this group
  <cr>

MLS _ 1(config)#$S BULLDOGS v3 auth sha CCNP priv aes 128 TIREDOFTYPING
MLS _ 1(config)#^Z
MLS _ 1#
Mar 26 10:16:25.467: Configuring snmpv3 USM user, persisting snmpEngineBoots.
```

Finally, we'll define the host to which to send traps.

```
MLS _ 1(config)#snmp-server host ?
```

```
WORD                                               IP/IPV6 address of
                                                   SNM notification host
http://<Hostname or A.B.C.D>[:<port number>][/<uri>]   HTTP address of XML
                                                   notification host

MLS _ 1(config)#snmp-server host 10.1.1.3 ?
  WORD      SNMPv1/v2c community string or SNMPv3 user name
  informs   Send Inform messages to this host
  traps     Send Trap messages to this host
  version   SNMP version to use for notification messages
  vrf       VPN Routing instance for this host

MLS _ 1(config)#snmp-server host 10.1.1.3 traps ?
  WORD      SNMPv1/v2c community string or SNMPv3 user name
  Version   SNMP version to use for notification messages

MLS _ 1(config)#snmp-server host 10.1.1.3 traps version ?
  1    Use SNMPv1
  2c   Use SNMPv2c
  3    Use SNMPv3

MLS _ 1(config)#snmp-server host 10.1.1.3 traps version 3 ?
  auth     Use the SNMPv3 authNoPriv Security Level
  noauth   Use the SNMPv3 noAuthNoPriv Security Level
  priv     Use the SNMPv3 authPriv Security Level

MLS _ 1(config)#snmp-server host 10.1.1.3 traps version 3 priv ?
  WORD SNMPv1/v2c community string or SNMPv3 user name

MLS _ 1(config)#snmp-server host 10.1.1.3 traps version 3 priv CHRIS ?

<about 45 options, too many to list here>
  <cr>

MLS _ 1(config)#snmp-server host 10.1.1.3 traps version 3 priv CHRIS
```

Whew! You obviously have to do some serious planning for SNMPv3, including the encryption type and bit level of same, but it pays off in the end with security that's far superior to earlier versions.

The Network Time Protocol

It's vital for our routers and switches to have a central time source that allows our network devices to synchronize their clocks. Doing so allows our *syslog* timestamps to have accurate and synched time throughout the network, making troubleshooting a lot less frustrating. Synched time is critical for digital certificate operation as well. If your certificate is good from 2015–2017, but your device thinks it's 2010, there's a problem!

NTP allows us to specify time sources for our switches and routers, whether that time source be another router in the same network or an external time source.

At the very top of our NTP hierarchy are stratum-0 devices, typically atomic clocks. You can't configure a Cisco router to get its time directly from a stratum-0 server.

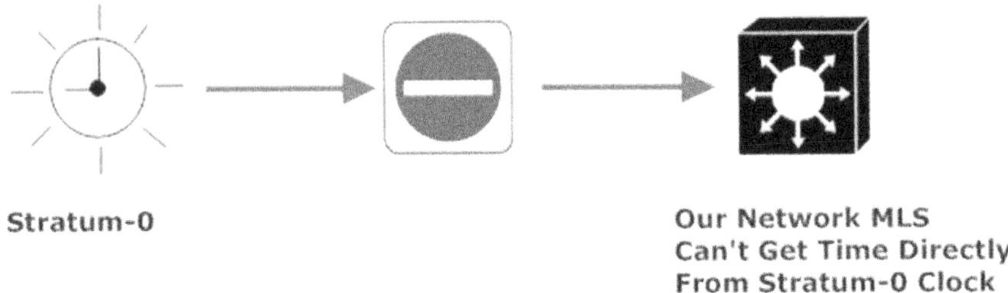

The number following "stratum" in nonstratum-0 devices indicates how many hops away the device is from a stratum-0 device. (And you thought you were done with hops in RIP!)

Stratum-1 servers are generally referred to as "time servers," and we *can* configure a Cisco router to get its time from a stratum-1 device.

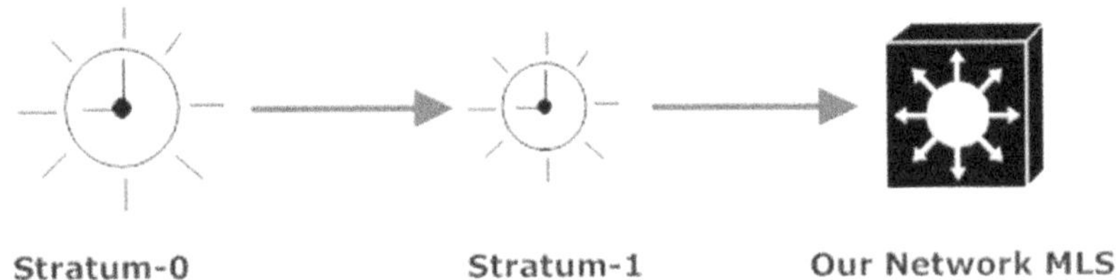

It's strongly recommended that your network's "outside" router receive its time from a public NTP timeserver. For the latest IP addresses of these servers, just run a search on the term *public NTP servers*. Be sure not to block UDP port 123 on that or other routers in your network—that's the port NTP uses.

Cisco routers can serve as NTP servers, clients, or peers. They can also depend on NTP broadcasts for the correct time. The NTP server-client relationship is as you'd expect, with the server giving the correct time to clients.

Clients accept the time-synch message from the server and set their internal clocks accordingly. Clients do *not* send NTP time-synch messages back to the server.

We're not limited to the traditional server/client relationship with NTP. *NTP peers* send NTP messages to each other, and either peer can send time-synch messages to the other.

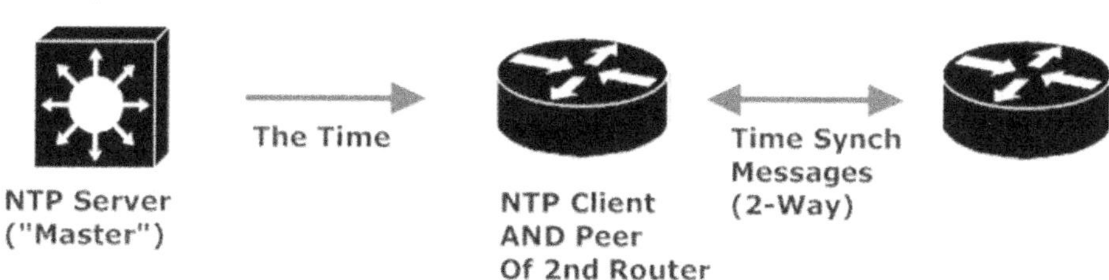

We can choose to run NTP in *broadcast mode* or *multicast mode*. With these methods, the server broadcasts or multicasts its NTP messages, which the clients must be able to receive—otherwise, we're wasting our time!

It's *highly* recommended an NTP public timeserver be used as your NTP Master time source. Should you choose to use one of your network routers as the NTP Master, it's imperative you use NTP authentication and/or ACLs to prevent routers from outside your network from attempting to synch with one of your routers.

In our lab, we'll configure MLS_1 as our NTP Master and a timeserver, with ROUTER_3 configured as a client of MLS_1. As always, the router number serves as the last octet of each IP address.

Let's check the clock on our NTP-Master-to-be:

```
MLS _ 1#show clock
09:25:29.167 EST Wed Mar 25 2015
```

Our *ntp master* options:

```
MLS _ 1(config)#ntp master ?
  <1-15> Stratum number
  <cr>
```

On R3, I'll use *ntp server* to point R3 to this switch as its time source.

```
ROUTER_3(config)#ntp server ?
  A.B.C.D               IP address of peer
  Hostname or A.B.C.D   IP address of supervisor (127.0.0.x)
  WORD                  Hostname of peer
  X:X:X:X::X            IPv6 address of peer
  ip                    Use IP for DNS resolution
  ipv6                  Use IPv6 for DNS resolution
  vrf                   VPN Routing/Forwarding Information

ROUTER_3(config)#ntp server 10.1.1.4
```

The commands *show ntp status* and *show ntp association* verify NTP's operation. There's a lot of information here, and the phrase we're looking for is "clock is synchronized." We're also looking for that asterisk next to the address in *show ntp association*, which indicates the synch is complete. Here's the output from the server's point of view, which includes the reference address 127.127.1.1, indicating the time source is the switch's internal clock.

```
MLS_1#show ntp association

  Address       ref clock     st      when     poll    reach   delay   offset    disp
*~127.127.1.1   .LOCL.         7        8       16      377    0.000    0.000    0.243
* sys.peer, # selected, + candidate, - outlyer, x falseticker, ~ configured

MLS_1#show ntp status
Clock is synchronized, stratum 8, reference is 127.127.1.1
nominal freq is 119.2092 Hz, actual freq is 119.2092 Hz, precision is 2**17
reference time is D8BD46F7.46BF9352 (09:38:47.276 EST Wed Mar 25 2015)
(Output truncated for clarity)
```

And from the client's point of view:

```
ROUTER_3#show ntp status
Clock is synchronized, stratum 9, reference is 10.1.1.4
nominal freq is 250.0000 Hz, actual freq is 250.0000 Hz, precision is 2**24
reference time is D8BD47D4.F3858835 (14:42:28.951 UTC Wed Mar 25 2015)
(Output truncated for clarity)

ROUTER_3#show ntp association

  Address       ref clock     st      when     poll    reach   delay   offset    disp
*~10.1.1.4      127.127.1.1    8       64       64       37    2.348  -66.425    439.77
* sys.peer, # selected, + candidate, - outlyer, x falseticker, ~ configured
```

If we're fortunate and smart enough to have NTP Master redundancy, we can configure our NTP clients to have more than one time server to choose from. We can also prefer one server over the other! Just use multiple *ntp server* commands while also using the *prefer* option to indicate the preferred server.

```
ROUTER_3(config)#ntp server 10.1.1.4 prefer
ROUTER_3(config)#ntp server 10.1.1.7
```

The NTP process likely strikes you as wide open to attack, since the only thing we're really telling the client is, "Hey, here's the IP address of the time server." Let's use NTP authentication to tie things down a bit. We'll enable this feature with *ntp authenticate*, then define a key and link that key to the *ntp server* command.

```
ROUTER_3(config)#ntp authenticate
ROUTER_3(config)#ntp authentication-key ?
    <1-4294967295> Key number

ROUTER_3(config)#ntp authentication-key 1 ?
  md5  MD5 authentication

ROUTER_3(config)#ntp authentication-key 1 md5 ?
  WORD Authentication key

ROUTER_3(config)#ntp authentication-key 1 md5 CCNP
ROUTER_3(config)#ntp trusted-key ?
    <1-4294967295> Key number

ROUTER_3(config)#ntp trusted-key 1
ROUTER_3(config)#ntp server 10.1.1.4 ?
  burst     Send a burst when peer is reachable
  iburst    Send a burst when peer is unreachable
  key       Configure peer authentication key
  maxpoll   Maximum poll interval
  minpoll   Minimum poll interval
  prefer    Prefer this peer when possible
  source    Interface for source address
  version   Configure NTP version
  <cr>

ROUTER_3(config)#ntp server 10.1.1.4 key ?
  <0-4294967295>    Peer key number

ROUTER_3(config)#ntp server 10.1.1.4 key 1
```

We'll need the same commands on the server (except the *ntp server* command, of course!):

```
MLS_1(config)#ntp authentication-key 1 md5 CCNP
MLS_1(config)#ntp authenticate
MLS_1(config)#ntp trusted-key 1
```

Verify NTP authentication with *show ntp association detail.* I've left out most of the output of this command, because when it says "detail," it means detail! The authentication verification is right at the top of the output:

```
ROUTER_3#show ntp association detail
10.1.1.4 configured, authenticated, our_master, sane, valid, stratum 8
ref ID 127.127.1.1      , time D8BE4169.4569D946 (08:27:21.271 UTC Thu Mar 26 2015)
```

That's all well and good, but NTP authentication isn't quite what it seems. I've just added another router to our lab, and it's able to get time from MLS_1 with no problem—and no authentication, either!

```
ROUTER_1(config)#ntp server 10.1.1.4

ROUTER_1#show ntp assoc

  Address      ref clock     st     when    poll    reach   delay   offset    disp
*~10.1.1.4     127.127.1.1    8       26      64       17   2.790    -8.124   939.53
 * sys.peer, # selected, + candidate, - outlyer, x falseticker, ~ configured

ROUTER_1#show ntp assoc detail
10.1.1.4 configured, our_master, sane, valid, stratum 8
ref ID 127.127.1.1      , time D8BE4561.46322015 (08:44:17.274 UTC Thu Mar 26 2015)
our mode client, peer mode server, our poll intvl 64, peer poll intvl 64
```

NTP authentication really just assures the client that it's talking to an NTP server that's under our administrative control. Enabling NTP authentication on the server does *not* require NTP clients to use authentication, as we've seen.

To further protect our NTP deployment, we'll configure an ACL on the server and use *ntp access-group* to apply it to NTP. Our ACL will permit only the source IP address 10.1.1.3 (Router_3), and we'll call that ACL in *ntp access-group.*

```
MLS_1(config)#access-list 22 permit host 10.1.1.3
MLS_1(config)#
MLS_1(config)#ntp access-group ?
  peer          Provide full access
  query-only    Allow only control queries
  serve         Provide server and query access
  serve-only    Provide only server access

MLS_1(config)#ntp access-group serve ?
  <1-99>        Standard IP access list
  <1300-1999>   Standard IP access list (expanded range)
  WORD          Named access list

MLS_1(config)#ntp access-group serve 22
```

debug ntp packets illustrates when MLS_1 receives an NTP message from the permitted IP address of 10.1.1.3, an NTP message is sent in reply. The debug shows an NTP message coming in from 10.1.1.1 as well, but that message is not answered due to the ACL and *ntp access-group* command.

```
MLS _ 1#debug ntp packet
NTP packets debugging is on
NTP message received from 10.1.1.3 on interface 'Vlan13' (10.1.1.4)
NTP message sent to 10.1.1.3, from interface 'Vlan13' (10.1.1.4)
NTP message received from 10.1.1.1 on interface 'Vlan13' (10.1.1.4)
NTP message received from 10.1.1.3 on interface 'Vlan13' (10.1.1.4)
NTP message sent to 10.1.1.3, from interface 'Vlan13' (10.1.1.4)
NTP message received from 10.1.1.1 on interface 'Vlan13' (10.1.1.4)
MLS _ 1#u all
All possible debugging has been turned off
```

While we're here, let's have a look at an NTP deployment using the broadcast model. All previous NTP configs have been removed. R2 is the NTP server, and R4 is the client. As you can see, R4 *needs* to be the client!

```
R2#show clock
*13:50:43.379 UTC Tue Sep 8 2015

R4#show clock
*01:25:52.223 UTC Thu Jan 1 1970
```

We'll set R2 up as a stratum-4 NTP server and then enable NTP broadcasts to be sent on that router's Fast0/0 interface.

```
R2(config)#ntp master 4

R2(config-if)#ntp broadcast ?
  client        Listen to NTP broadcasts
  destination   Configure broadcast destination address
  key           Configure broadcast authentication key
  version       Configure NTP version
  <cr>

R2(config-if)#ntp broadcast
```

With *ntp broadcast client* configured on R4's Fast0/0 interface, we should be able to bring R4 out of the 1970s. Let's run *debug ntp packet* to make sure the server and client are chatting.

```
R4(config)#int fast 0/0
R4(config-if)#ntp broadcast client

R4#debug ntp packet
NTP packets debugging is on
```

```
R4#show ntp assoc

  Address      ref clock     st      when     poll    reach   delay   offset    disp
* sys.peer, # selected, + candidate, - outlyer, x falseticker, ~ configured
R4#
*Jan 1 01:29:27.603: NTP message received from 10.1.1.2 on interface 'FastEther
net0/0' (255.255.255.255).
```

Nothing in *show ntp association* yet, but a message has come in from R2. Let's keep watching:

```
R4#show ntp assoc

  Address      ref clock     st      when     poll    reach   delay   offset    disp
10.1.1.2       .INIT.        16       -        64       0    0.000    0.000   16000.
* sys.peer, # selected, + candidate, - outlyer, x falseticker, ~ configured

*Jan  1 01:30:52.299: NTP message sent to 10.1.1.2, from interface 'FastEthernet
0/0' (10.1.1.4).
*Jan  1 01:30:52.299: NTP message received from 10.1.1.2 on interface 'FastEther
net0/0' (10.1.1.4).
*Jan  1 01:30:54.299: NTP message sent to 10.1.1.2, from interface 'FastEthernet
0/0' (10.1.1.4).
```

The timestamps haven't changed yet, but the exchange of NTP messages is encouraging. A few messages later…

```
Sep  8 14:11:52.088: NTP message received from 10.1.1.2 on interface 'FastEthern
et0/0' (255.255.255.255).
Sep  8 14:12:58.086: NTP message received from 10.1.1.2 on interface 'FastEthern
et0/0' (255.255.255.255).
R4#show ntp assoc

  Address      ref clock     st      when     poll    reach   delay   offset    disp
* 10.1.1.2     127.127.1.1    4        7       64     377    1.908   27.034   0.949
 * sys.peer, # selected, + candidate, - outlyer, x falseticker, ~ configured
```

…success! There's now an asterisk next to the address in the output of *show ntp association*, so we're gold. (No squiggly as in the previous lab, since we didn't manually configure the relationship.) Once the initial conversation between NTP client and server ends, we'll see the timestamps (and clock!) change to the server's time. Also, the client is no longer sending messages to the server; it's strictly the NTP server broadcasting from this point on.

Introduction to NetFlow and Flexible NetFlow

From Cisco's website: "NetFlow is an embedded instrumentation within Cisco IOS Software to characterize network operation."

Translation: "NetFlow lets you know what's happening on your network, both good and bad."

In all seriousness, NetFlow is a very impressive network monitoring tool, and it helps you spot issues before they become serious. Cisco's website lists the following as benefits of NetFlow, and I'm sure you'll agree with me that they are all great things to have.

- Analyze new applications and their network impact
- Reduction in peak WAN traffic
- Troubleshooting and understanding network pain points
- Detection of unauthorized WAN traffic
- Security and anomaly detection
- Validation of QoS parameters

The name is the recipe yet again as NetFlow analyzes flows of network traffic as they pass through a NetFlow-enabled router. NetFlow uses the following seven IP packet values to determine if traffic belongs to a particular flow, with the information regarding each flow kept in the NetFlow cache. The direction of the traffic flow is unchanged—NetFlow observes and reports but does not change anything.

- Source and destination IP address
- Source and destination port numbers
- Device interface upon which the packet was received
- L3 protocol type
- Class of Service (CoS)

The information collected by NetFlow can be accessed via *show* commands at the command-line interface or by sending the information to a NetFlow collector (a server) and accessing it there. We'll work with NetFlow at the command line and send the flow information to 172.12.123.1. First up, enable NetFlow on the Fast0/0 interface via the classic method:

```
R2(config)#int fast 0/0
R2(config-if)#ip route-cache ?
  cef             Enable Cisco Express Forwarding
  flow            Enable Flow fast-switching cache
  policy          Enable fast-switching policy cache for outgoing packets
  same-interface  Enable fast-switching on the same interface
  <cr>

R2(config-if)#ip route-cache flow
```

If there's a classic method, there must be a newer one! If your router is running IOS 12.2(14) S or later or 12.2(15) or later, you can use the *ip flow ingress* or *ip flow egress* command as shown here:

```
R2(config-if)#ip flow ?
  Egress          Enable outbound NetFlow
  Ingress         Enable inbound NetFlow
  Monitor         Apply a Flow Monitor to this interface
```

My router is running an IOS version that allowed it to run *ip flow ingress* (obviously!). It also allowed me to run *ip route-cache flow*. For your exam, I'd be familiar with both ways to enable NetFlow. The only real difference between the two is the newer *ip flow* command can be run on subinterfaces, while *ip route-cache flow* must go on the physical interface.

There's an important difference in requirements between *ip flow ingress* and *ip flow egress*. *ip flow egress* requires CEF or distributed CEF to be enabled both globally and on the interface...

```
R2(config)#ip cef
R2(config)#int fast 0/0
R2(config-if)#ip route-cache ?
  cef             Enable Cisco Express Forwarding
  flow            Enable Flow fast-switching cache
  policy          Enable fast-switching policy cache for outgoing packets
  same-interface  Enable fast-switching on the same interface
  <cr>

   R2(config-if)#ip route-cache cef
```

...while *ip flow ingress* requires CEF, distributed CEF, or fast switching (*ip route-cache*) to be enabled. If you're not getting the desired NetFlow info, *the first thing I'd check is whether CEF is on...*

```
R2#show ip cef
%IPv4 CEF not running
```

...or not!

ip flow-export destination command exports the NetFlow data to the IP address we specify.

```
R2(config)#ip flow-export ?
  Destination     Specify the Destination IP address
  interface-names Export interface names
  source          Specify the interface for source address
  template        Specify the template specific configurations
  version         Specify the version number
```

The other values are all optional. You can send the information to the same IP address on two UDP ports, but the router will call the duplicate IP address entry to your attention.

```
R2(config)#ip flow-export destination 172.12.123.1 9980
R2(config)#ip flow-export destination 172.12.123.1 9981
%Warning: Second destination address is the same as previous address 172.12.123.
1
```

Verify with *show ip flow export*. This is also a handy command to spot export packets being dropped for various reasons.

```
R2#show ip flow export
  Flow export v1 is enabled for main cache
  Export source and destination details :
  VRF ID : Default
    Destination(1)       172.12.123.1 (9980)
    Destination(2)       172.12.123.1 (9981)
  Version 1 flow records
  0 flows exported in 0 udp datagrams
  0 flows failed due to lack of export packet
  0 export packets were sent up to process level
  0 export packets were dropped due to no fib
  0 export packets were dropped due to adjacency issues
  0 export packets were dropped due to fragmentation failures
  0 export packets were dropped due to encapsulation fixup failures
```

NetFlow is a great feature, but there may be times that you don't want to analyze all of the traffic of a particular flow. Perhaps you'd like to sample the flow instead. That's where *NetFlow Random Sampling* comes in. With this feature, we'll create a NetFlow sampler map and apply it to an interface. This is just about the easiest "map" of any kind you'll ever write!

```
R2(config)#flow-sampler-map CCNP
R2(config-sampler)#?
Flow sampler configuration commands:
  exit      Exit from flow-sampler-map configuration mode
  mode      Mode of packet sampling for netflow processing

R2(config-sampler)#mode ?
  random    Random mode of sampling

R2(config-sampler)#mode random ?
  one-out-ofSelect one packet out of

R2(config-sampler)#mode random one-out-of ?
  <1-65535> number of sequential packets to select one packet from
```

```
R2(config-sampler)#mode random one-out-of 100 ?
  <cr>

R2(config-sampler)#mode random one-out-of 100
```

Not many options there! With this config, one out of every hundred packets will be sampled, and there will be no pattern to the sampling. One packet from 1–100 will be sampled, then 101–200, 201–300, and so forth. Apply it to the interface with *flow-sampler* and verify with *show flow-sampler.*

```
R2(config)#int serial 0/1/0
R2(config-if)#flow-sampler CCNP

R2#show flow-sampler

Sampler : CCNP, id : 1, packets matched : 0, mode : random sampling mode
  sampling interval is : 100
```

NetFlow is a powerful tool, but it is a tad inflexible at times. Perhaps we don't want to analyze every packet of a particular flow. Maybe we'd like to customize the NetFlow experience, if you will. Welcome to...

Flexible NetFlow

Flexible NetFlow uses the concept of traffic flows just like NetFlow but with greater flexibility (hence the name!). Flexible NetFlow allows customization of both the data analysis and data export processes as well as offering greater accounting capabilities than does "regular" NetFlow.

CEF or dCEF must be running in order to run Flexible NetFlow.

Flexible NetFlow has three main components, and all three do exactly what they sound like they do! *Flow monitors* are applied at the interface level and carry out the actual network monitoring and analysis. *Flow exporters*, well, they export the flow (!) to the collection device. The *flow sampler* determines how many packets are actually analyzed, which lowers the otherwise *massive* hit Flexible NetFlow delivers to our router resources when every packet is analyzed. Here's a sample flow sampler config:

```
R2(config)#sampler CCNP
R2(config-sampler)#mode ?
  deterministic   Deterministic mode of sampling
  random          Random mode of sampling

R2(config-sampler)#mode random ?
  <1-1>  number of packets to select per window

R2(config-sampler)#mode random 1 ?
  out-of  Select M packets out of an N packet window
```

```
R2(config-sampler)#mode random 1 out-of ?
  <2-32768>  window size to select packets from

R2(config-sampler)#mode random 1 out-of 10 ?
  <cr>

R2(config-sampler)#mode random 1 out-of 10
R2(config-sampler)#description sampling 10% of packets
```

After naming the sampler, you must choose either the deterministic or random mode of sampling. *Deterministic* means the same packet placement is sampled each time around; for example, if packet 1 is sampled here, then packets 11, 21, 31, 41, and so forth would also be sampled. Random means just that; a packet from 1–10 will be sampled, then a packet from 10–20, 20–30, 30–40, and onward. Verify the sample config with *show sampler.*

```
R2#show sampler
Sampler CCNP:
  ID:              1
  export ID:       0
  Description:     sampling 10% of packets
  Type:            random
  Rate:            1 out of 10
  Samples:         0
  Requests:        0
  Users (0):
```

Unicast Reverse Path Forwarding

Man, that name has *everything.* We got unicasts, we got something going in reverse, and then we got forwarding! This should be something!

Actually, it is something, and something you shouldn't get confused with plain old *reverse path forwarding* (RPF). RPF is a multicasting feature, and Unicast RPF is, well, a unicast feature. Unicast RPF enables a router to verify an incoming packet by ensuring its source IP address is reachable.

Unicast RPF will use its FIB to perform this check, so you know what that means...

```
R1(config)#ip cef
```

Cisco Express Forwarding must be up and running before you even get Unicast RPF started! After that, your choice is between *loose* and *strict* mode. With loose mode, the router will only check to be sure the source IP address of the incoming packet is reachable.

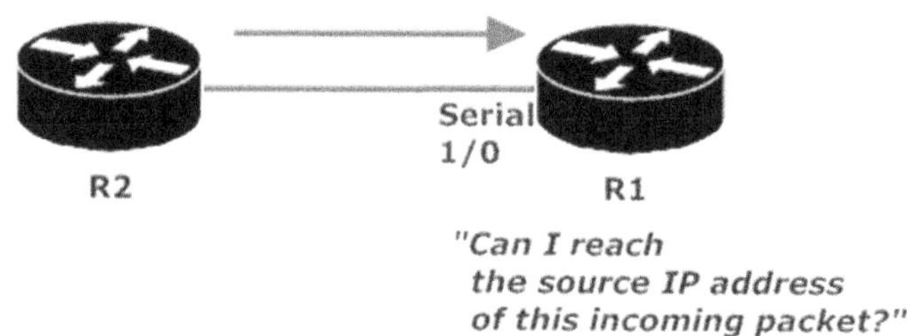

With strict mode, the verification is much tighter. The router must consider the source IP to be reachable *by the same interface the packet rode in on.*

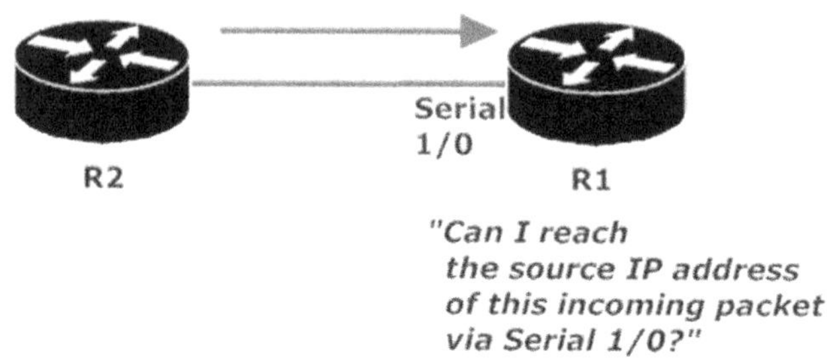

For either mode, the command is *ip verify unicast source reachable-via*. Follow that with *any* for loose mode and *rx* for strict mode. There was an *ip verify unicast reverse-path* command that's still present on many routers, but as IOS Help notes, that's the old command format.

```
R1(config)#int serial 1/0
R1(config-if)#ip verify unicast ?
  reverse-path  Reverse path validation of source address (old command format)
  source        Validation of source address

R1(config-if)#ip verify unicast source ?
  reachable-via  Specify reachability check to apply to the source address

R1(config-if)#ip verify unicast source reachable-via ?
   any  Source is reachable via any interface
   rx   Source is reachable via interface on which packet was received
```

Before we run a lab with this feature, check out *these* interesting options, particularly the bottom two.

```
R1(config-if)#ip verify unicast source reachable-via rx ?
  <1-199>          A standard IP access list number
  <1300-2699>      A standard IP expanded access list number
  allow-default    Allow default route to match when checking source address
  allow-self-ping  Allow router to ping itself (opens vulnerability in
                   verification)
```

The *allow-default* option exists because the default behavior of Unicast RPF is to *drop* packets that could meet verification only through the use of a default route. The *allow-self-ping* option means just what it says, but when IOS Help says "opens vulnerability in verification," I'd think thrice about using it.

We'll test the basic command and the *allow-default* option with this network:

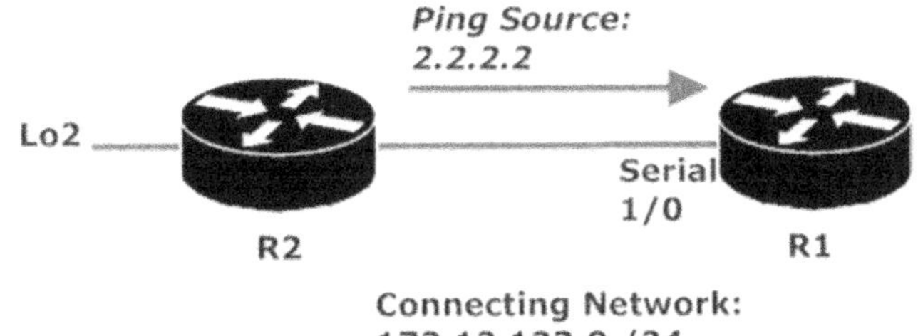

R2 has a loopback interface with the IP address 2.2.2.2, and we'll source the pings from that address to 172.12.123.1, R1's Serial 1/0 interface. Right now, R1 has no entry in its FIB for 2.2.2.2, but it *does* have a default route using 172.12.123.2 as the next-hop address.

```
R1#show ip cef
Prefix              Next Hop        Interface
0.0.0.0/0           172.12.123.2    Serial1/0
0.0.0.0/8           drop
0.0.0.0/32          receive
127.0.0.0/8         drop
(output truncated)
```

No trouble pinging 172.12.123.1 from 2.2.2.2...for now.

```
R2#ping 172.12.123.1 source 2.2.2.2
Packet sent with a source address of 2.2.2.2
!!!!!
Success rate is 100 percent (5/5), round-trip min/avg/max = 64/64/68 ms
```

Let's put Unicast RPF into action on R1's Serial 1/0 interface with the *any* option.

```
R1(config)#int serial 1/0
R1(config-if)#ip verify ?
  unicast   Enable per packet validation for unicast

R1(config-if)#ip verify unicast source ?
  reachable-via   Specify reachability check to apply to the source address

R1(config-if)#ip verify unicast source reachable-via ?
  any   Source is reachable via any interface
  rx    Source is reachable via interface on which packet was received
```

```
R1(config-if)#ip verify unicast source reachable-via any
```

Verify with *show cef interface.*

```
R1#show cef interface serial 1/0
Serial1/0 is up (if_number 6)
  Corresponding hwidb fast_if_number 6
  Corresponding hwidb firstsw->if_number 6
  Internet address is 172.12.123.1/24
  ICMP redirects are always sent
  Per packet load-sharing is disabled
  IP unicast RPF check is enabled
  (output truncated)
```

Let's send pings from R2!

```
R2#ping 172.12.123.1 source 2.2.2.2
Packet sent with a source address of 2.2.2.2
.....
Success rate is 0 percent (0/5)
```

The same pings that worked a few minutes ago now failed. We certainly have a good idea why, but just to verify that verification failed, let's run *show ip interface* on R1. This is a *seriously* verbose command, so let's use a little filtering so we can find the chase and cut right to it.

```
R1#show ip interface serial 1/0 | ?
  append    Append redirected output to URL (URLs supporting append operation
            only)
  begin     Begin with the line that matches
  exclude   Exclude lines that match
  include   Include lines that match
  redirect  Redirect output to URL
  section   Filter a section of output
  tee       Copy output to URL

R1#show ip interface serial 1/0 | include verification
5 verification drops
0 suppressed verification drops
```

You can see the number of verification drops on the router as a whole with *show ip traffic.*

```
R1#show ip traffic
IP statistics:
  Rcvd:  13831 total, 13816 local destination
         0 format errors, 0 checksum errors, 0 bad hop count
         2 unknown protocol, 0 not a gateway
```

```
        0 security failures, 0 bad options, 0 with options
  Opts: 0 end, 0 nop, 0 basic security, 0 loose source route
        0 timestamp, 0 extended security, 0 record route
        0 stream ID, 0 strict source route, 0 alert, 0 cipso, 0 ump
        0 other
  Frags: 0 reassembled, 0 timeouts, 0 couldn't reassemble
        0 fragmented, 0 fragments, 0 couldn't fragment
  Bcast: 13680 received, 16 sent
  Mcast: 0 received, 0 sent
  Sent:  132 generated, 0 forwarded
  Drop:  29 encapsulation failed, 0 unresolved, 0 no adjacency
        0 no route, 5 unicast RPF, 0 forced drop
```

Those five pings were definitely dropped due to failing verification, and we know why—by default, Unicast RPF doesn't allow the use of a default route to allow a packet to pass verification. To change that, we'll use the *allow-default* option.

```
R1(config-if)#ip verify unicast source reachable-via any allow-default

R2#ping 172.12.123.1 source 2.2.2.2
Packet sent with a source address of 2.2.2.2
!!!!!
Success rate is 100 percent (5/5), round-trip min/avg/max = 64/64/68 ms
```

The pings now zing right through!

The IP Helper Address Command

Cisco routers can't forward broadcasts, but this command enables a router to take an incoming UDP broadcast and forward it in unicast fashion to the address specified in the command. The *ip helper-address* command must be configured on the interface *receiving* the broadcasts that need forwarding.

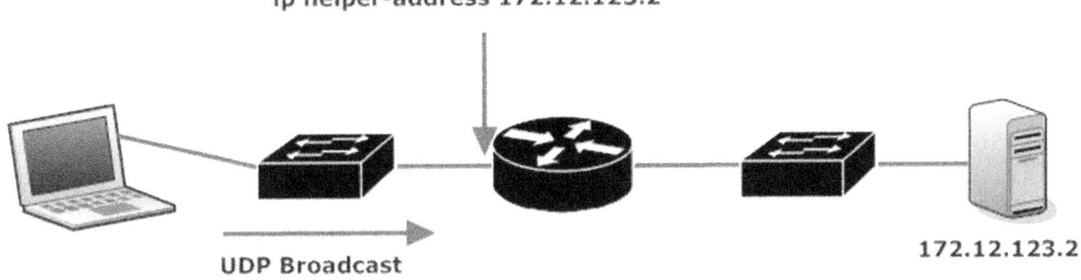

```
R1(config)#int fast 0/0
R1(config-if)#ip helper-address 172.12.123.2
```

Verify with *show ip interface*. You'll see the helper address near the top of this very long-winded show command.

```
R1#show ip interface
FastEthernet0/0 is up, line protocol is up
  Internet address is 10.1.1.1/24
  Broadcast address is 255.255.255.255
  Address determined by setup command
  MTU is 1500 bytes
  Helper address is 172.12.123.2
(output truncated)
```

This command is often used to allow a network segment with no DHCP server to successfully obtain IP addressing from a DHCP server on another segment. By default, this command actually forwards eight UDP broadcasts, and 'tis a good idea to know them all.

- TIME 37
- TACACS 49
- DNS 53
- BOOTP (DHCP Server) 67
- BOOTP (DHCP Client) 68
- TFTP 69
- NetBIOS Name Service 137
- NetBIOS Datagram Service 138

If the UDP broadcast that needs help isn't in that list, add it with the *ip forward-protocol udp* command. To remove a broadcast type from the list—you guessed it!—run *no ip forward-protocol*. This one's a global command, not an interface-level command. IOS Help will show you some of the more common UDP port numbers, but this is not an all-inclusive list.

```
R1(config)#ip forward-protocol udp ?
  <0-65535>       Port number
  biff            Biff (mail notification, comsat, 512)
  bootpc          Bootstrap Protocol (BOOTP) client (68)
  bootps          Bootstrap Protocol (BOOTP) server (67)
  discard         Discard (9)
  dnsix           DNSIX security protocol auditing (195)
  domain          Domain Name Service (DNS, 53)
  echo            Echo (7)
  isakmp          Internet Security Association and Key Management Protocol (500)
```

```
  mobile-ip       Mobile IP registration (434)
  nameserver      IEN116 name service (obsolete, 42)
  netbios-dgm     NetBios datagram service (138)
  netbios-ns      NetBios name service (137)
  netbios-ss      NetBios session service (139)
  non500-isakmp   Internet Security Association and Key Management Protocol
                  (4500)
  ntp             Network Time Protocol (123)
  pim-auto-rp     PIM Auto-RP (496)
  rip             Routing Information Protocol (router, in.routed, 520)
  snmp            Simple Network Management Protocol (161)
  snmptrap        SNMP Traps (162)
  sunrpc          Sun Remote Procedure Call (111)
  syslog          System Logger (514)
  tacacs          TAC Access Control System (49)
  talk            Talk (517)
  tftp            Trivial File Transfer Protocol (69)
  time            Time (37)
  who             Who service (rwho, 513)
  xdmcp           X Display Manager Control Protocol (177)
  <cr>
```

And speaking of port numbers...

The IP HTTP Secure-Port Command

We're saving most of the http secure configs and commands for your CCNA Security studies, but you should know how to view your router's current settings.

```
R1#show ip http server ?
  all             HTTP server all information
  connection      HTTP server connection information
  history         HTTP server history information
  secure          HTTP secure server status information
  session-module  HTTP server application session module information
  statistics      HTTP server statistics information
  status          HTTP server status information

R1#show ip http server secure ?
status Display HTTP secure server status

R1#show ip http server secure status
HTTP secure server status: Enabled
HTTP secure server port: 443
HTTP secure server ciphersuite: 3des-ede-cbc-sha des-cbc-sha rc4-128-md5 rc4-128
```

```
-sha
HTTP secure server client authentication: Disabled
HTTP secure server trustpoint:
HTTP secure server active session modules: ALL
```

You may have used a nondefault port number to SSH to a router, but have you ever changed the default port number on your own router? Here's how:

```
R1(config)#ip http secure-port ?
  443             Default secure port
  <1025-65535>    Secure port number range
```

ip http secure-port is kind enough to remind us of good ol' port 443, and on the occasions where you'll change this port, you can't set it to one of the well-known port numbers.

And yes, I know you know the well-known port numbers are 0–1024. You should also find the addresses in this ACL familiar:

```
R1(config)#access-list 111 deny ip 10.0.0.0 0.255.255.255 any
R1(config)#access-list 111 deny ip 172.16.0.0 0.15.255.255 any
R1(config)#access-list 111 deny ip 192.168.0.0 0.0.255.255 any
R1(config)#access-list 111 permit ip any any
```

The first three lines of that ACL deny the RFC 1918 private addresses, and this is an excellent ACL to place on your "outside" interface; that is, the interface on your router that's facing the outside world. You likely shouldn't use it on a network's internal routers, since you're probably using some of these addresses on your internal subnets!

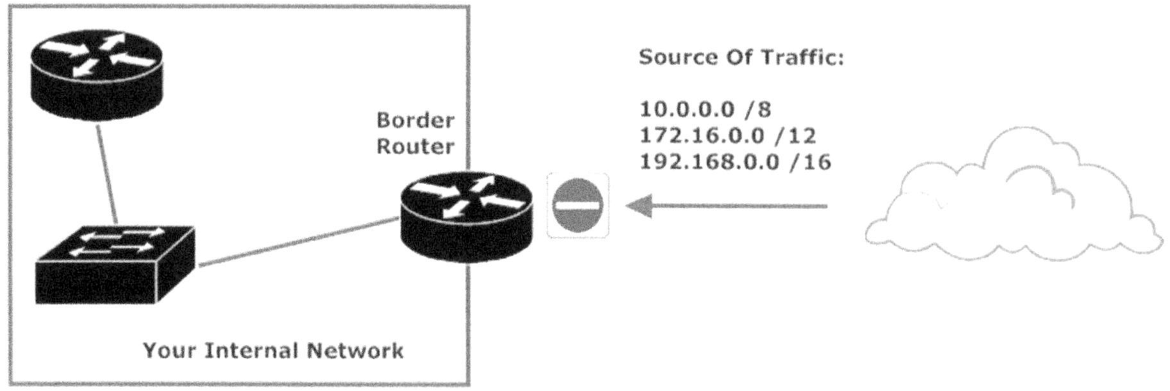

Giving debug ip packet a Little SUJ (Shut-Up Juice)

The *debug ip packet* command is a great t-shooting tool, but it gives you so much information that it can be hard to spot the information you need. On top of that, running this command in a production network (and some larger lab environments) can overwhelm the router to the point where the router cannot do its job. Here's the output of *show ip route* on R1, which at this point has a few OSPF adjacencies but isn't sending or receiving production traffic.

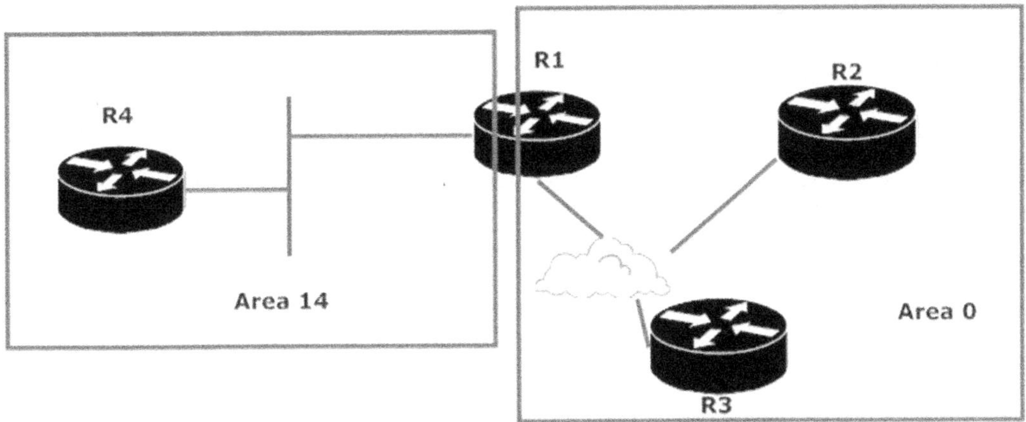


```
R1#debug ip packet
IP packet debugging is on
R1#
*Aug 20 07:35:57: IP: s=10.1.1.1 (local), d=224.0.0.5 (FastEthernet0/0), len
80, sending broad/multicast
*Aug 20 07:36:01: IP: s=10.1.1.4 (FastEthernet0/0), d=224.0.0.5, len 80, rcvd 0
*Aug 20 07:36:05: IP: s=172.12.123.3 (Serial1/0), d=172.12.123.1, len 80, rcvd 0
*Aug 20 07:36:07: IP: s=10.1.1.1 (local), d=224.0.0.5 (FastEthernet0/0), len
80, sending broad/multicast
*Aug 20 07:36:11: IP: s=10.1.1.4 (FastEthernet0/0), d=224.0.0.5, len 80, rcvd 0
*Aug 20 07:36:17: IP: s=10.1.1.1 (local), d=224.0.0.5 (FastEthernet0/0), len
80, sending broad/multicast
*Aug 20 07:36:20: IP: s=172.12.123.2 (Serial1/0), d=172.12.123.1, len 80, rcvd 0
*Aug 20 07:36:21: IP: s=10.1.1.4 (FastEthernet0/0), d=224.0.0.5, len 80, rcvd 0
*Aug 20 07:36:21: IP: s=172.12.123.1 (local), d=172.12.123.2 (Serial1/0), len 84,
sending
*Aug 20 07:36:21: IP: s=172.12.123.1 (local), d=172.12.123.3 (Serial1/0), len 84,
sending
*Aug 20 07:36:27: IP: s=10.1.1.1 (local), d=224.0.0.5 (FastEthernet0/0), len
80, sending broad/multicast
```

Mix a ping or two in there, and you have a *lot* of debugging going on!

```
R1#ping 10.1.1.4

Type escape sequence to abort.
Sending 5, 100-byte ICMP Echos to 10.1.1.4, timeout is 2 seconds:
!!!!!
Success rate is 100 percent (5/5), round-trip min/avg/max = 4/4/4 ms
R1#
*Aug 20 07:38:25: IP: s=10.1.1.4 (FastEthernet0/0), d=224.0.0.5, len 80, rcvd 0
```

```
*Aug 20 07:38:25: IP: tableid=0, s=10.1.1.1 (local), d=10.1.1.4 (FastEtherne
t0/0), routed via FIB
*Aug 20 07:38:25: IP: s=10.1.1.1 (local), d=10.1.1.4 (FastEthernet0/0), len
100, sending
*Aug 20 07:38:25: IP: tableid=0, s=10.1.1.4 (FastEthernet0/0), d=10.1.1.1 (F
astEthernet0/0), routed via RIB
*Aug 20 07:38:25: IP: s=10.1.1.4 (FastEthernet0/0), d=10.1.1.1 (FastEthernet
0/0), len 100, rcvd 3
*Aug 20 07:38:25: IP: tableid=0, s=10.1.1.1 (local), d=10.1.1.4 (FastEtherne
t0/0), routed via FIB
*Aug 20 07:38:25: IP: s=10.1.1.1 (local), d=10.1.1.4 (FastEthernet0/0), len
100, sending
*Aug 20 07:38:25: IP: tableid=0, s=10.1.1.4 (FastEthernet0/0), d=10.1.1.1 (F
astEthernet0/0), routed via RIB
*Aug 20 07:38:25: IP: s=10.1.1.4 (FastEthernet0/0), d=10.1.1.1 (FastEthernet
0/0), len 100, rcvd 3
*Aug 20 07:38:25: IP: tableid=0, s=10.1.1.1 (local), d=10.1.1.4 (FastEtherne
t0/0),
R1# routed via FIB
*Aug 20 07:38:25: IP: s=10.1.1.1 (local), d=10.1.1.4 (FastEthernet0/0), len
100, sending
```

On top of slamming the router, you're gonna go *blind* looking for a particular source or destination of traffic in that output. To specify the source or destination of traffic shown by *debug ip packet*, write an ACL identifying that traffic, and apply it when you write the *debug ip packet* command. We'll demo this with an ACL permitting traffic sourced *or* destined for 10.1.1.4. Be sure to run *show ip access-list* before writing this ACL, particularly at a client site.

```
R1#show ip access-list

R1#
```

There are no ACLs on this router, so we're clear to use any number we like.

```
R1(config)#access-list 124 permit ip host 10.1.1.4 any
R1(config)#access-list 124 permit ip any host 10.1.1.4
```

The first line permits traffic sourced from 10.1.1.4, and the second line permits traffic destined for 10.1.1.4. Now to debug!

```
R1#debug ip packet ?
  <1-199>        Access list
  <1300-2699>    Access list (expanded range)
  Detail         Print more debugging detail
  <cr>
```

```
R1#debug ip packet 124
IP packet debugging is on for access list 124

R1(config)#access-list 124 permit ip any host 10.1.1.4
R1(config)#access-list 124 permit ip host 10.1.1.4 any

R1#debug ip packet ?
  <1-199>         Access list
  <1300-2699>     Access list (expanded range)
  Detail          Print more debugging detail
  <cr>

R1#debug ip packet 124 ?
detail Print more debugging detail
<cr>

R1#debug ip packet 124
IP packet debugging is on for access list 124

*Aug 20 07:46:34: IP: s=10.1.1.4 (FastEthernet0/0), d=224.0.0.5, len 80, rcvd 0
*Aug 20 07:46:44: IP: s=10.1.1.4 (FastEthernet0/0), d=224.0.0.5, len 80, rcvd 0
*Aug 20 07:46:53: IP: s=10.1.1.4 (FastEthernet0/0), d=224.0.0.5, len 80, rcvd 0
*Aug 20 07:47:03: IP: s=10.1.1.4 (FastEthernet0/0), d=224.0.0.5, len 80, rcvd 0
```

We see the incoming OSPF hellos from R4 but not the OSPF hellos going from R1 to R4, since those have a destination address of 224.0.0.5. No traffic involving 172.12.123.2 or 172.12.123.3 is shown.

Let's send a ping from R1 to R4 and see what we see.

```
R1#ping 10.1.1.4

Type escape sequence to abort.
Sending 5, 100-byte ICMP Echos to 10.1.1.4, timeout is 2 seconds:
!!!!!
Success rate is 100 percent (5/5), round-trip min/avg/max = 4/4/4 ms
R1#
*Aug 20 07:47:12: IP: tableid=0, s=10.1.1.1 (local), d=10.1.1.4 (FastEtherne
t0/0), routed via FIB
*Aug 20 07:47:12: IP: s=10.1.1.1 (local), d=10.1.1.4 (FastEthernet0/0), len
100, sending
*Aug 20 07:47:12: IP: tableid=0, s=10.1.1.4 (FastEthernet0/0), d=10.1.1.1 (F
astEthernet0/0), routed via RIB
*Aug 20 07:47:12: IP: s=10.1.1.4 (FastEthernet0/0), d=10.1.1.1 (FastEthernet
0/0), len 100, rcvd 3
*Aug 20 07:47:12: IP: tableid=0, s=10.1.1.1 (local), d=10.1.1.4 (FastEtherne
t0/0), routed via FIB
```

```
*Aug 20 07:47:12: IP: s=10.1.1.1 (local), d=10.1.1.4 (FastEthernet0/0), len
100, sending
*Aug 20 07:47:12: IP: tableid=0, s=10.1.1.4 (FastEthernet0/0), d=10.1.1.1 (F
astEthernet0/0), routed via RIB
*Aug 20 07:47:12: IP: s=10.1.1.4 (FastEthernet0/0), d=10.1.1.1 (FastEthernet
0/0), len 100, rcvd 3
*Aug 20 07:47:12: IP: tableid=0, s
R1#=10.1.1.1 (local), d=10.1.1.4 (FastEthernet0/0), routed via FIB
*Aug 20 07:47:12: IP: s=10.1.1.1 (local), d=10.1.1.4 (FastEthernet0/0), len
100, sending
*Aug 20 07:47:12: IP: tableid=0, s=10.1.1.4 (FastEthernet0/0), d=10.1.1.1 (F
astEthernet0/0), routed via RIB
*Aug 20 07:47:12: IP: s=10.1.1.4 (FastEthernet0/0), d=10.1.1.1 (FastEthernet
0/0), len 100, rcvd 3
*Aug 20 07:47:12: IP: tableid=0, s=10.1.1.1 (local), d=10.1.1.4 (FastEtherne
t0/0), routed via FIB
*Aug 20 07:47:12: IP: s=10.1.1.1 (local), d=10.1.1.4 (FastEthernet0/0), len
100, sending
*Aug 20 07:47:12: IP: tableid=0, s=10.1.1.4 (FastEthernet0/0), d=10.1.1.1 (F
astEthernet0/0), routed via RIB
*Aug 20 07:47:12: IP: s=10.1.1.4 (FastEthernet0/0), d=10.1.1.1 (FastEthernet
0/0), len 100, rcvd 3
*Aug 20 07:47:12: IP: tableid=0, s=10.1.1.1 (local), d=10.1.1.4 (FastEtherne
t0/0), routed via FIB
*Aug 20 07:47:12: IP: s=10.1.1.1 (local), d=10.1.1.4 (FastEthernet0/0), len
100, sending
*Aug 20 07:47:12: IP: tableid=0, s=10.1.1.4 (FastEthernet0/0), d=10.1.1.1 (F
astEthernet0/0), routed via RIB
*Aug 20 07:47:12: IP: s=10.1.1.4 (FastEthernet0/0), d=10.1.1.1 (FastEthernet
0/0), len 100, rcvd 3
*Aug 20 07:47:12: IP: s=10.1.1.4 (FastEthernet0/0), d=224.0.0.5, len 80, rcv
d 0
```

This is a *great* way to debug a ping in a production network without getting a bunch of debug results you don't want. As always, you should turn off all debugs that you turned on before you leave, and that includes getting rid of any ACLs you used during the debug process. Removing the ACL you used should turn debugging off...

```
R1(config)#no access-list 124.
IP packet debugging is off
Turning off all possible debugging on ACL 124
```

...but verify with *show debug* and *show ip access-list.*

```
R1#show debug

R1#show ip access-list
```

You're good to go! But before we do just that, I want to answer a question I know a bunch of you are asking right now: "Hey, what kind of details do I get with *show ip debug detail*?"

```
R1#debug ip packet ?
  <1-199>        Access list
  <1300-2699>    Access list (expanded range)
  detail         Print more debugging detail
  <cr>

R1#debug ip packet 124 ?
  Detail   Print more debugging detail
  <cr>
```

Let's find out! I put ACL 124 back into place (not shown) and ran *debug ip packet 124 detail...*

```
R1#debug ip packet 124 ?
  detail   Print more debugging detail
  <cr>

R1#debug ip packet 124 detail
IP packet debugging is on (detailed) for access list 124
```

...and the truth is, you're not getting a ton of extra detail. You'll see some extra information regarding ICMP types and protocol numbers, but that's about it, as shown in this partial output of *debug ip packet 124 detail.*

```
*Aug 20 08:28:23.389: IP: s=10.1.1.4 (FastEthernet0/0), d=224.0.0.5, len 80, rcv
d 0, proto=89

*Aug 20 08:28:36.779: IP: s=10.1.1.1 (local), d=10.1.1.4 (FastEthernet0/0), len
100, sending
*Aug 20 08:28:36.779:          ICMP type=8, code=0
```

For most situations, the nondetailed *debug ip packet* will do just fine.

Spotting Memory Issues (Router Memory, That Is)

I often mention being careful about the load on your router's memory, but how do you know when you're starting to overload your router in that department? Cisco's website lists several signs that you just might have a problem:

- If your router rejects Telnet sessions... you might have a memory problem.
- If your router shows you the output of *show processor memory* regardless of the command you're actually entering...that, my friend, is a cry for help.

- If your router literally tells you "Low on memory" or "Unable to create EXEC—no memory or too many processes"...you *do* have a memory problem.

Other possible signs of memory issues include your *show* commands not showing you anything when you know darn well there is something to show you and your router just hanging when you try to connect via the console connection.

If you can't connect via the console port, Cisco recommends you disconnect both the WAN and LAN cables connected to the router (ouch!) and then try to get in. Since the router won't be processing packets, there's an excellent chance you'll be able to connect successfully. Cisco recommends you then run *show memory allocating-process totals* and *show logging*. If your router doesn't support *show memory allocating-process totals*, run *show memory summary*. Many routers support both.

```
R1#show memory allocating-process totals
                Head    Total(b)   Used(b)     Free(b)   Lowest(b)   Largest(b)
Processor   84A738A0    31419072  14112904    17306168    15647184     15634908
I/O          6700000    26214400   2094568    24119832    24114848     24119804




Allocator PC Summary for: Processor

     PC            Total    Count   Name
0x802D6124        1719452     201   Process Stack
0x822CB508        1469296       9   pak subblock chunk
0x821C9C14         526324      48   TCL Chunks
0x800E43E8         442540       6   MallocLite
```

(This will be followed by fifteen screens of information.)

Typically, you'll be making a copy of this information for a tech support specialist. That's true of the next topic as well!

Making a Core Dump

Defining a core dump is simple enough; it's a copy of the router's memory contents. Simple enough, indeed!

Generating a core dump is another matter. Here's what Cisco has to say about creating core dumps:

"CAUTION: Core dumps are not necessary to solve most crash cases. Creation of a core dump when the router is functioning in a network can disrupt network operation. Use... only under the direction of a technical support representative."

A core dump can be created via FTP, TFTP, RCP (Remote Copy Protocol), or via a flash disk. Obviously, the procedures are different depending on which method you use, but each will use the *exception core-file* and *exception region-size* commands.

```
R1(config)#exception ?
  core-file            Set name of core dump file
  crashinfo            Crashinfo collection
  data-corruption      Data error exception handling
  delay-dump           Pause dump (in the case of dump via peer)
  dump                 Set name of host to dump to
  flash                Set the device and erase permission
  memory               Memory leak debugging
  protocol             Set protocol for sending core file
  region-size          Size of region for exception-time memory pool
  spurious-interrupt   Crash after a given number of spurious interrupts
```

```
R1(config)#exception core-file ?
WORD Name of the core file
```

Use *exception core-file* to change the default name given to the core dump, which is "R1-core" in this case. The hostname always begins the core dump filename by default, followed by "-core."

```
R1(config)#exception region-size ?
  <1024-65536>    Region size
```

Speaking of memory (and we just were!), *exception region-size* reserves just a bit of memory to be used by the core dump in case the larger memory pool is corrupted. Otherwise, you have a good chance of a memory issue arising during the core dump creation, and that's the last thing you need. The default is 16384 bytes, and the larger this value, the better the chances of having an issue-free core dump.

You can test with *write core*, which creates a core dump and saves the file to the location specified.

```
R4#write core 10.1.1.1
Base name of core files to write [R4-core]?
```

Creating core dumps isn't something we do every day (thankfully), and certainly not something I'd run on any router without checking Cisco documentation on whether you actually need to run one.

Remember when VPN usage was rare in networking? Me either! (Just kidding. I was there. I admit it.) Today, VPNs are everywhere, including your ROUTE exam – and in the very next section of this study guide! Let's get to it!

Chapter 11:

VPNS AND IPSEC

In today's world, it's not enough to have remote communications at the touch of a button or the click of a mouse. We need those communications to be as secure as possible, and that's what Virtual Private Networks (VPNs) are all about. It's the "private" part of VPN that we're most concerned with, since VPNs bring security to a connection using a shared channel, treating that shared channel as though it were a private network.

VPNs are sometimes called *tunnels*, since the VPN is effectively tunneling through an existing communication outlet, such as a Serial interface on a Cisco router. We can apply security rules and policies to the tunnel without applying them to the connection we're tunneling through.

VPNs bring data origin authentication, encryption, and data integrity to the table. Data origin authentication allows the receiver to guarantee the source of the packet...

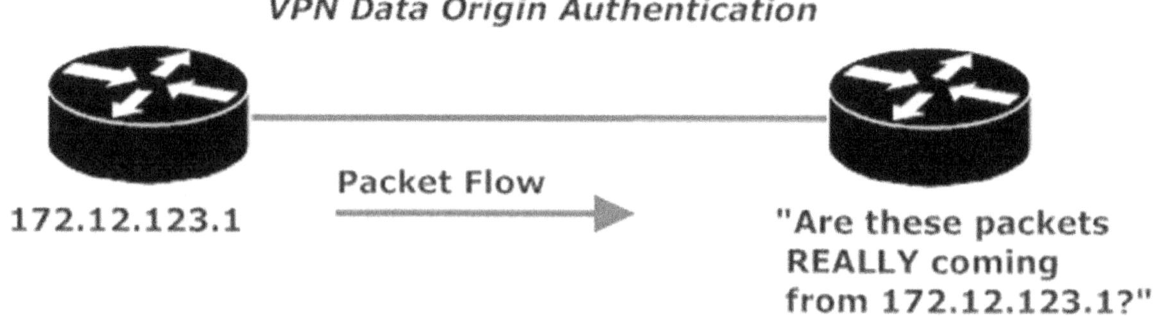

...encryption makes the contents of packets unreadable during transmission, making intercepted packets useless to the interceptor...

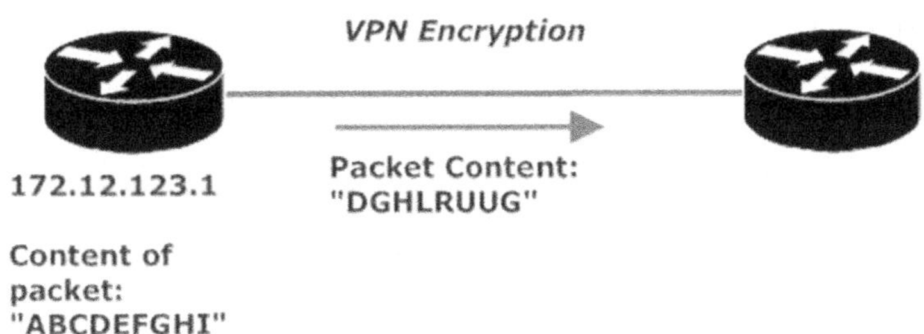

...and integrity is the receiver's ability to ensure the data was not tampered with during transmission.

One protocol we can use to build a tunnel is the *Generic Routing Encapsulation* (GRE). You may think, "Hey, I don't want to use generics on my network—I want the name-brand stuff!" That's not a good reason to not use GRE, but here's a reason that is—there's no encryption scheme in GRE. I'm sure you'll agree that's a pretty big drawback!

This huge security hole is corrected by IP Security, generally referred to as IPSec. (Be careful how you type that, stranger.) IPSec offers encryption and authentication and is a combination of three protocols:

- *Authentication Header* (AH), which defines a method for authentication and securing data
- *Encapsulating Security Payload* (ESP), which defines a method for authenticating, security, and encrypting data
- *Internet Key Exchange* (IKE), which negotiates the security parameters and authentication keys

The IPSec Packet Format

IP Header	AH	ESP Header	Data	ESP Trailer

Defined in RFC 2402, Authentication Header (AH) offers solid security, with data origin authentication and optional anti-replay protection. The drawback with AH is that the authentication it provides for the IP header is not complete. Some of the IP fields cannot be correctly predicted by the receiver, since some may change during transmission. AH will protect the IP packet's payload.

In short, AH offers data origin authentication, data integrity, and optional anti-replay protection. AH does not offer data confidentiality.

The Encapsulating Security Payload (ESP) does just that, with an ESP Header and Trailer encapsulating the data. ESP offers data origin authentication, anti-replay protection, and data confidentiality.

When comparing AH and ESP, you may have flashbacks to comparing TCP and UDP. TCP offers a ton of features that UDP doesn't, so why does any protocol or service use UDP instead of TCP? Overhead, of course! It's the same with ESP and AH. ESP is much more processor intensive than AH, and ESP requires strong cryptography, which isn't available everywhere and isn't allowed everywhere. AH has no such requirement. Still, the full encapsulation of data makes ESP a wise choice whenever it's feasible.

Both ESP and AH can be run in either tunnel mode or transport mode. In tunnel mode, the entire IPSec process is transparent to the end hosts, and specialized IPSec gateway devices handle that part of the load. Tunnel mode encrypts the entire IP packet, and then that encrypted packet is placed into another IP packet. That encapsulating packet will have the IP addresses configured on the tunnel endpoints, and it's those tunnel IP addresses that will be used to route the packet.

Transport mode encrypts the IP packet's payload, but the IPSec header is inserted directly after the IP header. As a result, there is no protection for the original IP address. It's the original IP address that's used for routing, and only data from the Transport layer up is protected by IPSec.

There are five main steps in creating an IPSec VPN. We start with *process initialization* via the receipt of interesting traffic, which is a really fancy way of saying, "The VPN creation process starts because traffic we said could, so we did." That interesting traffic is defined by a crypto access list. Next up is *IKE Phase 1,* where the IKE SA (Internet Key Exchange Security Association) is negotiated.

Next in line is *IKE Phase 2*, where the IPSec SA is negotiated. When this is completed, the IPSec tunnel (also called the IKE Phase 2 tunnel) build is complete.

The self-explanatory *data transfer* now takes place, and when that transfer is complete, the tunnel is torn down. This *tunnel termination* can be configured to happen after a certain number of bytes have passed through the tunnel or after the data transfer has been idle for a given period of time. If traffic is flowing through the tunnel at the same time the tunnel's supposed to come down, a new Security Association can be agreed upon while the existing one is still in place.

The VPN Build Process

'Nuff stuff! Let's get to the VPN build! We'll build a VPN between R1 and R3. R2 is still in the picture but not in the lab.

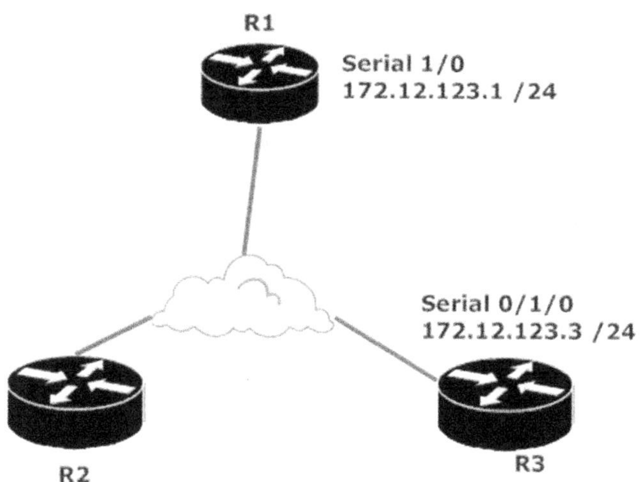

Let's get started!

Creating the IKE Policy

First things first—be sure the Internet Security Association and Key Management Protocol (ISAKMP) is on via the *crypto isakmp enable* command. It should be on by default. *Should* be.

```
R1(config)#crypto isakmp enable
```

To display the current IKE policies, run *show crypto isakmp policy.* Since we haven't created one yet, there won't be one...

```
R1#show crypto isakmp policy

Global IKE policy
Default protection suite
  encryption algorithm:       DES - Data Encryption Standard (56 bit keys).
  hash algorithm:             Secure Hash Standard
  authentication method:      Rivest-Shamir-Adleman Signature
  Diffie-Hellman group:       #1 (768 bit)
  lifetime:                   86400 seconds, no volume limit
```

...or *will* there? There's a default policy, but we're not going to use that one. Let's create our own with *crypto isakmp policy.*

```
R1(config)#crypto isakmp policy ?
  <1-10000>       Priority of protection suite
```

The first value to consider is the policy priority. The lower the number, the higher the priority, with "1" the best possible priority. This value cannot be set to zero, and there is no default, so you gotta put something in! Let's go with 100 and then use IOS Help to see the possibilities.

```
R1(config)#crypto isakmp policy 100
R1(config-isakmp)#?
ISAKMP commands:
  authentication   Set authentication method for protection suite
  default          Set a command to its defaults
  encryption       Set encryption algorithm for protection suite
  exit             Exit from ISAKMP protection suite configuration mode
  group            Set the Diffie-Hellman group
  hash             Set hash algorithm for protection suite
  lifetime         Set lifetime for ISAKMP security association
  no               Negate a command or set its defaults
```

Authentication is always good, so let's see the available options.

```
R1(config-isakmp)#authentication ?
  pre-share       Pre-Shared Key
  rsa-encr        Rivest-Shamir-Adleman Encryption
  rsa-sig         Rivest-Shamir-Adleman Signature
```

We'll go with preshared keys and then check out the encryption options.

```
R1(config-isakmp)#authentication pre-share
R1(config-isakmp)#encryption ?
  3des     Three key triple DES
  aes      AES - Advanced Encryption Standard.
  des      DES - Data Encryption Standard (56 bit keys).
```

We'll go with 3DES. What about the hash algorithm choices?

```
R1(config-isakmp)#encryption 3des
R1(config-isakmp)#hash ?
  md5     Message Digest 5
  sha     Secure Hash Standard
```

There's our old pal MD5 along with the Secure Hash Standard. We'll go with the devil we know and use MD5.

```
R1(config-isakmp)#encryption 3des
R1(config-isakmp)#hash ?
  md5     Message Digest 5
  sha     Secure Hash Standard

R1(config-isakmp)#hash md5
```

We'll set the SA lifetime with the lifetime option, setting it to the maximum number of seconds, which equals twenty-four hours.

```
R1(config-isakmp)#hash md5
R1(config-isakmp)#lifetime ?
  <60-86400>       lifetime in seconds

    R1(config-isakmp)#lifetime 86400
```

show crypto isakmp policy displays the default suite and the policy we just wrote.

```
R1#show crypto isakmp policy

Global IKE policy
Protection suite of priority 100
        encryption algorithm:     Three key triple DES
        hash algorithm:           Message Digest 5
        authentication method:    Pre-Shared Key
        Diffie-Hellman group:     #1 (768 bit)
        lifetime:                 86400 seconds, no volume limit
Default protection suite
        encryption algorithm:     DES - Data Encryption Standard (56 bit keys)
        hash algorithm:           Secure Hash Standard
        authentication method:    Rivest-Shamir-Adleman Signature
        Diffie-Hellman group:     #1 (768 bit)
        lifetime:                 86400 seconds, no volume limit
```

These policies are all part of IKE Phase 1. If Phase 1 goes badly, you will *not* have a Phase 2! Phase 1 begins with the connection initiator sending its policies to the desired VPN partner.

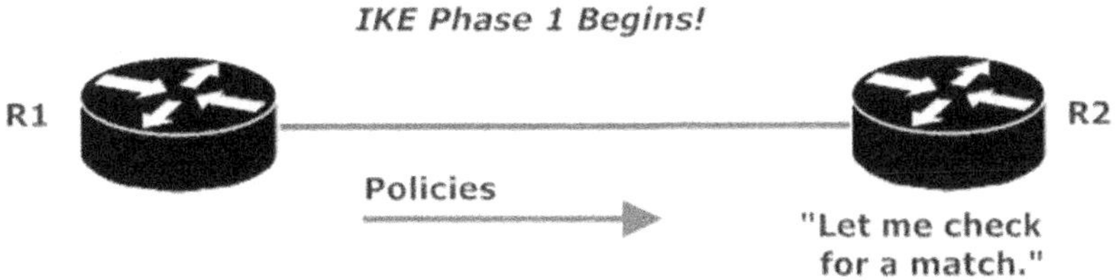

The recipient will then attempt to find a match for that policy among its own policies, starting with its lowest numbered policy. If that policy doesn't match, the recipient checks its *next* lowest numbered policy and so forth until a match is found (or not).

It would be intuitive to think the policy match has to be exact to move forward, but that's not quite the case. The hash, encryption, authentication, and Diffie-Hellman group number do all have to match. When it comes to the lifetime, though, the recipient policy must have a lifetime equal to or less than the initiator. If the recipient policy's lifetime is lower than the initiator, the lower value is used.

Hey, what about those preshared keys we mentioned in the policy? We'll make those with the *crypto isakmp key* command, choosing the encrypted password option (Always a good choice!), and *CCNP* will be the password.

```
R1(config)#crypto isakmp key ?
  0      Specifies an UNENCRYPTED password will follow
  6      Specifies an ENCRYPTED password will follow

R1(config)#crypto isakmp key 6 ?
  WORD   The HIDDEN user password string

R1(config)#crypto isakmp key 6 CCNP ?
  Address define shared key with IP address
  Hostname      define shared key with hostname

R1(config)#crypto isakmp key 6 CCNP address ?
  A.B.C.D Peer IP address

R1(config)#crypto isakmp key 6 CCNP address 172.12.123.3 ?
  A.B.C.D Peer IP subnet mask
  no-xauth      Bypasses XAuth for this peer
  <cr>

R1(config)#crypto isakmp key 6 CCNP address 172.12.123.3
```

Next up—the IPSec Transform Sets! Sounds complicated, but it's simply a group of individual parameters that will enforce a security policy. Unsurprisingly, the endpoints must agree exactly on which encryption and algorithms will be used to create the IPSec SA.

As with ISAKMP policies, multiple transform sets can be written and then sent to a remote peer. The remote peer compares each set received against its own transform sets, and when a match is found, the IPSec SA is built. We'll create a simple IPSec transform set right now via the *crypto ipsec transform-set* command. You do have to give it a name and then decide whether you're using ESP or AH.

```
R1(config)#crypto ipsec transform-set CCNP _ LAB ?
  ah-md5-hmac         AH-HMAC-MD5 transform
  ah-sha-hmac         AH-HMAC-SHA transform
  ah-sha256-hmac      AH-HMAC-SHA256 transform
  ah-sha384-hmac      AH-HMAC-SHA384 transform
  ah-sha512-hmac      AH-HMAC-SHA512 transform
  comp-lzs            IP Compression using the LZS compression algorithm
  esp-3des            ESP transform using 3DES(EDE) cipher (168 bits)
  esp-aes             ESP transform using AES cipher
  esp-des             ESP transform using DES cipher (56 bits)
  esp-gcm             ESP transform using GCM cipher
  esp-gmac            ESP transform using GMAC cipher
```

```
  esp-md5-hmac          ESP transform using HMAC-MD5 auth
  esp-null              ESP transform w/o cipher
  esp-seal              ESP transform using SEAL cipher (160 bits)
  esp-sha-hmac          ESP transform using HMAC-SHA auth
  esp-sha256-hmac       ESP transform using HMAC-SHA256 auth
  esp-sha384-hmac       ESP transform using HMAC-SHA384 auth
  esp-sha512-hmac       ESP transform using HMAC-SHA512 auth

R1(config)#crypto ipsec transform-set CCNP_LAB ah-md5-hmac
R1(cfg-crypto-trans)#mode ?
transport transport (payload encapsulation) mode
tunnel tunnel (datagram encapsulation) mode

R1(cfg-crypto-trans)#mode tunnel

R1(config)#crypto ipsec transform-set CCNP_LAB ah-md5-hmac
R1(cfg-crypto-trans)#mode tunnel
```

Now for the lifetime! The default lifetime of an IPSec SA is one hour, and that default can be adjusted with the following command. Note the command's time unit is seconds; you can also use kilobytes.

```
R1(config)#crypto ipsec ?
  client                    Configure a client
  df-bit                    Handling of encapsulated DF bit.
  Fragmentation             Handling of fragmentation of near-MTU sized packets
  nat-transparency          IPsec NAT transparency model
  optional                  Enable optional encryption for IPSec
  profile                   Configure an ipsec policy profile
  security-association      Security association parameters
  transform-set             Define transform and settings

R1(config)#crypto ipsec security-association ?
  idle-time       Automatically delete IPSec SAs after a given idle period.
  lifetime        security association lifetime
  replay          Set replay checking.

R1(config)#crypto ipsec security-association lifetime ?
  Kilobytes       Volume-based key duration
  Seconds         Time-based key duration

R1(config)#crypto ipsec security-association lifetime seconds ?
  <120-86400> Security association duration in seconds

R1(config)#crypto ipsec security-association lifetime seconds 1800
```

Now for some interesting traffic!

Crypto Access Lists

The crypto ACL is the exact same ACL that we've been writing our entire Cisco career, just put to a different use and a slightly different operation. A crypto ACL evaluating *outbound* traffic decides which traffic flows will be protected by IPSec and which ones will not. Traffic permitted by the ACL is protected, while flows denied by the ACL are transmitted without IPSec's protection.

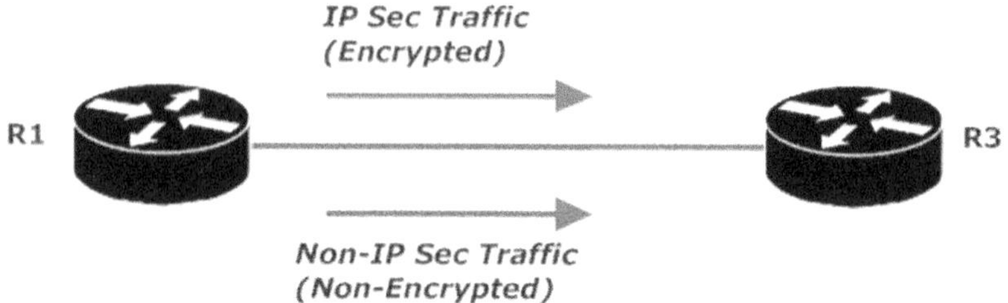

A crypto ACL "permit" on *inbound* traffic indicates traffic that should be IPSec protected when it arrives. If said traffic arrives and is not so protected, the router will drop that traffic.

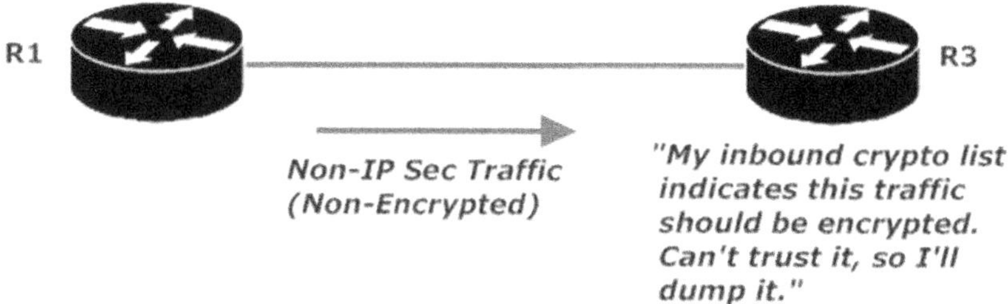

Crypto ACLs are used to evaluate both inbound and outbound traffic; there's no "in" or "out" when applying a crypto ACL to an interface. Basically, the same ACL is read forward for outbound traffic and backward for inbound traffic. Assume this ACL is on R1:

```
R1(config)#access-list 103 permit ip host 172.12.123.1 host 172.12.123.3
```

When it's part of a crypto map, ACL 103 is read forward for outgoing traffic...

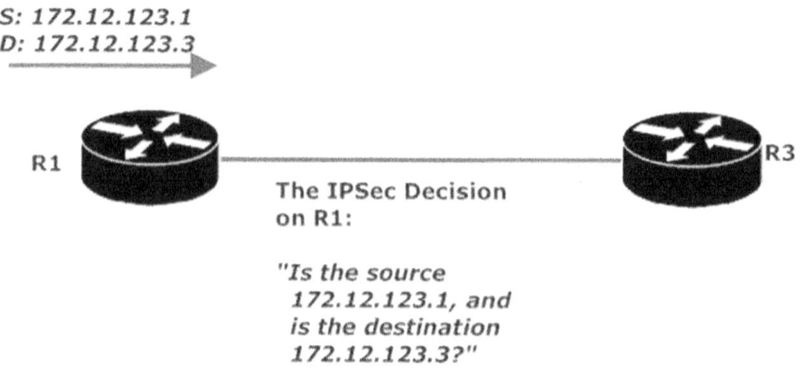

...and backward for incoming traffic.

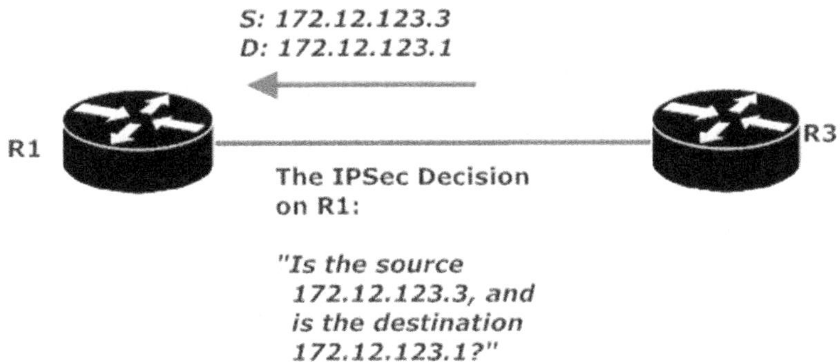

This behavior makes it vital to put a symmetrical ACL on the remote VPN endpoint, not an identical one. We can't just cut and paste this ACL from R1 to R3:

```
R1(config)#access-list 103 permit ip host 172.12.123.1 host 172.12.123.3
```

Instead, we need to put a mirror image of that ACL on R3.

```
R3(config)#access-list 103 permit ip host 172.12.123.3 host 172.12.123.1
```

There's no problem using *host* in a crypto ACL, but Cisco strongly recommends against using *any*, especially *permit any any.* You can end up with way too much encrypted traffic leaving the interface and/or dropping important but unencrypted incoming control traffic.

That's enough talk about ACL 103. Let's put it into action via a crypto map!

```
R1(config)#crypto map CCNP ?
  <1-65535>          Sequence to insert into crypto map entry
  client             Specify client configuration settings
  gdoi               Configure crypto map gdoi features
  isakmp             Specify isakmp configuration settings
  isakmp-profile     Specify isakmp profile to use
  local-address      Interface to use for local address for this crypto map
  redundancy         High availability options for this map

R1(config)#crypto map CCNP 100 ?
  gdoi              GDOI
  ipsec-isakmp      IPSEC w/ISAKMP
  ipsec-manual      IPSEC w/manual keying
  <cr>

R1(config)#crypto map CCNP 100 ipsec-isakmp ?
  dynamic      Enable dynamic crypto map support
  profile      Enable crypto map as a crypto-profile
  <cr>
```

```
R1(config)#crypto map CCNP 100 ipsec-isakmp
  % NOTE: This new crypto map will remain disabled until a peer and a valid
      access list have been configured.
R1(config-crypto-map)#
```

We've successfully created the crypto map CCNP and chosen sequence number 100, and this crypto map will use ISAKMP to establish the IPSec Security Association. After a gentle reminder from the router that this crypto map is useless until we set up a valid ACL and a peer has been named, we're in crypto map config mode. In this mode, we can identify the ACL, transform sets, and peers, and security association lifetimes for this map can be set.

```
R1(config)#crypto map CCNP 100 ipsec-isakmp
  % NOTE: This new crypto map will remain disabled until a peer and a valid
      access list have been configured.
R1(config-crypto-map)#match ?
  address Match address of packets to encrypt.

R1(config-crypto-map)#match address ?
  <100-199>          IP access-list number
  <2000-2699>        IP access-list number (expanded range)
  WORD               Access-list name

R1(config-crypto-map)#match address 103
R1(config-crypto-map)#set ?
  identity                      Identity restriction.
  ip                            Interface Internet Protocol config commands
  isakmp-profile                Specify isakmp Profile
  nat                           Set NAT translation
  peer                          Allowed Encryption/Decryption peer.
  pfs                           Specify pfs settings
  security-association          Security association parameters
  transform-set                 Specify list of transform sets in priority order

R1(config-crypto-map)#set peer 172.12.123.3
R1(config-crypto-map)#set transform-set CCNP_LAB
R1(config-crypto-map)#int serial 1/0
R1(config-if)#crypto map CCNP
R1(config-if)#
*Jul 13 18:41:49.870: %CRYPTO-6-ISAKMP_ON_OFF: ISAKMP is ON
```

This crypto map will encrypt traffic matching ACL 103, the peer 172.12.123.3 has been set, and the transform set we created earlier will be used. After applying the crypto map to Serial 1/0, we're told ISAKMP is on, and we're ready to test!

Before sending interesting traffic, I'll run *debug crypto ipsec*. The exclamation points returned by the ping are in the middle of the debug output. There's a lot of output here, so I've bolded the pertinent portions.

```
R1#debug crypto ipsec
Crypto IPSEC debugging is on

R1#ping 172.12.123.3

Type escape sequence to abort.
Sending 5, 100-byte ICMP Echos to 172.12.123.3, timeout is 2 seconds:

*Jul 15 02:56:03.074: IPSEC(sa _ request): ,
  (key eng. msg.) OUTBOUND local= 172.12.123.1, remote= 172.12.123.3,
   local _ proxy= 172.12.123.1/255.255.255.255/0/0 (type=1),
   remote _ proxy= 172.12.123.3/255.255.255.255/0/0 (type=1),
   protocol= AH, transform= ah-md5-hmac (Tunnel),
   lifedur= 1800s and 4608000kb,
   spi= 0x17D7E349(400024393), conn _ id= 0, keysize= 0, flags= 0x400A
*Jul 15 02:56:03.827: IPSEC(validate _ proposal _ request): proposal part #1,
  (key eng. msg.) INBOUND local= 172.12.123.1, remote= 172.12.123.3,
   local _ proxy= 172.12.123.1/255.255.255.255/0/0 (type=1),
   remote _ proxy= 172.12.123.3/255.255.255.255/0/0 (type=1),
   protocol= AH, transform= ah-md5-hmac (Tunnel),
   lifedur= 0s and 0kb,
   spi= 0x0(0), conn _ id= 0, keysize= 0, flags= 0x2
*Jul 15 02:56:03.827: Crypto mapdb : proxy _ match
      src addr        : 172.12.123.1
      dst addr        : 172.12.123.3
      protocol        : 0
      src port        : 0
      dst port        : 0
*Jul 15 02:56:03.835: IPS.!!! (Note - the actual pings. Two times out while the
tunnel was built. - CB) EC(key _ engine): got a queue event with 2 kei messag
   Es(
*Jul 15 02:56:03.835: IPSEC(initialize _ sas): ,
  (key eng. msg.) INBOUND local= 172.12.123.1, remote= 172.12.123.3,
   local _ proxy= 172.12.123.1/0.0.0.0/0/0 (type=1),
   remote _ proxy= 172.12.123.3/0.0.0.0/0/0 (type=1),
   protocol= AH, transform= ah-md5-hmac (Tunnel),
   lifedur= 1800s and 4608000kb,
   spi= 0x17D7E349(400024393), conn _ id= 0, keysize= 0, flags= 0x2
*Jul 15 02:56:03.835: IPSEC(initialize _ sas): ,
  (key eng. msg.) OUTBOUND local= 172.12.123.1, remote= 172.12.123.3,
   local _ proxy= 172.12.123.1/0.0.0.0/0/0 (type=1),
   remote _ proxy= 172.12.123.3/0.0.0.0/0/0 (type=1),
   protocol= AH, transform= ah-md5-hmac (Tunnel),
   lifedur= 1800s and 4608000kb,
   spi= 0x84455AC7(2219137735), conn _ id= 0, keysize= 0, flags= 0xA
!Jul 15 02:56:03.835: Crypto mapdb : proxy _ match
```

```
Success rate is 80 percent (4/5), round-trip min/avg/max = 92
        src addr           : 172.12.123.1
        dst addr           : 172.12.123.3
        protocol           : 0
        src port           : 0
        dst port           : 0
*Jul 15 02:56:03.839: IPSEC(crypto_ipsec_sa_find_ident_head): reconnecting
with the same proxies and 172.12.123.3
*Jul 15 02:56:03.839: IPSec: Flow_switching Allocated flow for sibling 80000002
*Jul 15 02:56:03.839: IPSEC(policy_db_add_ident): src 172.12.123.1, dest 172.12.
    123.3, dest_port 0

*Jul 15 02:56:03.839: IPSEC(create_sa): sa created,
   (sa) sa_dest= 172.12.123.1, sa_proto= 51, (AH uses protocol 51 - CB)
    sa_spi= 0x17D7E349(400024393),
    sa_trans= ah-md5-hmac , sa_conn_id= 2001
*Jul 15 02:56:03.839: IPSEC(create_sa): sa created,
   (sa) sa_dest= 172.12.123.3, sa_proto= 51,
    sa_spi= 0x84455AC7(2219137735),
    sa_trans= ah-md5-hmac , sa_conn_id= 2002/93/96 ms
```

show crypto isakmp sa verifies the SA is in place and is active. In this situation, active *is* what we want to see!

```
R1#show crypto isakmp sa
dst              src              state          conn-id slot  status
172.12.13.3      172.12.13.1      QM_IDLE              2    0  ACTIVE
```

For information on the IPSec SA, run *show crypto ipsec sa*. From top to bottom, you'll see the following:

The name of the crypto map (1)

The IP address of the current peer and the port number in use (2)

The number of packet encapsulations and deencapsulations (3)

The path MTU (4)

The remaining lifetime of the key in kilobytes and seconds (5)

The status of the SA (6)

```
R1#show crypto ipsec sa

interface: Serial1/0
     Crypto map tag: CCNP, local addr 172.12.123.1 (1)
```

```
protected vrf: (none)
local ident (addr/mask/prot/port): (172.12.123.1/255.255.255.255/0/0)
remote ident (addr/mask/prot/port): (172.12.123.3/255.255.255.255/0/0)
current _ peer 172.12.123.3 port 500 (2)
   PERMIT, flags={origin _ is _ acl,}
  #pkts encaps: 14, #pkts encrypt: 14, #pkts digest: 14 (3)
  #pkts decaps: 12, #pkts decrypt: 12, #pkts verify: 12
  #pkts compressed: 0, #pkts decompressed: 0
  #pkts not compressed: 0, #pkts compr. failed: 0
  #pkts not decompressed: 0, #pkts decompress failed: 0
  #send errors 1, #recv errors 0

   local crypto endpt.: 172.12.123.1, remote crypto endpt.: 172.12.123.3
   path mtu 1500, ip mtu 1500, ip mtu idb Serial1/0 (4)
   current outbound spi: 0x84455AC7(2219137735)

    inbound esp sas:

    inbound ah sas:
      spi: 0x17D7E349(400024393)
        transform: ah-md5-hmac ,
        in use settings ={Tunnel, }
        conn id: 2001, flow _ id: SW:1, crypto map: CCNP
        sa timing: remaining key lifetime (k/sec): (4562034/590) (5)
        replay detection support: Y
        Status: ACTIVE (6)

    inbound pcp sas:

    outbound esp sas:

    outbound ah sas:
      spi: 0x84455AC7(2219137735)
        transform: ah-md5-hmac ,
        in use settings ={Tunnel, }
        conn id: 2002, flow _ id: SW:2, crypto map: CCNP
        sa timing: remaining key lifetime (k/sec): (4562034/579)
        replay detection support: Y
        Status: ACTIVE

    outbound pcp sas:
```

We see nothing under the ESP fields for a very good reason—we didn't use ESP!

One final word on this build! When writing ACLs that will be permitting and blocking traffic on interfaces that will also have VPNs passing through, take care to leave protocols 50 and 51 unblocked as well as UDP port 500. Respectively, those numbers belong to ESP,

AH, and IKE. The "PCP" mentioned in that last *show* command refers to the *IP Payload Compression Protocol,* which uses IP protocol 108.

An Introduction to DMVPN

For the sake of clarity and sanity, I've left the cloud out of the following illustrations. We have six remote office spokes and one central office hub.

The first thing any of us learned about hub-and-spoke networks is that spoke-to-spoke communication has to go through the hub. To have our VPN traffic flow in the most efficient manner possible, we need to allow direct spoke-to-spoke VPNs that do *not* go through the hub.

We could implement a full mesh of VPNs, but as with static routing and BGP, a full mesh is a technically correct manner of getting things done that comes with a ton of overhead and some administrative nightmares on the side at no extra charge. Each spoke router would require us to configure five VPNs. Worse than the eventual troubleshooting that comes with that much static configuration is the fact that the VPNs will stay up even when there's no traffic going across. That's a real waste of router resources and bandwidth.

A much more efficient solution, *DMVPN (Dynamic Multipoint VPNs),* allows a spoke router to dynamically create a VPN to another spoke when the VPN is actually needed and then to tear that same VPN down when it's no longer needed.

DMVPN does not work in a vacuum. Far from it! For DMVPNs to work, we need the cooperation of the following:

- A stable dynamic routing protocol (and / or a static route)
- GRE (mGRE, to be specific)
- NHRP, the Next-Hop Routing Protocol
- IPSec

We're familiar with IPSec, and we'll discuss mGRE and NHRP in just a moment. Right now, a quick work regarding the routing protocol.

I know this is *really* obvious, but I'm mentioning it since it's easy to overlook the obvious. For a router to build a dynamic tunnel to another router, that router has to know how to reach the remote router. Remember, the hub's not getting directly involved in the tunnel build; the DMVPN goes directly from one spoke to another.

On a related point, if you see the tunnel bouncing or flapping—that is, going up, then down, then up, then down—that indicates the local router is able to reach the remote router only intermittently. That can be anything from a simple adjacency issue to an unstable OSPF area (and just about anything in between). In short, if your local router has issues reaching the remote router for any reason, that tunnel's going down. When it comes to troubleshooting DMVPN, I'd start with the connectivity (or lack of same) to the remote router, then mGRE, then IPSec.

And speaking of mGRE...

IPSec has one glaring weakness—the inability to protect multicast packets. However, GRE *can* encapsulate multicast packets, bringing us the unusual combination of GRE Over IPSec. Basically, we're encapsulating the multicast packet via GRE and then sending the encapsulated packet over an IPSec tunnel. GRE fills the gap for IPSec not being able to protect multicasts, and IPSec fills the gap for GRE lacking security.

mGRE really comes in handy in our dreaded hub-and-spoke network! Multipoint GRE makes it possible for the hub to use only one interface for as many tunnels as you need. Thing is, if we have a single multipoint interface on the hub router and multiple endpoints for our tunnels, we gotta have some kind of mapping in there. That's where the *Next Hop Resolution Protocol* (NHRP) comes in.

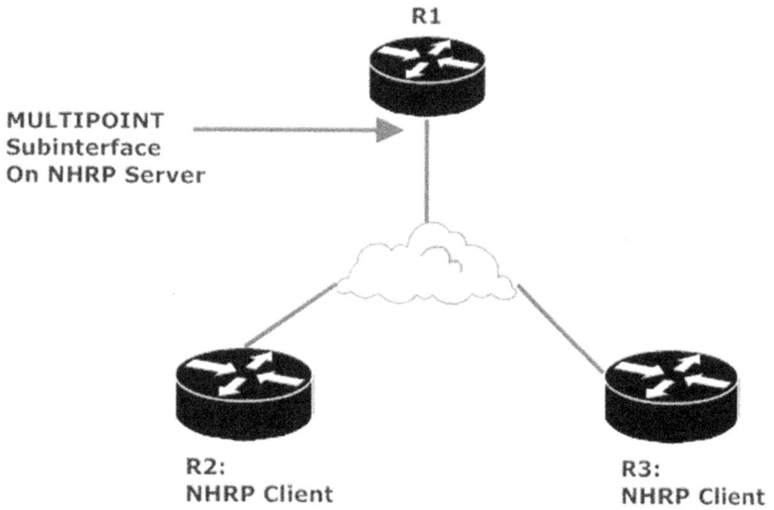

Our NHRP deployment uses the client-server model, with our hub as the server and the spokes as the client. The clients send two IP addresses to the server—one identifying the physical address used for the tunnel and the other the IP address assigned to the tunnel itself. The server puts this information in its NHRP database.

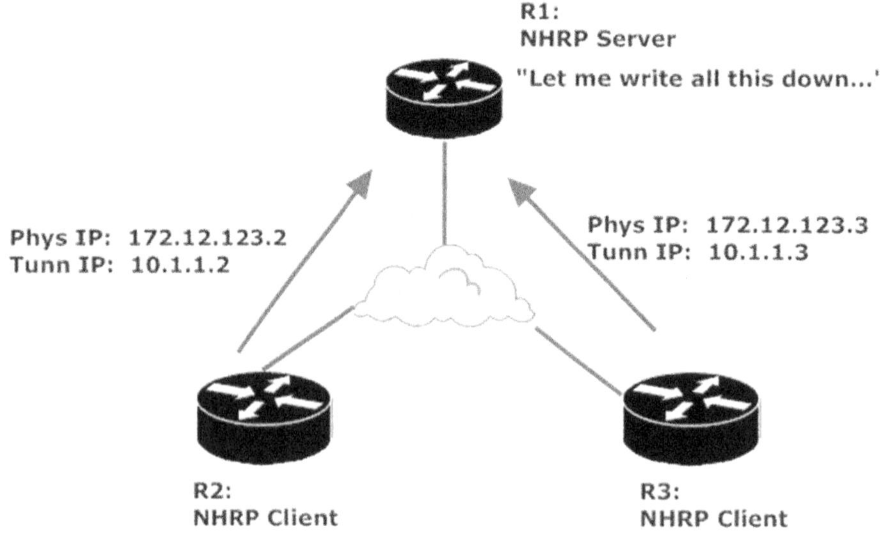

The database comes into play when one of our spokes needs to build a tunnel to another. When R2 wants to build a tunnel to R3, R2 will ask R1 what physical interface IP address is mapped to the tunnel IP address 10.1.1.3. R1 checks its NHRP database for the answer, R1 answers R2's query, and R2 can then successfully tunnel to R3. When NHRP information is received directly from the NHRP server, you'll see the *authoritative* flag set in the output of *show ip nhrp*.

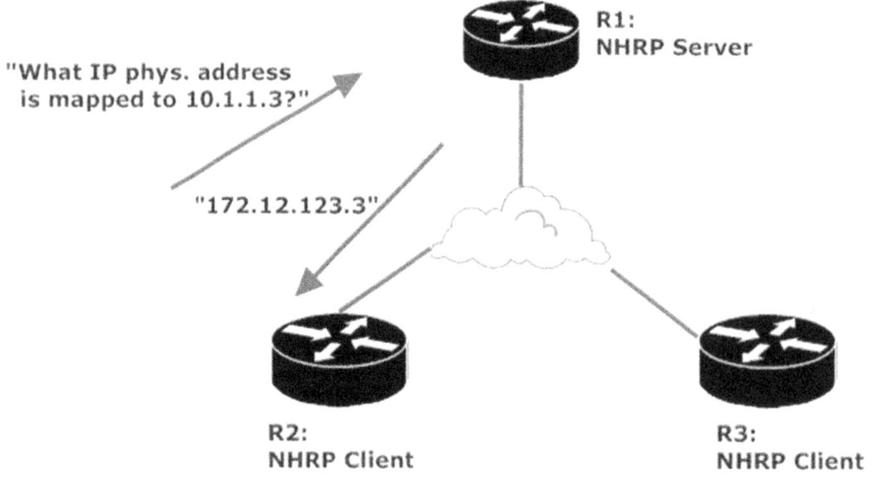

While NHRP acts in a similar fashion to ARP, it's much more complex to configure and troubleshoot. While we'll have to leave NHRP configuration for another day, I do want to point out the tunnel config on the hub. You'll configure the tunnel source as usual...

```
R1(config)#int tunnel 0
R1(config-if)#ip address 10.1.1.1 255.255.255.0
R1(config-if)#tunnel source serial 0/2/0.123
R1(config-if)#tunnel destination ?
```

```
  Hostname or A.B.C.D       ip address or host name
  X:X:X:X::X                IPv6 address
```

...but you will not put a single destination address, since an mGRE tunnel doesn't have a single destination. Instead, be sure to configure the tunnel mode as *gre multipoint.*

```
R1(config)#int tunnel 0
R1(config-if)#ip address 10.1.1.1 255.255.255.0
R1(config-if)#tunnel source serial 0/2/0.123
R1(config-if)#tunnel destination ?
  Hostname or A.B.C.D     ip address or host name
  X:X:X:X::X              IPv6 address

R1(config-if)#tunnel mode ?
  aurp        AURP TunnelTalk AppleTalk encapsulation
  cayman      Cayman TunnelTalk AppleTalk encapsulation
  dvmrp       DVMRP multicast tunnel
  eon         EON compatible CLNS tunnel
  gre         generic route encapsulation protocol
  ipip        IP over IP encapsulation
  ipsec       IPSec tunnel encapsulation
  iptalk      Apple IPTalk encapsulation
  ipv6        Generic packet tunneling in IPv6
  ipv6ip      IPv6 over IP encapsulation
  mpls        MPLS encapsulations
  nos         IP over IP encapsulation (KA9Q/NOS compatible)
  rbscp       RBSCP in IP tunnel

R1(config-if)#tunnel mode gre ?
  ip              over IP
  ipv6            over IPv6
  multipoint      over IP (multipoint)

R1(config-if)#tunnel mode gre multipoint ?
  <cr>

R1(config-if)#tunnel mode gre multipoint
```

One Final Word Regarding GRE

Don't block IP protocol 47 with your ACLs. If you do, you just killed GRE, and what did GRE ever do to you? (Seriously, you can't build a tunnel with IP protocol 47 blocked, and if you block if after the tunnel's built, the tunnel will come straight down.)

A Quick Intro to the World of Cisco Easy VPN

I get suspicious when I see the word "easy." It's like "low monthly payments." It's all relative, right? Easy VPN does make our life as network admins a little easier, though. Easy VPN uses the client-server model, and the festivities begin with the now-familiar IKE authentication, where the client sends its IKE proposals, and the server accepts the proposal that matches the ones configured on the server.

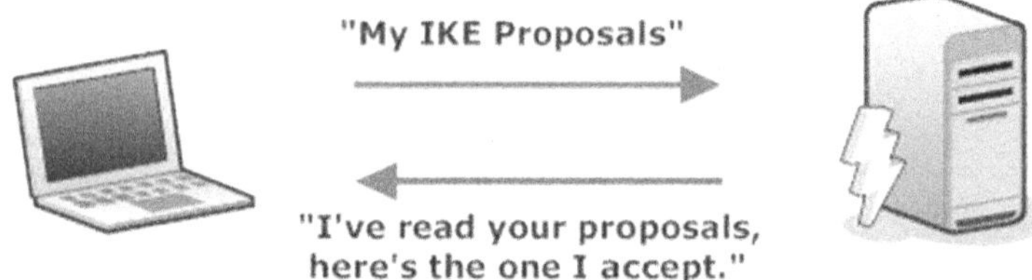

The server then authenticates the client via XAUTH, the IKE Extended Authentication. The first part of the authentication is a server-to-client challenge...

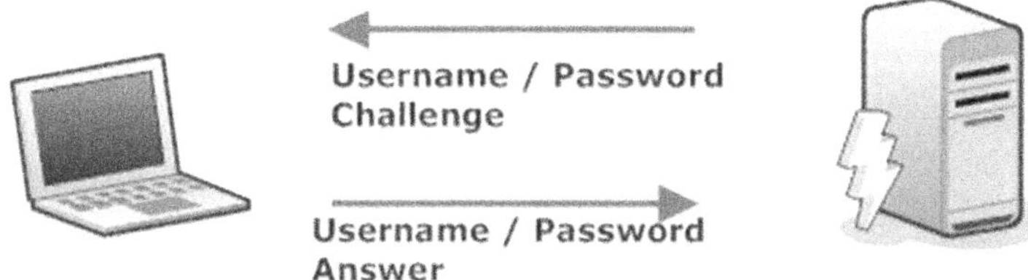

...and the client's response is checked against RADIUS or TACACS+, our AAA protocols. Assuming all is well, the server lets the client know that the client has successfully authenticated. The client will then request additional information from the server.

Once that information is received, the IPSec SA is put into place, and we're done! It really IS easy!

Virtual Routers and VRF Lite

Sometimes it's fine to let traffic types and flows mix, and sometimes it's not. Maybe you have some ultra-time-sensitive voice and video traffic and you want to keep it separate from the usual riff-raff traffic. Maybe you just want to keep a certain subnet's traffic separate from others in order to keep that subnet's existence as secret as possible. Whatever the reason, Virtual Routing and Forwarding can help. We're actually going to use a "lite" version here, cleverly known as VRF-Lite.

Here's the physical setup for this lab, along with the IP addresses.

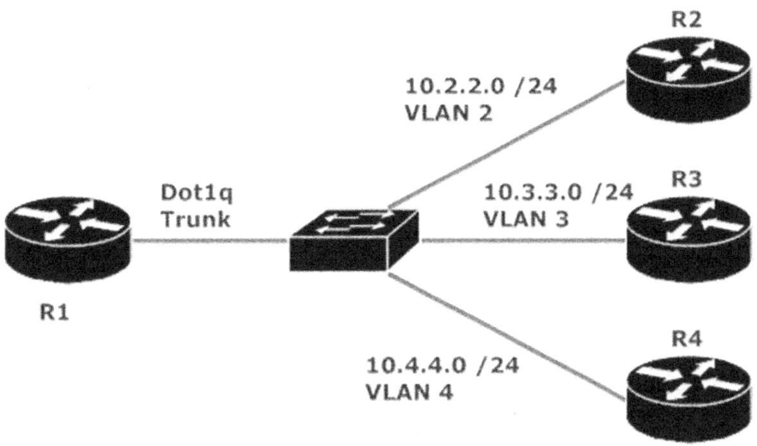

The configurations for this lab:

The switch:

```
interface FastEthernet0/1
switchport trunk encapsulation dot1q
switchport mode trunk
!
interface FastEthernet0/2
switchport access vlan 2
switchport mode access
!
interface FastEthernet0/3
switchport access vlan 3
switchport mode access
!
interface FastEthernet0/4
switchport access vlan 4
switchport mode access
```

R1:

```
interface FastEthernet0/0
no ip address
duplex auto
speed auto
!
interface FastEthernet0/0.2
encapsulation dot1Q 2
ip address 10.2.2.1 255.255.255.0
!
interface FastEthernet0/0.3
encapsulation dot1Q 3
ip address 10.3.3.1 255.255.255.0
!
interface FastEthernet0/0.4
 encapsulation dot1Q 4
 ip address 10.4.4.1 255.255.255.0
!
```

R2:

```
interface FastEthernet0/0
 ip address 10.2.2.2 255.255.255.0
```

R3:

```
interface FastEthernet0/0
 ip address 10.3.3.3 255.255.255.0
```

R4:

```
interface FastEthernet0/0
 ip address 10.4.4.4 255.255.255.0
```

We'll now create our first three VRFs, giving them boring but highly intuitive names.

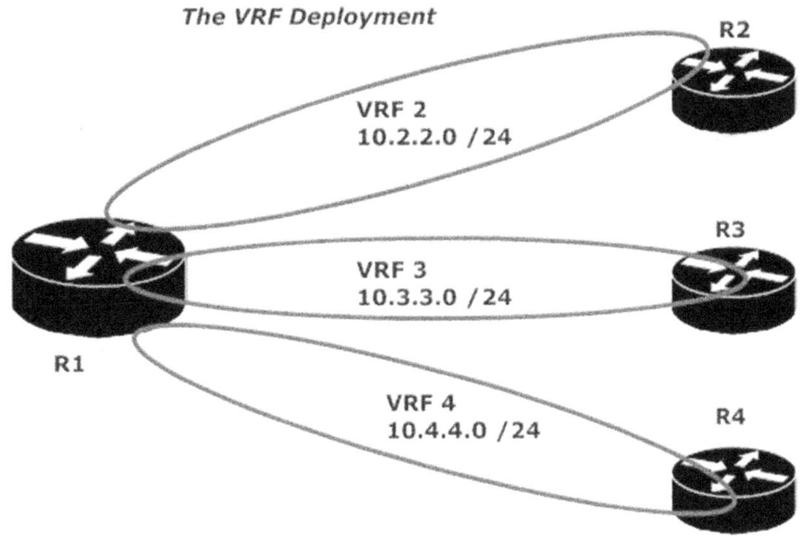


```
R1(config)#ip vrf ?
  WORD  VPN Routing/Forwarding instance name

R1(config)#ip vrf VRF2

R1(config)#ip vrf VRF3

R1(config)#ip vrf VRF4
```

With our three VRFs created, we'll assign each subinterface to its appropriate instance.

```
R1(config)#int fast 0/0.2
R1(config-subif)#ip vrf ?
  forwarding  Configure forwarding table
  receive     Add Interface Address into VRF Table
  sitemap     Configure route-map for routes received from this site

R1(config-subif)#ip vrf forwarding ?
  WORD Table name

R1(config-subif)#ip vrf forwarding VRF2
% Interface FastEthernet0/0.2 IP address 10.2.2.1 removed due to enabling VRF VR
F2
```

Hmm. Does that mean the address is actually removed, or that it's being moved to its own routing table? We'll check on that after putting the other two subinterfaces into their VRFs.

```
R1(config-subif)#ip vrf forwarding VRF3
% Interface FastEthernet0/0.3 IP address 10.3.3.1 removed due to enabling VRF VR
F3
```

```
R1(config-subif)#
R1(config-subif)#int fast 0/0.4
R1(config-subif)#ip vrf forwarding VRF4
% Interface FastEthernet0/0.4 IP address 10.4.4.1 removed due to enabling VRF VR
F4
```

Hmm. Not sure if I like all of these addresses being removed. Let's verify the VRF config with *show ip vrf.*

```
R1#show ip vrf
  Name                             Default RD          Interfaces
  VRF2                             <not set>           Fa0/0.2
  VRF3                             <not set>           Fa0/0.3
  VRF4                             <not set>           Fa0/0.4
```

Looks good, although no IP addresses are mentioned in this output. (The "Default RD" refers to a route descriptor, and that's a VRF topic for another day.) Let's look at the main route table.

```
R1#show ip route

Gateway of last resort is not set

R1#
```

Nothing—but VRF keeps a separate routing table for each instance. Perhaps the connected routes are there!

```
R1#show ip route ?
  Hostname or A.B.C.D  Network to display information about or hostname
  bgp                  Border Gateway Protocol (BGP)
  connected            Connected
  dhcp                 Show routes added by DHCP Server or Relay
  eigrp                Enhanced Interior Gateway Routing Protocol (EIGRP)
  isis                 ISO IS-IS
  list                 IP Access list
  mobile               Mobile routes
  odr                  On Demand stub Routes
  ospf                 Open Shortest Path First (OSPF)
  profile              IP routing table profile
  rip                  Routing Information Protocol (RIP)
  static               Static routes
  summary              Summary of all routes
  supernets-only       Show supernet entries only
  track-table          Tracked static table
  update-queue         Queue of RIB updates
  vrf                  Display routes from a VPN Routing/Forwarding instance
  |                    Output modifiers
  <cr>
```

```
R1#show ip route vrf ?
  WORD  VPN Routing/Forwarding instance name

R1#show ip route vrf VRF2

Routing Table: VRF2

Gateway of last resort is not set

(no routes)


R1#show ip route vrf VRF3

Routing Table: VRF3

Gateway of last resort is not set

(no routes)


R1#show ip route vrf VRF4

Routing Table: VRF4

(no routes)

Gateway of last resort is not set
```

Those connected routes have disappeared! The router is *haunted*!

Well, not quite. When the router told us the addresses were being removed, that's *exactly* what was going on. Often the order of commands doesn't matter on a Cisco router—*password* and *login* on VTY lines, for instance—but here, it does. If you enable VRF on the subinterfaces after the IP addresses have been applied, *you must reapply the addresses.*

```
R1(config)#int fast 0/0.2
R1(config-subif)#ip address 10.2.2.1 255.255.255.0
R1(config-subif)#int fast 0/0.3
R1(config-subif)#ip address 10.3.3.1 255.255.255.0
R1(config-subif)#int fast 0/0.4
R1(config-subif)#ip address 10.4.4.1 255.255.255.0

R1#show ip route vrf VRF2
Routing Table: VRF2
Gateway of last resort is not set
```

```
     10.0.0.0/24 is subnetted, 1 subnets
C       10.2.2.0 is directly connected, FastEthernet0/0.2

R1#show ip route vrf VRF3
Routing Table: VRF3

Gateway of last resort is not set

     10.0.0.0/24 is subnetted, 1 subnets
C       10.3.3.0 is directly connected, FastEthernet0/0.3

R1#show ip route vrf VRF4
Routing Table: VRF4
Gateway of last resort is not set

     10.0.0.0/24 is subnetted, 1 subnets
C       10.4.4.0 is directly connected, FastEthernet0/0.4
```

That's more like it! Each VRF now has its own routing table. Let's celebrate! Pings all around!

```
R1#ping 10.2.2.2
.....
Success rate is 0 percent (0/5)

R1#ping 10.3.3.3
.....
Success rate is 0 percent (0/5)

R1#ping 10.4.4.4
.....
Success rate is 0 percent (0/5)
```

Now *that's* strange. These are directly connected routes, so there's no issue with a routing protocol. There's no problem with the subinterfaces:

```
R1#show int fast 0/0.2
FastEthernet0/0.2 is up, line protocol is up
  Hardware is AmdFE, address is 000f.f7c4.09c0 (bia 000f.f7c4.09c0)
  Internet address is 10.2.2.1/24

R1#show int fast 0/0.3
FastEthernet0/0.3 is up, line protocol is up
  Hardware is AmdFE, address is 000f.f7c4.09c0 (bia 000f.f7c4.09c0)
  Internet address is 10.3.3.1/24

R1#show int fast 0/0.4
FastEthernet0/0.4 is up, line protocol is up
```

```
  Hardware is AmdFE, address is 000f.f7c4.09c0 (bia 000f.f7c4.09c0)
  Internet address is 10.4.4.1/24
```

Ladies and gentlemen of this supposed jury, this does *not make sense*!

Well, it actually *does* make sense when it comes to VRFs. You may never have even looked at the *ping* options, but there's one in there we need right now:

```
R1#ping ?
  WORD         Ping destination address or hostname
  appletalk    Appletalk echo
  clns         CLNS echo
  decent       DECnet echo
  ip           IP echo
  ipv6         IPv6 echo
  ipx          Novell/IPX echo
  srb          srb echo
  tag          Tag encapsulated IP echo
  vrf          Select VPN routing instance
  <cr>

R1#ping vrf ?
  WORD VPN Routing/Forwarding instance name

R1#ping vrf VRF2 ?
  WORD         Ping destination address or hostname
  appletalk    Appletalk echo
  clns         CLNS echo
  decent       DECnet echo
  ip           IP echo
  ipv6         IPv6 echo
  ipx          Novell/IPX echo
  srb          srb echo
  tag          Tag encapsulated IP echo
  <cr>

R1#ping vrf VRF2 10.2.2.2
!!!!!
Success rate is 100 percent (5/5), round-trip min/avg/max = 1/1/1 ms

R1#ping vrf VRF3 10.3.3.3
!!!!!
Success rate is 100 percent (5/5), round-trip min/avg/max = 1/2/4 ms

R1#ping vrf VRF4 10.4.4.4
!!!!!
Success rate is 100 percent (5/5), round-trip min/avg/max = 1/2/4 ms
```

With our connected routes taken care of, let's introduce OSPF to our VRF configuration.

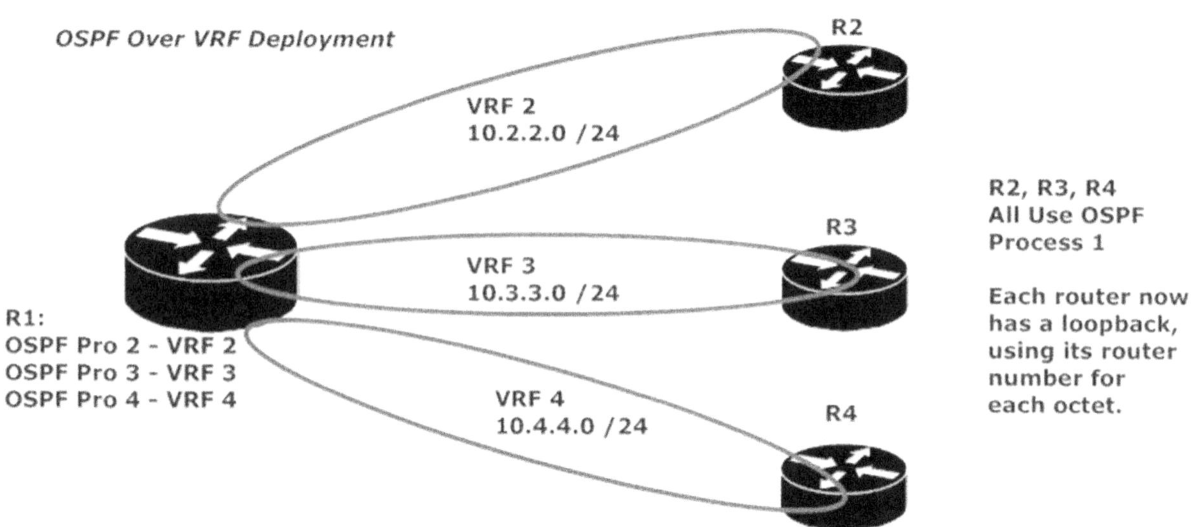

Just as we have three instances of VRF on R1, we need to create three separate instances of OSPF, and that means adding a little information to the usual *router ospf* command.

```
R1(config)#router ospf 2 ?
  vrf  VPN Routing/Forwarding Instance
  <cr>

R1(config)#router ospf 2 vrf ?
  WORD  VPN Routing/Forwarding Instance (VRF) name

R1(config)#router ospf 2 vrf VRF2
R1(config-router)#network 10.2.2.0 0.0.0.255 area 0

R1(config-router)#router ospf 3 vrf VRF3
R1(config-router)#network 10.3.3.0 0.0.0.255 area 0

R1(config-router)#router ospf 4 vrf VRF4
R1(config-router)#network 10.4.4.0 0.0.0.255 area 0

R2(config)#router ospf 1
R2(config-router)#network 10.2.2.0 0.0.0.255 area 0
%OSPF-5-ADJCHG: Process 1, Nbr 10.2.2.1 on FastEthernet0/0
 from LOADING to FULL, Loading Done

R3(config)#router ospf 1
R3(config-router)#network 10.3.3.0 0.0.0.255 area 0
%OSPF-5-ADJCHG: Process 1, Nbr 10.3.3.1 on FastEthernet0/0
 from LOADING to FULL, Loading Done
```

```
R4(config)#router ospf 1
R4(config-router)#network 10.4.4.0 0.0.0.255 area 0
%OSPF-5-ADJCHG: Process 1, Nbr 10.4.4.1 on FastEthernet0/0
 from LOADING to FULL, Loading Done
```

The adjacencies are in place!

```
R1#show ip ospf neighbor

Neighbor ID     Pri   State           Dead Time   Address         Interface
4.4.4.4           1   FULL/BDR        00:00:37    10.4.4.4        FastEthernet0/0.4
3.3.3.3           1   FULL/BDR        00:00:33    10.3.3.3        FastEthernet0/0.3
2.2.2.2           1   FULL/BDR        00:00:36    10.2.2.2        FastEthernet0/0.2
```

We'll add routes to our network by enabling OSPF on the loopbacks on R2, R3, and R4.

```
R2(config)#router ospf 1
R2(config-router)#network 2.2.2.0 0.0.0.255 area 2

R3(config)#router ospf 1
R3(config-router)#network 3.3.3.0 0.0.0.255 area 3

R4(config)#router ospf 1
R4(config-router)#network 4.4.4.0 0.0.0.255 area 4
```

The resulting VRF tables on R1:

```
R1#show ip route vrf VRF2

Routing Table: VRF2
Gateway of last resort is not set

     2.0.0.0/32 is subnetted, 1 subnets
O IA    2.2.2.2 [110/2] via 10.2.2.2, 00:01:32, FastEthernet0/0.2
     10.0.0.0/24 is subnetted, 1 subnets
C       10.2.2.0 is directly connected, FastEthernet0/0.2


R1#show ip route vrf VRF3

Routing Table: VRF3
Gateway of last resort is not set

     3.0.0.0/32 is subnetted, 1 subnets
O IA    3.3.3.3 [110/2] via 10.3.3.3, 00:01:26, FastEthernet0/0.3
     10.0.0.0/24 is subnetted, 1 subnets
C       10.3.3.0 is directly connected, FastEthernet0/0.3
```

```
R1#show ip route vrf VRF4

Routing Table: VRF4
Gateway of last resort is not set

      4.0.0.0/32 is subnetted, 1 subnets
O IA     4.4.4.4 [110/2] via 10.4.4.4, 00:01:18, FastEthernet0/0.4
      10.0.0.0/24 is subnetted, 1 subnets
C        10.4.4.0 is directly connected, FastEthernet0/0.4
```

Let's send some pings!

```
R1#ping vrf VRF2 2.2.2.2
!!!!!
Success rate is 100 percent (5/5), round-trip min/avg/max = 1/2/4 ms

R1#ping vrf VRF3 3.3.3.3
!!!!!
Success rate is 100 percent (5/5), round-trip min/avg/max = 1/2/4 ms

R1#ping vrf VRF4 4.4.4.4
!!!!!
Success rate is 100 percent (5/5), round-trip min/avg/max = 1/2/4 ms
```

And there we go!

There's always room for improvement, though, and *Easy Virtual Networking* (EVN) is an improvement over VRF Lite. The config is a lot simpler, too! Instead of creating the subinterfaces required in our VRF Lite lab, we'll have a *Virtual Network Trunk* (VNET) carry traffic tagged with—you guessed it!—a VNET tag.

Another EVN benefit, *route replication*, grants each virtual network access to the *Routing Information Base* (RIB) for *every* VRF. That really cuts down on the number of overall duplicate routing table entries, which in turn makes the overall process faster and lessens the hit to our router resources. This keeps each virtual network's traffic separate while making overall network operations much more efficient.

EVN configuration is beyond the scope of the exam, but I would recommend having a look at the following two-page PDF on Cisco's website:

http://www.cisco.com/c/dam/en/us/products/collateral/ios-nx-os-software/easy-virtual-network-evn/aag_c45-675118.pdf

To go with that, here's a quick list of EVN requirements, limitations, and benefits!

- Supports up to thirty-two virtual networks
- EVN trunks can be built on any interface that can run dot1q encapsulation

- However, EVN trunks do not support ACLs, NAT, NetFlow, or WCCP (Web Cache Communication Protocol)
- Is backward-compatible with VRF-Lite; however, you cannot configure VRF-Lite and EVN on the same interface
- Supports sharing of DNS, DHCP, and other network services via route replication
- EVN does not support OSPFv3 (OSPF for IP6), ISIS, or RIP

Let's take time right now to revisit two old friends...NAT and PAT!

Chapter 12:

NAT AND PAT

Network Address Translation

Network Address Translation takes a host's private IP address and translates it to a non-private, routable address. Without NAT, a host such as this one on the 10.1.1.0 /24 network couldn't communicate with the outside world.

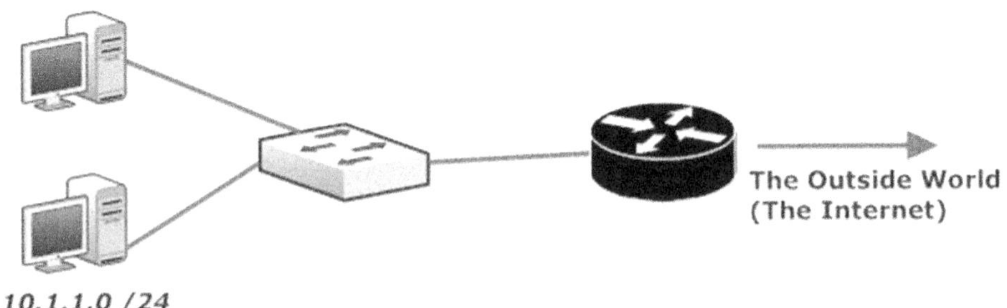

The addresses we'll be translating are from the RFC 1918 range of private addresses. Note the masks for these address ranges are not the same as those for the full Class A (/8), Class B (/16), and Class C (/24) address ranges.

Class A: 10.0.0.0 /8

Class B: 172.16.0.0 /12

Class C: 192.168.0.0 /16

The only thing that's even the *slightest* bit tricky about NAT is the names given to the addresses in the overall NAT process. We start with an *inside local address*, the address used by hosts on the local network to communicate with other hosts on the local network. The inside local address is the address being translated—locally. In this network, the inside local address is 10.1.1.1 /24.

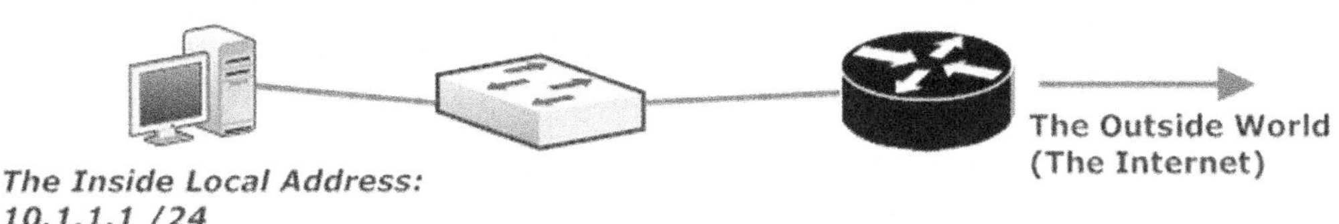

The inside local address is translated to an *inside global address*. In this case, that'll be 200.1.1.1 /24.

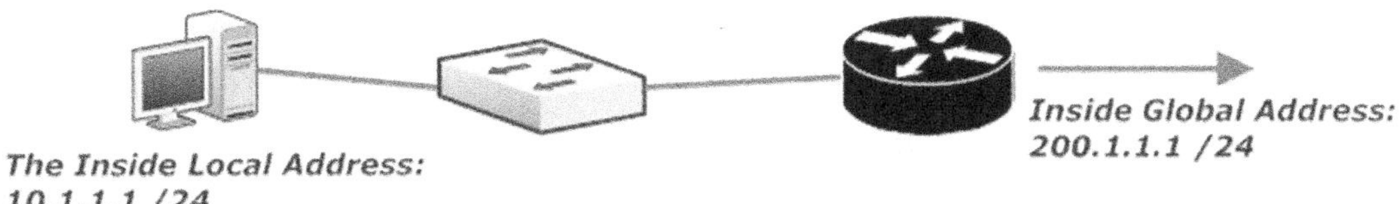

Outside local addresses are the nonroutable addresses of hosts on the remote network, while *outside global addresses* are the routable addresses assigned to hosts on a remote network. The terms "inside" and "outside" really depend on your perspective. If the address is in use on your network (global or local), it's an inside address. If it's in use by the other involved network, it's a global address.

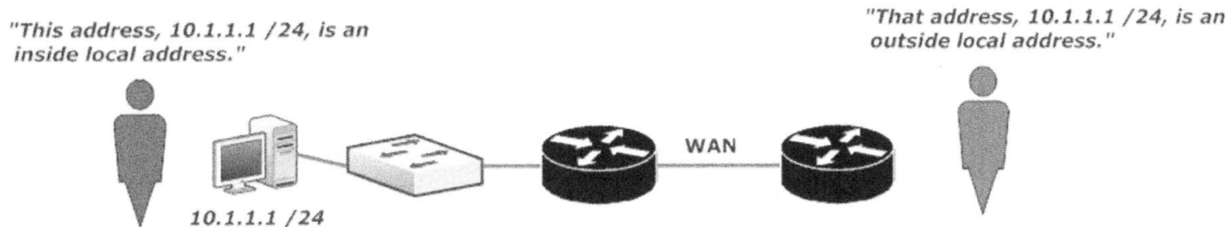

When a router performs NAT, that router makes an entry in its NAT translation table, mapping the inside local address to the assigned inside global address.

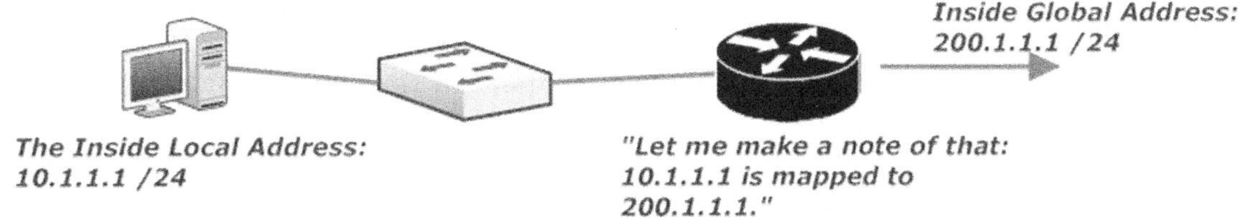

The private address is never seen outside the local network, and the host receiving these packets has no idea NAT has occurred. Actually, the host sending the packets doesn't know about NAT either! The only device that even knows this is going on is the NAT router.

When packets come back in with a routable address, the router checks its NAT table to see if another translation is in order. If so, the router translates the inside global address back to the appropriate inside local address and routes the packets accordingly.

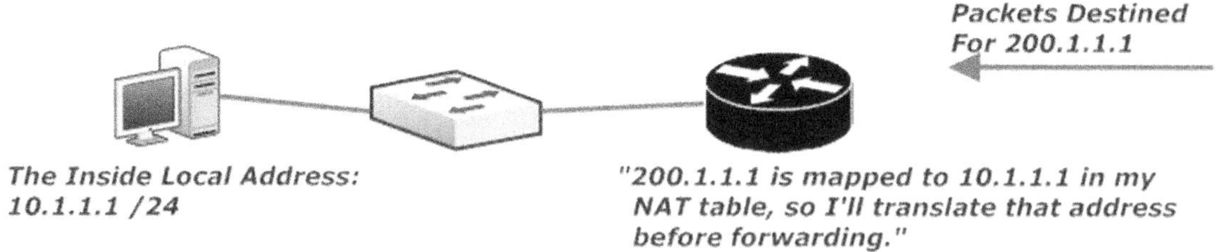

Let's have a look at the two main flavors of NAT.

Static NAT (SNAT)

If a limited number of hosts need NAT, static NAT may be the way to go. You could also have a server who will need to use NAT, and you don't want to pull a routable address from a NAT pool in that situation. You'd want a static address for that server, and static NAT gives you just that. SNAT is simply a one-on-one mapping of inside local to inside global addresses.

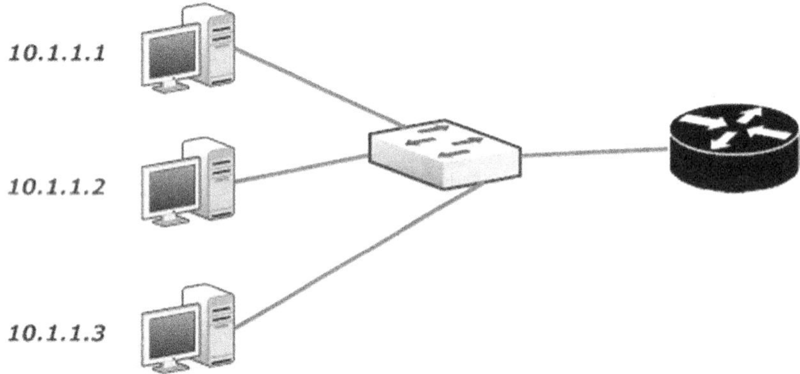

With this network, we'd need three mappings for SNAT. Before creating the mappings, I strongly recommend you configure the required *ip nat inside* and *ip nat outside* commands on the appropriate interfaces. You don't want to spend a half hour t-shooting your NAT mappings and then realize you forgot the interface-level commands! *ip nat inside* goes on the interface closest to the hosts having their addresses translated, and *ip nat outside* goes on the exit interface of the router performing NAT.

```
R1(config)#int fast 0/0
R1(config-if)#ip address 10.1.1.100 255.255.255.0
R1(config-if)#ip nat inside

R1(config-if)#int serial 1/0
R1(config-if)#ip address 172.12.123.1 255.255.255.0
R1(config-if)#ip nat outside
```

We'll drop back to global config more for the creation of the mappings via the *ip nat inside source* command.

```
R1(config)#ip nat inside ?
  destination        Destination address translation
  source             Source address translation

R1(config)#ip nat inside source ?
  list               Specify access list describing local addresses
  route-map          Specify route-map
  static             Specify static local->global mapping

R1(config)#ip nat inside source static ?
  A.B.C.D            Inside local IP address
  esp                IPSec-ESP (Tunnel mode) support
  network            Subnet translation
  tcp                Transmission Control Protocol
  udp                User Datagram Protocol

R1(config)#ip nat inside source static 10.1.1.1 ?
  A.B.C.D            Inside global IP address
  interface          Specify interface for global address

R1(config)#ip nat inside source static 10.1.1.1 200.1.1.1
R1(config)#ip nat inside source static 10.1.1.2 200.1.1.2
R1(config)#ip nat inside source static 10.1.1.3 200.1.1.3
```

Let's have a look at the NAT translation table.

```
R1#show ip nat translation
Pro Inside global      Inside local       Outside local      Outside global
--- 200.1.1.1          10.1.1.1           ---                ---
--- 200.1.1.2          10.1.1.2           ---                ---
--- 200.1.1.3          10.1.1.3           ---                ---
```

Looks good! On to dynamic NAT!

Dynamic NAT (DNAT)

The issue with static NAT is the issue with static *anything*, and that's scalability. If you have quite a few hosts that need address translation, dynamic NAT is the NAT for you. DNAT enables us to create a pool of inside global addresses. Those routable addresses are mapped to certain private addresses on an as-needed basis, and the mapping is dropped when the translation is no longer active.

In the following lab, the addresses 10.1.1.2 and 10.1.1.22 will need translation.

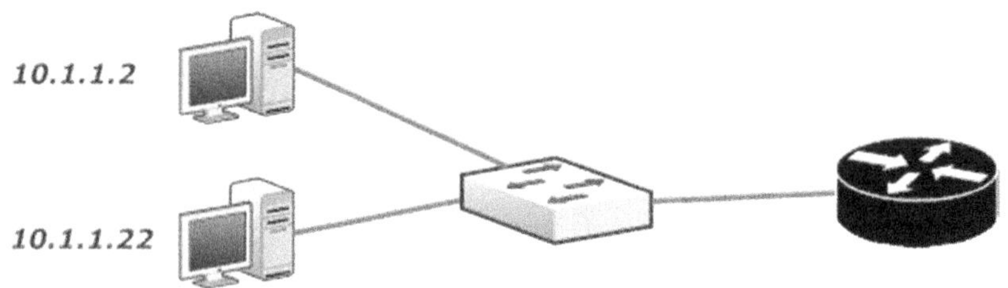

We'll need *ip nat inside* on the router's ethernet interface and *ip nat outside* on the serial interface.

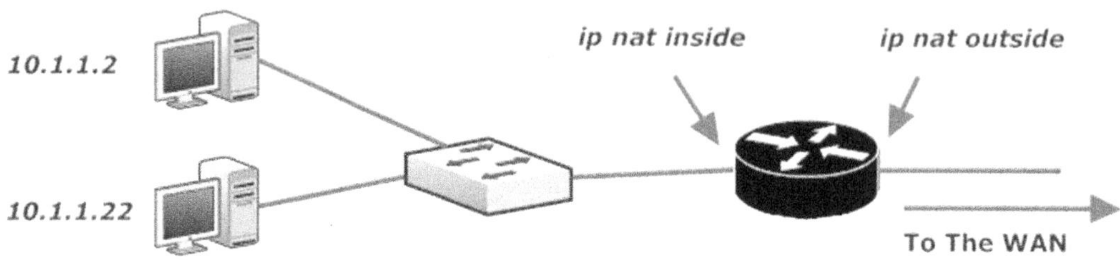

Assuming we have the 200.1.1.1–200.1.1.5 /24 address range available for our hosts, we'll put those addresses into the NAT pool.

```
R1(config)#ip nat ?
  Stateful          Stateful NAT configuration commands
  create            Create flow entries
  inside            Inside address translation
  log               NAT Logging
  outside           Outside address translation
  pool              Define pool of addresses
  service           Special translation for application using non-standard port
  source            Source address translation
  translation       NAT translation entry configuration

R1(config)#ip nat pool ?
  WORD Pool name

R1(config)#ip nat pool CCNP ?
  A.B.C.D           Start IP address
  netmask           Specify the network mask
  prefix-length     Specify the prefix length

R1(config)#ip nat pool CCNP 200.1.1.1 ?
  A.B.C.D End IP address

R1(config)#ip nat pool CCNP 200.1.1.1 200.1.1.5 ?
  Netmask           Specify the network mask
```

```
  prefix-length     Specify the prefix length

R1(config)#ip nat pool CCNP 200.1.1.1 200.1.1.5 netmask ?
  A.B.C.D Network mask

R1(config)#ip nat pool CCNP 200.1.1.1 200.1.1.5 netmask 255.255.255.0 ?
  Accounting        Specify the accounting
  add-route         Add special route to Virtual Interface
  type              Specify the pool type
  <cr>

R1(config)#ip nat pool CCNP 200.1.1.1 200.1.1.5 netmask 255.255.255.0
```

We'll now use an ACL to identify the interfaces that are allowed to draw an address from the NAT pool and follow that with *ip nat inside source*, with the source being that new ACL.

```
R1(config)#access-list 2 permit host 10.1.1.2
R1(config)#access-list 2 permit host 10.1.1.22

R1(config)#ip nat inside source ?
  list              Specify access list describing local addresses
  route-map         Specify route-map
  static            Specify static local->global mapping

R1(config)#ip nat inside source list ?
  <1-2699>          Access list number for local addresses
  WORD              Access list name for local addresses

R1(config)#ip nat inside source list 2 ?
  interface         Specify interface for global address
  pool              Name pool of global addresses

R1(config)#ip nat inside source list 2 pool ?
  WORD              Pool name for global addresses

R1(config)#ip nat inside source list 2 pool CCNP
```

Let's test by pinging 172.12.123.2 from both loopbacks.

```
R1#ping 172.12.123.2 source 10.1.1.2
Packet sent with a source address of 10.1.1.2
!!!!!
Success rate is 100 percent (5/5), round-trip min/avg/max = 64/65/68 ms

R1#ping 172.12.123.2 source 10.1.1.22
Packet sent with a source address of 10.1.1.22
  !!!!!
```

```
Success rate is 100 percent (5/5), round-trip min/avg/max = 64/65/69 ms

R1#show ip nat trans

Pro Inside global      Inside local     Outside local      Outside global
icmp 200.1.1.1:11      10.1.1.2:11      172.12.123.2:11    172.12.123.2:11
--- 200.1.1.1          10.1.1.2         ---                ---
icmp 200.1.1.2:12      10.1.1.22:12     172.12.123.2:12    172.12.123.2:12
--- 200.1.1.2          10.1.1.22        ---                ---
```

Success! The ICMP traffic from 10.1.1.2 were translated to inside global address 200.1.1.1, the first available address in the NAT pool. Pings sent from 10.1.1.22 directly after that were translated to 200.1.1.2. For more information on your NAT translations, run *show ip nat statistics.* This command displays the outside and inside interfaces, the number of active and expired translations, and information regarding the CCNP pool.

```
R1#show ip nat stat
Total active translations: 4 (0 static, 4 dynamic; 2 extended)
Outside interfaces:
Serial1/0
Inside interfaces:
Loopback2, Loopback22
Hits: 30 Misses: 0
CEF Translated packets: 15, CEF Punted packets: 0
Expired translations: 1
Dynamic mappings:
-- Inside Source
[Id: 2] access-list 2 pool CCNP refcount 4
pool CCNP: netmask 255.255.255.0
         start 200.1.1.1 end 200.1.1.5
         type generic, total addresses 5, allocated 2 (40%), misses 0
Appl doors: 0
Normal doors: 0
Queued Packets: 0
```

I then added another loopback and sent a ping to 172.12.123.2 from 222.2.2.2. The ping goes through, but even though I wrote *ip nat inside* on the new loopback, there is no NAT translation. Why?

```
R1(config)#int loopback222
R1(config-if)#ip address 222.2.2.2 255.255.255.0
R1(config-if)#ip nat inside

R1#ping 172.12.123.2 source 222.2.2.2
Packet sent with a source address of 222.2.2.2
!!!!!
Success rate is 100 percent (5/5), round-trip min/avg/max = 64/66/68 ms
```

```
R1#show ip nat trans
Pro Inside global      Inside local       Outside local      Outside global
--- 200.1.1.1          10.1.1.2           ---                ---
--- 200.1.1.2          10.1.1.22          ---                ---
```

The source address 222.2.2.2 doesn't match the ACL, so no NAT for you! (For 222.2.2.2, that is.)

Dynamic NAT is great as long as you have more routable addresses in the NAT pool than hosts who need them. Not all of us have a pool of routable addresses sitting around, though, and we may not have any addresses to spare at all. That's where Port Address Translation (PAT) comes in!

Port Address Translation

Generally referred to as "overloading," PAT allows the private IP addresses of inside hosts to be translated to a single routable address—the address already in use on the outside interface.

The private address is actually translated to that routable address and a port number, allowing the same routable IP address to be used by multiple inside hosts for NAT. PAT's easy to configure, too! Instead of referring to a NAT pool with the *ip nat inside source* command, just identify the outside interface and the word *overload*. You'll still need *ip nat inside* and *ip nat outside* on the appropriate interfaces.

Before proceeding with the PAT lab, I removed the *ip nat inside source* command that called the NAT pool. Check out the message I received when doing so:

```
R1(config)#no ip nat inside source list 2 pool CCNP

Dynamic mapping in use, do you want to delete all entries? [no]: yes
```

When a Cisco device asks you a question and the prompted answer is "no," you should think twice before answering. Perhaps even thrice! Since we're in a lab, I answered "yes" and then put in the new command. (There's a much kinder and gentler way of clearing your NAT translations that I'll share with you later in this section.)

```
R1(config)#ip nat inside source list 2 ?
  interface          Specify interface for global address
  pool               Name pool of global addresses

R1(config)#ip nat inside source list 2 interface serial 1/0 ?
  oer                Use with vtemplate only. On new translation, if OER BR
                     is UP, OER will select IP from outgoing Interface. All
                     packets matching translation are forwarded over Interface
                     for duration of translation.
```

```
  overload          Overload an address translation
  reversible        Allow out->in traffic
  vrf               Specify vrf
  <cr>

R1(config)#ip nat inside source list 2 interface serial 1/0 overload
```

Let's ping and zing!

```
R1#ping 172.12.123.2 source 10.1.1.2
Packet sent with a source address of 10.1.1.2
!!!!!
Success rate is 100 percent (5/5), round-trip min/avg/max = 64/66/68 ms

R1#ping 172.12.123.2 source 10.1.1.22
Packet sent with a source address of 10.1.1.22
!!!!!
Success rate is 100 percent (5/5), round-trip min/avg/max = 64/65/68 ms

R1#show ip nat trans
Pro Inside global       Inside local     Outside local       Outside global
icmp 172.12.123.1:14    10.1.1.2:14      172.12.123.2:14     172.12.123.2:14
icmp 172.12.123.1:15    10.1.1.22:15     172.12.123.2:15     172.12.123.2:15
```

Success! Both hosts have their IP addresses changed to the address already in use on Serial 1/0, just with different port numbers. *show ip nat stat* reflects the change to PAT by mentioning an interface in the inside source information area.

```
R1#show ip nat stat
Total active translations: 2 (0 static, 2 dynamic; 2 extended)
Outside interfaces:
  Serial1/0
Inside interfaces:
  Loopback2, Loopback22, Loopback222
Hits: 90 Misses: 0
CEF Translated packets: 45, CEF Punted packets: 0
Expired translations: 7
Dynamic mappings:
-- Inside Source
[Id: 3] access-list 2 interface Serial1/0 refcount 2
Appl doors: 0
Normal doors: 0
Queued Packets: 0
```

Before we move on, let me share with you that kinder and gentler way of terminating dynamic NAT translations. *One command to clear them all!*

```
R1#show ip nat trans
Pro Inside global      Inside local      Outside local      Outside global
icmp 172.12.123.1:18   10.1.1.22:18      172.12.123.2:18    172.12.123.2:18
icmp 172.12.123.1:19   10.1.1.22:19      172.12.123.2:19    172.12.123.2:19

R1#clear ip nat trans *

R1#show ip nat trans
```

I created two new translations so we'd have something to clear and then ran *clear ip nat trans *. show ip nat trans* verifies the clear! Here are your options for clearing translations:

```
R1#clear ip nat trans ?
  *              Delete all dynamic translations
  esp            Encapsulating Security Payload
  forced         Delete all dynamic translations (forcefully)
  inside         Inside addresses (and ports)
  outside        Outside addresses (and ports)
  tcp            Transmission Control Protocol
  udp            User Datagram Protocol
  vrf            Clear entries of VRF instance
```

And with that, we're done! Thanks for making TBA part of your success story, and be sure to use the following free resources to make the CCNP ROUTE exam even easier!

My YouTube channel, packed with free CCNP ROUTE videos!

https://www.youtube.com/user/ccie12933

My new CCNP-info-rich website, launching in April 2016.

http://www.bryantadvantage.com

Finally, let me hear from you via Twitter @ccie12933 when you nail the exam – and I know you will!

Chris B.